English / Cambodian

អង់គ្លេស / ខ្មែរ

THE OXFORD
Picture
Dictionary

NORMA SHAPIRO AND JAYME ADELSON-GOLDSTEIN

Translated by Techno-Graphics & Translations, Inc.

Oxford University Press

Oxford University Press
198 Madison Avenue, New York, NY 10016 USA
Great Clarendon Street, Oxford OX2 6DP England

Oxford New York
Athens Auckland Bangkok Bogotá Buenos Aires
Calcutta Cape Town Chennai Dar es Salaam
Delhi Florence Hong Kong Istanbul Karachi
Kuala Lumpur Madrid Melbourne Mexico City
Mumbai Nairobi Paris São Paulo Shanghai
Singapore Taipei Tokyo Toronto Warsaw

And associated companies in
Berlin Ibadan

OXFORD is a trademark of Oxford University Press.

Copyright © 1998 Oxford University Press

Library of Congress Cataloging-in-Publication Data

Shapiro, Norma.
    The Oxford picture dictionary: English/Cambodian/
Norma Shapiro and Jayme Adelson-Goldstein; translated
by Techno-Graphics and Translations, Inc.
        p.   cm.
    Includes bibliographical references and index.
    ISBN 0-19-435194-7
    1. English language—Dictionaries—Khmer.   2. Picture
    dictionaries, English.   3. Picture dictionaries, Khmer.
    I. Adelson-Goldstein, Jayme.   II. Title.
    PL4327.S53   1999   98-9378
    423'.95932—dc21

No unauthorized photocopying.

Translation reviewed by: Cambridge Translation Resources
Editorial Manager: Susan Lanzano
Art Director: Lynn Luchetti
Senior Editor: Eliza Jensen
Production Editor: Tyrone Prescod
Senior Designer: Susan P. Brorein
Art Buyer: Tracy A. Hammond
Cover Design Production: Brett Sonnenschein
Production Manager: Abram Hall
Production Controller: Georgiann Baran
Production Services by: Techno-Graphics and Translations, Inc.
Pronunciation Editor: Sharon Goldstein
Cover design by Silver Editions

Printing (last digit): 10 9 8 7 6 5 4 3 2

Printed in China

Illustrations by: David Aikins, Doug Archer, Craig Attebery,
Garin Baker, Sally Bensusen, Eliot Bergman, Mark Bischel, Dan
Brown / Artworks NY, Roy Douglas Buchman, George Burgos /
Larry Dodge, Carl Cassler, Mary Chandler, Robert Crawford, Jim
Delapine, Judy Francis, Graphic Chart and Map Co., Dale
Gustafson, Biruta Akerbergs Hansen, Marcia Hartsock, C.M.I.,
David Hildebrand, The Ivy League of Artists, Inc. / Judy
Degraffenreid, The Ivy League of Artists, Inc. / Tom Powers, The
Ivy League of Artists, Inc. / John Rice, Pam Johnson, Ed
Kurtzman, Narda Lebo, Scott A. MacNeill / MACNEILL &
MACINTOSH, Andy Lendway / Deborah Wolfe Ltd., Jeffrey
Mangiat, Suzanne Mogensen, Mohammad Mansoor, Tom
Newsom, Melodye Benson Rosales, Stacey Schuett, Rob
Schuster, James Seward, Larry Taugher, Bill Thomson, Anna
Veltfort, Nina Wallace, Wendy Wassink-Ackison, Michael
Wepplo, Don Wieland
Thanks to Mike Mikos for his preliminary architectural sketches
of several pieces.

References
Boyer, Paul S., Clifford E. Clark, Jr., Joseph F. Kett, Thomas L.
Purvis, Harvard Sitkoff, Nancy Woloch, *The Enduring Vision: A
History of the American People*, Lexington, Massachusetts:
D.C. Heath and Co., 1990.

Grun, Bernard, *The Timetables of History: A Horizontal Linkage
of People and Events,* (based on Werner Stein's Kulturfahrplan)
New York: A Touchstone Book, Simon and Schuster, 1946,
1963, 1975, 1979.

Statistical Abstract of the United States: 1996, 116th Edition,
Washington, DC: US Bureau of the Census, 1996.

The World Book Encyclopedia, Chicago: World Book Inc., a
Scott Fetzer Co., 1988 Edition.

Toff, Nancy, Editor-in-Chief, *The People of North America*
(Series), New York: Chelsea House Publishers, Main Line
Books, 1988.

Trager, James, *The People's Chronology, A Year-by-Year Record
of Human Events from Prehistory to the Present,* New York:
Henry Holt Reference Book, 1992.

Acknowledgments

The publisher and authors would like to thank the following people for reviewing the manuscript and/or participating in focus groups as the book was being developed:

Ana Maria Aguilera, Lubie Alatriste, Ann Albarelli, Margaret Albers, Sherry Allen, Fiona Armstrong, Ted Auerbach, Steve Austen, Jean Barlow, Sally Bates, Sharon Batson, Myra Baum, Mary Beauparlant, Gretchen Bitterlin, Margrajean Bonilla, Mike Bostwick, Shirley Brod, Lihn Brown, Trish Brys-Overeem, Lynn Bundy, Chris Bunn, Carol Carvel, Leslie Crucil, Robert Denheim, Joshua Denk, Kay Devonshire, Thomas Dougherty, Gudrun Draper, Sara Eisen, Lynda Elkins, Ed Ende, Michelle Epstein, Beth Fatemi, Andra R. Fawcett, Alice Fiedler, Harriet Fisher, James Fitzgerald, Mary Fitzsimmons, Scott Ford, Barbara Gaines, Elizabeth Garcia Grenados, Maria T. Gerdes, Penny Giacalone, Elliott Glazer, Jill Gluck de la Llata, Javier Gomez, Pura Gonzales, Carole Goodman, Joyce Grabowski, Maggie Grennan, Joanie Griffin, Sally Hansen, Fotini Haritos, Alice Hartley, Fernando Herrera, Ann Hillborn, Mary Hopkins, Lori Howard, Leann Howard, Pamela Howard, Rebecca Hubner, Jan Jarrell, Vicki Johnson, Michele Kagan, Nanette Kaska, Gena Katsaros, Evelyn Kay, Greg Keech, Cliff Ker, Gwen Kerner-Mayer, Marilou Kessler, Patty King, Linda Kiperman, Joyce Klapp, Susan Knutson, Sandy Kobrine, Marinna Kolaitis, Donna Korol, Lorraine Krampe, Karen Kuser, Andrea Lang, Nancy Lebow, Tay Lesley, Gale Lichter, Sandie Linn, Rosario Lorenzano, Louise Louie, Cheryl Lucas, Ronna Magy, Juanita Maltese, Mary Marquardsen, Carmen Marques Rivera, Susan McDowell, Alma McGee, Jerry McLeroy, Kevin McLure, Joan Meier, Patsy Mills, Judy Montague, Vicki Moore, Eneida Morales, Glenn Nadelbach, Elizabeth Neblett, Kathleen Newton, Yvonne Nishio, Afra Nobay, Rosa Elena Ochoa, Jean Owensby, Jim Park, John Perkins, Jane Pers, Laura Peskin, Maria Pick, Percy Pleasant, Selma Porter, Kathy Quinones, Susan Ritter, Martha Robledo, Maureen Rooney, Jean Rose, David Ross, Julietta Ruppert, Lorraine Ruston, Susan Ryan, Frederico Salas, Leslie Salmon, Jim Sandifer, Linda Sasser, Lisa Schreiber, Mary Segovia, Abe Shames, Debra Shaw, Stephanie Shipp, Pat Singh, Mary Sklavos, Donna Stark, Claire Cocoran Stehling, Lynn Sweeden, Joy Tesh, Sue Thompson, Christine Tierney, Laura Topete, Carmen Villanueva, Laura Webber, Renée Weiss, Beth Winningham, Cindy Wislofsky, Judy Wood, Paula Yerman.

A special thanks to Marna Shulberg and the students of the Saticoy Branch of Van Nuys Community Adult School.

We would also like to thank the following individuals and organizations who provided their expertise:

Carl Abato, Alan Goldman, Dr. Larry Falk, Caroll Gray, Henry Haskell, Susan Haskell, Los Angeles Fire Department, Malcolm Loeb, Barbara Lozano, Lorne Dubin, United Farm Workers.

Authors' Acknowledgments

Throughout our careers as English language teachers, we have found inspiration in many places—in the classroom with our remarkable students, at schools, conferences, and workshops with our fellow teachers, and with our colleagues at the ESL Teacher Institute. We are grateful to be part of this international community.

We would like to sincerely thank and acknowledge Eliza Jensen, the project's Senior Editor. Without Eliza, this book would not have been possible. Her indomitable spirit, commitment to clarity, and unwavering advocacy allowed us to realize the book we envisioned.

Creating this dictionary was a collaborative effort and it has been our privilege to work with an exceptionally talented group of individuals who, along with Eliza Jensen, make up the Oxford Picture Dictionary team. We deeply appreciate the contributions of the following people:

Lynn Luchetti, Art Director, whose aesthetic sense and sensibility guided the art direction of this book,

Susan Brorein, Senior Designer, who carefully considered the design of each and every page,

Klaus Jekeli, Production Editor, who pored over both manuscript and art to ensure consistency and accuracy, and

Tracy Hammond, Art Buyer, who skillfully managed thousands of pieces of art and reference material.

We also want to thank Susan Mazer, the talented artist who was by our side for the initial problem-solving and Mary Chandler who also lent her expertise to the project.

We have learned much working with Marjorie Fuchs, Lori Howard, and Renée Weiss, authors of the dictionary's ancillary materials. We thank them for their on-going contributions to the dictionary program.

We must make special mention of Susan Lanzano, Editorial Manager, whose invaluable advice, insights, and queries were an integral part of the writing process.

This book is dedicated to my husband, Neil Reichline, who has encouraged me to take the road less traveled, and to my sons, Eli and Alex, who have allowed me to sit at their baseball games with my yellow notepad. —NS

This book is lovingly dedicated to my husband, Gary and my daughter, Emily Rose, both of whom hugged me tight and let me work into the night. —JAG

A Letter to the Teacher

Welcome to The Oxford Picture Dictionary.

This comprehensive vocabulary resource provides you and your students with over 3,700 words, each defined by engaging art and presented in a meaningful context. *The Oxford Picture Dictionary* enables your students to learn and use English in all aspects of their daily lives. The 140 key topics cover home and family, the workplace, the community, health care, and academic studies. The topics are organized into 12 thematic units that are based on the curriculum of beginning and low-intermediate level English language coursework. The word lists of the dictionary include both single word entries and verb phrases. Many of the prepositions and adjectives are presented in phrases as well, demonstrating the natural use of words in conjunction with one another.

The Oxford Picture Dictionary uses a variety of visual formats, each suited to the topic being represented. Where appropriate, word lists are categorized and pages are divided into sections, allowing you to focus your students' attention on one aspect of a topic at a time.

Within the word lists:

- nouns, adjectives, prepositions, and adverbs are numbered,

- verbs are bolded and identified by letters, and

- targeted prepositions and adjectives within phrases are bolded.

The dictionary includes a variety of exercises and self-access tools that will guide your students toward accurate and fluent use of the new words.

- Exercises at the bottom of the pages provide vocabulary development through pattern practice, application of the new language to other topics, and personalization questions.

- An alphabetical index assists students in locating all words and topics in the dictionary.

- A phonetic listing for each word in the index and a pronunciation guide give students the key to accurate pronunciation.

- A verb index of all the verbs presented in the dictionary provides students with information on the present, past, and past participle forms of the verbs.

The Oxford Picture Dictionary is the core of *The Oxford Picture Dictionary Program* which includes a *Dictionary Cassette,* a *Teacher's Book* and its companion *Focused Listening Cassette, Beginning* and *Intermediate Workbooks, Classic Classroom Activities* (a photocopiable activity book), *Overhead Transparencies,* and two *Readers.* Bilingual editions of *The Oxford Picture Dictionary* are available in Spanish, Chinese, Vietnamese, and many other languages.

TEACHING THE VOCABULARY

Your students' needs and your own teaching philosophy will dictate how you use *The Oxford Picture Dictionary* with your students. The following general guidelines, however, may help you adapt the dictionary's pages to your particular course and students. (For topic-specific, step-by-step guidelines and activities for presenting and practicing the vocabulary on each dictionary page see the *Oxford Picture Dictionary Teacher's Book.*)

Preview the topic

A good way to begin any lesson is to talk with students to determine what they already know about the topic. Some different ways to do this are:

- Ask general questions related to the topic;

- Have students brainstorm a list of words they know from the topic; or

- Ask questions about the picture(s) on the page.

Present the vocabulary

Once you've discovered which words your students already know, you are ready to focus on presenting the words they need. Introducing 10–15 new words in a lesson allows students to really learn the new words. On pages where the word lists are longer, and students are unfamiliar with many of the words, you may wish to introduce the words by categories or sections, or simply choose the words you want in the lesson.

Here are four different presentation techniques. The techniques you choose will depend on the topic being studied and the level of your students.

- Say each new word and describe or define it within the context of the picture.

- Demonstrate verbs or verb sequences for the students, and have volunteers demonstrate the actions as you say them.

- Use Total Physical Response commands to build comprehension of the vocabulary: *Put the pencil on your book. Put it on your notebook. Put it on your desk.*

- Ask a series of questions to build comprehension and give students an opportunity to say the new words:

- ▶ Begin with *yes/no* questions. *Is #16 chalk?* (yes)

- ▶ Progress to *or* questions. *Is #16 chalk or a marker?* (chalk)

- ▶ Finally ask *Wh* questions.

  What can I use to write on this paper? (a marker/ Use a marker.)

Check comprehension

Before moving on to the practice stage, it is helpful to be sure all students understand the target vocabulary. There are many different things you can do to check students' understanding. Here are two activities to try:

- Tell students to open their books and point to the items they hear you say. Call out target vocabulary at random as you walk around the room checking to see if students are pointing to the correct pictures.

- Make true/false statements about the target vocabulary. Have students hold up two fingers for true, three fingers for false. *You can write with a marker.* [two fingers] *You raise your notebook to talk to the teacher.* [three fingers]

Take a moment to review any words with which students are having difficulty before beginning the practice activities.

Practice the vocabulary

Guided practice activities give your students an opportunity to use the new vocabulary in meaningful communication. The exercises at the bottom of the pages are one source of guided practice activities.

- **Talk about...** This activity gives students an opportunity to practice the target vocabulary through sentence substitutions with meaningful topics.

  e.g. **Talk about your feelings.**

  I feel _happy_ when I see my friends.

- **Practice...** This activity gives students practice using the vocabulary within common conversational functions such as making introductions, ordering food, making requests, etc.

  e.g. **Practice asking for things in the dining room.**

  Please pass _the platter_.

  May I have _the creamer_?

  Could I have _a fork_, please?

- **Use the new language.** This activity asks students to brainstorm words within various categories, or may

ask them to apply what they have learned to another topic in the dictionary. For example, on *Colors*, page 12, students are asked to look at *Clothing I*, pages 64–65, and name the colors of the clothing they see.

- **Share your answers.** These questions provide students with an opportunity to expand their use of the target vocabulary in personalized discussion. Students can ask and answer these questions in whole class discussions, pair or group work, or they can write the answers as journal entries.

Further guided and communicative practice can be found in the *Oxford Picture Dictionary Teacher's Book* and in *Classic Classroom Activities*. The *Oxford Picture Dictionary Beginning* and *Intermediate Workbooks* and *Read All About It 1* and *2* provide your students with controlled and communicative reading and writing practice.

We encourage you to adapt the materials to suit the needs of your classes, and we welcome your comments and ideas. Write to us at:

Oxford University Press
ESL Department
198 Madison Avenue
New York, NY 10016

Jayme Adelson-Goldstein

Norma Shapiro

A Letter to the Student

Dear Student of English,

Welcome to *The Oxford Picture Dictionary*. The more than 3,700 words in this book will help you as you study English.

Each page in this dictionary teaches about a specific topic. The topics are grouped together in units. All pages in a unit have the same color and symbol. For example, each page in the Food unit has this symbol:

On each page you will see pictures and words. The pictures have numbers or letters that match the numbers or letters in the word lists. Verbs (action words) are identified by letters and all other words are identified by numbers.

How to find words in this book

- Use the Table of Contents, pages ix–xi.
  Look up the general topic you want to learn about.

- Use the Index, pages 173–205.
  Look up individual words in alphabetical (A–Z) order.

- Go topic by topic.
  Look through the book until you find something that interests you.

How to use the Index

When you look for a word in the index this is what you will see:

the word   the number (or letter) in the word list

apples [ăp/əlz] **50**–4

the pronunciation   the page number

If the word is on one of the maps, pages 122–125, you will find it in the Geographical Index on pages 206–208.

How to use the Verb Guide

When you want to know the past form of a verb or its past participle form, look up the verb in the verb guide. The regular verbs and their spelling changes are listed on pages 170–171. The simple form, past form, and past participle form of irregular verbs are listed on page 172.

Workbooks

There are two workbooks to help you practice the new words:
The Oxford Picture Dictionary Beginning and *Intermediate Workbooks*.

As authors and teachers we both know how difficult English can be (and we're native speakers!). When we wrote this book, we asked teachers and students from the U.S. and other countries for their help and ideas. We hope their ideas and ours will help you. Please write to us with your comments or questions at:

Oxford University Press
ESL Department
198 Madison Avenue
New York, NY 10016

We wish you success!

Jayme Adelson-Goldstein   *Norma Shapiro*

លិខិតចំពោះសិស្ស

ចំពោះសិស្សរៀនភាសាអង់គ្លេស,

សូមស្វាគមន៍ រចនានុក្រមរូបភាព *The Oxford Picture Dictionary* ។ ចំនួនពាក្យជាង ៣,៧០០ នៅក្នុងសៀវភៅនេះនឹងជួយអ្នក នៅពេលអ្នករៀនភាសាអង់គ្លេស ។

ទំព័រនិមួយៗ ក្នុងរចនានុក្រមនេះ បង្ហាត់អំពីមុខវិជ្ជា ពិសេសៗ ។ មុខវិជ្ជាទាំងនេះត្រូវបានបែងចែកជាក្រុមៗ ក្នុង ជំពូកទាំងនោះ ។ ទំព័រទាំងអស់ ក្នុងជំពូក មានពាណ៌ និង សញ្ញាដូចគ្នា ។ ឧទាហរណ៍, ទំព័រនិមួយៗនៅក្នុង ជំពូកម្ហូបអាហារ មានសញ្ញាដូចនេះ:

នៅលើទំព័រនិមួយៗ អ្នកនឹងឃើញរូបភាព និងពាក្យ ។ រូបភាពទាំងនោះមានលេខ ឬគ្មអក្សរ ដែលត្រូវនឹងលេខ ឬគ្មអក្សរ ក្នុងបញ្ជីពាក្យទាំងនោះ ។ កិរិយាសព្ទ (ពាក្យ ដែលមានចលនា) ត្រូវបានសម្គាល់ដោយគ្មអក្សរ និង ពាក្យដំទៃទ្យេតទាំងអស់ ត្រូវបានសម្គាល់ដោយលេខ ។

វិធីរកពាក្យក្នុងសៀវភៅនេះ

- ការប្រើបញ្ជីរៀង, ទំព័រ ix – xi ។
  មើលមុខវិជ្ជាទូទៅ ដែលអ្នកចង់រៀន ។

- ការប្រើ លិបិក្រម (Index), ទំព័រ 173–205 ។
  មើលពាក្យនិមួយៗ តាមលំដាប់គ្មអក្សរ (A–Z) ។

- ពីមុខវិជ្ជាមួយទៅមុខវិជ្ជាមួយ ។
  រកមើលក្នុងសៀវភៅ លុះត្រាតែអ្នករកឃើញអ្វីដែល អ្នកចង់បាន ។

របៀបប្រើ លិបិក្រម

កាលណាអ្នករកមើលពាក្យ ក្នុងលិបិក្រម អ្នកនឹងឃើញ គ្មដូច្នេះ:

ពាក្យ   លេខ (ឬអក្សរ) ក្នុងបញ្ជីពាក្យ

apples [ăp/əlz] **50**–4

ការបញ្ចេញសម្លេង   លេខទំព័រ

បើប្រសិនជាពាក្យនេះ នៅលើទំព័រផែនទី, ទំព័រ 122–125, អ្នកអាចរកវាក្នុង Geographical Index នៅទំព័រ 206–208 ។

របៀបប្រើទម្រង់កិរិយាសព្ទ

កាលណាអ្នកចង់ដឹងពីទម្រង់អតីតកាលនៃកិរិយាសព្ទ ណាមួយ ឬ កិរិយាសព្ទណានៃអតីតកាលដែលទេបនឹងក្នុង សុតទៅ, ចូរមើលកិរិយាសព្ទនោះ ក្នុងទម្រង់កិរិយាសព្ទ ។ កិរិយាសព្ទសាមញ្ញ និង ការផ្លាស់ប្តូរគ្របគ្រប មានចុះ នៅលើទំព័រ 170–171 ។ ទម្រង់ធម្មតា, ទម្រង់អតីតកាល, ហើយនិងទម្រង់អតីតកាលទេបនឹងក្នុងសុតទៅនៃ កិរិយាសព្ទ មិនទេ្យង មានរាយនៅក្នុងទំព័រ 172 ។

សៀវភៅកិច្ចការ

មានសៀវភៅកិច្ចការពីរ ដែលអាចជួយអ្នកហ្វឹកហាត់ ពាក្យថ្មីៗគឺ:
The Oxford Picture Dictionary Beginning និង *Intermediate Workbooks.*

ក្នុងនាមជាអ្នកនិពន្ធ និងជាគ្រូបង្រៀន យើងដឹងច្បាស់ ណាស់ន្ទូវការពិបាក ក្នុងការរៀនភាសាអង់គ្លេស (ហើយ នេះជាភាសាកំណើតរបស់យើងស្រាប់ផង!) ។ នៅពេល ដែលយើងសរសេរសៀវភៅនេះ, យើងបានមកស្តាប់ លោកគ្រូ អ្នកគ្រូ និងសិស្សរាប់សិស្ស ពីសហរដ្ឋអាមេរិក និង ពីប្រទេសដទៃទេ្យត ដើម្បីជាជំនួយ និងគំនិត ។ យើង សង្ឃឹមថាគំនិតរបស់គេ និងរបស់យើង នឹងជួយអ្នកបាន ។ សូមសរសេរមកយើង បើប្រសិនជាអ្នកមានយោបល់ និងសំនួរផ្សេងៗ តាមអស័យដ្ឋានខាងក្រោមនេះ:

Oxford University Press
ESL Department
198 Madison Avenue
New York, NY 10016

សូមអោយបានសម្រេចជូនចប់បំណង!

Jayme Adelson-Goldstein   *Norma Shapiro*

Contents បញ្ជីរឿង

1. Everyday Language ភាសាប្រចាំថ្ងៃ

A Classroom បន្ទប់រៀន	2–3
Personal Information ពត៌មានផ្ទាល់ខ្លួន	4
School សាលារៀន	5
Studying រៀន	6–7
Everyday Conversation ការសន្ទនាប្រចាំថ្ងៃ	8
The Telephone ទូរស័ព្ទ	9
Weather ធាតុអាកាស	10
Describing Things រៀបរាប់ពីវត្ថុ	11
Colors ពណ៌	12
Prepositions អាយតនិបាត	13
Numbers and Measurements លេខ និង រង្វាស់	14–15
Time ពេលវេលា	16–17
The Calendar ប្រក្រតិទិន	18–19
Money ប្រាក់	20
Shopping ការទិញដូរ	21

2. People មនុស្ស

Age and Physical Description អាយុ និងលក្ខណៈរាងកាយ	22
Describing Hair រៀបរាប់អំពីសក់	23
Family គ្រួសារ	24–25
Daily Routines កិច្ចការប្រចាំថ្ងៃ	26–27
Life Events ដំណើរជីវិត	28–29
Feelings អារម្មណ៍	30–31
A Graduation ការបញ្ចប់កម្មវិធីសិក្សា	32–33

3. Housing ផ្ទះសម្បែង

Places to Live កន្លែងសំរាប់នៅ	34
Finding a Home រកផ្ទះនៅ	35
Apartments ផ្ទះល្វែងជួល	36–37
A House ផ្ទះ	38
A Yard ដីធ្លា	39
A Kitchen ផ្ទះបាយ	40
A Dining Area បន្ទប់បាយ	41
A Living Room បន្ទប់ទទួលភ្ញៀវ	42
A Bathroom បន្ទប់ទឹក	43
A Bedroom បន្ទប់គេង	44
A Children's Bedroom បន្ទប់គេងរបស់ក្មេង	45
Housework កិច្ចការក្នុងផ្ទះ	46
Cleaning Supplies សម្ភារៈសំរាប់សំអាត	47
Household Problems and Repairs បញ្ហាក្នុងផ្ទះ និង ការជួសជុល	48–49

4. Food មុខអាហារ

Fruit ផ្លែឈើ	50
Vegetables បន្លែ	51
Meat and Poultry សាច់ធម្មតា និងសាច់ បសុបក្សី	52
Deli and Seafood មុខម្ហូបនៃស្រេច និងម្ហូបសមុទ្រ	53
The Market ផ្សារ	54–55
Containers and Packaged Foods មុខនៅក្នុងធុង និងកញ្ចប់	56
Weights and Measures ទម្ងន់ និងរង្វាស់រង្វាល់	57
Food Preparation ការរៀបចំម្ហូប	58
Kitchen Utensils សម្ភារៈផ្ទះបាយ	59

Contents បញ្ជីរឿង

Fast Food   មុបធ្វើរហ័សៗ   60
A Coffee Shop Menu   មុបនៅក្តៀមការហ្វេ   61
A Restaurant   ភោជនិយដ្ឋាន   62–63

5. Clothing   សំលៀកបំពាក់

Clothing I   សំលៀកបំពាក់ ភាគ ១   64–65
Clothing II   សំលៀកបំពាក់ ភាគ ២   66
Clothing III   សំលៀកបំពាក់ ភាគ ៣   67
Shoes and Accessories   ស្រ្តនាប់ជើង និងសម្ភារៈបន្ថែម   68–69
Describing Clothes   អ្យេរាប់អំពីសំលៀកបំពាក់   70–71
Doing the Laundry   បោកខោអាវ   72
Sewing and Alterations   ការដេរបោះ និង សារើខោអាវ   73

6. Health   សុខភាព

The Body   រាងកាយ   74–75
Personal Hygiene   អនាម័យផ្ទាល់ខ្លួន   76–77
Symptoms and Injuries   អាការៈរោគ និងស្ពាមរបួស   78
Illnesses and Medical Conditions   ជម្ងឺ និងលក្ខណៈជម្ងឺ   79
Health Care   ការថែទាំសុខភាព   80–81
Medical Emergencies   ភាពអាសន្នផ្នែកពេទ្យ   82
First Aid   ការជួយសង្គ្រោះជាបន្ទាន់   83
Clinics   គិលានដ្ឋាន   84
Medical and Dental Exams   ការពិនិត្យគ្រេញ និងធ្មេញ   85
A Hospital   មន្ទីរពេទ្យ   86–87

7. Community   សហគមន៍

City Streets   ផ្លូវផ្សេល់ទីក្រុង   88–89
An Intersection   ផ្លូវប្រសព្វគ្នា   90–91
A Mall   ផ្សារធំ   92–93
A Childcare Center   មជ្ឈមណ្ឌលកុមារ   94–95
U.S. Mail   ស្ថានិយសំបុត្រសហរដ្ឋ   96
A Bank   ធនាគារ   97
A Library   បណ្ណាល័យ   98
The Legal System   ប្រព័ន្ធច្បាប់   99
Crime   បទឧក្រិដ្ឋ   100
Public Safety   សន្តិសុខសាធារណៈ   101
Emergencies and Natural Disasters   ភាពអាសន្ន និងមហន្តរាយធម្មជាតិ   102–103

8. Transportation   គមនាគម

Public Transportation   ការដឹកនាំសាធារណៈ   104
Prepositions of Motion   ពាក្យទាក់ទងនឹងចលនា   105
Cars and Trucks   ឡានតូច និងឡានអឺកទំនិញ   106
Directions and Traffic Signs   ទិស និងសញ្ញាចរាចរ   107
Parts of a Car and Car Maintenance   ផ្នែកគ្រឿងឡាន និងការថែទាំ   108–109
An Airport   អាកាសយានដ្ឋាន   110
A Plane Trip   ការធ្វើដំណើរតាមយន្តហោះ   111

9. Areas of Study   មុខវិជ្ជាសិក្សា

Types of Schools   ប្រភេទនៃសាលារៀន   112
English Composition   ការតែងសេចក្តីជាភាសាអង់គ្លេស   113
U.S. History   ប្រវត្តិសាស្ត្រនៃសហរដ្ឋអាមេរិក   114–115

U.S. Government and Citizenship	រដ្ឋាបាលអាមេរិកាំង និងការចូលសញ្ជាតិ	116
Geography	ភូមិសាស្ត្រ	117
Mathematics	គណិតសាស្ត្រ	118
Science	វិទ្យាសាស្ត្រ	119
Music	តន្ត្រី	120
More School Subjects	មុខវិជ្ជាសិក្សាផ្សេងៗទៀត	121
North America and Central America	អាមេរិកខាងជើង និង អាមេរិកកណ្ដាល	122–123
The World	ពិភពលោក	124–125
Energy and the Environment	ថាមពល និង បរិយាការ	126
The Universe	សាកលលោក	127

10. Plants and Animals រុក្ខជាតិ និងសត្វ

Trees and Plants	ដើមឈើ និង រុក្ខជាតិ	128
Flowers	ផ្កា	129
Marine Life, Amphibians, and Reptiles	សត្វសមុទ្រ, សត្វរស់ក្នុងទឹកនិងលើគោក, និង ឧរង្គសត្វ	130–131
Birds, Insects, and Arachnids	សត្វស្លាប, សត្វល្អិត និង អដ្ឋបាទិកសត្វ	132
Domestic Animals and Rodents	សត្វស្រុក និងសត្វកកេរ	133
Mammals	ថនិកសត្វ	134–135

11. Work កិច្ចការ

Jobs and Occupations, A–H	ការងារ និង មុខរបរ A–H	136–137
Jobs and Occupations, H–W	ការងារ និង មុខរបរ H–W	138–139
Job Skills	ជំនាញការផ្នែកការងារ	140
Job Search	រកការងារ	141
An Office	ការិយាល័យ	142–143
Computers	កុំព្យូទ័រ	144
A Hotel	សណ្ឋាគារ	145
A Factory	រោងចក្រ	146
Job Safety	ការពារគ្រោះថ្នាក់នៅកន្លែងធ្វើការ	147
Farming and Ranching	ការធ្វើស្រែចំការ និងការចិញ្ចឹមសត្វ	148
Construction	សំណង់	149
Tools and Building Supplies	ឧបករណ៍ និងសម្ភារៈសំណង់	150–151

12. Recreation ការកំសាន្ត

Places to Go	កន្លែងដែលគួរទៅ	152
The Park and Playground	ឧទ្យាន និង កន្លែងក្មេងលេង	153
Outdoor Recreation	ការកំសាន្តនៅក្រៅផ្ទះ	154
The Beach	មាត់សមុទ្រ	155
Sports Verbs	កិរិយាស័ព្ទទាក់ទងនឹងកីឡា	156–157
Team Sports	កីឡាជាក្រុម	158
Individual Sports	កីឡាម្នាក់ៗ	159
Winter Sports and Water Sports	កីឡានៅរដូវត្រជាក់ និងកីឡាក្នុងទឹក	160
Sports Equipment	សម្ភារៈកីឡា	161
Hobbies and Games	គ្រឿងកំសាន្ត និងល្បែង	162–163
Electronics and Photography	គ្រឿងអេឡិចត្រូនិច និង ការថតរូប	164–165
Entertainment	ការកំសាន្ត	166–167
Holidays	ថ្ងៃបុណ្យ	168
A Party	ការជប់លៀង	169
Verb Guide	ទម្រង់កិរិយាស័ព្ទ	170
Index	លិបិក្រម	173
Geographical Index	លិបិក្រម ភូមិសាស្ត្រ	206
Cambodian Index	លិបិក្រមខ្មែរ	209

1. chalkboard
ក្តារខៀន

2. screen
សំពត់សសំរាប់បញ្ចាំង

3. student
សិស្ស

4. overhead projector
ប្រដាប់បញ្ចាំងរូបភាពឆ្លុះឡើងលើ

5. teacher
គ្រូបង្រៀន

6. desk
តុសរសេរ

7. chair / seat
កៅអី

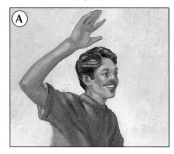

A. Raise your hand.
លើកដៃ ។

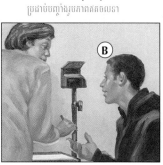

B. Talk to the teacher.
និយាយទៅគ្រូ ។

C. Listen to a cassette.
ស្តាប់កាសែត ។

D. Stand up.
ក្រោកឈរ ។

E. Sit down. / Take a seat.
អង្គុយចុះ ។

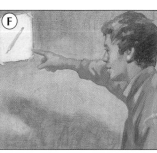

F. Point to the picture.
ចង្អុលទៅរូបភាព ។

G. Write on the board.
សរសេរលើក្តារខៀន ។

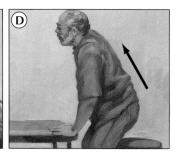

H. Erase the board.
លប់ក្តារខៀន ។

I. Open your book.
បើកសៀវភៅ ។

J. Close your book.
បិទសៀវភៅ ។

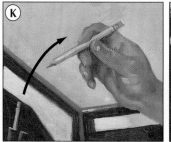

K. Take out your pencil.
យកខ្មៅដៃចេញ ។

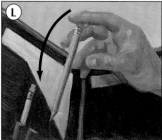

L. Put away your pencil.
ទុកខ្មៅដៃវិញ ។

8. bookcase
ទូសៀវភៅ

9. globe
ផែនទីមូល / ភូគោល

10. clock
នាឡិកា

11. cassette player
ម៉ាស៊ីនចាក់កាសែត

12. map
ផែនទី

13. pencil sharpener
ប្រដាប់ចិតខ្មៅដៃ

14. bulletin board
ក្ដារបិទប្រកាស

15. computer
កុំព្យូទ័រ

16. chalk
ដីស-

17. chalkboard eraser
ប្រដាប់លុបក្ដារខៀន

18. pen
ប៊ិច

19. marker
ម៉ាករ័

20. pencil
ខ្មៅដៃ

21. pencil eraser
ប្រដាប់លុបខ្មៅដៃ

22. textbook
សៀវភៅអាន

23. workbook
សៀវភៅមេរៀន

24. binder / notebook
សៀវភៅសរសេរ

25. notebook paper
សន្ទឹកសៀវភៅ

26. spiral notebook
សៀវភៅសរសេរស្គរ៉ាល់

27. ruler
បន្ទាត់

28. dictionary
វចនានុក្រម

29. picture dictionary
វចនានុក្រមរូបភាព

30. the alphabet
អក្ខរក្រម

31. numbers
លេខ

Use the new language.

1. Name three things you can open.

2. Name three things you can put away.

3. Name three things you can write with.

Share your answers.

1. Do you like to raise your hand?

2. Do you ever listen to cassettes in class?

3. Do you ever write on the board?

School Registration Form ក្រដាសចុះឈ្មោះចូលរៀន

1. name _Nguyen_ _____ _CHUng_
   ឈ្មោះ   **2.** first name   **3.** middle initial   **4.** last name
            នាមខ្លួន   នាមកណ្ដាល   នាមត្រកូល

5. address _5503 CEDAR LANE_ _____   **6.** apt. # * _____
   អាសយដ្ឋាន   បន្ទប់លេខ

7. city _Columbia_ _____   **8.** state _MN_ _____   **9.** ZIP code _21044_
   ទីក្រុង   រដ្ឋ   លេខកូដប៉ុស្ត

_(410)_ _____ _730 2051_ _____   _212 - 11 - 055_
10. area code   **11.** telephone number   **12.** sex: **13.** ☐ male   **15.** Social Security number
លេខក្បាលទូរស័ព្ទ   លេខទូរស័ព្ទ   ភេទ   ប្រុស   អត្តលេខសន្ដិសុខសង្គម
                                              14. ☑ female
                                                     ស្រី្ត

16. date of birth _11 10 1951_ _____   **17.** place of birth _____
   ខែថ្ងៃកំណើត   (month) (date) (year)   ទីកន្លែងកំណើត
               (ខែ)   (ថ្ងៃ)   (ឆ្នាំ)
                                          18. signature _____
                                               ហត្ថលេខា

* apt. # = apartment number

A. Spell your name.
ប្រកបឈ្មោះអ្នក ។

B. Fill out a form.
បំពេញក្រដាស ។

C. Print your name.
សរសេរឈ្មោះអ្នកជាអក្សរពុម្ព ។

D. Sign your name.
ចុះហត្ថលេខាឈ្មោះអ្នក ។

Talk about yourself.

My first name is <u>Sam</u>.

My last name is spelled <u>L-A-R-S-O-N</u>.

I come from <u>Ottawa</u>.

Share your answers.

1. Do you like your first name?

2. Is your last name from your mother? father? husband?

3. What is your middle name?

1. classroom
បន្ទប់រៀន

2. teacher
គ្រូ

3. auditorium
កន្លែងតំសំរាប់អង្គុយមើល / សវនដ្ឋាន

4. cafeteria
កន្លែងលក់អាហារដែលអ្នកទិញពិសេយកខ្លួនឯង

5. lunch benches
កៅអីវែងសម្រាប់អង្គុយញាំុំបាយ

6. library
បណ្ណាល័យ

7. lockers
បន្ទប់ទូមានសោរ

8. rest rooms
បង្គន់

9. gym
គ្រឹះស្ថានហាត់ប្រាណ

10. bleachers
កន្លែងអង្គុយមើលការប្រកួត

11. track
ផ្លូវរត់

12. field
ធ្នាក់ឡា

13. principal's office
ការិយាល័យចាងហ្វាង

14. principal
ចាងហ្វាង

15. counselor's office
ការិយាល័យអ្នកអោយឱវាទ

16. counselor
អ្នកអោយឱវាទ

17. main office
ការិយាល័យធំ

18. clerk
ស្មៀន

More vocabulary

instructor: teacher

coach: gym teacher

administrator: principal or other school supervisor

Share your answers.

1. Do you ever talk to the principal of your school?

2. Is there a place for you to eat at your school?

3. Does your school look the same as or different from the one in the picture?

Dictionary work កិច្ចការវចនានុក្រម

A. Look up a word.
បើកមើលពាក្យ ។

B. Read the word.
អានពាក្យ ។

C. Say the word.
ថាពាក្យ ។

D. Repeat the word.
ថាពាក្យម្ដងទៀត ។

E. Spell the word.
ប្រកបពាក្យ ។

F. Copy the word.
ចំឡងពាក្យ ។

Work with a partner ធ្វើជាមួយដៃគូ

G. Ask a question.
សួរសំណួរ ។

H. Answer a question.
ឆ្លើយសំណួរ ។

I. Share a book.
ចែកសៀវភៅគ្នាមើល ។

J. Help your partner.
ជួយដៃគូរបស់អ្នក ។

Work in a group ធ្វើជាក្រុម

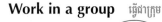

K. Brainstorm a list.
បញ្ចេញគំនិតគ្រប់ស្រាយ តំបញ្ជី ។

L. Discuss the list.
ពិភាក្សាពីបញ្ជី ។

M. Draw a picture.
គូររូប ។

N. Dictate a sentence.
ចំឡងតាមអានប្រយោគមួយ ។

Class work កិច្ចការធ្វើតាមថ្នាក់

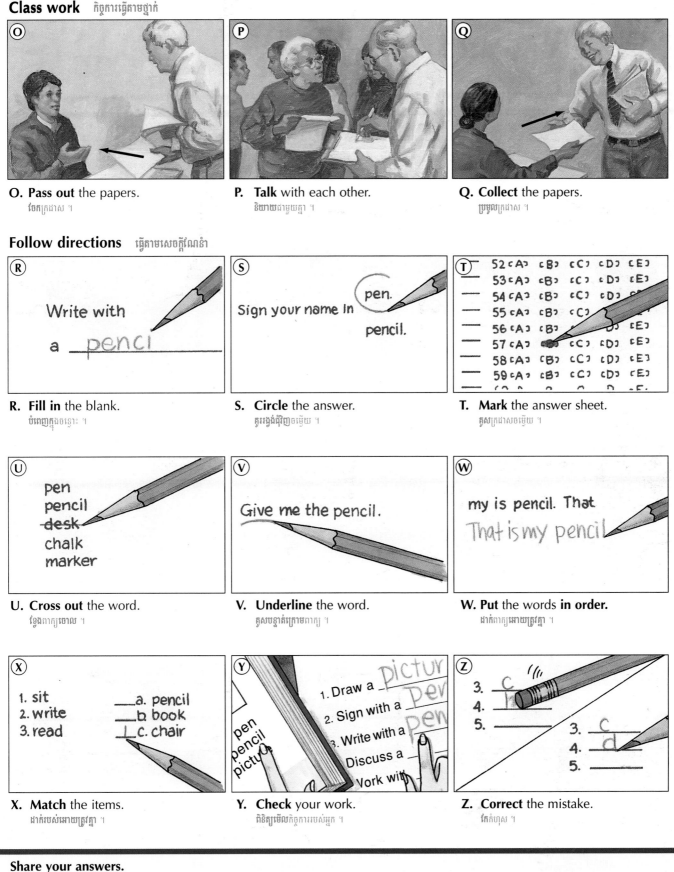

O. Pass out the papers.
ចែកក្រដាស ។

P. Talk with each other.
និយាយជាមួយគ្នា ។

Q. Collect the papers.
ប្រមូលក្រដាស ។

Follow directions ធ្វើតាមសេចក្តីណែនាំ

R. Fill in the blank.
បំពេញក្នុងចន្លោះ ។

S. Circle the answer.
គូរវង់ជុំវិញចម្លើយ ។

T. Mark the answer sheet.
គូសក្រដាសចម្លើយ ។

U. Cross out the word.
ខ្វែងពាក្យចោល ។

V. Underline the word.
គូសបន្ទាត់ក្រោមពាក្យ ។

W. Put the words **in order.**
ដាក់ពាក្យឲ្យត្រូវគ្នា ។

X. Match the items.
ដាក់របស់ឲ្យត្រូវគ្នា ។

Y. Check your work.
ពិនិត្យមើលកិច្ចការរបស់អ្នក ។

Z. Correct the mistake.
កែកំហុស ។

Share your answers.

1. Do you like to work in groups?

2. Do you like to share books?

3. Do you like to answer questions?

4. Is it easy for you to talk with your classmates?

5. Do you always check your work?

6. Do you cross out your mistakes or erase them?

A. greet someone
ជំរាបសួរនរណាម្នាក់

B. begin a conversation
ផ្តើមការសន្ទនា

C. end the conversation
បញ្ចប់ការសន្ទនា

D. introduce yourself
ប្រាប់ឈ្មោះអ្នក

E. make sure you **understand**
អោយជាក់ច្បាស់ថាអ្នកយល់

F. introduce your friend
ណែនាំមិត្តអ្នកអោយគេស្គាល់

G. compliment your friend
លើកសរសើរមិត្តអ្នក

H. thank your friend
អរគុណមិត្តអ្នក

I. apologize
សុំទោស

Practice introductions.

Hi, I'm <u>Sam Jones</u> and this is my friend, <u>Pat Green</u>.

 Nice to meet you. I'm <u>Tomas Garcia</u>.

Practice giving compliments.

That's a great <u>sweater</u>, <u>Tomas</u>.

 Thanks <u>Pat</u>. I like your <u>shoes</u>.

Look at **Clothing I,** pages **64–65** for more ideas.

1. telephone/phone
   ទូរស័ព្ទ

2. receiver
   ដងទូរស័ព្ទ

3. cord
   ខ្សែទូរស័ព្ទ

4. local call
   និយាយទូរស័ព្ទក្នុងតំបន់

5. long-distance call
   និយាយទូរស័ព្ទក្រៅតំបន់

6. international call
   និយាយទូរស័ព្ទឆ្លងប្រទេស

7. operator
   ទូរស័ព្ទការិ

8. directory assistance (411)
   អ្នកជំនួយខាងលេខទូរស័ព្ទ

9. emergency service (911)
   ហៅទូរស័ព្ទសម្រាប់ពេលអាសន្ន

10. phone card
    កាតទូរស័ព្ទ

11. pay phone
    ទូរស័ព្ទបង់ថ្លៃ

12. cordless phone
    ទូរស័ព្ទឥតខ្សែ

13. cellular phone
    ទូរស័ព្ទប្រើថ្ម

14. answering machine
    ម៉ាស៊ីនឆ្លើយទូរស័ព្ទ

15. telephone book
    សៀវភៅទូរស័ព្ទ

16. pager
    អេង្គ

Using a pay phone ប្រើទូរស័ព្ទបង់ថ្លៃ

A. **Pick up** the receiver.
   លើកដងទូរស័ព្ទ ។

B. **Listen** for the dial tone.
   ស្តាប់សំលេងទូរស័ព្ទរ ។

C. **Deposit** coins.
   ដាក់កាក់ ។

D. **Dial** the number.
   វៃលេខទូរស័ព្ទ ។

E. **Leave** a message.
   ទុកសារផ្ញើនៅក្នុងម៉ាស៊ីន ។

F. **Hang up** the receiver.
   ដាក់ដងទូរស័ព្ទចុះ ។

More vocabulary

When you get a person or place that you didn't want to call, we say you have the **wrong number.**

Share your answers.

1. What kinds of calls do you make?
2. How much does it cost to call your country?
3. Do you like to talk on the telephone?

9

Temperature
សីតុណ្ហភាព

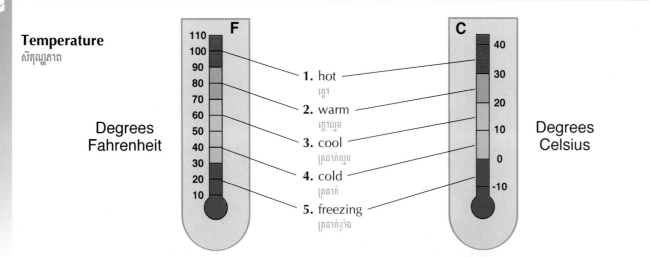

Degrees
Fahrenheit

Degrees
Celsius

1. hot
ក្តៅ

2. warm
ក្តៅល្មម

3. cool
ត្រជាក់ល្មម

4. cold
ត្រជាក់

5. freezing
ត្រជាក់ខ្លាំង

6. sunny / clear
បើកថ្ងៃ / មេឃស្រឡះ

7. cloudy
មេឃពពកច្រើន

8. raining
ភ្លៀង

9. snowing
ធ្លាក់ទឹកកក

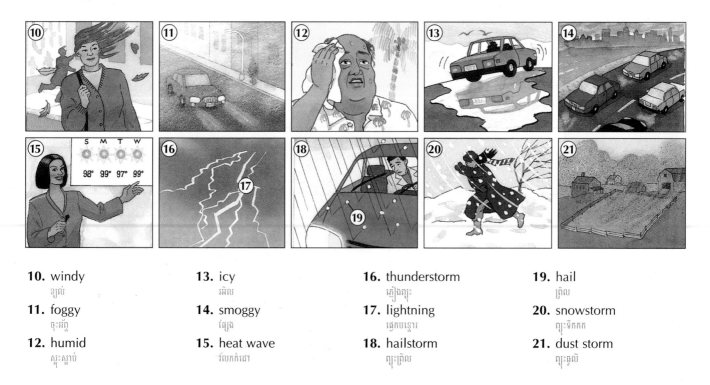

10. windy
ខ្យល់

11. foggy
ចុះអ័ព្ទ

12. humid
សុះស្ងាប់

13. icy
អើល

14. smoggy
ផ្សែង

15. heat wave
រលកក៏ដៅ

16. thunderstorm
ផ្គរលាន់

17. lightning
ផ្លេកបន្ទោរ

18. hailstorm
ព្យុះព្រិល

19. hail
ព្រិល

20. snowstorm
ព្យុះទឹកកក

21. dust storm
ព្យុះធូលី

Language note: *it is, there is*

For **1–14** we use, *It's <u>cloudy</u>.*

For **15–21** we use, *There's <u>a heat wave</u>.*
There's <u>lightning</u>.

Talk about the weather.

Today it's <u>hot</u>. It's <u>98 degrees</u>.

Yesterday it was <u>warm</u>. It was <u>85 degrees</u>.

1. **little** hand
   ដៃតូច
2. **big** hand
   ដៃធំ

3. **fast** driver
   អ្នកបើកឡានលឿន
4. **slow** driver
   អ្នកបើកឡានយឺត

5. **hard** chair
   កៅអីរឹង
6. **soft** chair
   កៅអីទន់

7. **thick** book /
   fat book
   សៀវភៅក្រាស់
8. **thin** book
   សៀវភៅស្តើង

9. **full** glass
   កែវពេញ
10. **empty** glass
    កែវទទេ

11. **noisy** children /
    loud children
    ក្មេងមាត់ច្រើន
12. **quiet** children
    ក្មេងស្ងាត់ស្ងៀម

13. **heavy** box
    ប្រអប់ធ្ងន់
14. **light** box
    ប្រអប់ស្រាល

15. **neat** closet
    ទូស្អាត
16. **messy** closet
    ទូរាយប៉ាយ

17. **good** dog
    ឆ្កែល្អ
18. **bad** dog
    ឆ្កែអាក្រក់

19. **expensive** ring
    ចិញ្ចៀនថ្លៃ
20. **cheap** ring
    ចិញ្ចៀនថោក

21. **beautiful** view
    ទេសភាពល្អ
22. **ugly** view
    ទេសភាពអាក្រក់

23. **easy** problem
    បញ្ហាស្រួល
24. **difficult** problem /
    hard problem
    បញ្ហាពិបាក

Use the new language.

1. Name three things that are thick.
2. Name three things that are soft.
3. Name three things that are heavy.

Share your answers.

1. Are you a slow driver or a fast driver?
2. Do you have a neat closet or a messy closet?
3. Do you like loud or quiet parties?

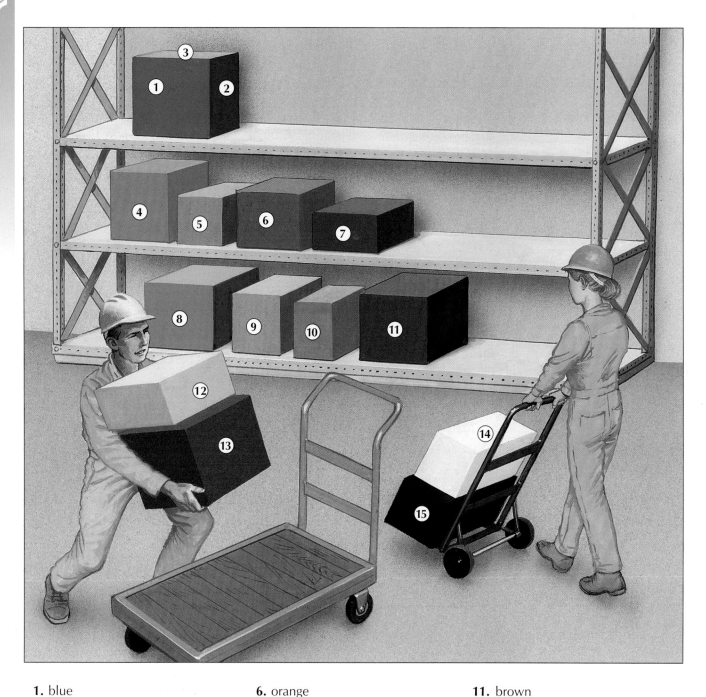

1. blue	**6.** orange	**11.** brown
ខៀវ	ស្វាយ៉ុ	ត្នោត
2. dark blue	**7.** purple	**12.** yellow
ខៀវក្រម៉ៅ	ស្វាយ	លឿង
3. light blue	**8.** green	**13.** red
ខៀវខ្ចី	បៃតង	ក្រហម
4. turquoise	**9.** beige	**14.** white
ខៀវ-បៃតង	ប្រផេះស្រអាប់	ស
5. gray	**10.** pink	**15.** black
ប្រផេះ	ផ្កាឈូក	ខ្មៅ

Use the new language.

Look at **Clothing I,** pages **64–65.**

Name the colors of the clothing you see.

That's a dark blue suit.

Share your answers.

1. What colors are you wearing today?

2. What colors do you like?

3. Is there a color you don't like? What is it?

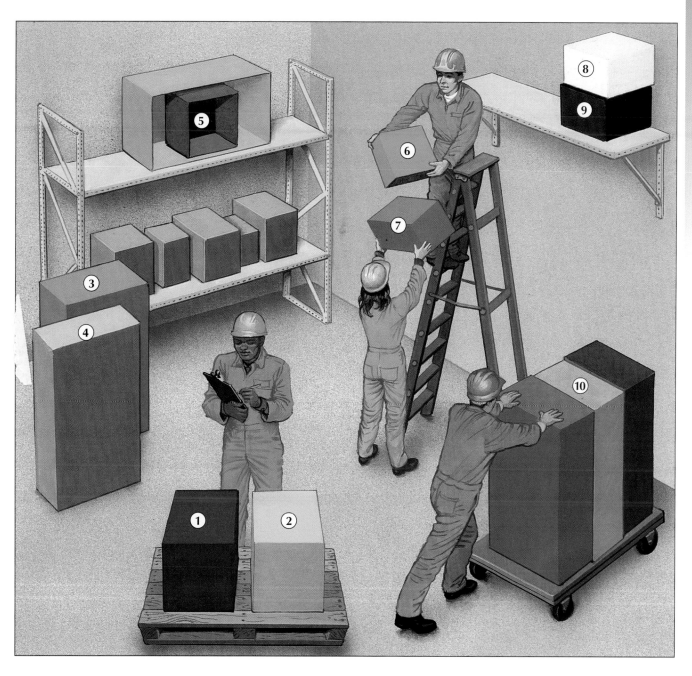

1. The red box is **next to** the yellow box, **on the left.**
   ប្រអប់ពណ៌ក្រហម **នៅវែក្បរ** ប្រអប់ពណ៌លឿង **នៅខាងឆ្វេង** ។

2. The yellow box is **next to** the red box, **on the right.**
   ប្រអប់ពណ៌លឿង **នៅវែក្បរ** ប្រអប់ពណ៌ក្រហម **នៅខាងស្តាំ** ។

3. The turquoise box is **behind** the gray box.
   ប្រអប់ពណ៌ខៀវរចាស់ **នៅពីក្រោយ** ប្រអប់ពណ៌ប្រផេះ ។

4. The gray box is **in front of** the turquoise box.
   ប្រអប់ពណ៌ប្រផេះ **នៅខាងមុខ** ប្រអប់ពណ៌ខៀវរចាស់ ។

5. The dark blue box is **in** the beige box.
   ប្រអប់ពណ៌ខៀវស្រអាប់ **នៅក្នុង** ប្រអប់ពណ៌ផ្កាត ។

6. The green box is **above** the orange box.
   ប្រអប់ពណ៌បៃតង **នៅពីលើ** ប្រអប់ពណ៌ស្វាយ ។

7. The orange box is **below** the green box.
   ប្រអប់ពណ៌ស្វាយ **នៅពីក្រោម** ប្រអប់ពណ៌បៃតង ។

8. The white box is **on** the black box.
   ប្រអប់ពណ៌ស **នៅលើ** ប្រអប់ពណ៌ខ្មៅ ។

9. The black box is **under** the white box.
   ប្រអប់ពណ៌ខ្មៅ **នៅក្រោម** ប្រអប់ពណ៌ស ។

10. The pink box is **between** the purple box and the brown box.
    ប្រអប់ពណ៌ផ្កាឈូក **នៅចន្លោះ** ប្រអប់ពណ៌ស្វាយ និងប្រអប់ពណ៌ត្នោត។

More vocabulary

near: in the same area
*The white box is **near** the black box.*

far from: not near
*The red box is **far from** the black box.*

Cardinals បរិមាណសំខ្យា

0 zero សូន្យ	11 eleven ដប់មួយ	21 twenty-one ម្ភៃមួយ	101 one hundred one មួយរយមួយ
1 one មួយ	12 twelve ដប់ពីរ	22 twenty-two ម្ភៃពីរ	1,000 one thousand មួយពាន់
2 two ពីរ	13 thirteen ដប់បី	30 thirty សាមសិប	1,001 one thousand one មួយពាន់មួយ
3 three បី	14 fourteen ដប់បួន	40 forty សែសិប	10,000 ten thousand ដប់ពាន់ / មួយម៉ឺន
4 four បួន	15 fifteen ដប់ប្រាំ	50 fifty ហាសិប	100,000 one hundred thousand មួយសែន
5 five ប្រាំ	16 sixteen ដប់ប្រាំមួយ	60 sixty ហុកសិប	1,000,000 one million មួយលាន
6 six ប្រាំមួយ	17 seventeen ដប់ប្រាំពីរ	70 seventy ចិតសិប	1,000,000,000 one billion មួយរយកោដិ
7 seven ប្រាំពីរ	18 eighteen ដប់ប្រាំបី	80 eighty ប៉ែតសិប	
8 eight ប្រាំបី	19 nineteen ដប់ប្រាំបួន	90 ninety កៅសិប	
9 nine ប្រាំបួន	20 twenty ម្ភៃ	100 one hundred មួយរយ	
10 ten ដប់			

Ordinals បូរណសំខ្យា

1st first ទីមួយ	8th eighth ទីប្រាំបី	15th fifteenth ទីដប់ប្រាំ
2nd second ទីពីរ	9th ninth ទីប្រាំបួន	16th sixteenth ទីដប់ប្រាំមួយ
3rd third ទីបី	10th tenth ទីដប់	17th seventeenth ទីដប់ប្រាំពីរ
4th fourth ទីបួន	11th eleventh ទីដប់មួយ	18th eighteenth ទីដប់ប្រាំបី
5th fifth ទីប្រាំ	12th twelfth ទីដប់ពីរ	19th nineteenth ទីដប់ប្រាំបួន
6th sixth ទីប្រាំមួយ	13th thirteenth ទីដប់បី	20th twentieth ទីម្ភៃ
7th seventh ទីប្រាំពីរ	14th fourteenth ទីដប់បួន	

Roman numerals លេខរ៉ូម៉ាំង

I	= 1	VII	= 7	XXX	= 30
II	= 2	VIII	= 8	XL	= 40
III	= 3	IX	= 9	L	= 50
IV	= 4	X	= 10	C	= 100
V	= 5	XV	= 15	D	= 500
VI	= 6	XX	= 20	M	= 1,000

Fractions ប្រភាគ

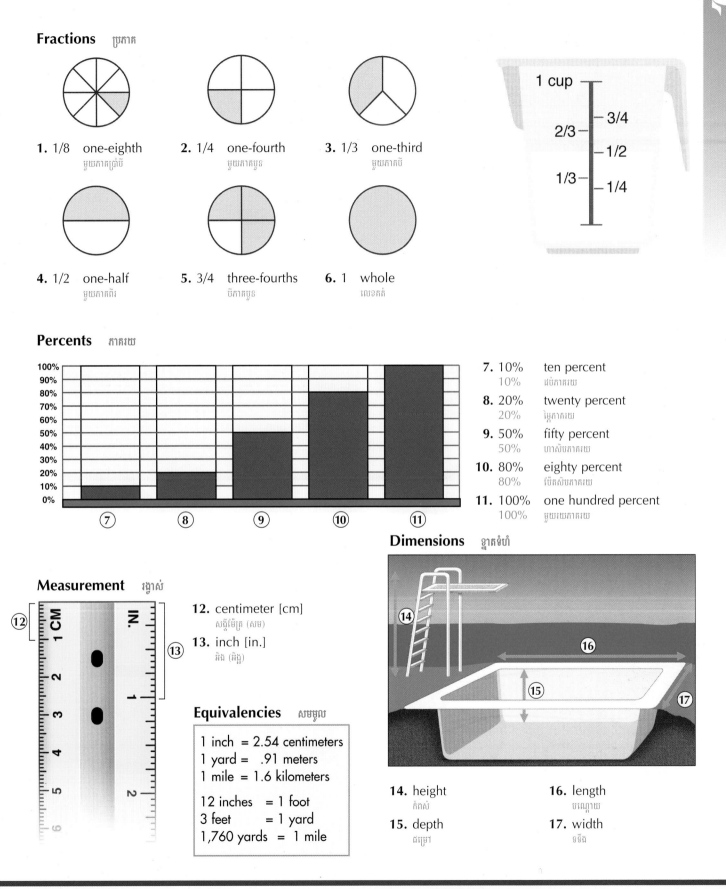

1. 1/8   one-eighth
មួយភាគប្រាំបី

2. 1/4   one-fourth
មួយភាគបួន

3. 1/3   one-third
មួយភាគបី

4. 1/2   one-half
មួយភាគពីរ

5. 3/4   three-fourths
បីភាគបួន

6. 1   whole
លេខគត់

1 cup
3/4
2/3
1/2
1/3
1/4

Percents ភាគរយ

100%
90%
80%
70%
60%
50%
40%
30%
20%
10%
0%

⑦   ⑧   ⑨   ⑩   ⑪

7. 10%   ten percent
10%   ដប់ភាគរយ

8. 20%   twenty percent
20%   ម្ភៃភាគរយ

9. 50%   fifty percent
50%   ហាសិបភាគរយ

10. 80%   eighty percent
80%   ប៉ែតសិបភាគរយ

11. 100%   one hundred percent
100%   មួយរយភាគរយ

Measurement រង្វាស់

12. centimeter [cm]
សង់ទីម៉ែត្រ (សម)

13. inch [in.]
អ៊ីង (អ៊ិង្ស)

Equivalencies សមមូល

1 inch	= 2.54 centimeters
1 yard	= .91 meters
1 mile	= 1.6 kilometers
12 inches	= 1 foot
3 feet	= 1 yard
1,760 yards	= 1 mile

Dimensions ខ្នាតទំហំ

14. height
កំពស់

15. depth
ជម្រៅ

16. length
បណ្ដោយ

17. width
ទទឹង

More vocabulary

measure: to find the size or amount of something

count: to find the total number of something

Share your answers.

1. How many students are in class today?

2. Who was the first person in class today?

3. How far is it from your home to your school?

A.M.

P.M.

1. second
វិនាទី

2. minute
នាទី

3. hour
ម៉ោង

4. 1:00
one o'clock
ម៉ោងមួយ

5. 1:05
one-oh-five
ម៉ោងមួយ ប្រាំនាទី
five after one
ម៉ោងមួយ ប្រាំនាទី

6. 1:10
one-ten
ម៉ោងមួយ ដប់នាទី
ten after one
ម៉ោងមួយ ដប់នាទី

7. 1:15
one-fifteen
ម៉ោងមួយ ដប់ប្រាំនាទី
a quarter after one
ម៉ោងមួយដប់ប្រាំនាទី

8. 1:20
one-twenty
ម៉ោងមួយ ម្ភៃនាទី
twenty after one
ម៉ោងមួយ ម្ភៃនាទី

9. 1:25
one twenty-five
ម៉ោងមួយ ម្ភៃប្រាំនាទី
twenty-five after one
ម៉ោងមួយ ម្ភៃប្រាំនាទី

10. 1:30
one-thirty
ម៉ោងមួយកន្លះ
half past one
ម៉ោងមួយកន្លះ

11. 1:35
one thirty-five
ម៉ោងមួយ សាមសិបប្រាំនាទី
twenty-five to two
ម៉ោងពីរខ្វះម្ភៃប្រាំនាទី

12. 1:40
one-forty
ម៉ោងមួយ សែសិបនាទី
twenty to two
ម៉ោងពីរខ្វះម្ភៃនាទី

13. 1:45
one forty-five
ម៉ោងមួយសែសិបប្រាំនាទី
a quarter to two
ម៉ោងពីរខ្វះ ដប់ប្រាំនាទី

14. 1:50
one-fifty
ម៉ោងមួយហាសិបនាទី
ten to two
ម៉ោងពីរខ្វះដប់នាទី

15. 1:55
one fifty-five
ម៉ោងមួយ ហាសិបប្រាំនាទី
five to two
ម៉ោងពីរ ខ្វះប្រាំនាទី

Talk about the time.

What time is it? It's <u>10:00 a.m.</u>

What time do you wake up on weekdays? At <u>6:30 a.m.</u>

What time do you wake up on weekends? At <u>9:30 a.m.</u>

Share your answers.

1. How many hours a day do you study English?

2. You are meeting friends at 1:00. How long will you wait for them if they are late?

16. morning
ព្រឹក

17. noon
ថ្ងៃត្រង់

18. afternoon
រសៀល

19. evening
ល្ងាច

20. night
យប់

21. midnight
ពាក់កណ្ដាលយប់

22. early
ភ្លាម

23. late
យឺត

TIME ZONES

ANCHORAGE ⓔ

㉕

㉖

㉗ EDMONTON

㉘

㉙

㉚

㉜ ㉝
October-April   April-October

VANCOUVER

WINNIPEG

ST. JOHN'S
㉛

MONTREAL HALIFAX

CHICAGO NEW YORK

SAN FRANCISCO DENVER WASHINGTON D.C.

LOS ANGELES

HOUSTON

MIAMI

PACIFIC OCEAN

㉔ HONOLULU

MEXICO CITY

ATLANTIC OCEAN

SAN SALVADOR

MANAGUA

CARACAS

24. Hawaii-Aleutian time
ម៉ោង ហាវ៉ៃ-អេល្យូទៀន

27. mountain time
ម៉ោងភ្នំ

30. Atlantic time
ម៉ោងអាត្លង់ទិក

33. daylight saving time
ពេលបន្ថយ/បន្ថែមម៉ោង

25. Alaska time
ម៉ោង អាឡាស្កា

28. central time
ម៉ោងកណ្ដាល

31. Newfoundland time
ម៉ោងនៅវហ្វិនឡិន ដ៍រកឃើញថ្មី

26. Pacific time
ម៉ោង ប៉ាស៊ីហ្វិក

29. eastern time
ម៉ោងភាគខាងកើត

32. standard time
ម៉ោងធម្មតា

More vocabulary

on time: not early and not late
He's on time.

Share your answers.

1. When do you watch television? study? do housework?

2. Do you come to class on time? early? late?

Days of the week
ថ្ងៃប្រចាំសប្ដាហ៍

1. Sunday
អាទិត្យ

2. Monday
ច័ន្ទ

3. Tuesday
អង្គារ

4. Wednesday
ពុធ

5. Thursday
ព្រហស្បតិ៍

6. Friday
សុក្រ

7. Saturday
សៅរ៍

8. year
ឆ្នាំ

9. month
ខែ

10. day
ថ្ងៃ

11. week
សប្ដាហ៍

12. weekdays
ថ្ងៃក្នុងសប្ដាហ៍

13. weekend
ចុងសប្ដាហ៍

14. date
ថ្ងៃខែឆ្នាំ

15. today
ថ្ងៃនេះ

16. tomorrow
ថ្ងៃស្អែក

17. yesterday
ម្សិលមិញ / ម្សិលម្ងៃ

18. last week
អាទិត្យមុន / សប្ដាហ៍មុន

19. this week
អាទិត្យនេះ / សប្ដាហ៍នេះ

20. next week
អាទិត្យក្រោយ / សប្ដាហ៍ក្រោយ

21. every day
រាល់ថ្ងៃ

22. once a week
មួយអាទិត្យម្ដង / មួយសប្ដាហ៍ម្ដង

23. twice a week
ពីរដងមួយសប្ដាហ៍ / ពីរដងមួយអាទិត្យ

24. three times a week
បីដងមួយសប្ដាហ៍ / បីដងមួយអាទិត្យ

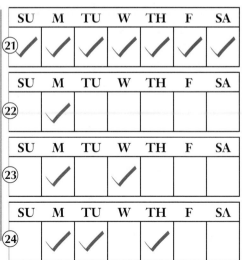

Talk about the calendar.

What's today's date? It's <u>March 10th</u>.

What day is it? It's <u>Tuesday</u>.

What day was yesterday? It was <u>Monday</u>.

Share your answers.

1. How often do you come to school?

2. How long have you been in this school?

2001

JAN 25
SUN	MON	TUE	WED	THU	FRI	SAT
	1	2	3	4	5	6
7	8	9	10	11	12	13
14	15	16	17	18	19	20
21	22	23	24	25	26	27
28	29	30	31			

FEB 26
SUN	MON	TUE	WED	THU	FRI	SAT
				1	2	3
4	5	6	7	8	9	10
11	12	13	14	15	16	17
18	19	20	21	22	23	24
25	26	27	28			

MAR 27
SUN	MON	TUE	WED	THU	FRI	SAT
				1	2	3
4	5	6	7	8	9	10
11	12	13	14	15	16	17
18	19	20	21	22	23	24
25	26	27	28	29	30	31

APR 28
SUN	MON	TUE	WED	THU	FRI	SAT
1	2	3	4	5	6	7
8	9	10	11	12	13	14
15	16	17	18	19	20	21
22	23	24	25	26	27	28
29	30					

MAY 29
SUN	MON	TUE	WED	THU	FRI	SAT
		1	2	3	4	5
6	7	8	9	10	11	12
13	14	15	16	17	18	19
20	21	22	23	24	25	26
27	28	29	30	31		

JUN 30
SUN	MON	TUE	WED	THU	FRI	SAT
					1	2
3	4	5	6	7	8	9
10	11	12	13	14	15	16
17	18	19	20	21	22	23
24	25	26	27	28	29	30

JUL 31
SUN	MON	TUE	WED	THU	FRI	SAT
1	2	3	4	5	6	7
8	9	10	11	12	13	14
15	16	17	18	19	20	21
22	23	24	25	26	27	28
29	30	31				

AUG 32
SUN	MON	TUE	WED	THU	FRI	SAT
			1	2	3	4
5	6	7	8	9	10	11
12	13	14	15	16	17	18
19	20	21	22	23	24	25
26	27	28	29	30	31	

SEP 33
SUN	MON	TUE	WED	THU	FRI	SAT
						1
2	3	4	5	6	7	8
9	10	11	12	13	14	15
16	17	18	19	20	21	22
23/30	24	25	26	27	28	29

OCT 34
SUN	MON	TUE	WED	THU	FRI	SAT
	1	2	3	4	5	6
7	8	9	10	11	12	13
14	15	16	17	18	19	20
21	22	23	24	25	26	27
28	29	30	31			

NOV 35
SUN	MON	TUE	WED	THU	FRI	SAT
				1	2	3
4	5	6	7	8	9	10
11	12	13	14	15	16	17
18	19	20	21	22	23	24
25	26	27	28	29	30	

DEC 36
SUN	MON	TUE	WED	THU	FRI	SAT
						1
2	3	4	5	6	7	8
9	10	11	12	13	14	15
16	17	18	19	20	21	22
23/30	24/31	25	26	27	28	29

MARCH 21
JUNE 21
SEPT. 21
DEC. 21

37
38
39
40

JUNE 5 — TIM!
41

MARCH 2 — ANNIVERSARY
42

JULY 4 — INDEPENDENCE DAY — STATE BANK — CLOSED-JULY 4
43

APRIL 4 — EASTER SUNDAY
44

MAY 17 — DOCTOR 4:30
45

AUGUST
46

Months of the year
ខែប្រចាំឆ្នាំ

25. January
មករា

26. February
កុម្ភៈ

27. March
មិនា

28. April
មេសា

29. May
ឧសភា

30. June
មិថុនា

31. July
កក្កដា

32. August
សីហា

33. September
កញ្ញា

34. October
តុលា

35. November
វិច្ឆិកា

36. December
ធ្នូ

Seasons
រដូវ

37. spring
រដូវផ្ការីក

38. summer
រដូវក្ដៅ

39. fall
រដូវស្លឹកឈើជ្រុះ

40. winter
រដូវរងា

41. birthday
ថ្ងៃកំណើត

42. anniversary
ថ្ងៃខួប

43. legal holiday
ថ្ងៃឈប់សម្រាកតាមច្បាប់

44. religious holiday
ថ្ងៃបុណ្យសាសនា

45. appointment
ពេលណាត់ជួប

46. vacation
វិស្សមកាល

Use the new language.

Look at the **ordinal numbers** on page **14**.

Use ordinal numbers to say the date.

It's June 5th. It's the fifth.

Talk about your birthday.

My birthday is in the winter.

My birthday is in January.

My birthday is on January twenty-sixth.

Money ប្រាក់

Coins កាក់

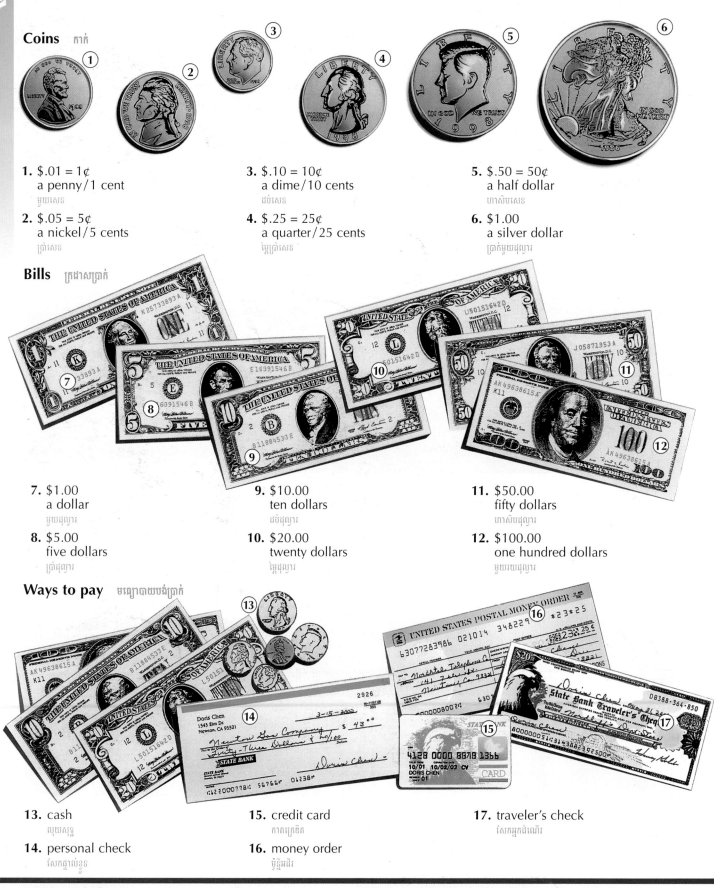

1. $.01 = 1¢
a penny / 1 cent
មួយសេន

2. $.05 = 5¢
a nickel / 5 cents
ប្រាំសេន

3. $.10 = 10¢
a dime / 10 cents
ដប់សេន

4. $.25 = 25¢
a quarter / 25 cents
ម្ភៃប្រាំសេន

5. $.50 = 50¢
a half dollar
ហាសិបសេន

6. $1.00
a silver dollar
ប្រាក់មួយដុល្លារ

Bills ក្រដាសប្រាក់

7. $1.00
a dollar
មួយដុល្លារ

8. $5.00
five dollars
ប្រាំដុល្លារ

9. $10.00
ten dollars
ដប់ដុល្លារ

10. $20.00
twenty dollars
ម្ភៃដុល្លារ

11. $50.00
fifty dollars
ហាសិបដុល្លារ

12. $100.00
one hundred dollars
មួយរយដុល្លារ

Ways to pay មធ្យោបាយបង់ប្រាក់

13. cash
លុយសុទ្ធ

14. personal check
សែកផ្ទាល់ខ្លួន

15. credit card
កាតក្រេឌិត

16. money order
ម៉ង់ឌេជ័រ

17. traveler's check
សែកអ្នកដំណើរ

More vocabulary

borrow: to get money from someone and return it later

lend: to give money to someone and get it back later

pay back: to retxurn the money that you borrowed

Other ways to talk about money:

a dollar bill or *a one*

a five-dollar bill or *a five*

a ten-dollar bill or *a ten*

a twenty-dollar bill or *a twenty*

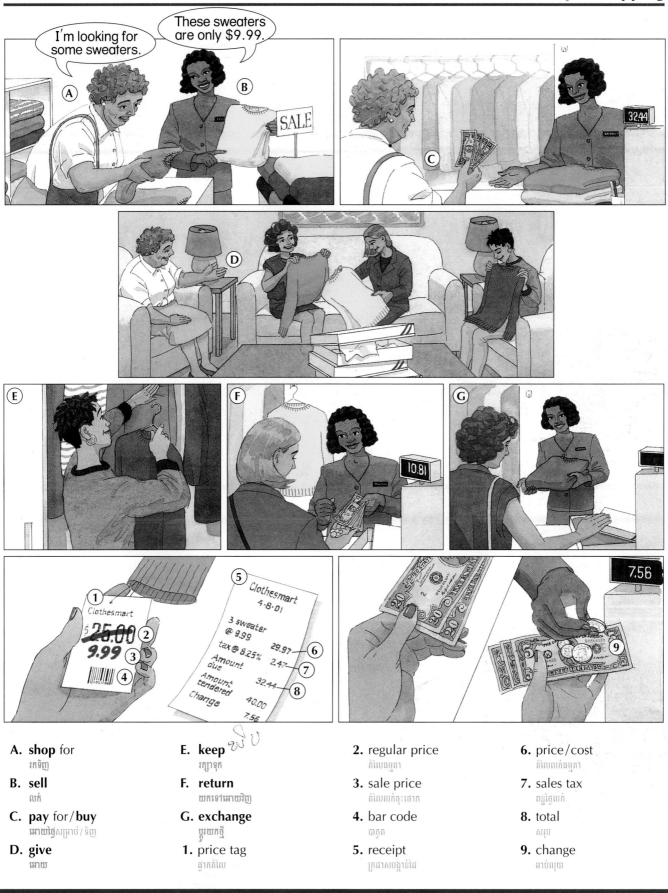

A. shop for
កេទិញ

B. sell
លក់

C. pay for/**buy**
ឆោយថ្លៃសម្រាប់/ទិញ

D. give
ឆោយ

E. keep
រក្សាទុក

F. return
យកទៅឆោយវិញ

G. exchange
ប្តូរយកថ្មី

1. price tag
ផ្លាកតំលៃ

2. regular price
តំលៃធម្មតា

3. sale price
តំលៃលក់ចុះថោក

4. bar code
បាកូត

5. receipt
ក្រដាសបង្កាន់ដៃ

6. price/cost
តំលៃលក់ធម្មតា

7. sales tax
ពន្ធថៃលក់

8. total
សរុប

9. change
អាប់លុយ

More vocabulary

When you use a credit card to shop, you get a **bill** in the mail. Bills list, in writing, the items you bought and the total you have to pay.

Share your answers.

1. Name three things you pay for every month.

2. Name one thing you will buy this week.

3. Where do you like to shop?

Age and Physical Description អាយុ និងលក្ខណៈរាងកាយ

1. children
ក្មេងក្មេង

2. baby
ទារក

3. toddler
ក្មេងក្មេង (អាយុពីរពីរទៅបីឆ្នាំ)

4. 6-year-old boy
ក្មេងប្រុសអាយុ ៦ ឆ្នាំ

5. 10-year-old girl
ក្មេងស្រីអាយុ ១០ ឆ្នាំ

6. teenagers
ក្មេងជំទង់

7. 13-year-old boy
ក្មេងប្រុសអាយុ ១៣ ឆ្នាំ

8. 19-year-old girl
ក្មេងស្រីអាយុ ១៩ ឆ្នាំ

9. adults
មនុស្សធំ

10. woman
ស្រី្ត

11. man
ប្រុស

12. senior citizen
មនុស្សចាស់ជរា

13. young
ក្មេង

14. middle-aged
ជាក់កណ្តាលអាយុ

15. elderly
មនុស្សចាស់ទុំ

16. tall
ខ្ពស់

17. average height
កំពស់មធ្យម

18. short
ទាប

19. pregnant
មានផ្ទៃពោះ

20. heavyset
ធាត់កំប៉ើង

21. average weight
ធាត់មធ្យម

22. thin/slim
ស្គម/ស្តើង

23. attractive
ដែលមេាក៏ចិត្ត

24. cute
ស្អាត

25. physically challenged
ពិការ

26. sight impaired/blind
មើលមិនឃើញ/ពិការភ្នែក

27. hearing impaired/deaf
ស្តាប់មិនឮ/ថ្លង់

Talk about yourself and your teacher.

I am young, average height, and average weight.

My teacher is a middle-aged, tall, thin man.

Use the new language.

Turn to **Hobbies and Games,** pages **162–163.**

Describe each person on the page.

He's a heavyset, short, senior citizen.

1. short hair
   សក់ខ្លី

2. shoulder-length hair
   សក់វែងប្រះស្មា

3. long hair
   សក់វែង

4. part
   ផ្នែកចំហៀង

5. mustache
   ពុកមាត់

6. beard
   ពុកចង្កា

7. sideburns
   ជើងសក់

8. bangs
   កាត់សក់សេះ

9. straight hair
   សក់សួត

10. wavy hair
    សក់អង្កាញ់

11. curly hair
    សក់ក្រញាញ់ / សក់រួញ

12. bald
    ទំពែក

13. gray hair
    សក់ស្កូវ

14. red hair
    សក់ក្រហម

15. black hair
    សក់ខ្មៅ

16. blond hair
    សក់ទងដែង

17. brown hair
    សក់ពណ៌ត្នោត

18. brush
    ច្រាស់សិតសក់

19. scissors
    កន្ត្រៃ

20. blow dryer
    ប្រដាប់ផ្លុំសក់

21. rollers
    ប្រដាប់មួរសក់

22. comb
    ក្រាស់

A. **cut** hair
   កាត់សក់

B. **perm** hair
   អ៊ុតសក់

C. **set** hair
   ក្រងសក់

D. **color** hair/**dye** hair
   លាបពណ៌សក់

More vocabulary

hair stylist: a person who cuts, sets, and perms hair

hair salon: the place where a hair stylist works

Talk about your hair.

My hair is <u>long</u>, <u>straight</u>, and <u>brown</u>.

I have <u>long</u>, <u>straight</u>, <u>brown</u> hair.

When I was a child my hair was <u>short</u>, <u>curly</u>, and <u>blond</u>.

Tom Lee's Family

1. grandparents
ជីដូនជីតា

Min   Lu

2. grandmother
ជីដូន

3. grandfather
ជីតា

4. parents
ឪពុកម្ដាយ

Rose   Chang

Helen   Daniel

Tom

5. mother
ម្ដាយ

6. father
ឪពុក

10. aunt
មីង / អុំ

11. uncle
ម៉ា (ញ) / អុំ

Lily   Alex

Emily

8. sister
បងស្រី (ប្អូនស្រី)

9. brother
បងប្រុស (ប្អូនប្រុស)

12. cousin
ជីដូនមួយ

7. (Min and Lu's)
grandson
(របស់មិន និង លូ) ចៅប្រុស

Berta   Mario   Ana Garcia's
Family

Ana

13. mother-in-law
ម្ដាយក្មេក

14. father-in-law
ឪពុកក្មេក

Marta   Carlos   Tito

20. (Tito's) wife
(របស់ទីតូ) ប្រពន្ធ

15. sister-in-law
បង / ប្អូនថ្លៃស្រី

16. brother-in-law
បង / ប្អូនថ្លៃប្រុស

19. husband
ប្ដី

Alice   Eddie   Sara   Felix

17. niece
ក្មួយស្រី

18. nephew
ក្មួយប្រុស

21. daughter
កូនស្រី

22. son
កូនប្រុស

More vocabulary

Lily and Emily are Min and Lu's **granddaughters.**

Daniel is Min and Lu's **son-in-law.**

Ana is Berta and Mario's **daughter-in-law.**

Share your answers.

1. How many brothers and sisters do you have?

2. What number son or daughter are you?

3. Do you have any children?

Lisa Smith's Family

23. married
អៀបការគ្នា

Carol   Dan

Lisa

24. divorced
លែងលះគ្នា

25. single mother
ម្ដាយប៉ុស្តិ៍លែង

26. single father
ឪពុកប្រពន្ធលែង

27. remarried
អៀបការឡើងវិញ

Rick   Carol

Dan   Sue

Rick   Carol

28. stepfather
ឪពុកចុង

David   Mary

Lisa

Dan   Sue

31. stepmother
ម្ដាយចុង

Kim   Bill

29. half brother
បង/ប្អូនប្រុស ឪពុក
ឬម្ដាយតែមួយ

30. half sister
បង/ប្អូនស្រី
ឪពុកឬម្ដាយតែមួយ

32. stepsister
បង/ប្អូនស្រី
ដែលជាកូនឪពុក ឬម្ដាយចុង

33. stepbrother
បង/ប្អូនប្រុស ដែលជាកូន
ឪពុក ឬម្ដាយចុង

More vocabulary

Carol is Dan's **former wife.**

Sue is Dan's **wife.**

Dan is Carol's **former husband.**

Rick is Carol's **husband.**

Lisa is the **stepdaughter** of both Rick and Sue.

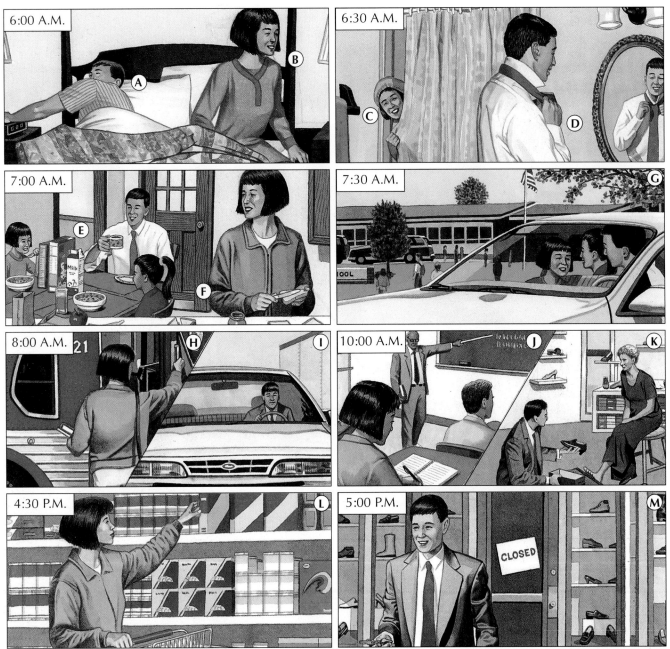

A. **wake up**
ភ្ញាក់ដឹងខ្លួន

B. **get up**
ក្រោកឡើង

C. **take** a shower
ងូតទឹក

D. **get dressed**
ស្លៀកពាក់

E. **eat** breakfast
ស្រង់ស្រូបអាហារពេលព្រឹក

F. **make** lunch
រៀបបាយ

G. **take** the children to school
យកកូនទៅសាលា

H. **take** the bus to school
ជិះឡានឈ្នួលទៅសាលា

I. **drive** to work/**go** to work
បើកឡានទៅធ្វើការ/ទៅធ្វើការ

J. **be** in school
រៀន/នៅសាលា

K. **work**
ធ្វើការ

L. **go** to the market
ទៅផ្សារ

M. **leave** work
ចេញពីធ្វើការ

Grammar point: 3rd person singular

For **he** and **she**, we add **-s** or **-es** to the verb.

He/She wake**s** up.

He/She watch**es** TV.

These verbs are different (irregular):

be	He/She **is** in school at 10:00 a.m.
have	He/She **has** dinner at 6:30 p.m.

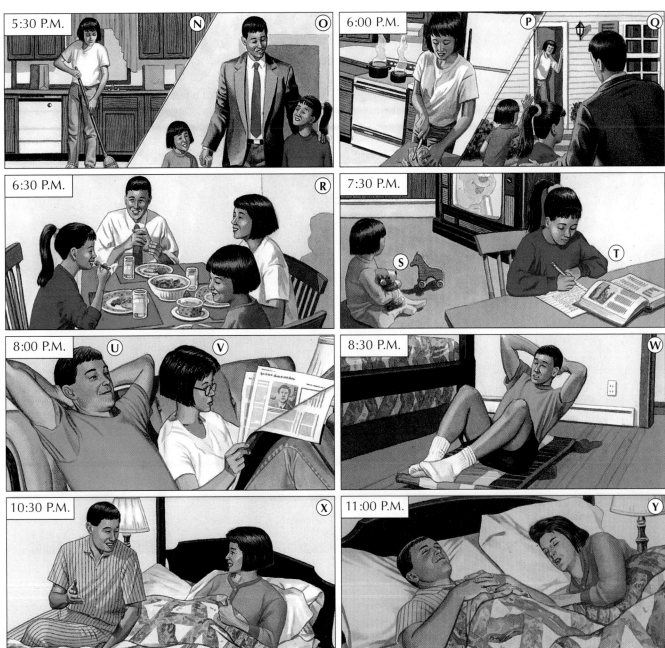

N. clean the house
ផុតផ្ទះ / សំអាតផ្ទះ

O. pick up the children
ទៅយកកូន

P. cook dinner
ធ្វើម្ហូបពេលល្ងាច

Q. come home / **get** home
មកផ្ទះ

R. have dinner
ពិសារបាយពេលល្ងាច

S. watch TV
មើលទូរទស្សន៍

T. do homework
ធ្វើកិច្ចការសាលា

U. relax
សំរាក

V. read the paper
អានកាសែត

W. exercise
ហាត់ប្រាណ

X. go to bed
ទៅសំរាន្ត / ទៅផ្ទែ

Y. go to sleep
ទៅដេក ឬទៅគេង

Talk about your daily routine.

I take a shower in the morning.
I go to school in the evening.
I go to bed at 11 o'clock.

Share your answers.

1. Who makes dinner in your family?
2. Who goes to the market?
3. Who goes to work?

Life Events ដំណើរជីវិត

A. **be born**
កើត

B. **start** school
ចាប់ផ្ដើមចូលរៀន

C. **immigrate**
ចាកចេញពីប្រទេស

D. **graduate**
ចប់ការសិក្សា

E. **learn** to drive
រៀនបើកបរ

F. **join** the army
ចូលផ្ទៃទាហាន

G. **get** a job
បានការងារ

H. **become** a citizen
ចូលសញ្ជាតិ

I. **rent** an apartment
ផ្ទះបន្ទប់ស្នាក់

J. **go** to college
ទៅរៀននៅមហាវិទ្យាល័យ

K. **fall in love**
ធ្លាក់ក្នុងក្ដីស្នេហា

L. **get married**
រៀបការ

A — 1925
B — 1930
C — DEPARTMENT OF IMMIGRATION — 1940
D — 1942
E — 1943
F — 1944
G — 1948
H — 1949
I — 1951
J — CITY COLLEGE — 1956
K — 1957
L — 1958

Grammar point: past tense

start		immigrate	
learn		graduate	
join	+ed	move	+d
rent		retire	
travel		die	

These verbs are different (irregular):

be	—	was	have	—	had
get	—	got	buy	—	bought
become	—	became			
go	—	went			
fall	—	fell			

28

M. have a baby
មានកូន

N. travel
ធ្វើដំណើរ

O. buy a house
ទិញផ្ទះ

P. move
ផ្លាស់លំនៅ

Q. have a grandchild
មានចៅ

R. die
ស្លាប់

1. birth certificate
សំបុត្រកំណើត

2. diploma
សញ្ញាប័ត្រមធ្យមសិក្សា

3. Resident Alien card
កាតផ្តល់សិទ្ធិរស់នៅ

4. driver's license
ប័ណ្ណបើកបរ

5. Social Security card
កាតសន្តិសុខសង្គម

6. Certificate of Naturalization
សំបុត្របញ្ជាក់ចូលសញ្ជាតិ

7. college degree
សញ្ញាប័ត្រមហាវិទ្យាល័យ

8. marriage license
សំបុត្រអាពាហ៍ពិពាហ៍

9. passport
លិខិតឆ្លងដែន

More vocabulary

When a husband dies, his wife becomes a **widow.**

When a wife dies, her husband becomes a **widower.**

When older people stop working, we say they **retire.**

Talk about yourself.

I was born in 1968.

I learned to drive in 1987.

I immigrated in 1990.

1. hot
   ក្ដៅ

2. thirsty
   ស្រេក

3. sleepy
   ងុយដេក

4. cold
   ត្រជាក់

5. hungry
   ឃ្លាន

6. full
   ឆ្អែត

7. comfortable
   ស្រួល

8. uncomfortable
   មិនស្រួល

9. disgusted
   ឆ្អើម / ខ្ពើម

10. calm
    ស្ងប់ស្ងៀម

11. nervous
    អន្ទះអន្ទែង

12. in pain
    ចុកចាប់

13. worried
    ព្រួយ

14. sick
    ឈឺ

15. well
    ជា

16. relieved
    ធូរស្បើយ

17. hurt
    ឈឺចាប់

18. lonely
    ឯកោ / ឯការ

19. in love
    ស្រឡាញ់

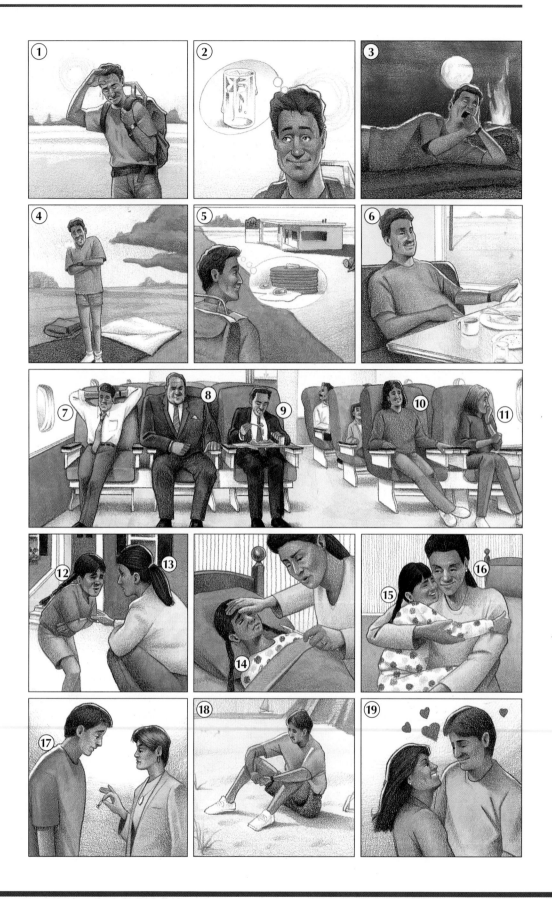

More vocabulary

furious: very angry

terrified: very scared

overjoyed: very happy

exhausted: very tired

starving: very hungry

humiliated: very embarrassed

Talk about your feelings.

I feel _happy_ when I see _my friends_.

I feel _homesick_ when I think about _my family_.

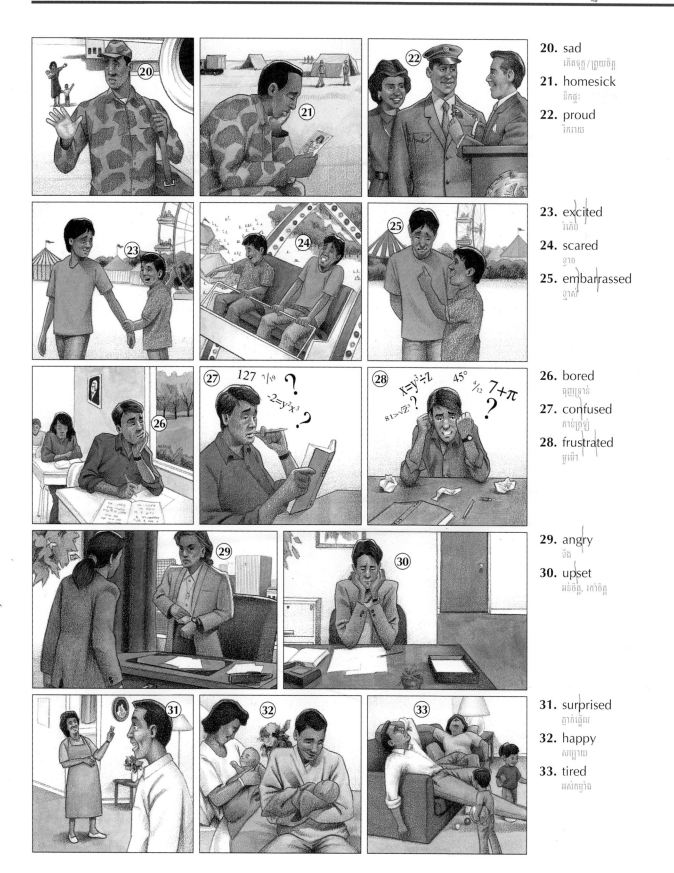

20. sad
កើតទុក្ខ/ព្រួយចិត្ត
21. homesick
នឹកផ្ទះ
22. proud
រីករាយ
23. excited
រំភើប
24. scared
ខ្លាច
25. embarrassed
ខ្មាស់
26. bored
ធុញទ្រាន់
27. confused
ភាន់ច្រឡំ
28. frustrated
អន់ចិត្ត
29. angry
ខឹង
30. upset
អន់ចិត្ត, រកាចិត្ត
31. surprised
ភ្ញាក់ផ្អើល
32. happy
សប្បាយ
33. tired
អស់កម្លាំង

Use the new language.

Look at **Clothing I**, page **64**, and answer the questions.

1. How does the runner feel?

2. How does the man at the bus stop feel?

3. How does the woman at the bus stop feel?

4. How do the teenagers feel?

5. How does the little boy feel?

A Graduation ការបញ្ចប់កម្មវិធីសិក្សា

The Ceremony

1. graduating class
   ថ្នាក់ត្រូវបញ្ចប់ការសិក្សា

2. gown
   អាវវែង

3. cap
   មួក

4. stage
   វិការដ្ឋាន

5. podium
   អធិកា

6. graduate
   អ្នកចប់ការសិក្សា

7. diploma
   សញ្ញាបត្រមធ្យមសិក្សា

8. valedictorian
   សិស្សដែលថ្លែងសុន្ទរកថា
   ពេលបញ្ចប់ការសិក្សា

9. guest speaker
   ធ្វើវាគ្មិន

10. audience
    ទស្សនិកជន

11. photographer
    អ្នកថតរូប

A. graduate
   ចប់ការសិក្សា

B. applaud / clap
   ទះដៃ

C. cry
   យំ

D. take a picture
   ថតរូប

E. give a speech
   ថ្លែងសុន្ទរកថា

Talk about what the people in the pictures are doing.

She is
- taking a picture.
- giving a speech.
- smiling.
- laughing.

He is
- making a toast.
- clapping.

They are
- graduating.
- hugging.
- kissing.
- applauding.

32

The Party

12. caterer អ្នកផ្គត់ផ្គង់មួបអាហារ	**15.** banner បដា	**18.** gifts អំណោយ	**H.** laugh សើច
13. buffet មួបដុសឆ្ងាញ់ខ្លួនឯង	**16.** dance floor កម្រាលរាំ	**F.** kiss ថើប	**I.** make a toast គោះកែវ / ទទួចកែវគ្នា
14. guests ភ្ញៀវ	**17.** DJ (disc jockey) ឌី ថេ	**G.** hug ឱប	**J.** dance រាំ

Share your answers.

1. Did you ever go to a graduation? Whose?

2. Did you ever give a speech? Where?

3. Did you ever hear a great speaker? Where?

4. Did you ever go to a graduation party?

5. What do you like to eat at parties?

6. Do you like to dance at parties?

Places to Live កន្លែងរស់នៅ។

1. the city / an urban area
ទីក្រុង / តំបន់ទីក្រុង

2. the suburbs
ជាយក្រុង

3. a small town
ក្រុងតូចៗ

4. the country / a rural area
ស្រុកស្រែចំការ / ជនបទ

5. apartment building
ផ្ទះល្វែងជួល

6. house
ផ្ទះ

7. townhouse
ផ្ទះក្រុង

8. mobile home
ផ្ទះចល័ត

9. college dormitory
សយនដ្ឋាននិស្សិតមហាវិទ្យាល័យ

10. shelter
ជម្រក

11. nursing home
មន្ទីរក្សាជនជរា-ពិការ

12. ranch
ក្រោលសត្វ

13. farm
ដីស្រែចំការ

More vocabulary

duplex house: a house divided into two homes

condominium: an apartment building where each apartment is owned separately

co-op: an apartment building owned by the residents

Share your answers.

1. Do you like where you live?

2. Where did you live in your country?

3. What types of housing are there near your school?

34

Renting an apartment ជួលផ្ទះល្វែង

A. look for a new apartment
រកផ្ទល់ ផ្ទះល្វែងថ្មី

B. talk to the manager
និយាយជាមួយអ្នកមើលការអុស្រត្រូវផ្ទះជួល

C. sign a rental agreement
ចុះហត្ថលេខាលើកិច្ចព្រមព្រៀងជួលផ្ទះ

D. move in
ចូលទៅ

E. unpack
រើវ៉ាន់ចេញ

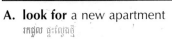

F. pay the rent
បង់ថ្លៃជួលផ្ទះ

Buying a house ទិញផ្ទះ

G. talk to the Realtor
និយាយជាមួយអ្នកលក់-ទិញផ្ទះបូរី

H. make an offer
ភង្ថ ទិញ

I. get a loan
ខ្ចីប្រាក់

J. take ownership
ឈរឈ្មោះជាម្ចាស់

K. arrange the furniture
រៀបចំ គ្រឿងតុប

L. pay the mortgage
បង់ថ្លៃបំណុល

More vocabulary

lease: a rental agreement for a specific period of time

utilities: gas, water, and electricity for the home

Practice talking to an apartment manager.

How much is the rent?

Are utilities included?

When can I move in?

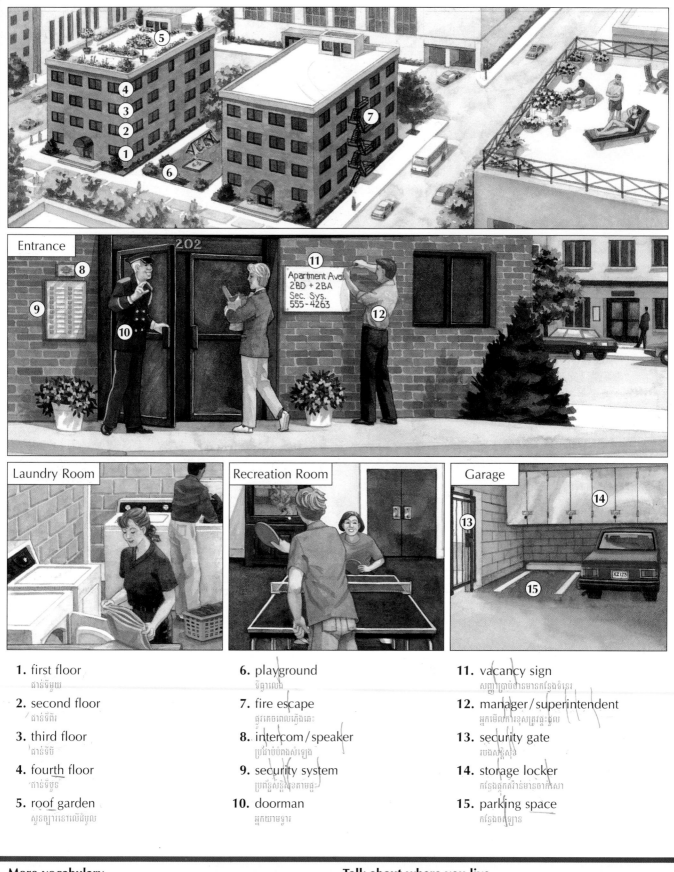

1. **first floor**
   ជាន់ទីមួយ

2. **second floor**
   ជាន់ទីពីរ

3. **third floor**
   ជាន់ទីបី

4. **fourth floor**
   ជាន់ទីបួន

5. **roof garden**
   សួនឧទ្យាននៅលើដំបូល

6. **playground**
   ទីធ្លាលេង

7. **fire escape**
   ផ្លូវគេចពេលឆេះកើតរោះ

8. **intercom / speaker**
   ប្រដាប់បំពងសំរទ្បុង

9. **security system**
   ប្រព័ន្ធសុវត្ថិភាពតាមផ្ទះ

10. **doorman**
    អ្នកយាមទ្វារ

11. **vacancy sign**
    សញ្ញាប្រាប់ថានមានកន្លែងទំនេរ

12. **manager / superintendent**
    អ្នកមើលការខុសត្រូវផ្ទះជួល

13. **security gate**
    របងសុវត្ថិភាព

14. **storage locker**
    កន្លែងទុកសំរាប់មានទ្វារជាក់សោ

15. **parking space**
    កន្លែងចតឡាន

More vocabulary

rec room: a short way of saying **recreation room**

basement: the area below the street level of an apartment or a house

Talk about where you live.

I live in Apartment 3 near the entrance.

I live in Apartment 11 on the second floor near the fire escape.

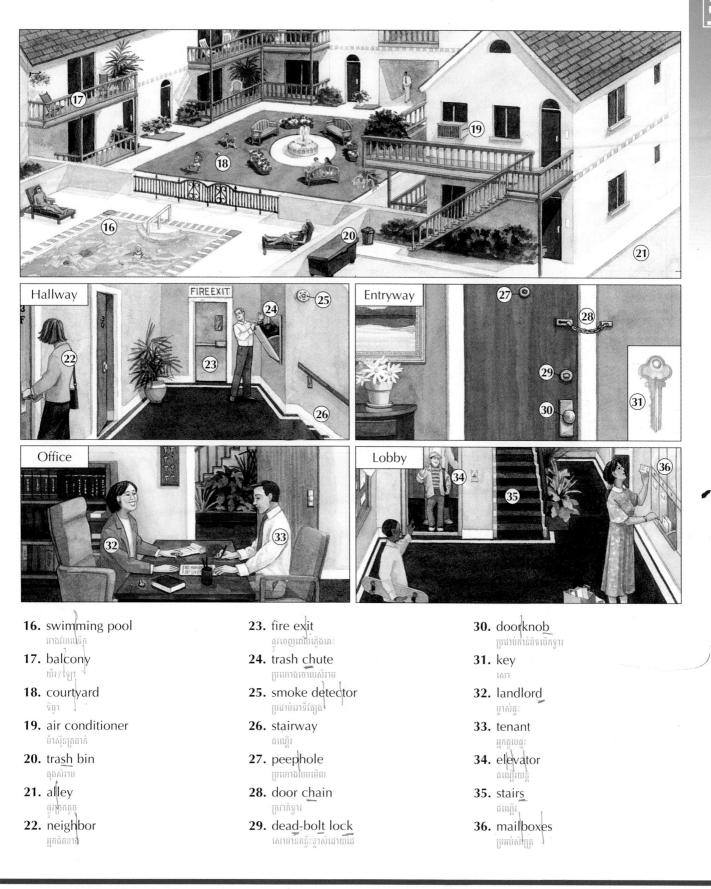

16. swimming pool អាងហែលទឹក	**23.** fire exit ផ្លូវចេញពេលភ្លើងឆេះ	**30.** doorknob ប្រដាប់កាន់បិទបើកទ្វារ
17. balcony យ៉ែរ/ផ្លា	**24.** trash chute ប្រហោងចោលសំរាម	**31.** key កូនសោ
18. courtyard ទីធ្លា	**25.** smoke detector ប្រដាប់ដោះទីផ្សែង	**32.** landlord ម្ចាស់ផ្ទះ
19. air conditioner ម៉ាស៊ីនត្រជាក់	**26.** stairway ជណ្ដើរ	**33.** tenant អ្នកជួលផ្ទះ
20. trash bin ធុងសំរាម	**27.** peephole ប្រហោងបែបមើល	**34.** elevator ជណ្ដើរយន្ត
21. alley ផ្លូវក្រោយ	**28.** door chain ច្រវាក់ទ្វារ	**35.** stairs ជណ្ដើរ
22. neighbor អ្នកជិតខាង	**29.** dead-bolt lock សោរមានគន្លឹះខ្ទាស់ដោយខ្លួនឯង	**36.** mailboxes ប្រអប់សំបុត្រ

Grammar point: *there is, there are*

singular: *there is*   plural: *there are*

There is *a fire exit in the hallway.*

There are *mailboxes in the lobby.*

Talk about apartments.

My apartment has <u>an elevator</u>, <u>a lobby</u>, and <u>a rec room</u>.

My apartment doesn't have <u>a pool</u> or <u>a garage</u>.

My apartment needs <u>air conditioning</u>.

37

1. **floor plan**
   ប្លង់បន្ទប់ ប្លង់ផ្ទះ

2. **backyard**
   ទិដ្ឋភាពខាងក្រោយ

3. **fence**
   របង

4. **mailbox**
   ប្រអប់សំបុត្រ

5. **driveway**
   ផ្លូវឡានចូល

6. **garage**
   រោងឡាន

7. **garage door**
   ទ្វាររោងឡាន

8. **screen door**
   ទ្វារស័ណ្ដាញ់

9. **porch light**
   គ្រឿងភ្លើងហាល

10. **doorbell**
    កណ្តឹងទ្វារ

11. **front door**
    ទ្វារមុខ

12. **storm door**
    ទ្វារក្រៅ

13. **steps**
    កាំជណ្តើរ

14. **front walk**
    ផ្លូវដើរខាងមុខ

15. **front yard**
    ទិដ្ឋភាពខាងមុខ

16. **deck**
    រានហាល

17. **window**
    បង្អួច

18. **shutter**
    បង្អួច (បង្អួច)

19. **gutter**
    ។

20. **roof**
    ដំបូល

21. **chimney**
    បំពង់ផ្សែង

22. **TV antenna**
    អង់តែនទូរទស្សន៍

More vocabulary

two-story house: a house with two floors

downstairs: the bottom floor

upstairs: the part of a house above the bottom floor

Share your answers.

1. What do you like about this house?

2. What's something you don't like about the house?

3. Describe the perfect house.

1. **hedge**
   របងដើមឈើ

2. **hammock**
   អ្រែង

3. **garbage can**
   ធុងសំរាម

4. **leaf blower**
   ម៉ាស៊ីនផ្លុំស្លឹកឈើ

5. **patio furniture**
   គ្រឿងអរនៅរោងហាល

6. **patio**
   រោងហាលជាប់និងដី

7. **barbecue grill**
   ចង្ក្រានអាំង

8. **sprinkler**
   ប្រដាប់បាញ់ទឹកស្រោចស្មៅ

9. **hose**
   បំពង់ទឹក

10. **compost pile**
    គំនរសំរាមធ្វើជី

11. **rake**
    រនាស់

12. **hedge clippers**
    កន្ត្រៃកាត់គុម្ពឈើ

13. **shovel**
    ប៉ែល

14. **trowel**
    ស្មាប់ព្រាបាយអរ ។

15. **pruning shears**
    កន្ត្រៃកាត់មែកឈើ

16. **wheelbarrow**
    រទេះរុញកង់មួយ

17. **watering can**
    ធុងស្រោចផ្កា

18. **flowerpot**
    ថើងផ្កា

19. **flower**
    ផ្កា

20. **bush** (rose)
    គម្ពោតផ្កា

21. **lawn**
    ស្មៅ

22. **lawn mower**
    ម៉ាស៊ីនកាត់ស្មៅ

A. **weed** the flower bed
   ដកស្មៅចេញពីក្បាលផ្កា

B. **water** the plants
   ស្រោចដើមឈើ

C. **mow** the lawn
   កាត់ស្មៅ

D. **plant** a tree
   ដាំដើមឈើ

E. **trim** the hedge
   តម្រឹមស្លឹកឈើ

F. **rake** the leaves
   រាស់ប្រមូលស្លឹកឈើ

Talk about your yard and gardening.

I like to plant trees.

I don't like to weed.

I like/don't like to work in the yard/garden.

Share your answers.

1. What flowers, trees, or plants do you see in the picture? (Look at **Trees, Plants, and Flowers,** pages **128–129** for help.)

2. Do you ever use a barbecue grill to cook?

1. cabinet	**8.** shelf	**15.** toaster oven	**22.** counter
ទូដាក់របស់របរនៅផ្ទះបាយ	ធ្នើ	ទូរអាំងនំបុ័ង	គុជាប់និងជញ្ជាំង
2. paper towels	**9.** refrigerator	**16.** pot	**23.** drawer
ក្រដាសជូតភ្នែ	ទូទឹកកក	ឆ្នាំង	ថត
3. dish drainer	**10.** freezer	**17.** teakettle	**24.** pan
របសម្រោះចាន	ម៉ាស៊ីនធ្វើអោយកក	កំសេ្យវរៃ	ខ្ទះ
4. dishwasher	**11.** coffeemaker	**18.** stove _RANGE_	**25.** electric mixer
ម៉ាស៊ីនលាងចាន	ប្រដាប់ធ្វើកាហ្វេ	ចង្ក្រានម៉ាស៊ូ	ម៉ាស៊ីនលាយក្រឡៀង
5. garbage disposal	**12.** blender	**19.** burner	**26.** food processor
ម៉ាស៊ីនកិនកាកសំណល់	ម៉ាស៊ីនកិន	ក្បាលចង្ក្រានឧតឧស្ម័ន	ម៉ាស៊ីនកិនសាច់ / បន្លែ
6. sink	**13.** microwave oven	**20.** oven	**27.** cutting board
អាងលាងចាន	ម៉ៃក្រវ៉េវ	ម្	ក្ដារ
7. toaster	**14.** electric can opener	**21.** broiler	
ប្រដាប់អាំងនំបុ័ង	ប្រដាប់បើកកំប៉ុង (ប្រើភ្លើង)	ចង្ក្រានអាំងសាច់	

Talk about the location of kitchen items.

The toaster oven is on the counter near the stove.

The microwave is above the stove.

Share your answers.

1. Do you have a garbage disposal? a dishwasher? a microwave?

2. Do you eat in the kitchen?

1. **china cabinet**
   ទូចានមកពិចិន
2. **set of dishes**
   ចានចម្រុះ
3. **platter**
   ចានសំរាប់តែគត់
4. **ceiling fan**
   កង្ហាល់ពិដាន
5. **light fixture**
   គ្រឿងភ្លើង
6. **serving dish**
   ចានត្រដាក់ម្ហូប
7. **candle**
   ទៀន

8. **candlestick**
   ជើងទ្រទៀន
9. **vase**
   ថូ
10. **tray**
    ថាស
11. **teapot**
    ប៉័ន់តែ
12. **sugar bowl**
    ចានស្ករ
13. **creamer**
    ថូដាក់ក្រម
14. **saltshaker**
    ប្រដាប់រោយអំបិល

15. **pepper shaker**
    ប្រដាប់រោយម្រេច
16. **dining room chair**
    កៅអីញ៉ាំបាយ
17. **dining room table**
    តុបាយ
18. **tablecloth**
    កម្រាលតុ
19. **napkin**
    ក្រដាសជូតដៃ
20. **place mat**
    ទ្រនាប់ចាន
21. **fork**
    សម

22. **knife**
    កាំបិត
23. **spoon**
    ស្លាបព្រា
24. **plate**
    ចានសំរាប់បិក/ចានទទាប
25. **bowl**
    ចានគោម/ចានរង្គ្រា
26. **glass**
    កែវ
27. **coffee cup**
    ពែងកាហ្វេ
28. **mug**
    កែរប្បែពែងគំ

Practice asking for things in the dining room.

Please pass the platter.

May I have the creamer?

Could I have a fork, please?

Share your answers.

1. What are the women in the picture saying?
2. In your home, where do you eat?
3. Do you like to make dinner for your friends?

A Living Room បន្ទប់ទទួលភ្ញៀវ

1. bookcase ទូសៀវភៅ	**8. mantel** ឃ្នងដើងក្រោនត្រ	**15. floor lamp** ចង្កៀងខ្ពស់ដាក់ផ្ទាល់កម្រាល	**22. magazine holder** ប្រដាប់ដាក់ទស្សនាវដ្ដី
2. basket ល្អី	**9. fireplace** ចង្ក្រានអុតអុស	**16. drapes** វាំងននបង្អួច	**23. coffee table** តុការកាហ្វេ
3. track lighting ភ្លើងមានអំពូលច្រើន	**10. fire** ភ្លើង	**17. window** បង្អួច	**24. armchair/easy chair** កៅអីមានភ្នាក់ដៃ
4. lightbulb អំពូលភ្លើង	**11. fire screen** សំណាញ់បាំងភ្លើង	**18. plant** ដើមរោជ	**25. love seat** កៅអីអង្គុយភ្ជាប់ពីរនាក់
5. ceiling ពិតាន	**12. logs** ឧស	**19. sofa/couch** សូហ្វា/កៅអីវែង	**26. TV (television)** ទូរទស្សន៍
6. wall ជញ្ជាំង	**13. wall unit** ទូអាក់កាំងក្នុងបន្ទប់ទទួលភ្ញៀវ	**20. throw pillow** ខ្នើយខ្ទើយ	**27. carpet** កម្រាលព្រំ
7. painting គំនូរ	**14. stereo system** គ្រឿងស្តេរេអូ	**21. end table** តុឯកកុ	

Use the new language.

Look at **Colors, page 12,** and describe this room.

There is <u>a gray sofa</u> and <u>a gray armchair</u>.

Talk about your living room.

In my living room I have <u>a sofa</u>, <u>two chairs</u>, and <u>a coffee table</u>.

I don't have <u>a fireplace</u> or <u>a wall unit</u>.

1. hamper
   កន្ត្រាដាក់ខោអាវប្រឡាក់

2. bathtub
   អាងងូតទឹក

3. rubber mat
   កម្រាលជាប់ក្នុងអាងងូតទឹកកុំអោយរអិល

4. drain
   កន្លែងបង្ហូរទឹក

5. hot water
   ទឹកក្តៅ

6. faucet
   ក្បាលប៉ាស៊ីនទឹក

7. cold water
   ទឹកត្រជាក់

8. towel rack
   ប្រដាប់ព្យួរកន្សែង

9. tile
   ផ្ទាំងកឿផ្ទែក្នុងបន្ទប់ងូតទឹក

10. showerhead
    ក្បាលទឹកផ្កាឈូក

11. (mini)blinds
    នៅវាំងនន

12. bath towel
    កន្សែងជូតខ្លួន

13. hand towel
    កន្សែងជូតដៃ

14. washcloth
    កូនកន្សែងជូតមុខ

15. toilet paper
    ក្រដាសបង្គន់

16. toilet brush
    ច្រាសបង្គន់

17. toilet
    បង្គន់

18. mirror
    កញ្ចក់

19. medicine cabinet
    ទូដាក់ថ្នាំ

20. toothbrush
    ច្រាសដុសធ្មេញ

21. toothbrush holder
    ប្រដាប់ដាក់ច្រាសដុសធ្មេញ

22. sink
    អាងលាងដៃ

23. soap
    សាប៊ូ

24. soap dish
    ចានសាប៊ូ

25. wastebasket
    ធុងចោលសំរាម

26. scale
    ជញ្ជីងថ្លឹង

27. bath mat
    កម្រាលជូតជើង

More vocabulary

half bath: a bathroom without a shower or bathtub

linen closet: a closet or cabinet for towels and sheets

stall shower: a shower without a bathtub

Share your answers.

1. Do you turn off the water when you brush your teeth?
   wash your hair? shave?

2. Does your bathroom have a bathtub or a stall shower?

1. mirror កញ្ចក់	**8.** bed គ្រែ	**15.** headboard ក្បាលគ្រែ	**22.** dust ruffle កម្រាលរំលេចជាយ
2. dresser / bureau ទូខោអាវមានគ្រឿងសំអិតសំអាង	**9.** pillow ខ្នើយ	**16.** clock radio វិទ្យុមាននាឡិកា	**23.** rug ព្រំ
3. drawer ថត	**10.** pillowcase ស្រោមខ្នើយ	**17.** lamp ចង្កៀង	**24.** floor កម្រាលឥដ្ឋ
4. closet កន្លែងព្យួរខោអាវ	**11.** bedspread កម្រាលពូក	**18.** lampshade គំរបចង្កៀង	**25.** mattress ពូក
5. curtains វាំងនន	**12.** blanket ភួយ	**19.** light switch កុងតាក់ភ្លើង	**26.** box spring ប្រអប់ទ្រនាប់ពូក
6. window shade រនាំងបាំងបង្អួច	**13.** flat sheet កម្រាលពូកខាងលើ	**20.** outlet កន្លែងដោតភ្លើង	**27.** bed frame ក្របគ្រែ
7. photograph រូបថត	**14.** fitted sheet កម្រាលពូកខាងក្រោម	**21.** night table តុនៅជាប់ជិតក្បាលគ្រែ	

Use the new language.

Describe this room. (See **Describing Things**, page **11**, for help.)

I see a soft pillow and a beautiful bedspread.

Share your answers.

1. What is your favorite thing in your bedroom?

2. Do you have a clock in your bedroom? Where is it?

3. Do you have a mirror in your bedroom? Where is it?

1. bunk bed
ត្រែពីរជាន់

2. comforter
ភួយញាត់សំឡី

3. night-light
ចង្កៀងពេលយប់

4. mobile
ប្រដាប់ព្យួរសម្រាប់ក្មេងរាំមើល

5. wallpaper
ផ្ទាំងក្រដាស

6. crib
ត្រែក្មេងៗ

7. bumper pad
ពូកយ៉ាងកុំអោយទង្គិចនឹងត្រែ

8. chest of drawers
ទូមានថតច្រើន

9. baby monitor
ប្រដាប់ចាប់សំលេងក្មេង

10. teddy bear
ក្លនខ្លាឃ្មុំាត់សំឡី

11. smoke detector
ប្រដាប់រាវរីផ្សែង

12. changing table
តុដូរកន្ទប

13. diaper pail
ធុងកន្ទប

14. dollhouse
ផ្ទះកុក្កតា

15. blocks
ដុំឈើត្រង

16. ball
បាល់

17. picture book
សៀវភៅរូបភាព

18. doll
កូនកុក្កតា

19. cradle
អង្រឹងឆក់ខ្សែ

20. coloring book
សៀវភៅរំសាប់ពណ៌

21. crayons
ខ្មៅដៃពណ៌

22. puzzle
ល្បែងផ្គុំៗ

23. stuffed animals
សត្វញាត់សំឡី

24. toy chest
ធុងដាក់របស់ក្មេងលេង

Talk about where items are in the room.

The dollhouse is near the coloring book.
The teddy bear is on the chest of drawers.

Share your answers.

1. Do you think this is a good room for children? Why?
2. What toys did you play with when you were a child?
3. What children's stories do you know?

A. dust the furniture
បោសសំអាតគ្រឿងទ្រ

B. recycle the newspapers
ក្រដាសកាសែតយកទៅធ្វើម្តងទៀត

C. clean the oven
សំអាតចង្ក្រានអាំង

D. wash the windows
លាងបង្អួច

E. sweep the floor
ផ្តុកម្រាល

F. empty the wastebasket
ចាលសំរាម

G. make the bed
រៀបគ្រែ

H. put away the toys
ទុករបស់ក្មេងលេង

I. vacuum the carpet
ម្បាគ្រាំ

J. mop the floor
ផ្តលាងកម្រាល

K. polish the furniture
ផ្តខាត់គ្រឿងទ្រ

L. scrub the floor
ដុសផ្តុកម្រាល

M. wash the dishes
លាងចាន

N. dry the dishes
សម្ងួតចាន

O. wipe the counter
ផ្តុកុបំផញ្ញ៉ាង

P. change the sheets
ផ្លូវកម្រាល

Q. take out the garbage
អាតសំរាមទៅចោល

Talk about yourself.

I wash the dishes every day.

I change the sheets every week.

I never dry the dishes.

Share your answers.

1. Who does the housework in your family?

2. What is your favorite cleaning job?

3. What is your least favorite cleaning job?

1. feather duster
   អំបោសស្លាបសត្វ

2. recycling bin
   ធុងដាក់របស់សម្រាប់ធ្វើឡើងវិញម្ដងទៀត

3. oven cleaner
   ថ្នាំលាងចង្ក្រានអាំង

4. rubber gloves
   ស្រោមដៃកៅស៊ូ

5. steel-wool soap pads
   អាចម៍ដែកសម្រាប់ដុសឆ្នាំង

6. rags
   ក្រណាត់សំរាប់ជូតធូលី

7. stepladder
   ជណ្ដើរ

8. glass cleaner
   ថ្នាំលាងកញ្ចក់

9. squeegee
   ប្រដាប់ជូត

10. broom
    អំបោស

11. dustpan
    ប្រដាប់កើបសំរាម

12. trash bags
    ថង់សំរាម

13. vacuum cleaner
    ម៉ាស៊ីនបូមសំរាម

14. vacuum cleaner attachments
    ដងម៉ាស៊ីនបូមសំរាម

15. vacuum cleaner bag
    ថង់ម៉ាស៊ីនបូមសំរាម

16. wet mop
    អំបោសជូតទឹកសើម

17. dust mop
    អំបោសបោសធូលី

18. furniture polish
    ថ្នាំជូតគ្រឿងអាយរលោង

19. scrub brush
    ច្រាសដុស

20. bucket/pail
    ធុង

21. dishwashing liquid
    ទឹកសាប៊ូម៉ាស៊ីនលាងចាន

22. dish towel
    កន្សែងជូតចាន

23. cleanser
    ម្សៅ ឬទឹកសំរាប់ដុសលោង

24. sponge
    អេប៉ុង

Practice asking for the items.

I want to <u>wash the windows</u>.
Please hand me <u>the squeegee</u>.

I have to <u>sweep the floor</u>.
Can you get me <u>the broom</u>, please?

1. The water heater is **not working**.
   ធុងទឹកក្ដៅខូច ។

2. The power is **out**.
   ភ្លើងដាច់ (លេត់) ។

3. The roof is **leaking**.
   ដំបូលលិច ។

4. The wall is **cracked**.
   ជញ្ជាំងប្រះបែក ។

5. The window is **broken**.
   បង្អួចបាក់ ។

6. The lock is **broken**.
   សោខូច ។

7. The steps are **broken**.
   ជណ្ដើរបាក់ ។

8. roofer
   អ្នកធ្វើដំបូលផ្ទះ

9. electrician
   ជាងភ្លើង

10. repair person
    អ្នកជួសជុល

11. locksmith
    ជាងធ្វើសោ

12. carpenter
    ជាងពេលើ

13. fuse box
    ប្រអប់ហ្វុស្យ

14. gas meter
    នាឡិកាវាស់ឧស្ម័ន

Use the new language.

Look at **Tools and Building Supplies,** pages **150–151.**

Name the tools you use for household repairs.

I use a hammer and nails to fix a broken step.

I use a wrench to repair a dripping faucet.

15. The furnace is **broken**.
ម៉ាស៊ីនកំដៅខូច ។

16. The faucet is **dripping**.
ក្បាលរ៉ូប៊ីណេស្រក់ទឹក ។

17. The sink is **overflowing**.
អាងលាងដៃ មានទឹកហៀរហួរ ។

18. The toilet is **stopped up**.
បង្គន់ស្អះចាល់ ។

19. The pipes are **frozen**.
បំពង់ទឹកកកស្អះ ។

20. plumber
ជាងបំពង់

21. exterminator
អ្នកសម្លាប់សត្វល្អិត

Household pests
សត្វចង្រៃក្នុងផ្ទះ

22. termite(s)
កណ្ដៀរ

23. flea(s)
ចៃឆ្កែ

24. ant(s)
ស្រមោច

25. cockroach(es)
កន្លាត

26. mice*
កណ្ដុរ

27. rat(s)
កណ្ដុរប្រែង

*Note: *one mouse, two mice*

More vocabulary

fix: to repair something that is broken

exterminate: to kill household pests

pesticide: a chemical that is used to kill household pests

Share your answers.

1. Who does household repairs in your home?

2. What is the worst problem a home can have?

3. What is the most expensive problem a home can have?

49

1. grapes
ទំពាំងបាយជូរ

2. pineapples
ម្នាស់

3. bananas
ចេក

4. apples
ផ្លែប៉ោម

5. peaches
ភិច

6. pears
ផ្លែរ៉ា

7. apricots
អាប្រ៊ីកុត

8. plums
ផ្លែឈ្លុំ

9. grapefruit
ក្រូចថ្លុង

10. oranges
ក្រូចពោធិសាត់

11. lemons
ក្រូចឆ្មារលឿង

12. limes
ក្រូចឆ្មារ

13. tangerines
ក្រូចឃ្វិច

14. avocadoes
អាវ៉ូកាដូ

15. cantaloupes
ត្រសក់ស្រូវ កង្កិប្ប

16. cherries
ផ្លែឈេរីរ៉ី

17. strawberries
ស្ត្របឺរី

18. raspberries
ផ្លែរ៉ាស់បឺរី

19. blueberries
ប៊្លូបឺរី

20. papayas
ល្ហុង

21. mangoes
ស្វាយ

22. coconuts
ដូង

23. nuts
ផ្លែណាត

24. watermelons
ឪឡឹក

25. dates
ល្ពៅ

26. prunes
ផ្លែព្រ៊ុន

27. raisins
ទំពាំងបាយជូរក្រៀម

28. not ripe
មិនទាន់ទុំ

29. ripe
ទុំ

30. rotten
ស្អុយ រលួយ

Language note: *a bunch of*
We say *a bunch of grapes* and *a bunch of bananas*.

Share your answers.

1. Which fruits do you put in a fruit salad?

2. Which fruits are sold in your area in the summer?

3. What fruits did you have in your country?

1. lettuce
សាឡាត់

2. cabbage
ស្ពៃក្តោប

3. carrots
ការ៉ុត

4. zucchini
ហ្សុកនី

5. radishes
រ៉ាឌី

6. beets
ប៊ីត

7. sweet peppers
ម្ទេសផ្អែក

8. chili peppers
ម្ទេសហិរ

9. celery
សែលរ្យ៉ាំ

10. parsley
វ៉ាន់ស៊ុយបារាំង

11. spinach
ស្ពីណាត់

12. cucumbers
ត្រសក់

13. squash
ល្ពៅ

14. turnips
ខៃចារមួល

15. broccoli
ខាត់ណាអាមេរិកាំង

16. cauliflower
ផ្កាស្ពៃស

17. scallions
ដើមខ្ទឹម

18. eggplants
ត្រប់សណ្ដាយ

19. peas
សណ្ដែកបារាំង

20. artichokes
អាទិឆក

21. potatoes
ដំឡូងបារាំង

22. yams
ដំឡូងផ្ធា

23. tomatoes
ប៉េងប៉ោះ

24. asparagus
ទំពាំងបារាំង

25. string beans
សណ្ដែកកួ

26. mushrooms
ផ្សិត

27. corn
ពោត

28. onions
ខ្ទឹមបារាំង

29. garlic
ខ្ទឹមស

Language note: *a bunch of, a head of*

We say *a bunch of carrots, a bunch of celery,* and *a bunch of spinach.*

We say *a head of lettuce, a head of cabbage,* and *a head of cauliflower.*

Share your answers.

1. Which vegetables do you eat raw? cooked?

2. Which vegetables need to be in the refrigerator?

3. Which vegetables don't need to be in the refrigerator?

MEAT

POULTRY

Beef សាច់គោ

1. roast beef
សាច់គោសំរាប់អាំង

2. steak
សាច់បន្ទះ

3. stewing beef
សាច់គោកាត់ជាអុំត្លួចៗ

4. ground beef
សាច់គោកិន

5. beef ribs
ឆ្អឹងជំនីរគោ

6. veal cutlets
សាច់គូនគោកាត់បន្ទះស្តើងៗ

7. liver
ថ្លើម

8. tripe
ពោះគោ

Pork សាច់ជ្រូក

9. ham
សាច់ភ្លៅ

10. pork chops
សាច់ជាប់ឆ្អឹងជំនីជ្រូកកាត់ជុំៗ

11. bacon
សាច់ជ្រូកបីជាន់

12. sausage
សាច់ក្រក

Lamb សាច់ចៀម

13. lamb shanks
សាច់កំភួនជើងចៀម

14. leg of lamb
ជើងចៀម

15. lamb chops
សាច់ឆ្អឹងជំនីចៀមកាត់ជុំៗ

16. chicken
សាច់មាន់

17. turkey
មាន់បារាំង

18. duck
ទា

19. breasts
សាច់ទ្រូង

20. wings
ស្លាប

21. thighs
ភ្លៅ

22. drumsticks
កំភួនជើងមាន់

23. gizzards
ពោះមាន់

24. **raw** chicken
សាច់មាន់ឆៅ

25. **cooked** chicken
សាច់មាន់ឆ្អិន

More vocabulary

vegetarian: a person who doesn't eat meat
Meat and poultry without bones are called **boneless**.
Poultry without skin is called **skinless**.

Share your answers.

1. What kind of meat do you eat most often?
2. What kind of meat do you use in soup?
3. What part of the chicken do you like the most?

1. white bread
និបុ័ងស

2. wheat bread
និបុ័ងស្រូវសាឡី

3. rye bread
និបុ័ងគ្រាប់ធញ្ញជាតិ

4. smoked turkey
មាន់បារាំងឆ្អើរ

5. salami
សាឡាមី

6. pastrami
ប៉ាស្ត្រាមី

7. roast beef
សាច់គោវាំង

8. corned beef
សាច់គោស្ងោរ

9. American cheese
ឈីស្យ អាមេរិកាំង

10. cheddar cheese
ឈីស្យ ឈីជា

11. Swiss cheese
ឈីស្យ ស្ម៊ីស

12. jack cheese
ឈីស្យ ចែក

13. potato salad
សាឡាត់ដំឡូងបារាំង

14. coleslaw
កុលស្ល

15. pasta salad
សាឡាត់ ប៉ាស្ត្រា

Fish ត្រី

16. trout
ត្រីម៉្យាងស្រដៀងនឹងត្រីព្រួល

17. catfish
ត្រីអណ្ដែង

18. whole salmon
ត្រីស្ម៊ុងទាំងមូល

19. salmon steak
សាច់ត្រីស្ម៊ុងបន្ទះៗ

20. halibut
ត្រី ហាលីបាត់

21. filet of sole
សាច់ត្រីអណ្ដាតឆ្កែបង្វះ

Shellfish សត្វសត្ថានខ្យងខ្ចៅ

22. crab
ក្ដាម

23. lobster
បង្កងសមុទ្រ

24. shrimp
កម្ពិស

25. scallops
ត្រីសមុទ្រ

26. mussels
ត្រីចំបុះទា

27. oysters
ត្រីសមុទ្រម៉្យាង

28. clams
លាសសមុទ្រ

29. fresh fish
ត្រីស្រស់

30. frozen fish
ត្រីកក

Practice ordering a sandwich.

I'd like roast beef and American cheese on rye bread.

Tell what you want on it.

Please put tomato, lettuce, onions, and mustard on it.

Share your answers.

1. Do you like to eat fish?

2. Do you buy fresh or frozen fish?

1. bottle return ដបយកត្រឡប់មកវិញ	**3.** shopping cart រទេះដាក់ឥវ៉ាន់	**6.** baked goods ម្ហូបដុត	**9.** dairy section កន្លែងលក់ប្រេងទឹកដោះ
2. meat and poultry section កន្លែងលក់សាច់ និងសាច់បសុបក្សី	**4.** canned goods ម្ហូបកំប៉ុង	**7.** shopping basket កន្ត្រកដាក់ឥវ៉ាន់	**10.** pet food ម្ហូបសត្វ
	5. aisle ច្រកដើរ / ផ្លូវដើរ	**8.** manager អ្នកគ្រប់គ្រងទិញ	**11.** produce section កន្លែងបន្លែផ្លែឈើ

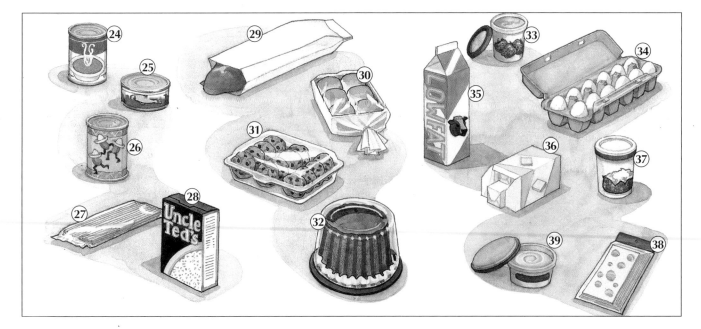

24. soup សម្ល / ស៊ុបកំប៉ុង	**28.** rice អង្ករ	**32.** cake នំ	**36.** butter ប៊ីរ
25. tuna ត្តូណា	**29.** bread នំប៉័ង	**33.** yogurt យ៉ូហ្គ័រ	**37.** sour cream ក្រែមជូរ
26. beans សណ្ដែកកំប៉ុង	**30.** rolls នំប៉័ងមូលៗ	**34.** eggs ពង / ស៊ុត	**38.** cheese ឈីស្ស
27. spaghetti ស្ប៉ាហ្គេទី	**31.** cookies នំឃុកឃី	**35.** milk ទឹកដោះគោ	**39.** margarine ម៉ាហ្គារីន

12. frozen foods អូបតក	**15.** beverages គ្រឿងភេសជ្ជៈ	**18.** cash register ម៉ាស៊ីនគិតលុយ	**21.** bagger អ្នកច្រកគ្រឿង
13. baking products គ្រឿងសំរាប់ដុត អាំង	**16.** snack foods ចំណីស្រស់ស្រូប	**19.** checker អ្នកគិតលុយ	**22.** paper bag ថង់ក្រដាស
14. paper products គ្រឿងក្រដាស	**17.** checkstand កន្លែងគិតលុយ	**20.** line ជួរ	**23.** plastic bag ថង់ប្លាស្ទិក

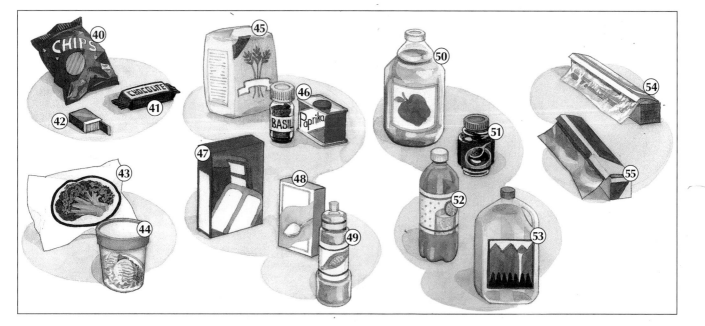

40. potato chips ដំឡូងបំពង	**44.** ice cream ការ៉េមកក	**48.** sugar ស្ករ	**52.** soda ស៊ូដា
41. candy bar ស្ករអំបុ	**45.** flour ម្សៅ	**49.** oil ប្រេង	**53.** bottled water ទឹកដប
42. gum ស្ករកៅស៊ូ	**46.** spices គ្រឿងទេស	**50.** apple juice ទឹកផ្លែប៉ោម	**54.** plastic wrap ថង់ប្លាស្ទិកសំរាប់ខ្ចប់
43. frozen vegetables បន្លែកក	**47.** cake mix ម្សៅសំរាប់ធ្វើនំ	**51.** instant coffee កាហ្វេកិនស្រេច	**55.** aluminum foil ក្រដាសអាលុមីញ៉ូម

1. bottle
ដប

2. jar
កែវ

3. can
កំប៉ុង

4. carton
កាតុង

5. container
ធុង

6. box
ប្រអប់

7. bag
ថង់

8. package
កញ្ចប់

9. six-pack
ក្រមមួយដប / កំប៉ុង

10. loaf
ដុំ

11. roll
រំុ

12. tube
បំពង់

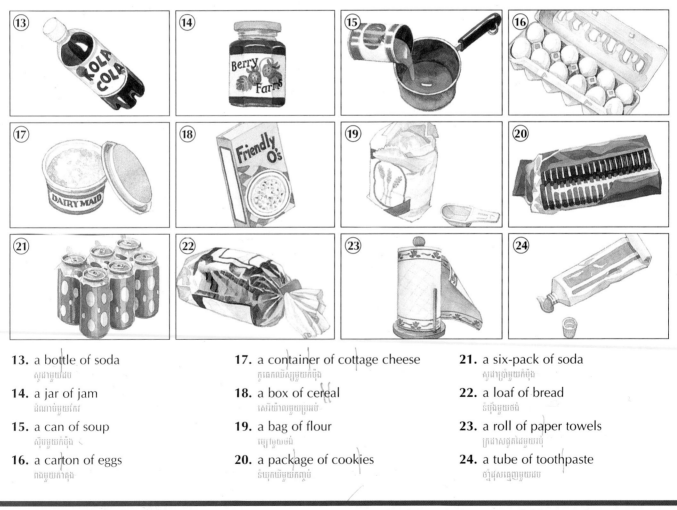

13. a bottle of soda
សូដាមួយដប

14. a jar of jam
ដំណាប់មួយកែវ

15. a can of soup
ស៊ុបមួយកំប៉ុង

16. a carton of eggs
ពងមួយកាតុង

17. a container of cottage cheese
ឈីសឆ្អិនមួយធុងកំប៉ុង

18. a box of cereal
សេរ៊ីយ៉ាលមួយប្រអប់

19. a bag of flour
ម្សៅមួយថង់

20. a package of cookies
នំឃុកឃីមួយកញ្ចប់

21. a six-pack of soda
សូដាក្រមមួយកំប៉ុង

22. a loaf of bread
នំប៉័ងមួយដុំ

23. a roll of paper towels
ក្រដាសជូតដៃមួយរំុ

24. a tube of toothpaste
ថ្នាំដុសធ្មេញមួយដប

Grammar point: *How much? How many?*

Some foods can be counted: *one apple, two apples.*

How many apples do you need? I need ***two*** apples.

Some foods cannot be counted, like liquids, grains, spices, or dairy foods. For these, count containers: *one box of rice, two boxes of rice.*

How much rice do you need? I need ***two boxes.***

56

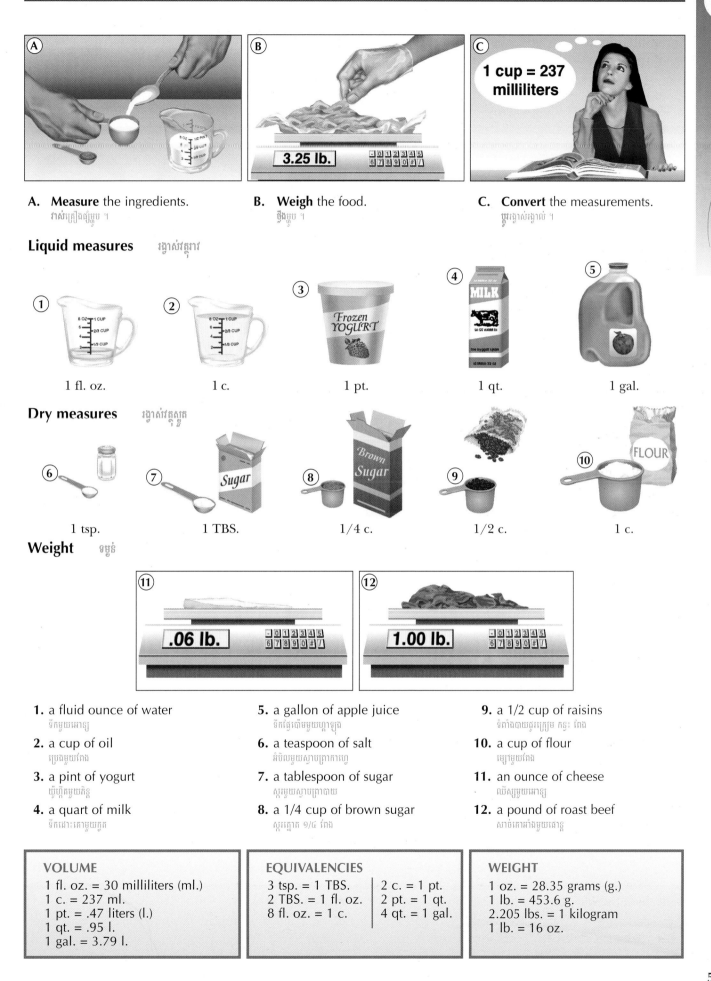

A. **Measure** the ingredients.
វាស់គ្រឿងផ្សំមុខ ១

B. **Weigh** the food.
ថ្លឹងមុខ ១

C. **Convert** the measurements.
ប្ដូររង្វាស់រង្វាល់ ។

C
1 cup = 237 milliliters

Liquid measures   រង្វាស់វត្ថុរាវ

1. 1 fl. oz.
2. 1 c.
3. 1 pt.
4. 1 qt.
5. 1 gal.

Dry measures   រង្វាស់វត្ថុស្ងួត

6. 1 tsp.
7. 1 TBS.
8. 1/4 c.
9. 1/2 c.
10. 1 c.

Weight   ទម្ងន់

11. .06 lb.
12. 1.00 lb.

1. a fluid ounce of water
ទឹកមួយអោ

2. a cup of oil
ប្រេងមួយពែង

3. a pint of yogurt
យ៉ូហ្គិតមួយភិន្ត

4. a quart of milk
ទឹកដោះគោមួយក្វត

5. a gallon of apple juice
ទឹកផ្លែបោមមួយហ្គាឡុង

6. a teaspoon of salt
អំបិលមួយស្លាបព្រាកាហ្វេ

7. a tablespoon of sugar
ស្ករមួយស្លាបព្រាបាយ

8. a 1/4 cup of brown sugar
ស្ករវត្ថាត ៩/៤ ពែង

9. a 1/2 cup of raisins
ទំពាំងបាយជូរក្រៀម កន្លះ ពែង

10. a cup of flour
ម្សៅមួយពែង

11. an ounce of cheese
ឈីស្សមួយអោ

12. a pound of roast beef
សាច់គោអាំងមួយផោន

VOLUME
1 fl. oz. = 30 milliliters (ml.)
1 c. = 237 ml.
1 pt. = .47 liters (l.)
1 qt. = .95 l.
1 gal. = 3.79 l.

EQUIVALENCIES	
3 tsp. = 1 TBS.	2 c. = 1 pt.
2 TBS. = 1 fl. oz.	2 pt. = 1 qt.
8 fl. oz. = 1 c.	4 qt. = 1 gal.

WEIGHT
1 oz. = 28.35 grams (g.)
1 lb. = 453.6 g.
2.205 lbs. = 1 kilogram
1 lb. = 16 oz.

Scrambled eggs ពងទាវាយបញ្ចូលគ្នា

A. **Break** 3 eggs.
ចំបែកពងទាបី ។

B. **Beat** well.
វាយអោយសព្វ ។

C. **Grease** the pan.
លាបខ្លាញ់ខ្ទះ ។

D. **Pour** the eggs into the pan.
ចាក់ពងទាចូលខ្ទះ ។

E. **Stir.**
គ្រវី ។

F. **Cook** until done.
ចំអិនទាល់តែឆ្អិនល្អ ។

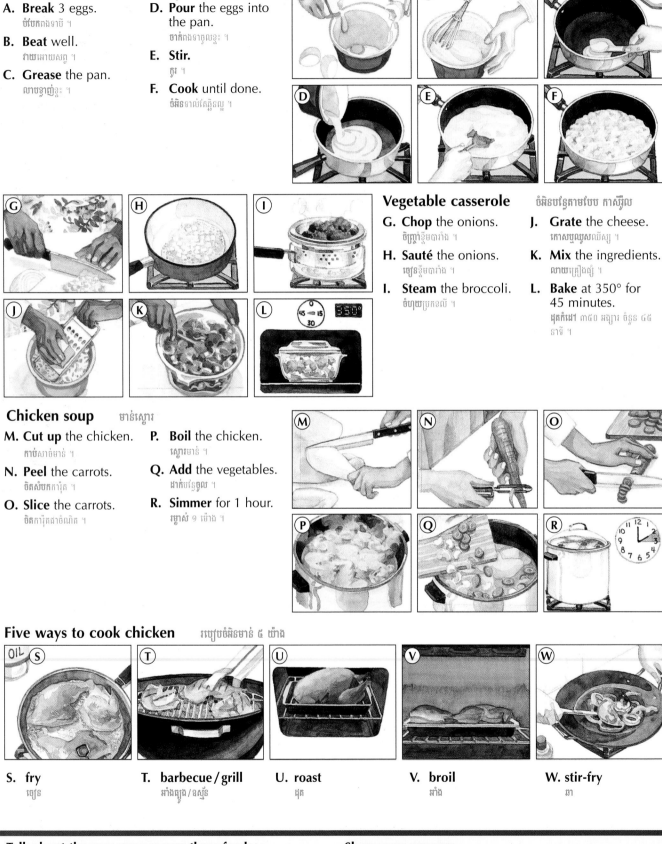

Vegetable casserole ចំអិនបន្លែតាមបែប កាស៊ីរ៉ូល

G. **Chop** the onions.
ចិញ្ច្រាំខ្ទឹមបារាំង ។

H. **Sauté** the onions.
ឆ្អើរខ្ទឹមបារាំង ។

I. **Steam** the broccoli.
ចំហុយប្រូកូលី ។

J. **Grate** the cheese.
កោសបួលឈីស ។

K. **Mix** the ingredients.
លាយគ្រឿងផ្សំ ។

L. **Bake** at 350° for 45 minutes.
ដុតកំដៅ ៣៥០ អង្សារ ចំនួន ៤៥ នាទី ។

Chicken soup ម្ហូបស្ងោរ

M. **Cut up** the chicken.
កាប់សាច់មាន់ ។

N. **Peel** the carrots.
ចិតសំបកការ៉ុត ។

O. **Slice** the carrots.
ចិតការ៉ុតជាចំណិត ។

P. **Boil** the chicken.
ស្ងោរមាន់ ។

Q. **Add** the vegetables.
ដាក់បន្លែចូល ។

R. **Simmer** for 1 hour.
រម្ងាស់ ១ ម៉ោង ។

Five ways to cook chicken របៀបចំអិនមាន់ ៥ យ៉ាង

S. fry
ចៀន

T. barbecue / grill
អាំងឆ្អុក / ឧស្ម័ន

U. roast
ដុត

V. broil
អាំង

W. stir-fry
ឆា

Talk about the way you prepare these foods.

I _fry_ eggs.

I _bake_ potatoes.

Share your answers.

1. What are popular ways in your country to make rice? vegetables? meat?

2. What is your favorite way to cook chicken?

1. **can opener**
   ប្រដាប់ភ្ជាប់កំប៉ុង

2. **grater**
   ប្រដាប់ឈ្លេស / ចិត

3. **plastic storage container**
   ចាន / ផុងប្លាស្ទិក

4. **steamer**
   ប្រដាប់ចំហុយ

5. **frying pan**
   ខ្ទះចៀន / ឆា

6. **pot**
   ឆ្នាំង

7. **ladle**
   វែក

8. **double boiler**
   ឆ្នាំងទ្វេរជាន់ / ឆ្នាំងទ្យោស្ទឹង

9. **wooden spoon**
   វែកឈើ

10. **garlic press**
    ប្រដាប់គាប ឬសង្កត់ខ្ទឹម

11. **casserole dish**
    ចានកាស្រ៊ិល

12. **carving knife**
    កាំបិតកាត់សាច់

13. **roasting pan**
    ថាសសាច់

14. **roasting rack**
    ចន្ទាសអាំង

15. **vegetable peeler**
    ប្រដាប់ចិតសម្បកបន្លែ

16. **paring knife**
    កូនកាំបិត

17. **colander**
    ប្រដាប់សំរេច់ទឹក

18. **kitchen timer**
    នាឡិកាជាំស្ស

19. **spatula**
    វែកគ្រ

20. **eggbeater**
    ប្រដាប់វាយ / វៃវាងទា

21. **whisk**
    ប្រដាប់វាយកងទារដោយដៃ

22. **strainer**
    តម្រង

23. **tongs**
    ដង្គៀប

24. **lid**
    គំរប

25. **saucepan**
    កូនឆ្នាំង

26. **cake pan**
    ថាសដុតន

27. **cookie sheet**
    ក្រដាសទ្រនាប់ន

28. **pie pan**
    ថាសដុតនំថាយ

29. **pot holders**
    ទ្រនាប់ឆ្នាំង

30. **rolling pin**
    ប្រដាប់លុញម្សៅ

31. **mixing bowl**
    ចានលាយគ្រឿង

Talk about how to use the utensils.

You use a peeler to peel potatoes.

You use a pot to cook soup.

Use the new language.

Look at **Food Preparation**, page **58**.

Name the different utensils you see.

1. hamburger ហាំប៊ឺហ្គឺ	**8.** green salad សាឡាត់
2. french fries ដំឡូងបំពង	**9.** taco ថាកូ
3. cheeseburger ឈីសប៊ឺហ្គឺ	**10.** nachos ណាឆូ
4. soda សូដា	**11.** frozen yogurt ការ៉េមយ៉ូហ្គិត
5. iced tea តែទឹកកក	**12.** milk shake ទឹកដោះគោក្រឡុក
6. hot dog ហុត ដក	**13.** counter គ្នាងមុខ / គុទទួល
7. pizza ភីតសា	**14.** muffin ម៉ាហ្វិន

15. doughnut នំដូណាត់	**22.** sugar substitute ស្ករជំនួស
16. salad bar កន្លែងដាក់សាឡាត់	**23.** ketchup ទឹកប៉េងប៉ោះ
17. lettuce ស្លឹកសាឡាត់	**24.** mustard ទឹកម៉្វីតាក / គេឡ្យាត់
18. salad dressing ទឹកសាឡាត់	**25.** mayonnaise ម៉ាយ៉ូរនេស
19. booth កន្លែងអង្គុយញ៉ាំ	**26.** relish គ្រឿងបន្ថែមលើម្ហូប
20. straw បំពង់បឺត	**A.** eat ញ៉ាំ
21. sugar ស្ករ	**B.** drink ផឹក

More vocabulary

donut: doughnut (spelling variation)

condiments: relish, mustard, ketchup, mayonnaise, etc.

Share your answers.

1. What would you order at this restaurant?

2. Which fast foods are popular in your country?

3. How often do you eat fast food? Why?

Breakfast

Lunch

Dinner

Desserts

Beverages

1. scrambled eggs
   ពងទារាយបញ្ចលេគ្នា

2. sausage
   សាច់ក្រក

3. toast
   នំបុ័ងឆ្អើរ/ដុត

4. waffles
   នំក្រម្ម

5. syrup
   ស៊ីរ៉ុប

6. pancakes
   នំចាក់ចួល

7. bacon
   បន្ទះសាច់ជ្រូកបិជាន់

8. grilled cheese
   sandwich
   សែនវិចឆ្អាក់ឈីស្ស្យ

9. chef's salad
   សាឡាត់ពិសេស

10. soup of the day
    ស៊ុប (ប្រចាំថ្ងៃ)

11. mashed potatoes
    ដំឡូងកិន

12. roast chicken
    មាន់អាំង

13. steak
    បន្ទះសាច់គោអាំង

14. baked potato
    ដំឡូងដុត

15. pasta
    ប៉ាស្ដា

16. garlic bread
    នំបុ័ងលាយខ្ទឹម

17. fried fish
    ត្រីចៀន

18. rice pilaf
    បាយ ភីឡាហ្វ

19. cake
    នំ

20. pudding
    បង្អែមផ្ទៀង

21. pie
    នំផាយ

22. coffee
    កាហ្វេ

23. decaf coffee
    កាហ្វេ ឌិកាហ្វ

24. tea
    តែ

Practice ordering from the menu.

I'd like <u>a grilled cheese sandwich</u> and <u>some soup</u>.

I'll have <u>the chef's salad</u> and <u>a cup of decaf coffee</u>.

Use the new language.

Look at **Fruit,** page **50.**

Order a slice of pie using the different fruit flavors.

Please give me a slice of <u>apple</u> pie.

1. **hostess**
   អ្នកទទួលភ្ញៀវ

2. **dining room**
   បន្ទប់ទទួលទានអាហារ

3. **menu**
   បញ្ជីម្ហូប

4. **server/waiter**
   អ្នកបរិវេ/អ្នកបរិវេប្រុស

5. **patron/diner**
   អ្នកមកញ៉ាំ

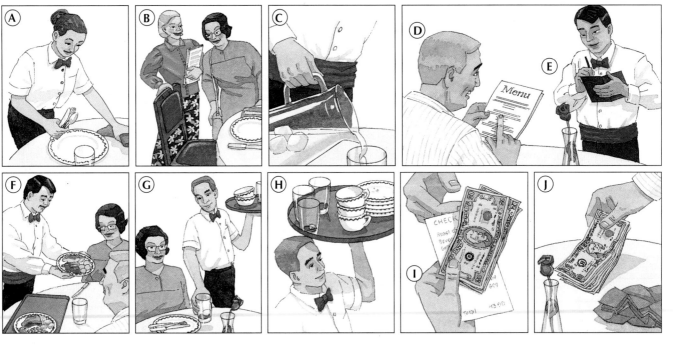

A. set the table
រៀបតុ

B. seat the customer
អញ្ជើញអាយអ្នកទិញអង្គុយ

C. pour the water
ចាក់ទឹក

D. order from the menu
ហៅម្ហូបម្ហូប

E. take the order
ទទួលការបញ្ជាយកតមុខម្ហូប

F. serve the meal
បរិម្ហូប

G. clear the table
សំអាតតុ

H. carry the tray
កាន់ថាស

I. pay the check
បង់ថ្លៃម្ហូប

J. leave a tip
ដាក់ប្រាក់ទឹកតែ

More vocabulary

eat out: to go to a restaurant to eat

take out: to buy food at a restaurant and take it home
to eat

Practice giving commands.

Please <u>set the table</u>.

I'd like you to <u>clear the table</u>.

It's time to <u>serve the meal</u>.

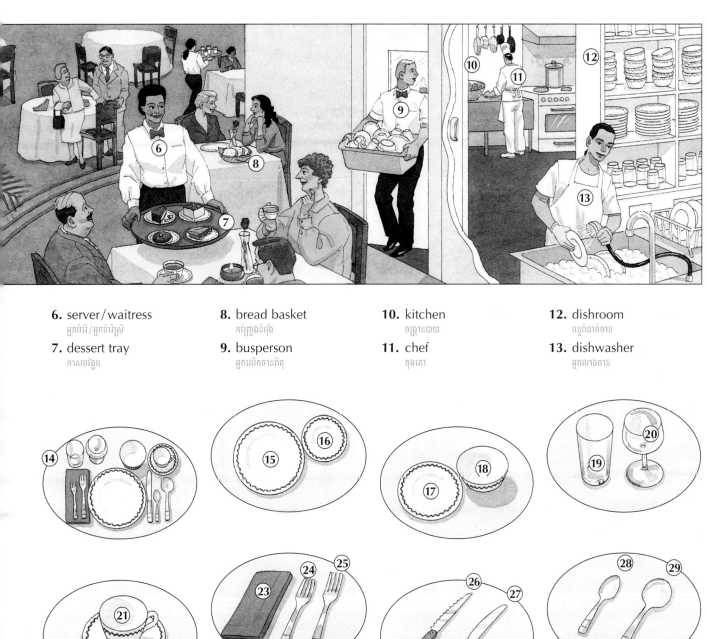

6. server / waitress	10. kitchen
អ្នកបម្រើ/អ្នកបម្រើស្រី	ចង្ក្រានបាយ
7. dessert tray	11. chef
ថាសបង្អែម	ចុងភៅ
8. bread basket	12. dishroom
កញ្ច្រែងនំបុ័ង	បន្ទប់ដាក់ចាន
9. busperson	13. dishwasher
អ្នករើកចានពិតុ	អ្នកលាងចាន

14. place setting	18. soup bowl
រៀបចានស្លាបព្រា	ចានស៊ុប
15. dinner plate	19. water glass
ចានឆ្លៀប	កែវទឹក
16. bread-and-butter plate	20. wine glass
ចាននំបុ័ង-ប៊ឺ	កែវស្រា
17. salad plate	21. cup
ចានសាឡាត់	កែវ

22. saucer	26. steak knife
ទ្រនាប់កែវ	កាំបិតកាត់សាច់
23. napkin	27. knife
ក្រដាសសជូតដៃ	កាំបិត
24. salad fork	28. teaspoon
សមសាឡាត់	ស្លាបព្រាការហ្វេ
25. dinner fork	29. soupspoon
សម	ស្លាបព្រាស៊ុប

Talk about how you set the table in your home.

The glass is on the right.

The fork goes on the left.

The napkin is next to the plate.

Share your answers.

1. Do you know anyone who works in a restaurant? What does he or she do?

2. In your opinion, which restaurant jobs are hard? Why?

1. **three-piece suit**
   អាវធំមានទាំងអាវកាក់

2. **suit**
   ខោអាវមួយសំរាប់

3. **dress**
   សំពត់រ៉ូប

4. **shirt**
   អាវសេមីស

5. **jeans**
   ខោខូវប៊យ

6. **sports coat**
   អាវកិឡាធំ

7. **turtleneck**
   អាវយឺតមូរក

8. **slacks/pants**
   ខោជើងវែង

9. **blouse**
   អាវស្រី

10. **skirt**
    សំពត់បៀប

11. **pullover sweater**
    អាវយឺតគ្រោស់

12. **T-shirt**
    អាវយឺតស្តើងៗ

13. **shorts**
    ខោជើងខ្លី

14. **sweatshirt**
    អាវកិឡាបៃដៃវែង

15. **sweatpants**
    ខោកិឡាជើងវែង

More vocabulary:

outfit: clothes that look nice together

When clothes are popular, they are **in fashion.**

Talk about what you're wearing today and what you wore yesterday.

I'm wearing <u>a gray sweater</u>, <u>a red T-shirt</u>, and <u>blue jeans</u>.

Yesterday I wore <u>a green pullover sweater</u>, <u>a white shirt</u>, and <u>black slacks</u>.

16. jumpsuit
អាវជាប់ខោ

17. uniform
ឯកសណ្ឋាន

18. jumper
អាវអៀមក្នុង

19. maternity dress
សំលៀកបំពាក់ស្ត្រីមានផ្ទៃពោះ

20. knit shirt
អាវចាក់

21. overalls
ខោអៀម

22. tunic
អាវជាយ

23. leggings
ខោរឹបជើង

24. vest
អាវកាក់

25. split skirt
ខោសំពត់

26. sports shirt
អាវយឺតកីឡា

27. cardigan sweater
អាវយឺតខាងមិនាន

28. tuxedo
អាវតុកស្តូវ

29. evening gown
អាវដែងសម្រាប់រាត្រីសមោសរ

Use the new language.

Look at **A Graduation**, pages **32–33.**

Name the clothes you see.

The man at the podium is wearing <u>a suit</u>.

Share your answers.

1. Which clothes in this picture are in fashion now?

2. Who is the best-dressed person in this line? Why?

3. What do you wear when you go to the movies?

1. hat
   មួក

2. overcoat
   អាវរងាវែង

3. leather jacket
   អាវរងាស្បែក

4. wool scarf/muffler
   កន្សែងរុំក

5. gloves
   ស្រោមដៃ

6. cap
   មួកក្លិប

7. jacket
   អាវរងា

8. parka
   អាវរងាមានមួក

9. mittens
   ស្រោមដៃច្រក

10. ski cap
    មួកជិះស្គី

11. tights
    ខោយឺតវែង

12. earmuffs
    ប្រដាប់បិទត្រចៀក

13. down vest
    អាវកាក់រងាត់ដៃ

14. ski mask
    ម៉ាស់ពាក់ការពារមុខជិះស្គី

15. down jacket
    អាវរងាធ្វីក្រាស់

16. umbrella
    ឆ័ត្រ

17. raincoat
    អាវភ្លៀង

18. poncho
    ក្រណាត់ការពារភ្លៀង

19. rain boots
    ស្បែកជើងវែងសំរាប់ការពារភ្លៀង

20. trench coat
    អាវភ្លៀងវែង

21. sunglasses
    វ៉ែនតាពាក់ការពារវ៉ៃថ្ងៃ

22. swimming trunks
    ខោងុតទឹក

23. straw hat
    មួកស្បូវ

24. windbreaker
    អាវទប់ខ្យល់

25. cover-up
    អាវវែងពាក់ខាងក្រៅ

26. swimsuit/bathing suit
    សំលៀកបំពាក់ងូតទឹក

27. baseball cap
    មួកក្លិបបេសបល្ល

Use the new language.

Look at **Weather**, page **10**.

Name the clothing for each weather condition.

Wear a jacket when it's windy.

Share your answers.

1. Which is better in the rain, an umbrella or a poncho?
2. Which is better in the cold, a parka or a down jacket?
3. Do you have more summer clothes or winter clothes?

1. leotard
សំលៀកបំពាក់ហាត់ប្រាណ

2. tank top
អាវយឺតកិឡ្លាវៃលរៃក

3. bike shorts
ខោខ្លីជិះកង់

4. pajamas
ពិសាម៉ា

5. nightgown
សំលៀកបំពាក់គេងស្ត្រី

6. slippers
ទ្រនាប់ជើង

7. blanket sleeper
អាវគ្រុសំរាប់ក្មេង

8. bathrobe
អាវពាក់ទៅបន្ទប់ទឹក

9. nightshirt
អាវពាក់ពេលយប់

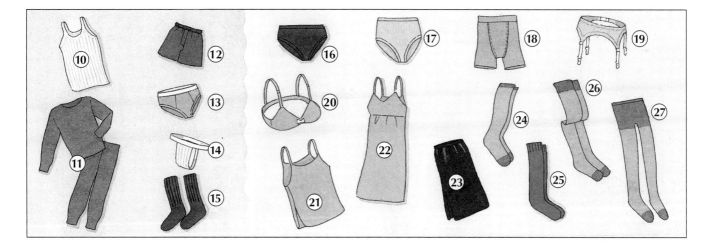

10. undershirt
អាវយឺតទ្រនាប់ពៀលរៃក

11. long underwear
ខោអាវពាក់ក្នុង

12. boxer shorts
ខោទ្រនាប់ខ្លី

13. briefs
ខោទ្រនាប់ប្រុស / ខោស្លិបប្រុស

14. athletic supporter / jockstrap
ខោទ្រនាប់អ្នកកិឡ្លា

15. socks
ស្រោមជើង

16. (bikini) panties
ខោទ្រនាប់បីយីនី

17. briefs / underpants
ខោទ្រនាប់ស្រី / ខោស្លិបស្រី

18. girdle
ខោវែតក្រក្រេក

19. garter belt
ខ្សែកោស្បីបស្រោមជើង

20. bra
អាវទ្រនាប់ស្រី

21. camisole
អាវទ្រនាប់វៃង / អាវពៀលភ្លៀកស្រី

22. full slip
អាវនិងសំពត់ទ្រនាប់ជាប់គ្នា

23. half slip
សំពត់ទ្រនាប់

24. knee-highs
ស្រោមជើងលើផងង

25. kneesocks
ស្រោមជើងត្រឹមផង្កង

26. stockings
ស្រោមជើងវៃងត្រឹមភ្លៅ

27. pantyhose
ស្រោមជើងនិងឡ្លុងស្តិ្ងមានខោ

More vocabulary

lingerie: underwear or sleepwear for women

loungewear: clothing (sometimes sleepwear) people wear around the home

Share your answers.

1. What do you wear when you exercise?

2. What kind of clothing do you wear for sleeping?

Shoes and Accessories ទ្រនាប់ជើង និងសម្ភារៈបន្ថែម

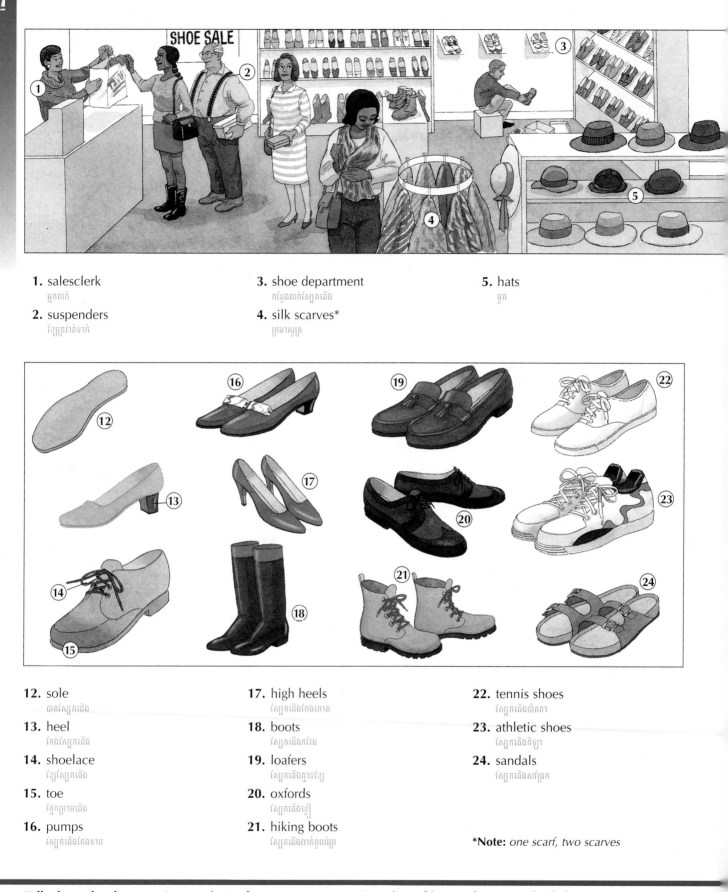

1. **salesclerk**
   អ្នកលក់

2. **suspenders**
   ខ្សែក្រវាត់ទាក់

3. **shoe department**
   ផ្នែកលក់ស្បែកជើង

4. **silk scarves***
   ក្រមាសូត្រ

5. **hats**
   មួក

12. **sole**
    បាតស្បែកជើង

13. **heel**
    កែងស្បែកជើង

14. **shoelace**
    ខ្សែស្បែកជើង

15. **toe**
    ថ្នក់ច្រាមជើង

16. **pumps**
    ស្បែកជើងកែងទាប

17. **high heels**
    ស្បែកជើងកែងចោត

18. **boots**
    ស្បែកជើងកវែង

19. **loafers**
    ស្បែកជើងគ្មានខ្សែ

20. **oxfords**
    ស្បែកជើងខ្លី

21. **hiking boots**
    ស្បែកជើងពាក់ឡើងភ្នំ

22. **tennis shoes**
    ស្បែកជើងប៉ិកតា

23. **athletic shoes**
    ស្បែកជើងកីឡា

24. **sandals**
    ស្បែកជើងសង្រែក

*Note: one scarf, two scarves

Talk about the shoes you're wearing today.

I'm wearing a pair of <u>white sandals</u>.

Practice asking a salesperson for help.

Could I try on these <u>sandals</u> in size <u>10</u>?

Do you have any <u>silk scarves</u>?

Where are <u>the hats</u>?

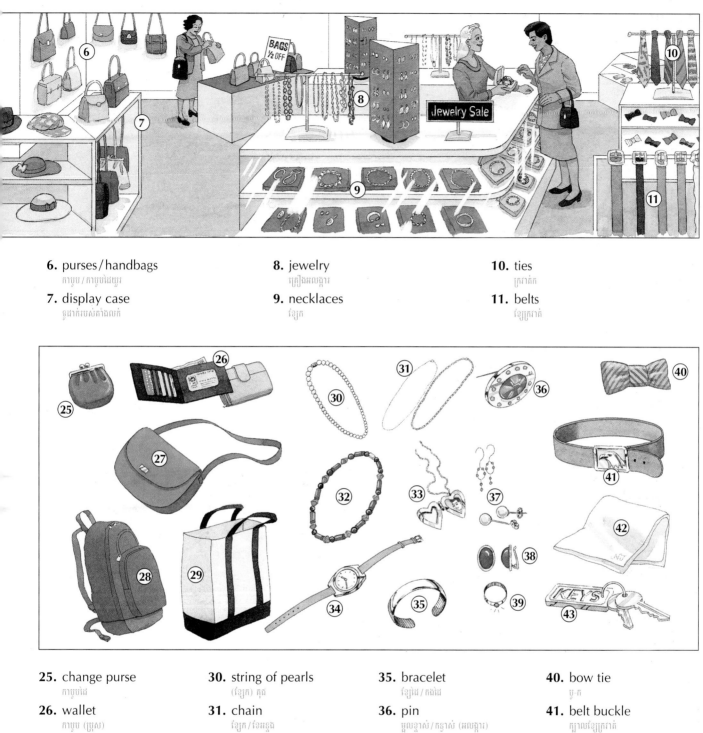

6. purses / handbags
កាបូប / កាបូបដៃស្ត្រី

7. display case
ទូដាក់របស់តាំងលក់

8. jewelry
គ្រឿងអលង្ការ

9. necklaces
ខ្សែក

10. ties
ក្រវាត់ក

11. belts
ខ្សែក្រវាត់

---

25. change purse
កាបូបដៃ

26. wallet
កាបូប (ប្រុស)

27. shoulder bag
កាបូបស្មាយ

28. backpack / bookbag
កាបូបស្ពាយពីក្រោយ

29. tote bag
កាបូបស្ពាន់

30. string of pearls
(ខ្សែក) គុជ

31. chain
ខ្សែក / ខ្សែអន្ទង

32. beads
អង្គាំ

33. locket
បន្ទោងខ្សែក

34. (wrist)watch
នាឡិកា(ដៃ)

35. bracelet
ខ្សែដៃ / កងដៃ

36. pin
ម្ជុលខ្លាស់ / កន្ទ្រាស់ (អលង្ការ)

37. pierced earrings
ក្រវិល

38. clip-on earrings
ក្រវិលគិប

39. ring
ចិញ្ចៀន

40. bow tie
ប៉ូក

41. belt buckle
ក្បាលខ្សែក្រវាត់

42. handkerchief
កន្សែងដៃ

43. key chain
ក្រវិលបេសោ

Share your answers.

1. Which of these accessories are usually worn by women? by men?

2. Which of these do you wear every day?

3. Which of these would you wear to a job interview? Why?

4. Which accessory would you like to receive as a present? Why?

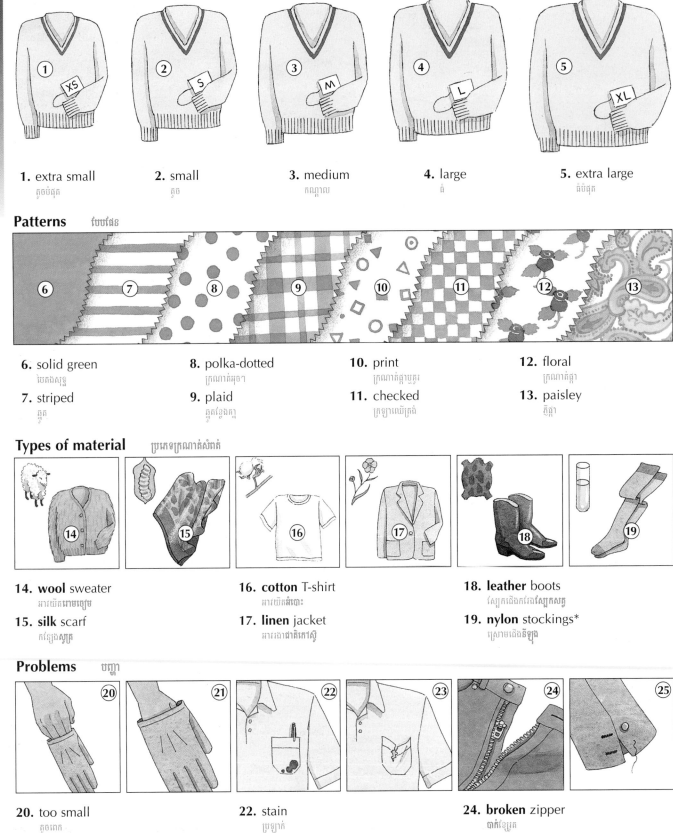

Describing Clothes របៀបរាប់អំពីសំលៀកបំពាក់

Sizes ទំហំ

1. extra small
គួចបំផុត

2. small
គួច

3. medium
កណ្តាល

4. large
ធំ

5. extra large
ធំបំផុត

Patterns របៀបផ្ទៃ

6. solid green
បៃតងសុទ្ធ

7. striped
ឆ្នូត

8. polka-dotted
ក្រឡាត់អុចៗ

9. plaid
ឆ្នូតខ្វែងគ្នា

10. print
ក្រឡាត់ផ្ការឬក្បូរ

11. checked
ក្រឡាលើបីក្រង់

12. floral
ក្រឡាត់ផ្កា

13. paisley
គ្រិផ្កា

Types of material ប្រភេទក្រឡាត់សំពត់

14. wool sweater
អាវយឺត**រោមចៀម**

15. silk scarf
កន្សែង**ស្ទូត**

16. cotton T-shirt
អាវយឺត**អំបោះ**

17. linen jacket
អាវធាជាតិកោ1ស៊ី

18. leather boots
ស្បែកជើងវែង**ស្បែកសត្វ**

19. nylon stockings*
ស្រោមជើង**នីឡុង**

Problems បញ្ហា

20. too small
គួចពេក

21. too big
ធំពេក

22. stain
ប្រឡាក់

23. rip/tear
ដាច់/រហែក

24. broken zipper
បាក់ខ្យួរ

25. missing button
បាត់ឡេវ

*****Note:** Nylon, polyester, rayon, and plastic are synthetic materials.

70

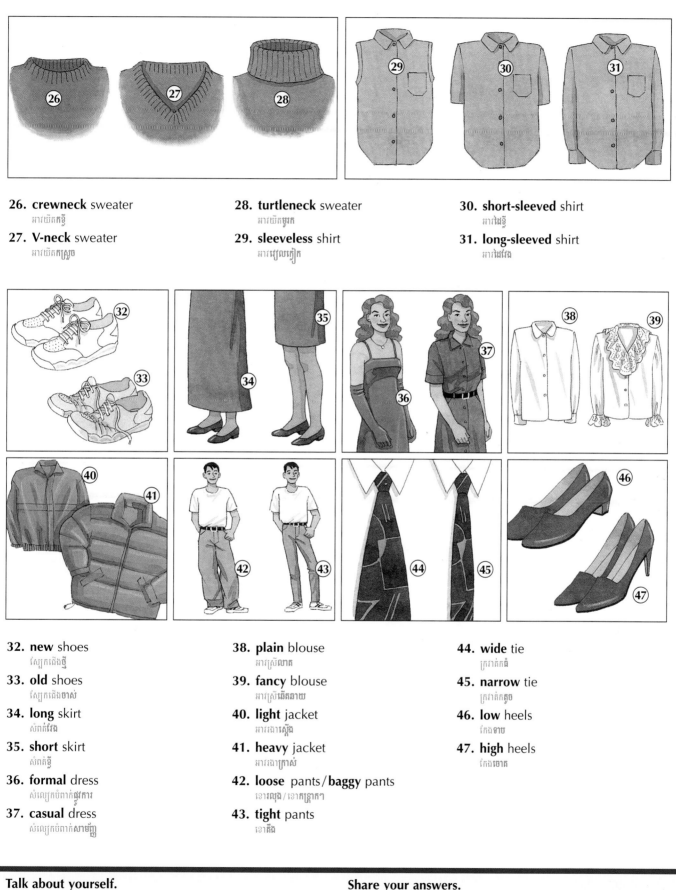

26. **crewneck** sweater
អាវយឹត**កខ្លី**

27. **V-neck** sweater
អាវយឹត**កស្រួច**

28. **turtleneck** sweater
អាវយឹត**កមួរក**

29. **sleeveless** shirt
អាវ**ឥតដៃ**

30. **short-sleeved** shirt
អាវ**ដៃខ្លី**

31. **long-sleeved** shirt
អាវ**ដៃវែង**

32. **new** shoes
ស្បែកជើង**ថ្មី**

33. **old** shoes
ស្បែកជើង**ចាស់**

34. **long** skirt
សំពត់**វែង**

35. **short** skirt
សំពត់**ខ្លី**

36. **formal** dress
សំលៀកបំពាក់**ផ្លូវការ**

37. **casual** dress
សំលៀកបំពាក់**សាមញ្ញ**

38. **plain** blouse
អាវស្រី**លៀត**

39. **fancy** blouse
អាវស្រី**លឿតឆោយ**

40. **light** jacket
អាវជារ**ស្តើង**

41. **heavy** jacket
អាវជា**ក្រាស់**

42. **loose** pants/**baggy** pants
ខោ**រលុង**/ខោ**កន្ត្រាកៗ**

43. **tight** pants
ខោ**តឹង**

44. **wide** tie
ក្រវ៉ាត់ក**ធំ**

45. **narrow** tie
ក្រវ៉ាត់ក**តូច**

46. **low** heels
កែង**ទាប**

47. **high** heels
កែង**ចោត**

Talk about yourself.

I like <u>long-sleeved</u> shirts and <u>baggy</u> pants.

I like <u>short skirts</u> and <u>high heels</u>.

I usually wear <u>plain</u> clothes.

Share your answers.

1. What type of material do you usually wear in the summer? in the winter?

2. What patterns do you see around you?

3. Are you wearing casual or formal clothes?

Doing the Laundry បោកខោអាវ

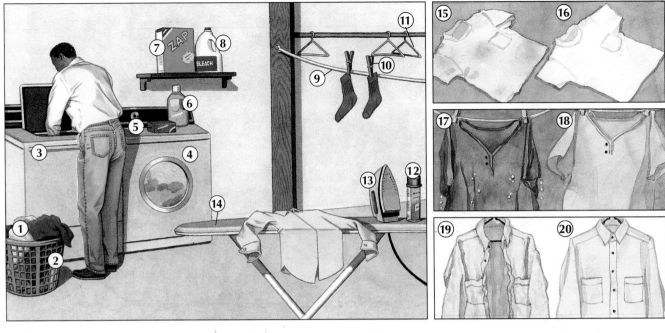

1. laundry
   ខោអាវបោកគក់

2. laundry basket
   កន្ត្រែងដាក់ខោអាវបោកគក់

3. washer
   ម៉ាស៊ីនបោក

4. dryer
   ម៉ាស៊ីនហាលខោអាវ

5. dryer sheets
   ក្រដាស់ក្រអូបធ្វើអោយខោអាវទន់

6. fabric softener
   ទឹកក្រអូបធ្វើអោយខោអាវទន់

7. laundry detergent
   សាប៊ូបោកខោអាវ

8. bleach
   សាប៊ូកាត់

9. clothesline
   ស្រូវហាលខោអាវ

10. clothespin
    ដង្កៀបហាលខោអាវ

11. hanger
    ប្រដាប់ព្យួរខោអាវ

12. spray starch
    ម្សៅអ៊ុត

13. iron
    ឆ្នាំងអ៊ុត

14. ironing board
    ក្តារអ៊ុតខោអាវ

15. **dirty** T-shirt
    អាវយឹតប្រឡាក់

16. **clean** T-shirt
    អាវយឹតស្អាត

17. **wet** T-shirt
    អាវយឹតសើម

18. **dry** T-shirt
    អាវយឹតស្ងួត

19. **wrinkled** shirt
    អាវញ

20. **ironed** shirt
    អាវអ៊ុតហើយ

A. **Sort** the laundry.
   ជ្រើសខោអាវទុកដោយឡែកៗ ។

B. **Add** the detergent.
   ថែមសាប៊ូ ។

C. **Load** the washer.
   ដាក់/បញ្ចូលខោអាវក្នុងម៉ាស៊ីនបោក ។

D. **Clean** the lint trap.
   សំអាតកម្រងម៉ាស៊ីនហាល ។

E. **Unload** the dryer.
   យកខោអាវចេញពីម៉ាស៊ីនហាល ។

F. **Fold** the laundry.
   បត់ខោអាវ ។

G. **Iron** the clothes.
   អ៊ុតខោអាវ ។

H. **Hang up** the clothes.
   ព្យួរខោអាវ ។

More vocabulary

dry cleaners: a business that cleans clothes using chemicals, not water and detergent

 wash in cold water only

 no bleach

▢ line dry

◯ dry-clean only, do not wash

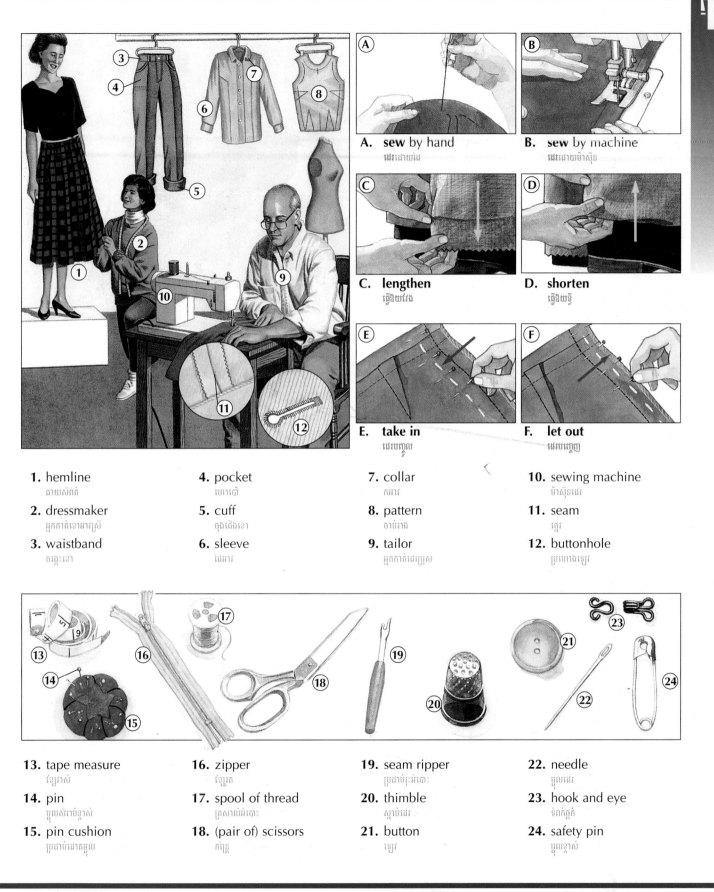

A. **sew** by hand
ដេរដោយដៃ

B. **sew** by machine
ដេរដោយម៉ាស៊ីន

C. **lengthen**
ធ្វើឱ្យវែង

D. **shorten**
ធ្វើឱ្យខ្លី

E. **take in**
ដេរបញ្ចូល

F. **let out**
ដេរបញ្ចេញ

1. hemline
ជាយសំពត់

2. dressmaker
អ្នកកាត់ខោអាវស្រី

3. waistband
ចង្កេះខោ

4. pocket
ហោប៉ៅ

5. cuff
កុងដើងខោ

6. sleeve
ដៃអាវ

7. collar
កអាវ

8. pattern
ចាប់រាង

9. tailor
អ្នកកាត់ដេរប្រុស

10. sewing machine
ម៉ាស៊ីនដេរ

11. seam
ថ្នេរ

12. buttonhole
ប្រហោងឆ្នូត

13. tape measure
ខ្សែវាស់

14. pin
មូលសំរាប់ខ្ទាស់

15. pin cushion
ប្រដាប់ដោតម្ជុល

16. zipper
ខ្សែរូត

17. spool of thread
ត្រសាល់អំបោះ

18. (pair of) scissors
កន្ត្រៃ

19. seam ripper
ប្រដាប់អុះអំបោះ

20. thimble
ស្នាប់ដេរ

21. button
ឆ្នូត

22. needle
មូលដេរ

23. hook and eye
ទំពក់ផ្គូរ

24. safety pin
មូលខ្ទាស់

More vocabulary

pattern maker: a person who makes patterns

garment worker: a person who works in a clothing factory

fashion designer: a person who makes original clothes

Share your answers.

1. Do you know how to use a sewing machine?

2. Can you sew by hand?

73

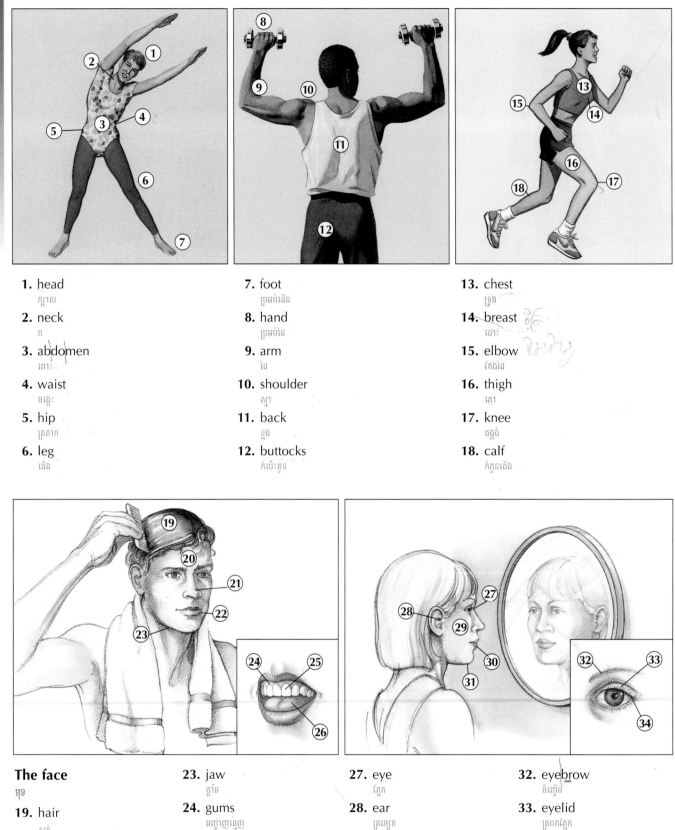

1. head
ក្បាល

2. neck
ក

3. abdomen
ពោះ

4. waist
ចង្កេះ

5. hip
ត្រគាក

6. leg
ជើង

7. foot
ប្រអប់ជើង

8. hand
ប្រអប់ដៃ

9. arm
ដៃ

10. shoulder
ស្មា

11. back
ខ្នង

12. buttocks
គំបើះគូទ

13. chest
ទ្រូង

14. breast
ដោះ

15. elbow
កែងដៃ

16. thigh
ភ្លៅ

17. knee
ជង្គង់

18. calf
កំភួនជើង

The face
មុខ

19. hair
សក់

20. forehead
ថ្ងាស

21. nose
ច្រមុះ

22. mouth
មាត់

23. jaw
ថ្គាម

24. gums
អញ្ចាញធ្មេញ

25. teeth
ធ្មេញ

26. tongue
អណ្តាត

27. eye
ភ្នែក

28. ear
ត្រចៀក

29. cheek
ថ្ពាល់

30. lip
បបូរមាត់

31. chin
ចង្កា

32. eyebrow
ចិញ្ចើម

33. eyelid
ត្របកភ្នែក

34. eyelashes
រោមភ្នែក

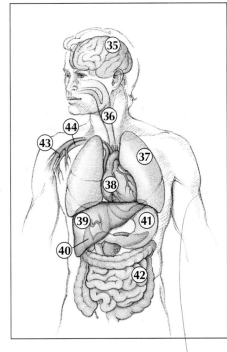

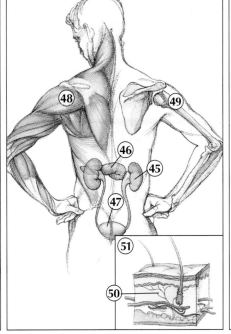

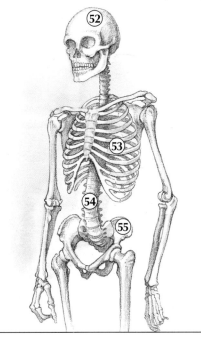

Inside the body
ខាងក្នុងរាងកាយ

35. brain
ខួរក្បាល

36. throat
បំពង់ក

37. lung
សួត

38 heart
បេះដូង

39. liver
ថ្លើម

40. gallbladder
ប្រម៉ាត់

41. stomach
ក្រពះ

42. intestines
ពោះវៀន

43. artery
សរសៃឈាមក្រហម

44. vein
សរសៃឈាមខៀ

45. kidney
ក្រលៀន

46. pancreas
លំពែង

47. bladder
ប្លោកនោម

48. muscle
សាច់ដុំ

49. bone
ឆ្អឹង

50. nerve
សរសៃប្រសាទ

51. skin
ស្បែក

The skeleton
គ្រោងឆ្អឹង

52. skull
ឆ្អឹងលលាដ៍ក្បាល

53. rib cage
ប្រអប់ឆ្អឹងជំនី

54. spinal column
ឆ្អឹងខ្នង

55. pelvis
ឆ្អឹងត្រគាក

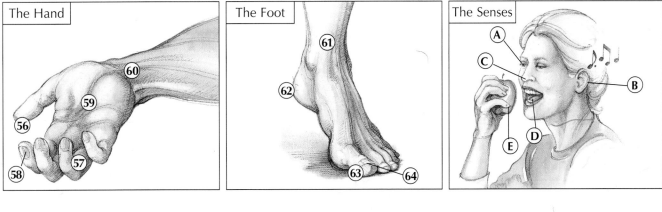

| The Hand | The Foot | The Senses |

56. thumb
មេដៃ

57. fingers
ម្រាមដៃ

58. fingernail
ក្រចកដៃ

59. palm
បាតដៃ

60. wrist
កដៃ

61. ankle
កជើង

62. heel
កែងជើង

63. toe
ម្រាមជើង

64. toenail
ក្រចកជើង

A. see
មើល / ឃើញ

B. hear
ឮ

C. smell
ហិតក្លិន / ក្លិន

D. taste
ភ្លក់ / រសជាតិ

E. touch
ប៉ះ / ពាល់

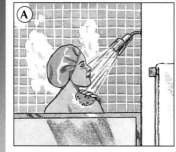

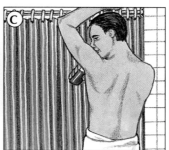

A. take a shower
ងូតទឹក (ផ្កាឈូក)

B. bathe / take a bath
ងូតទឹក

C. use deodorant
ប្រើប៉ូលោបក្លៀក

D. put on sunscreen
លាបថ្នាំសំរាប់ការពារវ៉ែលក

1. **shower cap**
អ្នកស្រោបក្បាល (ងូតទឹក)

2. **soap**
សាប៊ូ

3. **bath powder / talcum powder**
ម្សៅងូតទឹក

4. **deodorant**
ថ្នាំលាបក្លៀក

5. **perfume / cologne**
ទឹកអប់ / ទឹកអប់កូឡូញ

6. **sunscreen**
ថ្នាំលាបសំរាប់ការពារវ៉ែលក

7. **body lotion**
ទ្បស្យុងលាបខ្លួន

8. **moisturizer**
ថ្នាំផ្លើមស្បែក

 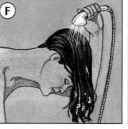   

E. wash...hair
កក់...សក់

F. rinse...hair
លាង...សក់

G. comb...hair
សិត...សក់

H. dry...hair
ផ្លុំ...សក់

I. brush...hair
សិត...សក់

9. **shampoo**
សាប៊ូកក់សក់

10. **conditioner**
សាប៊ូធ្វើឱ្យសក់ទន់

11. **hair gel**
ថ្នាំលាបសក់អោយរឹង

12. **hair spray**
ថ្នាំបាញ់សក់

13. **comb**
ក្រាស់

14. **brush**
ច្រាស់សិតសក់

15. **curling iron**
ប្រដាប់អ៊ុតសក់

16. **blow dryer**
ប្រដាប់ផ្លុំសក់

17. **hair clip**
គ្រឡេតសក់

18. **barrette**
ដង្កៀបសក់

19. **bobby pins**
ដង្កៀបសក់ក្បាលា

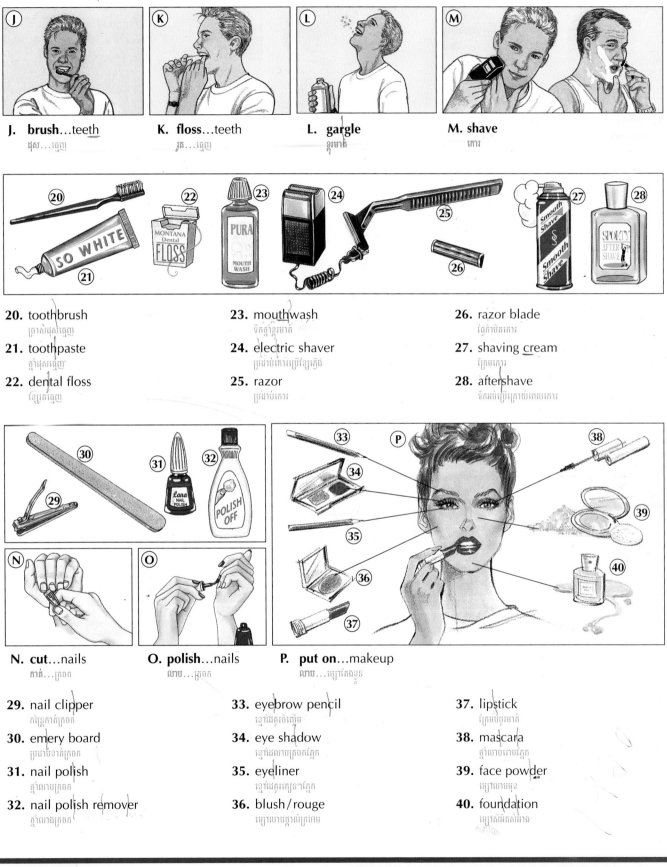

J. brush…teeth
ដុស…ធ្មេញ

K. floss…teeth
រត់…ធ្មេញ

L. gargle
ខ្លុរមាត់

M. shave
កោរ

20. toothbrush
ច្រាស់ដុសធ្មេញ

21. toothpaste
ថ្នាំដុសធ្មេញ

22. dental floss
ខ្សែរត់ធ្មេញ

23. mouthwash
ទឹកថ្លាខ្លុរមាត់

24. electric shaver
ម៉ាស៊ីនកោរប្រើខ្សែភ្លើង

25. razor
ប្រដាប់កោរ

26. razor blade
ផ្លែកាំបិតកោរ

27. shaving cream
ក្រែមកោរ

28. aftershave
ទឹកអប់ប្រើក្រោយពេលកោរ

N. cut…nails
កាត់…ក្រចក

O. polish…nails
លាប…ក្រចក

P. put on…makeup
លាប…ម្សៅតែងខ្លួន

29. nail clipper
កន្ត្រៃកាត់ក្រចក

30. emery board
ប្រដាប់ខាត់ក្រចក

31. nail polish
ថ្នាំលាបក្រចក

32. nail polish remover
ថ្នាំលាងក្រចក

33. eyebrow pencil
ខ្មៅដៃគូចិញ្ចើម

34. eye shadow
ខ្មៅដៃលាបគ្របភ្នែក

35. eyeliner
ខ្មៅដៃគូរក្បៀវភ្នែក

36. blush/rouge
ម្សៅលាបថ្ពាល់ក្រហម

37. lipstick
ក្រែមបបូរមាត់

38. mascara
ថ្នាំលាបរោមភ្នែក

39. face powder
ម្សៅលាបមុខ

40. foundation
ម្សៅស្អិតសំរាប់អាង

More vocabulary

A product without perfume or scent is **unscented.**

A product that is better for people with allergies is **hypoallergenic.**

Share your answers.

1. What is your morning routine if you stay home? if you go out?

2. Do women in your culture wear makeup? How old are they when they begin to use it?

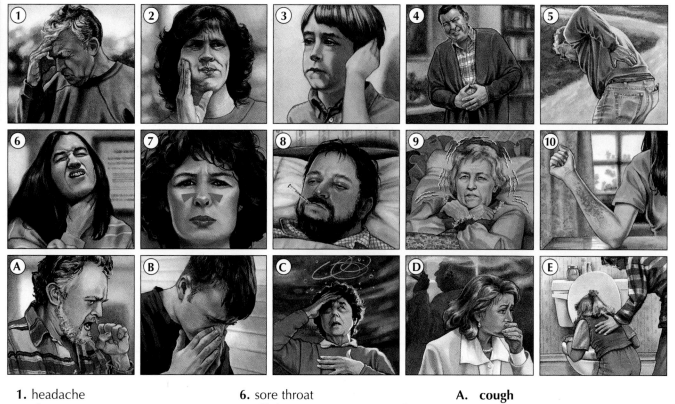

1. headache
ឈឺក្បាល

2. toothache
ឈឺធ្មេញ

3. earache
ឈឺត្រចៀក

4. stomachache
ឈឺពោះ / ឈឺក្រពះ

5. backache
ឈឺខ្នង

6. sore throat
ឈឺបំពង់ក

7. nasal congestion
គាំងច្រមុះ

8. fever/temperature
គ្រុន

9. chills
គ្រុនរងា

10. rash
ឡើងមោស់ / ឡើងកន្ទួល

A. **cough**
ក្អក

B. **sneeze**
កណ្ដាស់

C. **feel** dizzy
វិលមុខ

D. **feel** nauseous
ចង់ក្អួត

E. **throw up/vomit**
ក្អួត / ចង្អោរ

   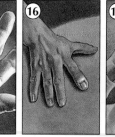  

11. insect bite
សត្វល្អិតទេច / ខាំ

12. bruise
ជាំស្បែក

13. cut
មុត

14. sunburn
រលាកកំដៅថ្ងៃ

15. blister
ពងបែក

16. **swollen** finger
ហើមម្រាមដៃ

17. **bloody** nose
ឈាមច្រមុះ

18. **sprained** ankle
ត្រេចកជើង

Use the new language.

Look at **Health Care,** pages **80–81.**

Tell what medication or treatment you would use for each health problem.

Share your answers.

1. For which problems would you go to a doctor? use medication? do nothing?

2. What do you do for a sunburn? for a headache?

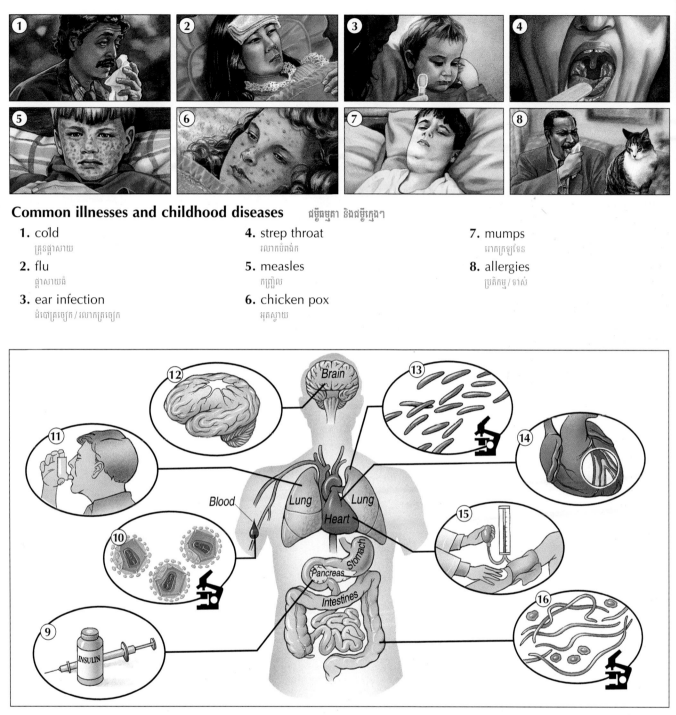

Common illnesses and childhood diseases   ជម្ងឺធម្មតា និងជម្ងឺក្មេងៗ

1. cold
ត្រជាក់ផ្តាសាយ

2. flu
ផ្តាសាយផ្តិ

3. ear infection
ដំបៅត្រចៀក / ឈឺត្រចៀក

4. strep throat
រលាកបំពង់ក

5. measles
កញ្ជ្រិល

6. chicken pox
អុតស្វាយ

7. mumps
រោគក្រមួនទេះ

8. allergies
ប្រតិកម្ម / ទាស់

Medical conditions and serious diseases   លក្ខណៈជម្ងឺ និង ជម្ងឺធ្ងន់ធ្ងរ

9. diabetes
ជម្ងឺទឹកនោមផ្អែម

10. HIV (human immunodeficiency virus)
រោគ HIV

11. asthma
ហឺត

12. brain cancer
មហារីកខួរក្បាល

13. TB (tuberculosis)
ជម្ងឺរបេង

14. heart disease
ជម្ងឺបេះដូង

15. high blood pressure
រោគលើសឈាម

16. intestinal parasites
បរាសិតក្នុងពោះវៀន

More vocabulary

AIDS (acquired immunodeficiency syndrome): a medical condition that results from contracting the HIV virus

influenza: flu

hypertension: high blood pressure

infectious disease: a disease that is spread through air or water

Share your answers.

Which diseases on this page are infectious?

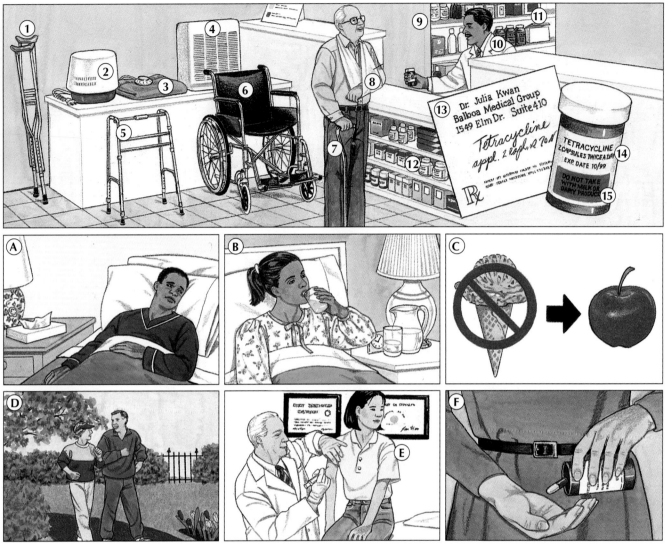

1. crutches
   ឈើច្រត់

2. humidifier
   ម៉ាស៊ីនផ្សើម

3. heating pad
   ទ្រនាប់កំដៅ

4. air purifier
   ម៉ាស៊ីនបន្សុតខ្យល់

5. walker
   ឈើបំបែរ

6. wheelchair
   កៅអីអ្នកពិការ

7. cane
   ឈើច្រត់

8. sling
   ខ្សែស្ពាយដៃ/ទ្រដៃ

9. pharmacy
   ហាងថ្នាំ/ឱសថស្ថាន

10. pharmacist
    ឱសថការី

11. prescription medication
    ថ្នាំមានសំបុត្រពេទ្យ

12. over-the-counter medication
    ថ្នាំឥតមានសំបុត្រពេទ្យ

13. prescription
    សំបុត្រឲ្យញថ្នាំ

14. prescription label
    ផ្លាកសំបុត្រថ្នាំ

15. warning label
    ផ្លាកប្រាម

A. **Get** bed rest.
    សំរាកលើគ្រែ ។

B. **Drink** fluids.
    ញ៉ាំជាតិទឹក ។

C. **Change** your diet.
    ផ្លាស់ប្ដូរអ្នកបរិភោគ ។

D. **Exercise.**
    ហាត់ប្រាណ ។

E. **Get** an injection.
    ចាក់ថ្នាំ ។

F. **Take** medicine.
    លេបថ្នាំ ។

More vocabulary

dosage: how much medicine you take and how many times a day you take it

expiration date: the last day the medicine can be used

treatment: something you do to get better

Staying in bed, drinking fluids, and getting physical therapy are treatments.

An injection that stops a person from getting a serious disease is called **an immunization** or **a vaccination.**

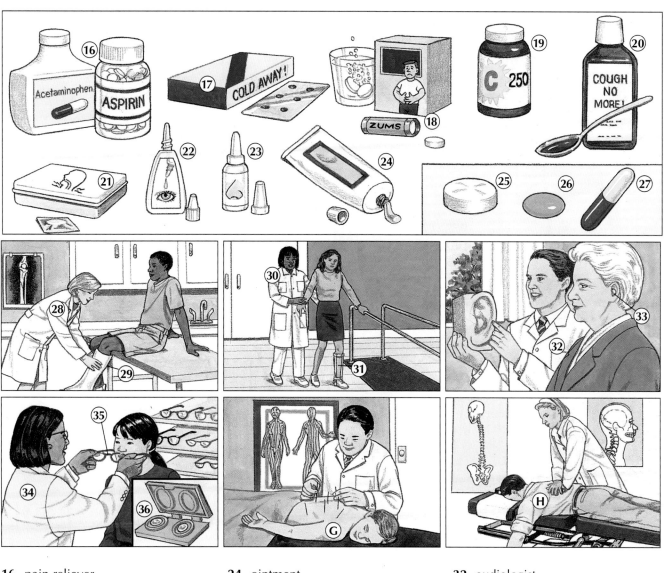

16. pain reliever
ថ្នាំម្សៅបំបាត់ការឈឺចាប់

17. cold tablets
ថ្នាំផ្តាសាយ

18. antacid
ថ្នាំប្រឆាំងជាតិអាស៊ីដ (អាន់តាស៊ីដ)

19. vitamins
វីតាមីន

20. cough syrup
ថ្នាំក្អក

21. throat lozenges
គ្រាប់ថ្នាំបំបាត់ឈឺបំពង់ក

22. eyedrops
ថ្នាំបន្តក់ភ្នែក

23. nasal spray
ថ្នាំបាញ់ច្រមុះ

24. ointment
ថ្នាំលាប / ថ្នាំក្រមួន

25. tablet
ថ្នាំគ្រាប់មូល

26. pill
ថ្នាំគ្រាប់ទ្រវែង

27. capsule
គ្រាប់ថ្នាំមួលទ្រវែងមានស្រោម

28. orthopedist
គ្រូពេទ្យវះកាត់ព្យាបាលឆ្អឹង

29. cast
រណបបុកបំបិទឆ្អឹង

30. physical therapist
អ្នកព្យាបាលរោគប្រើកាយាយាត

31. brace
ប្រដាប់ក្រៀក

32. audiologist
គ្រូពេទ្យឯកទេសត្រចៀក

33. hearing aid
ប្រដាប់ជំនួយត្រចៀក

34. optometrist
គ្រូពេទ្យពិនិត្យវ៉ែនតា

35. (eye)glasses
វ៉ែនតាជំនួយវ៉ែនតា

36. contact lenses
កែវជំនួយវ៉ែនតា

G. Get acupuncture.
ចាក់ម្ជុលវិទ្យាសាស្ត្រ ។

H. Go to a chiropractor.
ទៅជួបគ្រូពេទ្យចាប់សរសៃ ។

Share your answers.

1. What's the best treatment for a headache? a sore throat? a stomachache? a fever?

2. Do you think vitamins are important? Why or why not?

3. What treatments are popular in your culture?

A. **be injured / be hurt**
ត្រូវរបួស / ឈឺ

B. **be** unconscious
ត្រូវសន្លប់មិនដឹងខ្លួន

C. **be** in shock
ត្រូវស្លុតស្មារតី

D. **have** a heart attack
គាំងបេះដូង

E. **have** an allergic reaction
មានប្រតិកម្មនឹងការមិនត្រូវធាតុ

F. **get** an electric shock
ខ្សែភ្លើងឆក់

G. **get** frostbite
ត្រជាក់ឈាប់ស្បែក

H. **burn** (your)self
រលាក (ខ្លួនឯង)

I. **drown**
លង់ទឹក

J. **swallow** poison
លេបថ្នាំពុល

K. **overdose** on drugs
លេបថ្នាំហួសកម្រិត

L. **choke**
ស្អះ / ឈ្លក់ / អូរ

M. **bleed**
ចេញឈាម

N. **can't breathe**
ដកដង្ហើមមិនរួច

O. **fall**
ធ្លាក់ / ដួល

P. **break** a bone
បាក់ឆ្អឹង

Grammar point: past tense

burn	— burned	choke	— choked	bleed	— bled
drown	— drowned	be	— was, were	can't	— couldn't
swallow	— swallowed	have	— had	fall	— fell
overdose	— overdosed	get	— got	break	— broke

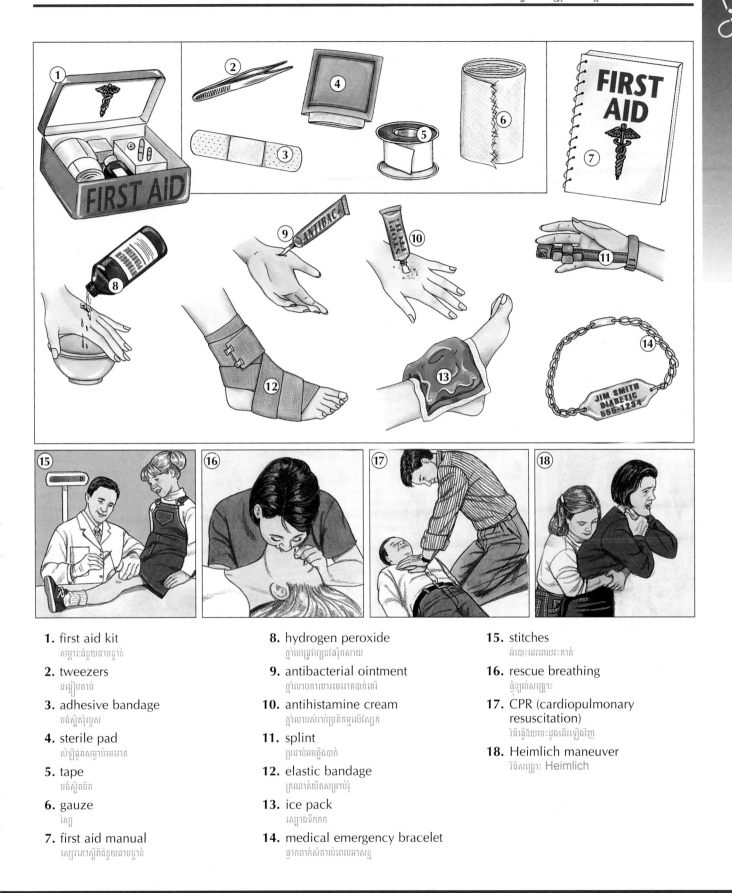

1. **first aid kit**
   សម្ភារៈជំនួយជាបន្ទាន់

2. **tweezers**
   ដង្កៀបចាប់

3. **adhesive bandage**
   បង់ស្អិតបិទរបួស

4. **sterile pad**
   សំឡីជូតសម្លាប់មេរោគ

5. **tape**
   បង់ស្អិតបិទ

6. **gauze**
   សំឡី

7. **first aid manual**
   សៀវភៅស្ដីពីជំនួយជាបន្ទាន់

8. **hydrogen peroxide**
   ថ្នាំហៃដ្រូហៀនផៃរ៉ុកសាយ

9. **antibacterial ointment**
   ថ្នាំលាបការពារមេរោគបាក់តេរី

10. **antihistamine cream**
    ថ្នាំលាបសំរាប់ប្រតិកម្មលើស្បែក

11. **splint**
    ប្រដាប់អមឆ្អឹងបាក់

12. **elastic bandage**
    ក្រណាត់យឺតសម្រាប់រុំ

13. **ice pack**
    ស្បៀងទឹកកក

14. **medical emergency bracelet**
    ផ្នាកពាក់សំគាល់ពេលអាសន្ន

15. **stitches**
    អំបោះដេរពេលរបួសកាត់

16. **rescue breathing**
    ផ្លុំខ្យល់សង្រ្គោះ

17. **CPR (cardiopulmonary resuscitation)**
    វិធីផ្ដុំឱ្យបេះដូងដេរឡើងវិញ

18. **Heimlich maneuver**
    វិធីសង្រ្គោះ Heimlich

Important Note: Only people who are properly trained should give stitches or do CPR.

Share your answers.

1. Do you have a First Aid kit in your home? Where can you buy one?

2. When do you use hydrogen peroxide? an elastic support bandage? antihistamine cream?

3. Do you know first aid? Where did you learn it?

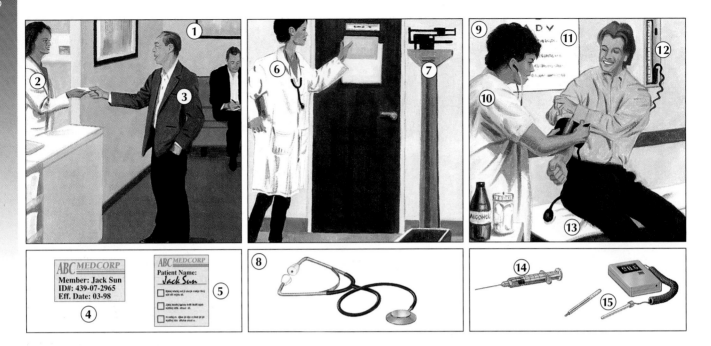

Medical clinic គិលានដ្ឋានពេទ្យ

1. **waiting room**
   បន្ទប់រង់ចាំ

2. **receptionist**
   អ្នកទទួលភ្ញៀវ

3. **patient**
   អ្នកជំងឺ

4. **insurance card**
   ប័ណ្ណធានារ៉ាប់រង

5. **insurance form**
   ក្រដាសធានារ៉ាប់រង

6. **doctor**
   គ្រូពេទ្យ

7. **scale**
   ជញ្ជីង

8. **stethoscope**
   ប្រដាប់ស្តាប់បេះដូង

9. **examining room**
   បន្ទប់ពិនិត្យ

10. **nurse**
    គិលានុបដ្ឋាយិកា

11. **eye chart**
    តារាងស្ទង់ភ្នែក

12. **blood pressure gauge**
    ប្រដាប់ស្ទង់ឈាម

13. **examination table**
    គ្រែសំរាប់ពិនិត្យ

14. **syringe**
    ម្ជុលចាក់ថ្នាំ

15. **thermometer**
    ប្រដាប់ស្ទង់កំដៅ

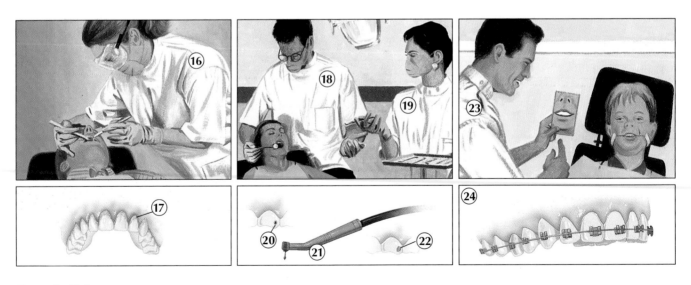

Dental clinic គិលានដ្ឋានធ្មេញ

16. **dental hygienist**
    អ្នកសំអាតធ្មេញ

17. **tartar**
    ក្រមរធ្មេញ

18. **dentist**
    ពេទ្យធ្មេញ

19. **dental assistant**
    អ្នកជំនួយពេទ្យធ្មេញ

20. **cavity**
    ធ្មេញជុំរុយស៊ី

21. **drill**
    ប្រដាប់ខូងធ្មេញ

22. **filling**
    បំពេញប្រហោង (ធ្មេញ)/ប៉ះធ្មេញ

23. **orthodontist**
    គ្រូពេទ្យរៀបកូនធ្មេញ

24. **braces**
    គ្រឿងស្រោបកាត់ធ្មេញ

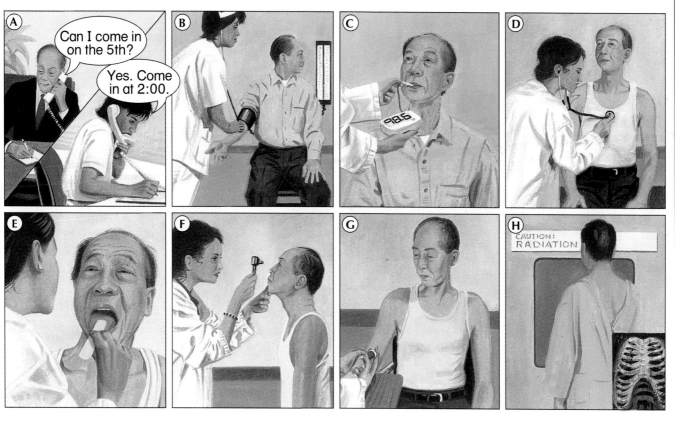

A. make an appointment
ធ្វើការណាត់ជួប

B. check...blood pressure
ពិនិត្យ...កម្រិតឈាម

C. take...temperature
ស្ទង់...កំដៅ

D. listen to...heart
ស្តាប់...បេះដូង

E. look in...throat
មើលក្នុង...បំពង់ក

F. examine...eyes
ពិនិត្យមើល...ភ្នែក

G. draw...blood
បូមយក...ឈាម

H. get an X ray
ថ្លុះខ្នងដោយរស្មី X

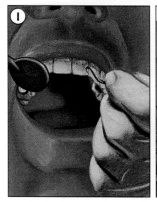
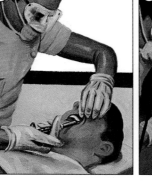
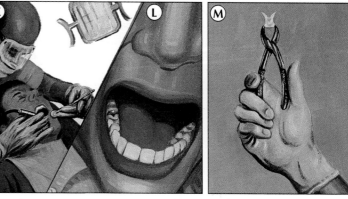

I. clean...teeth
សំអាត...ធ្មេញ

J. give...a shot of anesthetic
ចាក់...ថ្នាំស្ពឹក / សន្លប់

K. drill a tooth
ខៃធ្មេញ

L. fill a cavity
បំ៖ធ្មេញដុងរណ្ដៅ

M. pull a tooth
ដកធ្មេញ

More vocabulary

get a checkup: to go for a medical exam

extract a tooth: to pull out a tooth

Share your answers.

1. What is the average cost of a medical exam in your area?

2. Some people are nervous at the dentist's office. What can they do to relax?

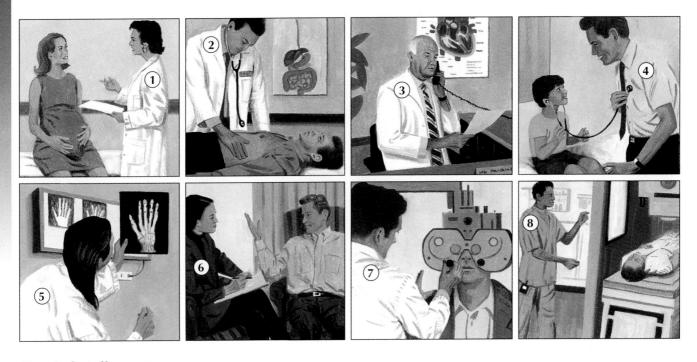

Hospital staff   បុគ្គលិកពេទ្យ

1. obstetrician
គ្រូពេទ្យផ្នែកស្ត្រីមានផ្ទៃពោះ

2. internist
គ្រូពេទ្យរោគវិនិច្ឆ័យផ្នែកក្នុងរាងកាយ

3. cardiologist
គ្រូពេទ្យផ្នែកបេះដូង

4. pediatrician
គ្រូពេទ្យកុមារក្មេង

5. radiologist
គ្រូពេទ្យកាំរស្មី

6. psychiatrist
គ្រូពេទ្យផ្នែកជំងឺសរសៃអារម្មណ៍

7. ophthalmologist
គ្រូពេទ្យផ្នែកជម្ងឺភ្នែក

8. X-ray technician
អ្នកឯកទេសផ្នែកកាំរស្មី

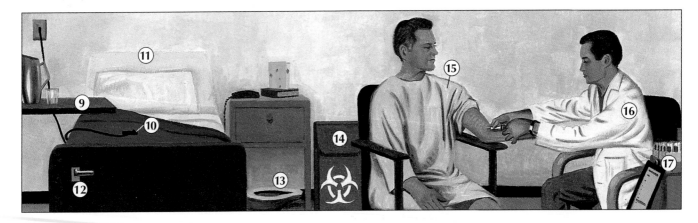

Patient's room   បន្ទប់អ្នកជម្ងឺ

9. bed table
តុសម្រាប់ដាក់របស់នៅលើគ្រែ

10. call button
គន្លឹះចុចហៅ

11. hospital bed
គ្រែពេទ្យ

12. bed control
ប្រដាប់ចុចបិទបើកគ្រែ

13. bedpan
កន្ទោរអ្នកជំងឺ

14. medical waste disposal
ធុងកាកសំណល់ពេទ្យ

15. hospital gown
អាវអ្នកជម្ងឺក្នុងពេទ្យ

16. lab technician
អ្នកឯកទេសខាងពិសោធន៍

17. blood work/blood test
យកឈាមមកពិសោធន៍

More vocabulary

nurse practitioner: a nurse licensed to give medical exams

specialist: a doctor who only treats specific medical problems

gynecologist: a specialist who examines and treats women

nurse midwife: a nurse practitioner who examines pregnant women and delivers babies

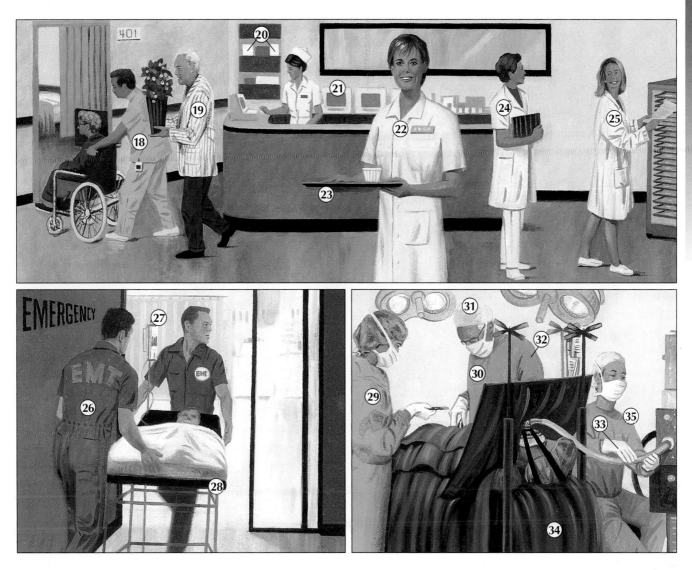

Nurse's station
កន្លែងតិលានុបដ្ឋាយិកា

18. orderly
អ្នកជួយធ្វើការពេទ្យ

19. volunteer
អ្នកស្ម័គ្រចិត្ត

20. medical charts
តារាងពេទ្យ

21. vital signs monitor
ប្រដាប់ត្រាប់សញ្ញាស់ខាវ់

22. RN (registered nurse)
តិលានុបដ្ឋាយិកាពេញច្បាប់ (RN)

23. medication tray
ថាសថ្នាំ

24. LPN (licensed practical nurse)/
LVN (licensed vocational nurse)
គុលានុបដ្ឋាយិកា អនុគ្រុប្តផ្ដេកវិជ្ជាជីរ:/
គុលានុបដ្ឋាយិកាអនុគ្រុប្ត ផ្ដេកពេទ្យ

25. dietician
ពេទ្យផ្ដេកចំណីអាហារ

Emergency room
បន្ទប់ភាពអាសន្ន

26. emergency medical technician
(EMT)
អ្នកជំងឺទេសពេទ្យសង្គ្រោះក្នុងពេលអាសន្ន (EMT)

27. IV (intravenous drip)
ថង់ថ្នាំសរិរ/IV/សេរ៉ូម

28. stretcher/gurney
រទេះដាក់អ្នកជម្ងឺ

Operating room
បន្ទប់វះកាត់

29. surgical nurse
តិលានុបដ្ឋាយិកាវះកាត់

30. surgeon
គ្រូពេទ្យផ្ដេកវះកាត់

31. surgical cap
អ្នករះកាត់

32. surgical gown
ខោអាវរោាក់វះកាត់

33. latex gloves
ស្រោមដៃកៅស៊ូ

34. operating table
គុរះកាត់/ប៉ុគ្រះកាត់

35. anesthesiologist
គ្រូពេទ្យផ្ដេកថ្នាំសន្លប់

Practice asking for the hospital staff.

Please get the nurse. I have a question for her.

Where's the anesthesiologist? I need to talk to her.

I'm looking for the lab technician. Have you seen him?

Share your answers.

1. Have you ever been to an emergency room? Who helped you?

2. Have you ever been in the hospital? How long did you stay?

1. fire station
   ស្ថានីយពន្លត់ភ្លើង

2. coffee shop
   ឆ្មែមកាហ្វេ

3. bank
   ធនាគារ

4. car dealership
   ហាងលក់ឡាន

5. hotel
   សណ្ឋាគារ

6. church
   ព្រះវិហារគ្រឹស្ត

7. hospital
   មន្ទីរពេទ្យ

8. park
   សួនកំសាន្ត

9. synagogue
   សាលាប្រជុំរបស់ជនជ្វីហ្វ

10. theater
    រោងល្ខោន

11. movie theater
    រោងភាពយន្ត

12. gas station
    ស្ថានីយសាំង

13. furniture store
    ហាងលក់គ្រឿងសង្ហារឹម

14. hardware store
    ហាងលក់គ្រឿងដែក

15. barber shop
    ហាងកាត់សក់

More vocabulary

skyscraper: a very tall office building

downtown / city center: the area in a city with the city hall, courts, and businesses

Practice giving your destination.

I'm going to go <u>downtown</u>.

I have to go to <u>the post office</u>.

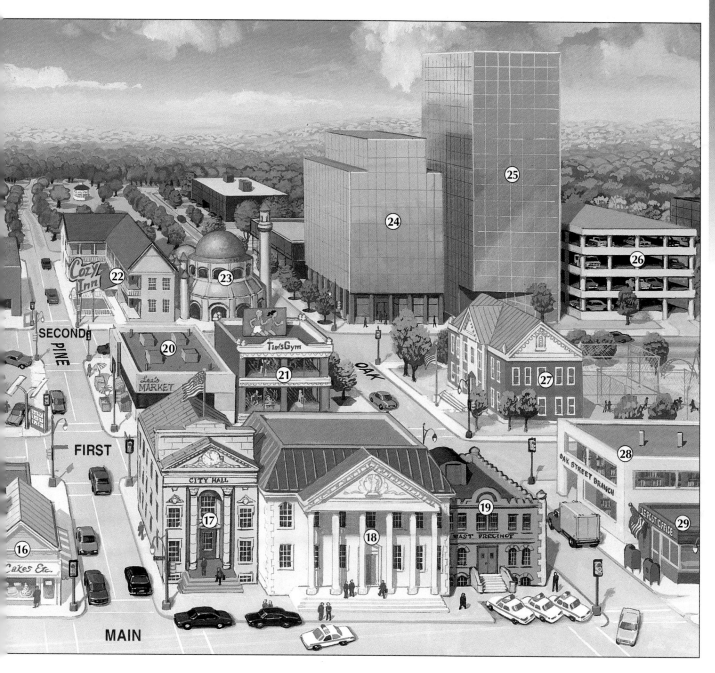

16. bakery
ហាងនំប៉័ង

17. city hall
សាលាក្រុង

18. courthouse
សាលាវិនិច្ឆ័យ

19. police station
ស្ថានីយតម្រួត

20. market
ផ្សារ

21. health club
ក្លិបហាត់ប្រាណ

22. motel
សណ្ឋាគារតូច

23. mosque
ព្រះវិហារឥស្លាម

24. office building
អគារការិយាល័យ

25. high-rise building
អគារខ្ពស់ៗ

26. parking garage
កន្លែងចតឡាន

27. school
សាលារៀន

28. library
បណ្ណាល័យ

29. post office
ប៉ុស្តិ៍ប្រៃសណីយ៍

Practice asking for and giving the locations of buildings.

Where's <u>the post office</u>?

It's on <u>Oak Street</u>.

Share your answers.

1. Which of the places in this picture do you go to every week?

2. Is it good to live in a city? Why or why not?

3. What famous cities do you know?

1. Laundromat
   កន្លែងបោកខោអាវ

2. drugstore / pharmacy
   ហាងលក់ថ្នាំពេទ្យ / ឱសថស្ថាន

3. convenience store
   ហាងលក់ទំនិញគ្រប់ចាយាយស្រួល

4. photo shop
   ហាងថតរូប

5. parking space
   ចំណតរថយន្ត

6. traffic light
   ភ្លើងចរាចរ

7. pedestrian
   អ្នកដើរ

8. crosswalk
   ផ្លូវឆ្លងកាត់

9. street
   ផ្លូវថ្នល់

10. curb
    ចិញ្ចើមផ្លូវ

11. newsstand
    កូនបេឡាកាសែត

12. mailbox
    ប្រអប់សំបុត្រ

13. drive-thru window
    ទិញអ្វីមួចតាមបង្អួចបើកឡាន

14. fast food restaurant
    ហាងលក់ម្ហូបរហ័ស

15. bus
    ឡានឈ្នួល

A. **cross** the street
   ឆ្លងថ្នល់

B. **wait** for the light
   រង់ចាំភ្លើងសញ្ញា

C. **drive** a car
   បើកឡាន

More vocabulary

neighborhood: the area close to your home

do errands: to make a short trip from your home to buy or pick up something

Talk about where to buy things.

You can buy <u>newspapers</u> at <u>a newsstand</u>.

You can buy <u>donuts</u> at <u>a donut shop</u>.

You can buy <u>food</u> at <u>a convenience store</u>.

16. bus stop
កន្លែងចាំឡានឧបon្តុ/រថយន្តក្រុង

17. corner
កាច់ជ្រុង

18. parking meter
ក្នុងម៉ែ៉ាក់កាក់ចតឡ្លាន

19. motorcycle
ម៉ូតូ

20. donut shop
ហាងដូណាត់

21. public telephone
ទូរស័ព្ទសាធារណៈ

22. copy center/print shop
ហាងថតឯកសារ និងថតក្រដាសបោះពុម្ព

23. streetlight
ភ្លើងផ្លូវ

24. dry cleaners
ហាងបោកអ៊ុតខោអាវប្រើកំដៅ

25. nail salon
ហាងធ្វើក្រចក

26. sidewalk
ចិញ្ចើមថ្នល់ / ផ្លូវដើរ

27. garbage truck
ឡ្លានដឹកសំរាម

28. fire hydrant
ក្បាលម៉ាស៊ីនទឹកពន្លត់ភ្លើង

29. sign
សញ្ញា

30. street vendor
អ្នកលក់តាមផ្លូវ

31. cart
រទេះដឹកឥវ៉ាន់

D. **park** the car
ចតឡ្លាន

E. **ride** a bicycle
ជិះកង់

Share your answers.

1. Do you like to do errands?

2. Do you always like to go to the same stores?

3. Which businesses in the picture are also in your neighborhood?

4. Do you know someone who has a small business? What kind?

5. What things can you buy from a street vendor?

1. music store
ហាងលក់គ្រឿងភ្លេង

2. jewelry store
ហាងគ្រឿងអលង្ការ

3. candy store
ហាងស្ករគ្រាប់

4. bookstore
បណ្ណាគារ

5. toy store
ហាងលក់វត្ថុងក្មេងលេង

6. pet store
ហាងលក់សត្វចិញ្ចឹម

7. card store
ហាងលក់បណ្ណផ្សេងៗ

8. optician
ហាងលក់វ៉ែនតា

9. travel agency
កន្លែងលក់សំបុត្រធ្វើដំណើរ

10. shoe store
ហាងលក់ស្បែកជើង

11. fountain
ក្បាលបាចបាញ់ទឹកលម្អ

12. florist
ហាងលក់ផ្កា

More vocabulary

beauty shop: hair salon

men's store: a store that sells men's clothing

dress shop: a store that sells women's clothing

Talk about where you want to shop in this mall.

Let's go to the card store.

I need to buy a card for Maggie's birthday.

13. department store
ហាងលក់សំល្យេកបំពាក់

14. food court
ទីលក់ម្ហូប

15. video store
ហាងលក់វិដេអ៊ុ

16. hair salon
ហាងធ្វើសក់

17. maternity shop
ហាងសំរាប់ស្ត្រីមានផ្ទៃពោះ

18. electronics store
ហាងលក់គ្រឿងអគ្គិសនី

19. directory
ស្បៀវភៅរាយឈ្មោះហាង

20. ice cream stand
តូបលក់ការ៉េម

21. escalator
ជណ្តើរយន្ត

22. information booth
កន្លែងសំរាប់ពត៌មាន

Practice asking for and giving the location of different shops.

Where's the maternity shop?

  It's on the first floor, next to the hair salon.

Share your answers.

1. Do you like shopping malls? Why or why not?

2. Some people don't go to the mall to shop. Name some other things you can do in a mall.

1. parent
ឪពុក / ម្ដាយ

2. stroller
រទេះរុញ

3. childcare worker
អ្នកថែក្មេង

4. cubby
បន្ទប់កូនក្មេង

5. toys
របស់ក្មេងលេង

6. rocking chair
កៅអីបះបើក

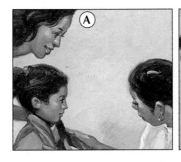

A. drop off
ទម្លាក់ទុក / ដាក់ចុះ

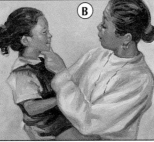

B. hold
កាន់

C. nurse
គិលានុបផ្ដាយិកា

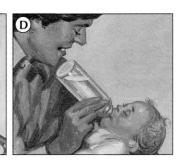

D. feed
បំបៅ

E. change diapers
ផ្ដូរកន្ទប

F. read a story
អានរឿង

G. pick up
ទៅយក

H. rock
យោល

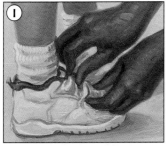

I. tie shoes
ចងខ្សែស្បែកជើង

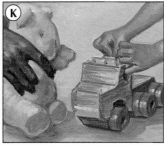

J. dress
ស្លៀកពាក់

K. play
លេង

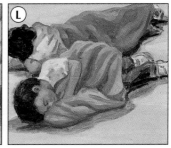

L. take a nap
ដេកថ្ងៃ

7. high chair
កៅអីខ្ពស់

8. bib
ស្រង-ក / កម្រង-ក

9. changing table
តុប្ដូរកន្ថបក្មេង

10. potty seat
កៅអីសម្រាប់ទារកបន្ទោរផុះ

11. playpen
ទ្រុងក្មេងលេង

12. walker
ក្យែក

13. car safety seat
កៅអីក្មេងក្នុងឡាន

14. baby carrier
ប្រដាប់ដាក់កូនឆ្អាម្យូរ

15. baby backpack
ប្រដាប់ស្ពាយកូនពីក្រោយ

16. carriage
រទេះរុញ

17. wipes
ប្រដាប់ផ្ដក

18. baby powder
ម្សៅកូនង្ហា

19. disinfectant
ម្សៅសម្លាប់មេរោគ

20. disposable diapers
កន្ថបប្រើហើយបោះចោល

21. cloth diapers
កន្ថបក្រណាត់

22. diaper pins
ប្រដាប់ខ្ទាស់កន្ថប

23. diaper pail
ធុងកន្ថប

24. training pants
ខោទារកវៀនស្ងៀក

25. formula
ទឹកដោះគោ

26. bottle
ដប

27. nipple
ក្បាលដោះ

28. baby food
ម្ហូបកូនង្ហា

29. pacifier
កៅស៊ូក្បាលដោះ

30. teething ring
កងកករ

31. rattle
ប្រដាប់អង្រួនលេង

1. envelope
ស្រោមសំបុត្រ

2. letter
សំបុត្រ

3. postcard
កាតប៉ូស្ដាល់

4. greeting card
ប័ណ្ណជូនពរ

5. package
កញ្ចប់

6. letter carrier
អ្នកដាក់សំបុត្រ

7. return address
អាសយដ្ឋានអ្នកផ្ញើ

8. mailing address
អាសយដ្ឋានអ្នកទទួល

9. postmark
ត្រាប៉ូស្ដ៍

10. stamp/postage
តែម

11. certified mail
សំបុត្រអនុសិដ្ឋ

12. priority mail
សំបុត្រផ្ញើបានលឿន

13. air letter/aerogramme
សំបុត្រផ្ញើតាមផ្លូវអាកាស

14. ground post/
parcel post
ប៉ូស្តផ្ញើកញ្ចប់របស់

15. Express Mail/
overnight mail
សំបុត្ររហ័ស/សំបុត្រផ្ញើមួយយប់ដល់

A. **address** a postcard
ចារអាសយដ្ឋានលើប៉ូស្ដ៍កាត

B. **send** it/**mail** it
ផ្ញើសំបុត្រ

C. **deliver** it
ចែកសំបុត្រ

D. **receive** it
ទទួលសំបុត្រ

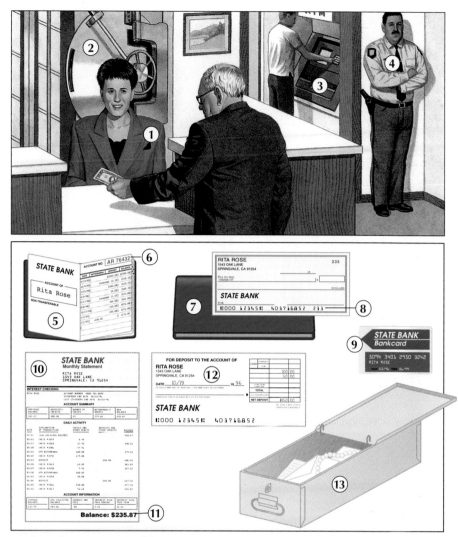

1. teller
   អ្នកលើកឬទូលប្រាក់
2. vault
   ទូដែលដាក់ប្រាក់
3. ATM (automated teller machine)
   ម៉ាស៊ីនដាក់កាតដកលុយ
4. security guard
   អ្នកយាម

5. passbook
   សៀវភៅធនាគារ
6. savings account number
   លេខគណនីសន្សំ
7. checkbook
   សៀវភៅសែក
8. checking account number
   លេខគណនីសែក
9. ATM card
   កាតសំរាប់ដកលុយពីម៉ាស៊ីន
10. monthly statement
    សំបុត្រគណនេយ្យប្រចាំខែ
11. balance
    ចំនួនប្រាក់នៅសល់ / គុណអ្នការ
12. deposit slip
    បណ្ណដាក់ប្រាក់កក់
13. safe-deposit box
    ទូដែលសម្រាប់ដាក់ប្រាក់

Using the ATM machine   ការប្រើម៉ាស៊ីនដាក់កាតដកលុយ

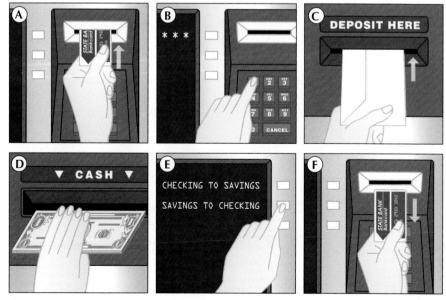

A. **Insert** your ATM card.
   បញ្ចូលកាតដាក់លុយរបស់អ្នកក្នុងម៉ាស៊ីន ។
B. **Enter** your PIN number.*
   ចុចលេខសំគាល់ខ្លួន ។
C. **Make** a deposit.
   ដាក់ប្រាក់កក់ ។

D. **Withdraw** cash.
   ដកប្រាក់ ។
E. **Transfer** funds.
   ផ្ទេរប្រាក់ ។
F. **Remove** your ATM card.
   ដកកាតដាក់លុយរបស់អ្នកចេញពីម៉ាស៊ីន ។

*PIN: personal identification number

More vocabulary

overdrawn account: When there is not enough money in an account to pay a check, we say the account is overdrawn.

Share your answers.

1. Do you use a bank?
2. Do you use an ATM card?
3. Name some things you can put in a safe-deposit box.

1. **reference librarian**
   បណ្ណារក្សឯកសារឆ្លាប់

2. **reference desk**
   តុឯកសារឆ្លាប់យោង

3. **atlas**
   សៀវភៅផែនទី

4. **microfilm reader**
   ម៉ាស៊ីនមើលមីក្រូហ្វីល

5. **microfilm**
   មីក្រូហ្វីល

6. **periodical section**
   កន្លែងដាក់ទស្សនាវដ្ដី

7. **magazine**
   ទស្សនាវដ្ដី

8. **newspaper**
   សារពត៌មាន

9. **online catalog**
   បញ្ជីរាយឈ្មោះរបស់តាមកុំព្យូ័រ

10. **card catalog**
    ការតរាយឈ្មោះរបស់

11. **media section**
    កន្លែងពត៌មានប្រចាំថ្ងៃ

12. **audiocassette**
    កាសែតចាក់ស្ដាប់

13. **videocassette**
    កាសែតវីឌីអូ

14. **CD (compact disc)**
    ថាស CD

15. **record**
    ថាសចិរ្យេង

16. **checkout desk**
    កន្លែងផែកយកសៀវភៅចេញ

17. **library clerk**
    ស្មៀនបណ្ណាល័យ

18. **encyclopedia**
    សារានុក្រម / សព្ទនានាធិប្បាយ

19. **library card**
    ប័ណ្ណបណ្ណាល័យ

20. **library book**
    សៀវភៅបណ្ណាល័យ

21. **title**
    ចំណងជើង

22. **author**
    អ្នកនិពន្ធ

More vocabulary

check a book out: to borrow a book from the library

nonfiction: real information, history or true stories

fiction: stories from the author's imagination

Share your answers.

1. Do you have a library card?

2. Do you prefer to buy books or borrow them from the library?

A. **arrest** a suspect
ចាប់ជនដែលគេសង្ស័យ
1. police officer
ភ្នាក់ងារ / តម្រួត / ប៉ូលិស
2. handcuffs
ខ្នោះដៃ

B. **hire** a lawyer / **hire** an attorney
ផ្ទល់មេធាវី
3. guard
អ្នកយាម
4. defense attorney
មេធាវីរបស់ចុងចោទ

C. **appear** in court
បង្ហាញមុខចំពោះតុលាការ
5. defendant
ចុងចោទ
6. judge
ចៅក្រម

D. **stand trial**
ការកាត់ក្ដី
7. courtroom
បន្ទប់តុលាការ

8. jury
ក្រុមវិនិច្ឆ័យ
9. evidence
កស្តុតាង

10. prosecuting attorney
មេធាវីរដ្ឋ / រដ្ឋអាជ្ញា
11. witness
សាក្សី

12. court reporter
អ្នកកត់សេចក្ដីនៃតុលាការ
13. bailiff
អាជ្ញាសាលា

E. **give** the verdict*
បេញសាលក្រម

F. **sentence** the defendant
កាត់ទោសអ្នកចុងចោទ

G. **go** to jail / **go** to prison
ជាប់គុក / រន្ធនាគារ
14. convict
កាត់អោយជាប់ទោស

H. **be released**
ត្រូវដោះលែង

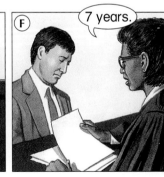

*Note: There are two possible verdicts, "guilty" and "not guilty."

Share your answers.

1. What are some differences between the legal system in the United States and the one in your country?

2. Do you want to be on a jury? Why or why not?

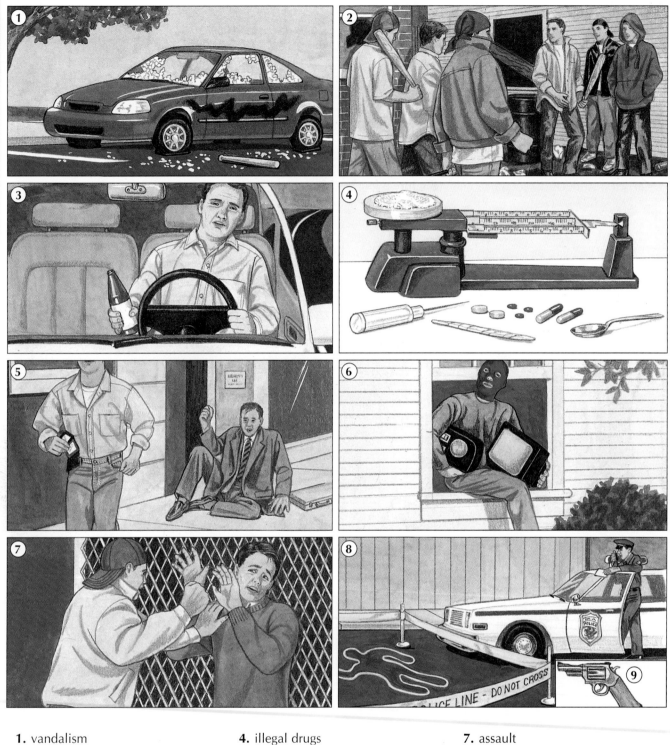

1. **vandalism**
   ការបំផ្លាញទ្រព្យងរដ្ឋ ឬសាធារណៈ

2. **gang violence**
   អំពើហិង្សាអោយនៃជនពាល

3. **drunk driving**
   បើកបរទាំងស្រវឹង

4. **illegal drugs**
   ថ្នាំខុសច្បាប់

5. **mugging**
   ការវាយប្លន់

6. **burglary**
   ការចូលប្លន់

7. **assault**
   ការបំពានបំពារ

8. **murder**
   ឃាតកម្ម

9. **gun**
   កាំភ្លើង

More vocabulary

commit a crime: to do something illegal

criminal: someone who commits a crime

victim: someone who is hurt or killed by someone else

Share your answers.

1. Is there too much crime on TV? in the movies?

2. Do you think people become criminals from watching crime on TV?

A. **Walk** with a friend.
ត្រូវដើរជាមួយមិត្តភ័ក្តិ ។

B. **Stay** on well-lit streets.
ត្រូវដើរតាមផ្លូវដែលមានភ្លើងភ្លឺច្បាស់ ។

C. **Hold** your purse close to your body.
ត្រូវកាន់កាបូបជាប់នឹងខ្លួន ។

D. **Protect** your wallet.
ត្រូវការពារកាបូបអ្នក ។

E. **Lock** your doors.
ត្រូវចាក់សោទ្វារ ។

F. **Don't open** your door to strangers.
កុំបើកទ្វារឲ្យមនុស្សចម្លែកចូល ។

G. **Don't drink** and **drive**.
កុំផឹកហើយបើកបរ ។

H. **Report** crimes to the police.
ត្រូវរាយការណ៍ប្រាប់អំពើឧក្រិដ្ឋទៅប៉ូលិស ។

More vocabulary

Neighborhood Watch: a group of neighbors who watch for criminals in their neighborhood

designated drivers: people who don't drink alcoholic beverages so that they can drive drinkers home

Share your answers.

1. Do you feel safe in your neighborhood?

2. Look at the pictures. Which of these things do you do?

3. What other things do you do to stay safe?

101

1. lost child
បាត់ក្មេង

2. car accident
គ្រោះថ្នាក់ឡាន

3. airplane crash
កញ្ចាល់បោះធ្លាក់

4. explosion
ផ្ទុះ

5. earthquake
រញ្ជួយផែនដី

6. mudslide
ដីបាក់ផ្លូវៗ

7. fire
ភ្លើងកើត

8. firefighter
អ្នកពន្លត់ភ្លើង

9. fire truck
ឡានពន្លត់ភ្លើង

Practice reporting a fire.

This is <u>Lisa Broad</u>. There is a fire.

The address is <u>323 Oak Street</u>.

Please send someone quickly.

Share your answers.

1. Can you give directions to your home if there is a fire?

2. What information do you give to the other driver if you are in a car accident?

10. drought
ភាពរាំងស្ងួត

11. blizzard
ព្យុះទឹកកក

12. hurricane
ខ្យល់កំបុតក្បាង

13. tornado
ព្យុះសង្ឃរា

14. volcanic eruption
ភ្នំភ្លើងផ្ទុះ

15. tidal wave
រលកសមុទ្រជោរ

16. flood
ទឹកជំនន់

17. search and rescue team
ក្រុមស្វែងរក និងសង្គ្រោះ

Share your answers.

1. Which disasters are common in your area? Which never happen?

2. What can you do to prepare for emergencies?

3. Do you have emergency numbers near your telephone?

4. What organizations will help you in an emergency?

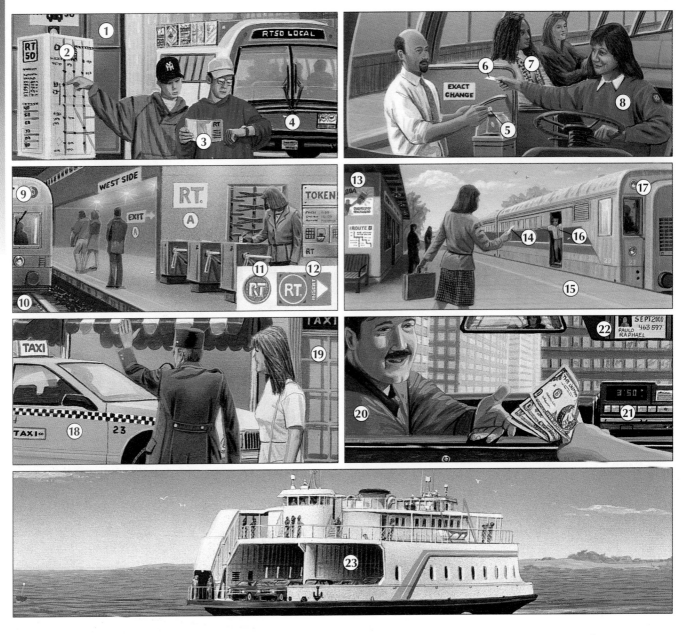

1. **bus stop**
   ចំណតឡានក្រុង

2. **route**
   ផ្លូវ

3. **schedule**
   កំណត់ពេល

4. **bus**
   ឡានក្រុង

5. **fare**
   ថ្លៃឈ្នួលធ្វើដំណើរ

6. **transfer**
   សំបុត្របន្ត

7. **passenger**
   អ្នកដំណើរ

8. **bus driver**
   អ្នកបើកឡានក្រុង

9. **subway**
   រថភ្លើងក្រោមដី

10. **track**
    ផ្លូវដែក

11. **token**
    កាក់ផ្ទឹះឡាន

12. **fare card**
    ប័ណ្ណផ្ទឹះឡាន

13. **train station**
    ស្ថានីយរថភ្លើង

14. **ticket**
    សំបុត្រ

15. **platform**
    កន្លែងចាំ

16. **conductor**
    អ្នកដែកសំបុត្រ

17. **train**
    រថភ្លើង

18. **taxi/cab**
    តាក់ស៊ី

19. **taxi stand**
    ចំណតតាក់ស៊ី

20. **taxi driver**
    អ្នកបើកតាក់ស៊ី

21. **meter**
    នាឡិកាគិតថ្លៃឈ្នួល

22. **taxi license**
    ប័ណ្ណបើកតាក់ស៊ី

23. **ferry**
    នាវាចម្លង/សាឡាង

More vocabulary

hail a taxi: to get a taxi driver's attention by raising your hand

miss the bus: to arrive at the bus stop late

Talk about how you and your friends come to school.

I take <u>the bus</u> to school.   *He <u>drives</u> to school.*

You take <u>the train</u>.   *She <u>walks</u> to school.*

We take <u>the subway</u>.   *They <u>ride</u> bikes.*

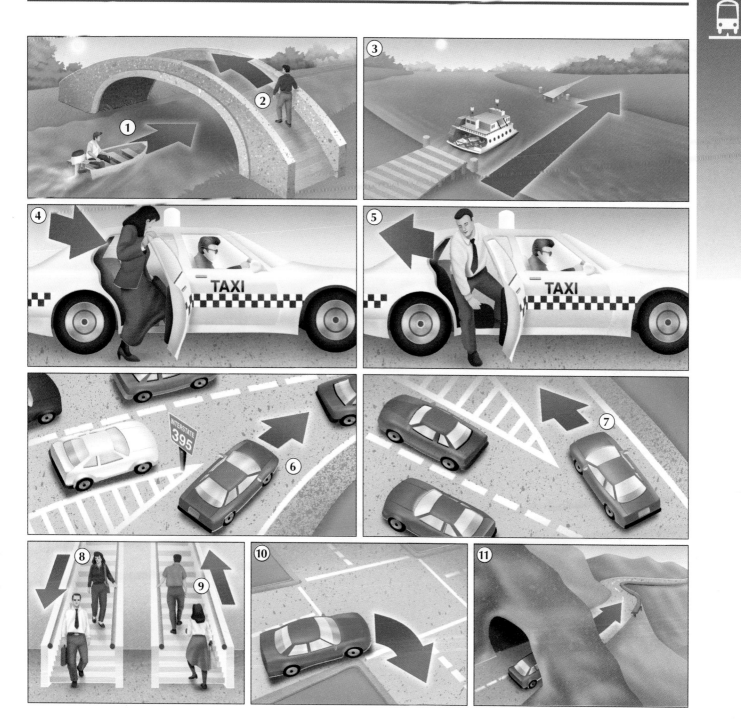

1. **under** the bridge
   ក្រោមស្ពាន
2. **over** the bridge
   លើស្ពាន
3. **across** the water
   ឆ្លងទឹក
4. **into** the taxi
   ចូលក្នុងតាក់ស៊ី

5. **out of** the taxi
   ចុះពីតាក់ស៊ី
6. **onto** the highway
   ចូលមហាវិថី
7. **off** the highway
   ចេញពីមហាវិថី
8. **down** the stairs
   ចុះជណ្តើរ

9. **up** the stairs
   ឡើងជណ្តើរ
10. **around** the corner
    ជុំវិញកាច់ជ្រុង
11. **through** the tunnel
    តាមផ្លូវក្រោមដី

Grammar point: *into, out of, on, off*

We say, *get **into** a taxi or a car.*
But we say, *get **on** a bus, a train, or a plane.*

We say, *get **out of** a taxi or a car.*
But we say, *get **off** a bus, a train, or a plane.*

1. subcompact
   ឡានតូចតូច

2. compact
   ឡានតូច

3. midsize car
   ឡានតូចកណ្ដាល

4. full-size car
   ឡានតូចធំ

5. convertible
   ឡានបើកដំបូល

6. sports car
   ឡានកីឡា

7. pickup truck
   ឡានដឹកឥវ៉ាន់

8. station wagon
   ឡានបិទាំង

9. SUV (sports utility
   vehicle)
   ឡានគ្រឿងកីឡា

10. minivan
    ឡានអ៊ីនតូច

11. camper
    ឡានសម្រាប់កំសាន្ត

12. dump truck
    ឡានដឹកដី

13. tow truck
    ឡានសណ្ដោង

14. moving van
    ឡានផ្ទុះ

15. tractor trailer / semi
    ឡានអូសឥវ៉ាន់កណ្ដាល

16. cab
    ក្បាលឡាន / ជាំងមុខ

17. trailer
    រថសណ្ដោងសំរាប់ដឹកទំនិញ

More vocabulary

make: the name of the company that makes the car

model: the style of car

Share your answers.

1. What is your favorite kind of car?

2. What kind of car is good for a big family? for a
   single person?

Directions ទិស

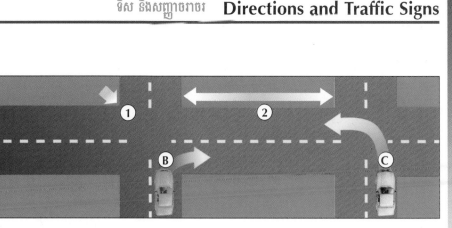

A. go straight
ទៅត្រង់

B. turn right
បត់ស្ដាំ

C. turn left
បត់ឆ្វេង

1. corner
កាច់ជ្រុង

2. block
ប្លុក

Signs សញ្ញា

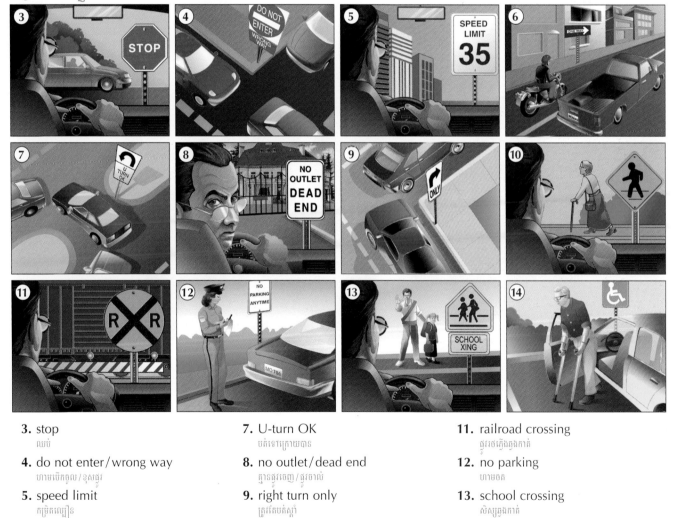

3. stop
ឈប់

4. do not enter / wrong way
ហាមបើកចូល / ខុសផ្លូវ

5. speed limit
កម្រិតល្បឿន

6. one way
ផ្លូវឯកទិស

7. U-turn OK
បត់ទៅក្រោយបាន

8. no outlet / dead end
គ្មានផ្លូវចេញ / ផ្លូវចាល់

9. right turn only
ត្រូវតែបត់ស្ដាំ

10. pedestrian crossing
អ្នកថ្មើរជើងឆ្លងកាត់

11. railroad crossing
ផ្លូវរថភ្លើងឆ្លងកាត់

12. no parking
ហាមចត

13. school crossing
សិស្សឆ្លងកាត់

14. handicapped parking
ចំណតជនពិការ

More vocabulary

right-of-way: the right to go first

yield: to give another person or car the right-of-way

Share your answers.

1. Which traffic signs are the same in your country?

2. Do pedestrians have the right-of-way in your city?

3. What is the speed limit in front of your school? your home?

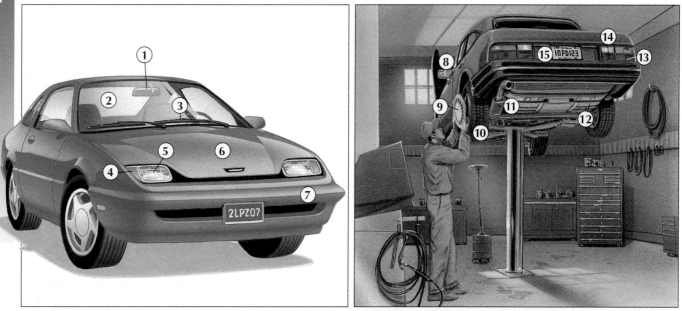

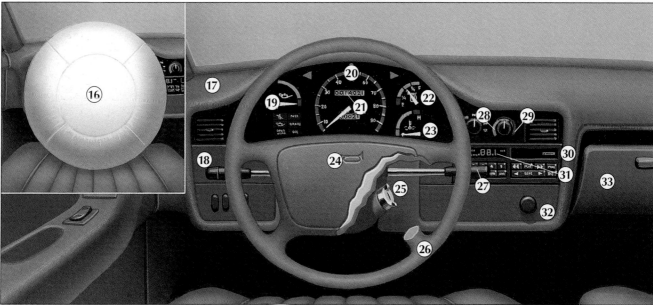

1. rearview mirror	**9. hubcap**	**18. turn signal**	**26. steering wheel**
កញ្ចក់មើលក្រោយ	គម្របកង់	ភ្លើងបត់	ចង្កូត
2. windshield	**10. tire**	**19. oil gauge**	**27. gearshift**
កញ្ចក់មុខ	កង់ឡាន	ប្រដាប់វាស់ប្រេង	ប្រដាប់ដាក់លេខ
3. windshield wipers	**11. muffler**	**20. speedometer**	**28. air conditioning**
ប្រដាប់ជូតកញ្ចក់ / ប្រដាប់បក់ទឹក	បំពង់ផ្សែង / ឧបរ្ករណ៍បន្ធូរសូរ	នាឡិកាល្បឿន	ម៉ាស៊ីនត្រជាក់
4. turn signal	**12. gas tank**	**21. odometer**	**29. heater**
ភ្លើងបត់	ធុងសាំង	នាឡិកាវាស់ចម្ងាយ	ម៉ាស៊ីនកំដៅ
5. headlight	**13. brake light**	**22. gas gauge**	**30. tape deck**
ចង្កៀងមុខ	ភ្លើងហ្រ្វាំង	ប្រដាប់វាស់ប្រេងសាំង	ម៉ាញ៉េឡាន
6. hood	**14. taillight**	**23. temperature gauge**	**31. radio**
គម្របម៉ាស៊ីន	ចង្កៀងក្រោយ	នាឡិកាវាស់កំដៅ	វិទ្យុ
7. bumper	**15. license plate**	**24. horn**	**32. cigarette lighter**
ជើងមុខរថយន្ត	ផ្ទាកលេខឡាន	ស៊ុងផ្លុំ	ប្រដាប់អុជបារី
8. sideview mirror	**16. air bag**	**25. ignition**	**33. glove compartment**
កញ្ចក់ចំហៀង	ថង់ខ្យល់	សោរពេ្ចាះម៉ាស៊ីន	ឃុបខាងមុខ
	17. dashboard		
	ចាំងបរិធានស្ទង់		

34. lock
សោឡាន

35. front seat
កៅអីមុខ

36. seat belt
ខ្សែក្រវាត់

37. shoulder harness
ប្រដាប់ស្ពាក

38. backseat
កៅអីក្រោយ

39. child safety seat
កៅអីក្មេង

40. fuel injection system
ប្រព័ន្ធបញ្ចេញប្រេង

41. engine
ម៉ាស៊ីន

42. radiator
រ៉ាឌីយ៉ាទ័រ

43. battery
អាគុយ

44. emergency brake
ប្រាំងពេលមានអាសន្ន

45. clutch*
អំប្រាយ៉ាហ្ស

46. brake pedal
ឈ្នាន់ប្រាំង

47. accelerator/gas pedal
ឈ្នាន់ល្បឿន

48. stick shift
ប្រដាប់ប្តូរលេខដៃ

49. trunk
កុងឡាន

50. lug wrench
ប្រដាប់មូលវង់

51. jack
ដែកគ្រីប

52. jumper cables
ខ្សែភ្ជាប់ចរិឌបូមអាគុយ

53. spare tire
កង់បង្គារ/សាគួរ

54. The car needs **gas**.
ឡានត្រូវការ**សាំង** ។

55. The car needs **oil**.
ឡានត្រូវការ**ប្រេង** ។

56. The radiator needs **coolant**.
រ៉ាឌីយ៉ាទ័រត្រូវការ**ប្រេងត្រជាក់** ។

57. The car needs a **smog check**.
ឡានត្រូវការ "**ពិនិត្យមើលផ្សែង**" ។

58. The battery needs **recharging**.
អាគុយត្រូវការ**សាកបញ្ចូលភ្លើង** ។

59. The tires need **air**.
កង់ត្រូវការ**ខ្យល់** ។

***Note:** Standard transmission cars have a clutch; automatic transmission cars do not.

1. airline terminal
ចំណតអាកាសយាន

2. airline representative
អ្នកតំណាងអាកាសយាន

3. check-in counter
កន្លែងឆែកសំបុត្រ

4. arrival and departure monitors
កុំព្យូទ័របង្ហាញពិពេលចេញ និងពេលមកដល់

5. gate
ច្រកចូល

6. boarding area
កន្លែងចូលយន្តហោះ

7. control tower
ប៉មបញ្ជាយន្តហោះ

8. helicopter
ឧទ្ធម្ភាគចក្រ

9. airplane
យន្តហោះ

10. overhead compartment
ធ្នើខាងលើ

11. cockpit
កន្លែងអ្នកបើកយន្តហោះ

12. pilot
អ្នកបើកយន្តហោះ

13. flight attendant
អ្នកបំរើក្នុងយន្តហោះ

14. oxygen mask
ម្រដាប់ដកដង្ហើម / ម៉ាស់អ្នកស៊ីសែន

15. airsickness bag
ថង់សម្រាប់អ្នកពុលយន្តហោះ

16. tray table
ថាសម្ហូប

17. baggage claim area
កន្លែងយកឥវ៉ាន់

18. carousel
ម៉ាស៊ីនទទួលទាំឥវ៉ាន់

19. luggage carrier
រទេះដឹកឥវ៉ាន់

20. customs
គយពិនិត្យ

21. customs officer
ភ្នាក់ងារគយ

22. declaration form
ត្រដាសម្រាបប្រកាសបញ្ជាក់

23. passenger
អ្នកដំណើរ

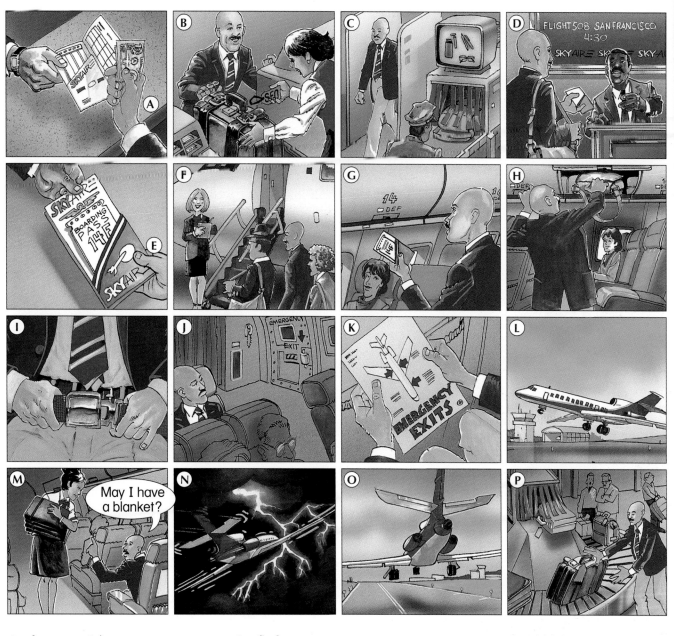

A. **buy** your ticket
ទិញសំបុត្រ

B. **check** your bags
ពិនិត្យមើលឥវ៉ាន់

C. **go through** security
ឆ្លងកាត់ម៉ាស៊ីនត្រួតពិនិត្យ

D. **check in** at the gate
បង្ហាញសំបុត្រនៅច្រកចូល

E. **get** your boarding pass
យកសំបុត្រឡើងយន្តហោះ

F. **board** the plane
ឡើងជិះយន្តហោះ

G. **find** your seat
រកកៅអីអង្គុយ

H. **stow** your carry-on bag
ទុកថង់យួររបស់អ្នក

I. **fasten** your seat belt
រឹតខ្សែក្រវ៉ាត់

J. **look for** the emergency exit
រកមើលច្រកចេញពេលអាសន្ន

K. **look at** the emergency card
មើលស្យៀវភៅរំលឹកវិធីភាពអាសន្ន

L. **take off** / **leave**
យន្តហោះឡើង / ចេញ

M. **request** a blanket
សុំភួយ

N. **experience** turbulence
ផ្ទប្រទះការរលាក់ខ្លាំង

O. **land** / **arrive**
ចុះ / មកដល់

P. **claim** your baggage
រកឥវ៉ាន់

May I have a blanket?

More vocabulary

destination: the place the passenger is going

departure time: the time the plane takes off

arrival time: the time the plane lands

direct flight: a plane trip between two cities with no stops

stopover: a stop before reaching the destination, sometimes to change planes

1. public school
សាលាសាធារណៈ

2. private school
សាលាឯកជន

3. parochial school
សាលាសាសនា

4. preschool
មត្តេយ្យសាលា

5. elementary school
សាលាបឋមសិក្សា

**6. middle school/
junior high school**
អនុវិទ្យាល័យ

7. high school
វិទ្យាល័យ

8. adult school
សាលាមនុស្សចាស់

9. vocational school/trade school
សាលាហ្វឹកហ្វឺនការងារ/ពាណិជ្ជកម្ម

10. college/university
មហាវិទ្យាល័យ/សាកលវិទ្យាល័យ

Note: In the U.S. most children begin school at age 5 (in kindergarten)
and graduate from high school at 17 or 18.

More vocabulary

When students graduate from a college or university
they receive a **degree**:

Bachelor's degree—usually 4 years of study

Master's degree—an additional 1–3 years of study

Doctorate—an additional 3–5 years of study

community college: a two-year college where students
can get an Associate of Arts degree

graduate school: a school in a university where students
study for their master's degrees and doctorates

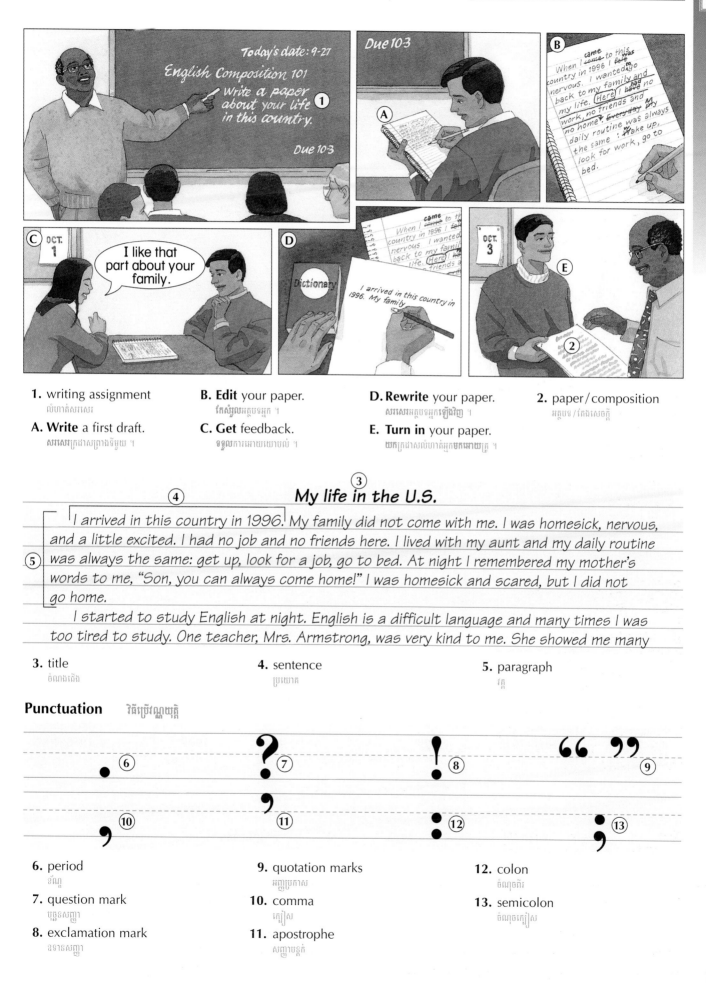

1. writing assignment
លំហាត់សរសេរ

A. Write a first draft.
សរសេរក្រដាសព្រាងទីមួយ ។

B. Edit your paper.
កែសម្រួលអត្ថបទអ្នក ។

C. Get feedback.
ទទួលការអោយយោបល់ ។

D. Rewrite your paper.
សរសេរអត្ថបទអ្នកឡើងវិញ ។

E. Turn in your paper.
យកក្រដាសលំហាត់អ្នកមកអោយគ្រូ ។

2. paper / composition
អត្ថបទ / រៀបសេចក្ដី

My life in the U.S.

I arrived in this country in 1996. My family did not come with me. I was homesick, nervous, and a little excited. I had no job and no friends here. I lived with my aunt and my daily routine was always the same: get up, look for a job, go to bed. At night I remembered my mother's words to me, "Son, you can always come home!" I was homesick and scared, but I did not go home.

I started to study English at night. English is a difficult language and many times I was too tired to study. One teacher, Mrs. Armstrong, was very kind to me. She showed me many

3. title
ចំណងជើង

4. sentence
ប្រយោគ

5. paragraph
វគ្គ

Punctuation វិធីប្រើវណ្ណយុត្តិ

6. period
ខ័ណ្ឌ

7. question mark
បុច្ឆនសញ្ញា

8. exclamation mark
ឧទានសញ្ញា

9. quotation marks
អព្ភប្រកាស

10. comma
ក្បៀស

11. apostrophe
សញ្ញាធ្នាក់

12. colon
ចំណុចពីរ

13. semicolon
ចំណុចក្បៀស

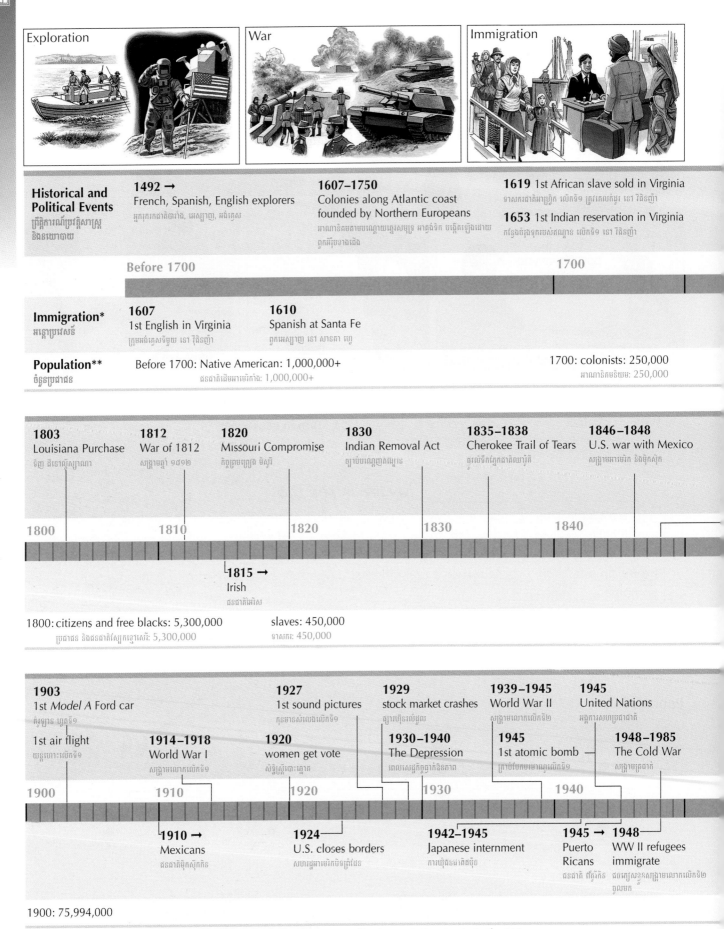

Exploration

War

Immigration

| **Historical and Political Events** ព្រឹត្តិការណ៍ប្រវត្តិសាស្ត្រ និងនយោបាយ | **1492 →** French, Spanish, English explorers អ្នករុករកជាតិបារាំង, អេស្ប៉ាញ, អង់គ្លេស | **1607–1750** Colonies along Atlantic coast founded by Northern Europeans អាណានិគមតាមបណ្ដោយឆ្នេរសមុទ្រ អាត្លង់ទិក បង្កើតឡើងដោយ ពួកអឺរ៉ុបខាងជើង | **1619** 1st African slave sold in Virginia ទាសករជាតិអាហ្វ្រិក លើកទី១ ត្រូវគេលក់ក្នុង នៅ វ៉ិជិនញ៉ា **1653** 1st Indian reservation in Virginia កន្លែងបំរុងទុកសំរាប់សណ្ឋាន លើកទី១ នៅ វ៉ិជិនញ៉ា |

Before 1700

1700

| **Immigration*** អន្តោប្រវេសន៍ | **1607** 1st English in Virginia ក្រុមអង់គ្លេសទីមួយ នៅ វ៉ិជិនញ៉ា | **1610** Spanish at Santa Fe ពួកអេស្ប៉ាញ នៅ សានតា ហ្វេ | **1700: colonists: 250,000** |
| **Population**** ចំនួនប្រជាជន | Before 1700: Native American: 1,000,000+ ជនជាតិដើមអាមេរិកាំង: 1,000,000+ | | 1700: colonists: 250,000 អាណានិគមនិយម: 250,000 |

| **1803** Louisiana Purchase ទិញ ឡ្វីស្យ៉ាណា | **1812** War of 1812 សង្គ្រាមឆ្នាំ ១៨១២ | **1820** Missouri Compromise កិច្ចព្រមព្រៀង មិស្សួរី | **1830** Indian Removal Act ច្បាប់បណ្ដេញជនឥណ្ឌា | **1835–1838** Cherokee Trail of Tears ផ្លូវទឹកភ្នែកជាតិឆេរ៉ូគី | **1846–1848** U.S. war with Mexico សង្គ្រាមអាមេរិក និងម៉ិកស៊ិក |

1800 **1810** **1820** **1830** **1840**

1815 → Irish ជនជាតិអៃរីស

1800: citizens and free blacks: 5,300,000 ប្រជាជន និងជនជាតិស្បែកខ្មៅសេរី: 5,300,000

slaves: 450,000 ទាសករ: 450,000

| **1903** 1st *Model A* Ford car ឡានម៉ាក ហ្វដ្ឋ៍១ | | **1927** 1st sound pictures កុនមានសំលេងលើកទី១ | **1929** stock market crashes ផ្សារហ៊ុនរលំផុត | **1939–1945** World War II សង្គ្រាមលោកលើកទី២ | **1945** United Nations អង្គការសហប្រជាជាតិ |
| 1st air flight យន្តហោះលើកទី១ | **1914–1918** World War I សង្គ្រាមលោកលើកទី១ | **1920** women get vote សិទ្ធិស្ត្រីបោះឆ្នោត | **1930–1940** The Depression ពេលសេដ្ឋកិច្ចធ្លាក់ចុះនិងភាព | **1945** 1st atomic bomb — គ្រាប់បែកបរមាណូលើកទី១ | **1948–1985** The Cold War សង្គ្រាមត្រជាក់ |

1900 **1910** **1920** **1930** **1940**

1910 → Mexicans ជនជាតិម៉ិកស៊ិកកាន់

1924 U.S. closes borders សហរដ្ឋអាមេរិកបិទព្រំដែន

1942–1945 Japanese internment ការឃុំឃាំងជនជាតិជប៉ុន

1945 → Puerto Ricans ជនជាតិ ព័រតូរិកោ

1948 WW II refugees immigrate ជនភៀសខ្លួនពីសង្គ្រាមលោកលើកទី២ ចូលមក

1900: 75,994,000

*Immigration dates indicate a time when large numbers of that group first began to immigrate to the U.S.
**All population figures before 1790 are estimates. Figures after 1790 are based on the official U.S. census.

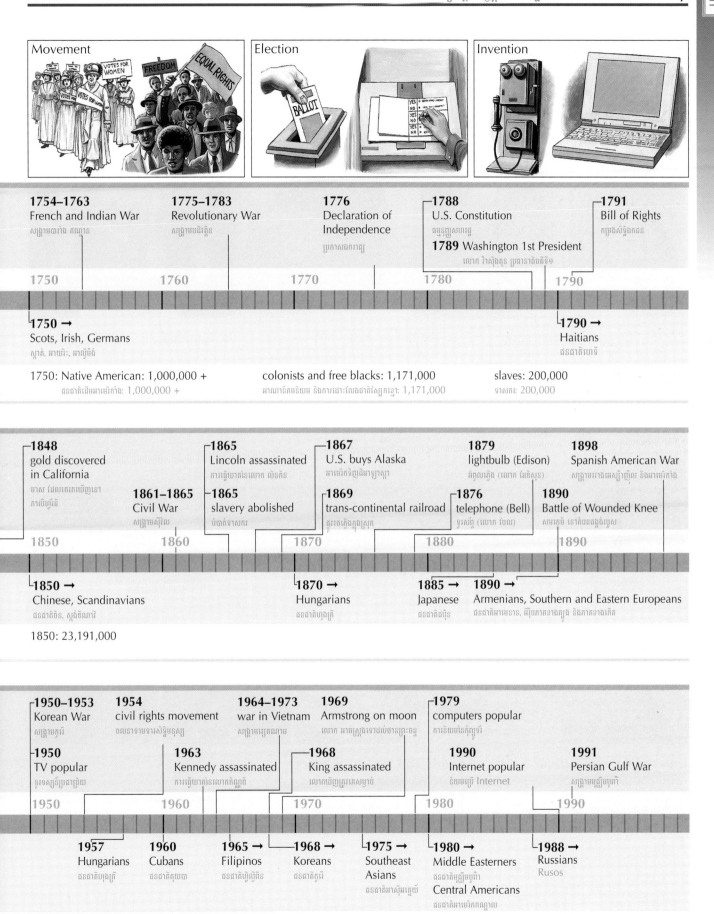

Movement

Election

Invention

1754–1763
French and Indian War
សង្គ្រាមជាវ៉ាំង ឥណ្ឌាន

1775–1783
Revolutionary War
សង្គ្រាមបដិវត្តន៍

1776
Declaration of Independence
ប្រកាសឯករាជ្យ

1788
U.S. Constitution
ធម្មនុញ្ញសហរដ្ឋ

1789 Washington 1st President
លោក វ៉ាស៊ុងតុន ប្រធានាធិបតីទី១

1791
Bill of Rights
កម្រងសិទ្ធិពលរដ្ឋ

1750   1760   1770   1780   1790

1750 →
Scots, Irish, Germans
ស្កុត, អាយរ៍, អាល្លឺម៉ង់

1790 →
Haitians
ជនជាតិហេទី

1750: Native American: 1,000,000 +
ជនជាតិដើមអាមេរិកាំង: 1,000,000 +

colonists and free blacks: 1,171,000
អាណានិគមនិយម និងការរំដោះមេលជនជាតិស្បែកខ្មៅ: 1,171,000

slaves: 200,000
ទាសករ: 200,000

1848
gold discovered in California
មាស ដែលគេរកឃើញនៅការលីហ្វ័រនី

1861–1865
Civil War
សង្គ្រាមស៊ីវិល

1865
Lincoln assassinated
ការធ្វើឃាតនៃលោក លិនកុិន

1865
slavery abolished
បំបាត់ទាសករ

1867
U.S. buys Alaska
អាមេរិកទិញដីអាឡាស្កា

1869
trans-continental railroad
ផ្លូវរថភ្លើងឆ្លងទ្វីប

1879
lightbulb (Edison)
អំពូលភ្លើង (លោក អែឌិសុន)

1876
telephone (Bell)
ទូរស័ព្ទ (លោក បែល)

1898
Spanish American War
សង្គ្រាមរវាងអេស្ប៉ាញ៉ុល និងអាមេរិកាំង

1890
Battle of Wounded Knee
សមរភូមិ នៅគីបនជង្គង់របួស

1850   1860   1870   1880   1890

1850 →
Chinese, Scandinavians
ជនជាតិចិន, ស្កង់ឌីណាវ៉ី

1870 →
Hungarians
ជនជាតិហុងគ្រី

1885 →
Japanese
ជនជាតិជប៉ុន

1890 →
Armenians, Southern and Eastern Europeans
ជនជាតិអាមេនាន, អឺរ៉ុបភាគខាងត្បូង និងភាគខាងកើត

1850: 23,191,000

1950–1953
Korean War
សង្គ្រាមកូរ៉េ

1954
civil rights movement
ចលនាចលាចលសិទ្ធិមនុស្ស

1964–1973
war in Vietnam
សង្គ្រាមវៀតណាម

1969
Armstrong on moon
លោក អាមស្ត្រុងទៅដល់ចានព្រះច័ន្ទ

1979
computers popular
ការនិយមនៃកុំព្យូទ័រ

1950
TV popular
ទូរទស្សន៍ប្រជាប្រិយ

1963
Kennedy assassinated
ការធ្វើឃាតនៃលោកកិណ្ណឌី

1968
King assassinated
លោកឃីញត្រូវគេសម្លាប់

1990
Internet popular
និយមធ្វើ Internet

1991
Persian Gulf War
សង្គ្រាមឈូងសមុទ្រពែរ្ស

1950   1960   1970   1980   1990

1957
Hungarians
ជនជាតិហុងគ្រី

1960
Cubans
ជនជាតិគុយបា

1965 →
Filipinos
ជនជាតិហ្វីលីពិន

1968 →
Koreans
ជនជាតិកូរ៉េ

1975 →
Southeast Asians
ជនជាតិអាស៊ីអាគ្នេយ៍

1980 →
Middle Easterners
ជនជាតិមជ្ឈិមបូព៌ា
Central Americans
ជនជាតិអាមេរិកកណ្តាល

1988 →
Russians
Rusos

1950: 150,697,000

1990: 248,700,000

BRANCHES OF GOVERNMENT

Legislative · Executive · Judicial

1. The House of Representatives
សភាតំណាងរាស្ត្រ

2. congresswoman / congressman
សមាជិកសភាស្រី / សមាជិកសភាប្រុស

3. The Senate
ព្រឹទ្ធសភា

4. senator
សមាជិកព្រឹទ្ធសភា

5. The White House
សេតវិមាន

6. president
ប្រធានាធិបតី

7. vice president
អនុប្រធានាធិបតី

8. The Supreme Court
តុលាការកំពូល

9. chief justice
ចៅក្រមកំពូល

10. justices
ចៅក្រម

Citizenship application requirements
ច្បាប់តម្រូវចូលសញ្ជាតិ

A. **be** 18 years old
ត្រូវមានអាយុ ១៨ ឆ្នាំ

B. **live** in the U.S. for five years
រស់នៅក្នុងសហរដ្ឋចំនួនប្រាំឆ្នាំ

C. **take** a citizenship test
ប្រឡងចូលសញ្ជាតិ

Rights and responsibilities
សិទ្ធិ និងការទទួលខុសត្រូវ

D. **vote**
បោះឆ្នោត

E. **pay** taxes
បង់ពន្ធ

F. **register** with Selective Service*
ចុះឈ្មោះក្នុងកងទ័ព

G. **serve** on a jury
បំរើ នៅក្នុងគណៈវិនិច្ឆ័យ

H. **obey** the law
គោរពច្បាប់

*Note: All males 18 to 26 who live in the U.S. are required to register with Selective Service.

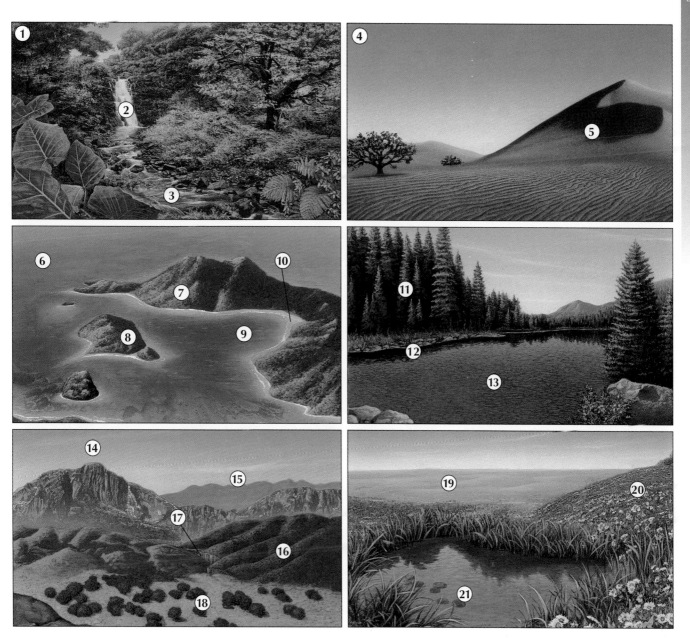

1. rain forest ព្រៃ	**7.** peninsula ឈូងទ្វីប	**13.** lake បឹង	**19.** plains ទីរាប
2. waterfall ល្បាក់ទឹក / ទឹកធ្លាក់	**8.** island កោះ	**14.** mountain peak កំពូលភ្នំ	**20.** meadow វាលស្មៅ
3. river ស្ទឹង	**9.** bay ឈូងសមុទ្រ	**15.** mountain range ជួរភ្នំ	**21.** pond ត្រពាំង
4. desert វាលខ្សាច់	**10.** beach មាត់ទន្លេ / ឆ្នេរសមុទ្រ	**16.** hills ជិទួល / កូនភ្នំ	
5. sand dune ផ្លុកខ្សាច់	**11.** forest ព្រៃឈើ	**17.** canyon ជ្រលងជ្រោះ	
6. ocean មហាសមុទ្រ	**12.** shore ច្រាំងសមុទ្រ	**18.** valley ជ្រលងភ្នំ	

More vocabulary

a body of water: a river, lake, or ocean

stream/creek: a very small river

Talk about where you live and where you like to go.

I live in a valley. There is a lake nearby.

I like to go to the beach.

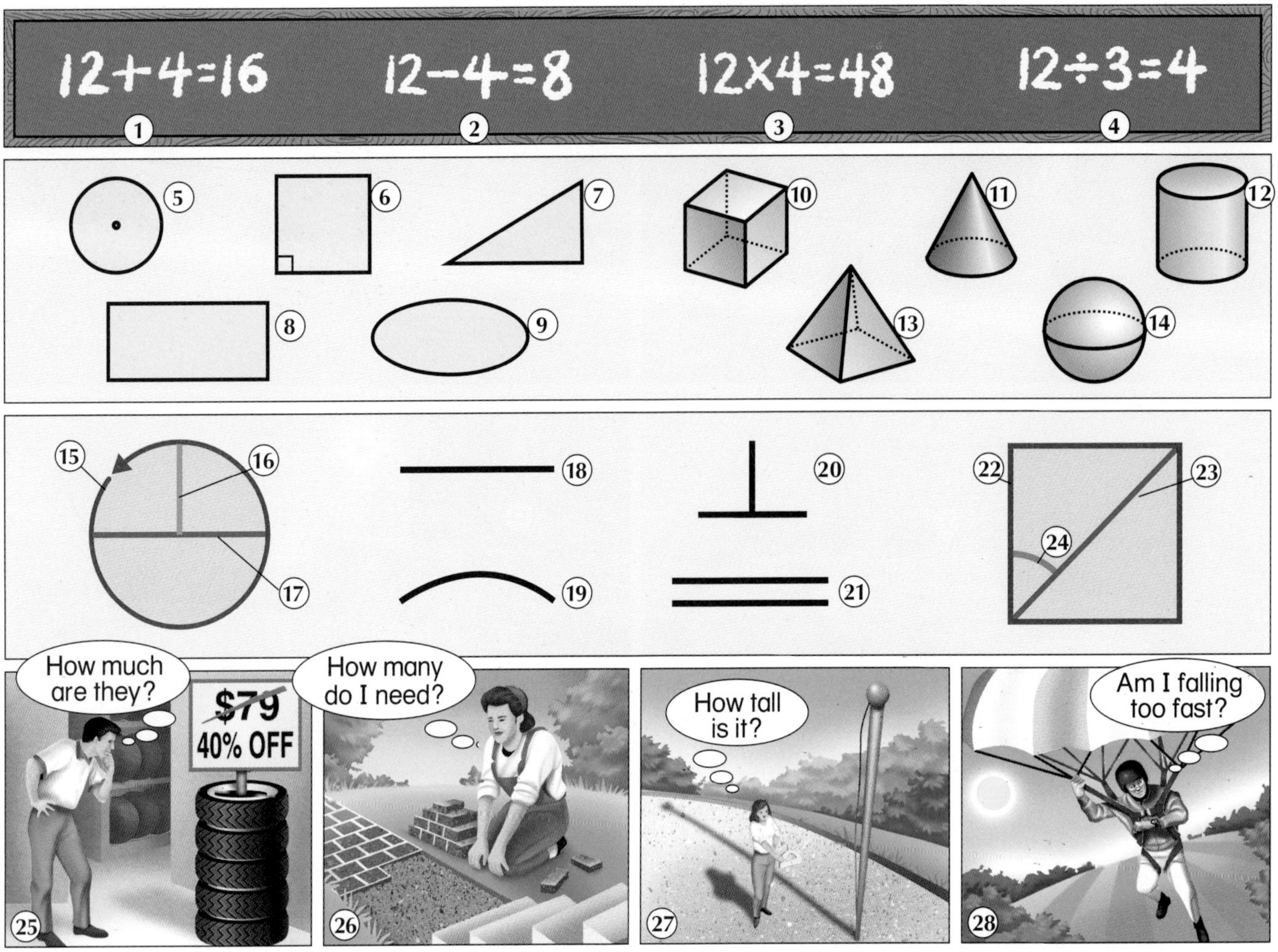

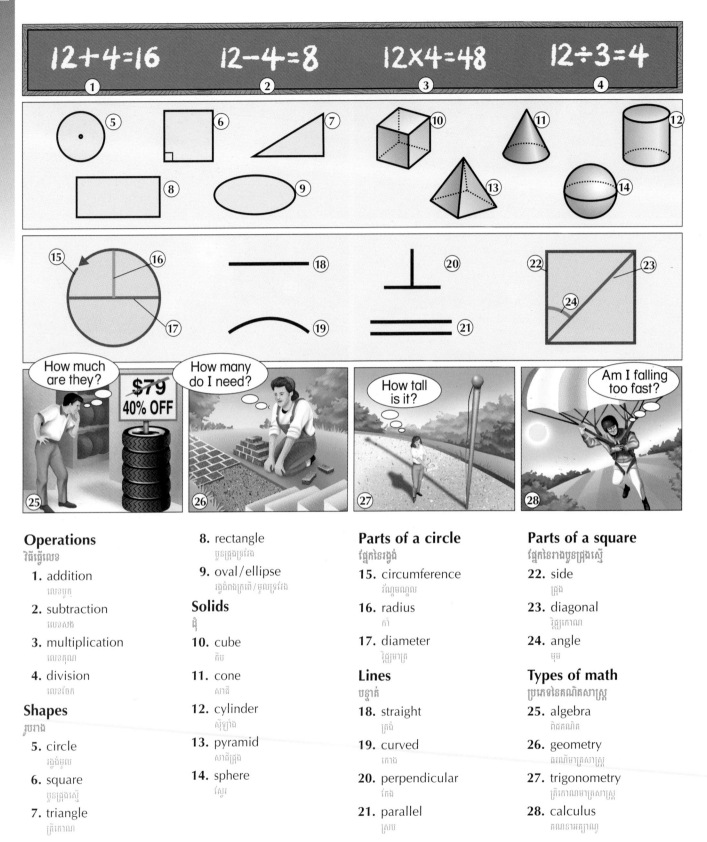

Operations
វិធីធ្វើលេខ

1. addition
   លេខបូក
2. subtraction
   លេខសង
3. multiplication
   លេខគុណ
4. division
   លេខចែក

Shapes
រូបរាង

5. circle
   រង្វង់មូល
6. square
   បួនជ្រុងស្មើ
7. triangle
   ត្រីកោណ
8. rectangle
   បួនជ្រុងទ្រវែង
9. oval/ellipse
   រង្វង់ពងក្រពើ / មូលទ្រវែង

Solids
ដុំ

10. cube
    គីប
11. cone
    សាជី
12. cylinder
    ស៊ីឡាំង
13. pyramid
    សាជីជ្រុង
14. sphere
    ស្វ៊ែរ

Parts of a circle
ផ្នែកនៃរង្វង់

15. circumference
    វ័ណ្ឌមណ្ឌល
16. radius
    កាំ
17. diameter
    វិជ្ឈមាត្រ

Lines
បន្ទាត់

18. straight
    ត្រង់
19. curved
    កោង
20. perpendicular
    កែង
21. parallel
    ស្រប

Parts of a square
ផ្នែកនៃរាងបួនជ្រុងស្មើ

22. side
    ជ្រុង
23. diagonal
    វិជ្ឈកោណ
24. angle
    មុម

Types of math
ប្រភេទនៃគណិតសាស្ត្រ

25. algebra
    ពិជគណិត
26. geometry
    ធរណីមាត្រសាស្ត្រ
27. trigonometry
    ត្រីកោណមាត្រសាស្ត្រ
28. calculus
    គណនាអត្យាណូ

More vocabulary

total: the answer to an addition problem

difference: the answer to a subtraction problem

product: the answer to a multiplication problem

quotient: the answer to a division problem

pi (π): the number when you divide the circumference of a circle by its diameter (approximately = 3.14)

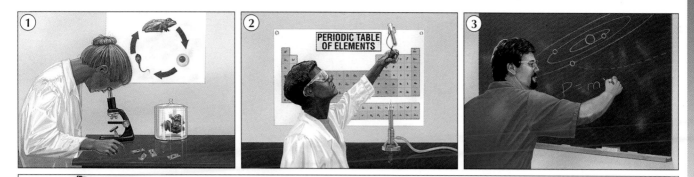

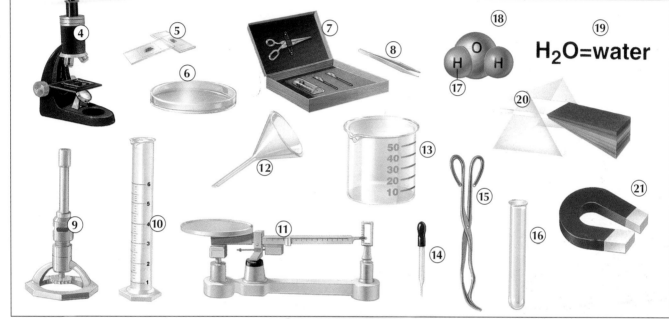

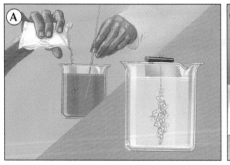

1. biology
ជីវសាស្ត្រ

2. chemistry
គីមី

3. physics
រូបវិទ្យា

4. microscope
អតិសុខុមទស្សន៍

5. slide
បន្ទះកែវ

6. petri dish
ចានពិសោធមេរោគ

7. dissection kit
ប្រដាប់សំរាប់វះកាត់

8. forceps
ដង្កៀប

9. Bunsen burner
ចង្ក្រានដុត

10. graduated cylinder
កែវវិភាគ

11. balance
ជញ្ជីង

12. funnel
ជីវឡាវ

13. beaker
កែវចំណុះ

14. dropper
ប្រដាប់បន្តក់ថ្នាំ

15. crucible tongs
ដង្កៀបវែង

16. test tube
កែវវិសោធន៍

17. atom
អាតូម

18. molecule
ម៉ូលេគុល

19. formula
រូបមន្ត

20. prism
ត្រីស្តី

21. magnet
មេដែក

A. **do** an experiment
ធ្វើការពិសោធន៍

B. **observe**
សង្កេតមើល

C. **record** results
កត់ត្រាលទ្ធផល

119

A. play an instrument
លេងភ្លេង

B. sing a song
ច្រៀងចំរៀង

1. orchestra
វង់ភ្លេង

2. rock band
វង់ភ្លេងរ៉ក

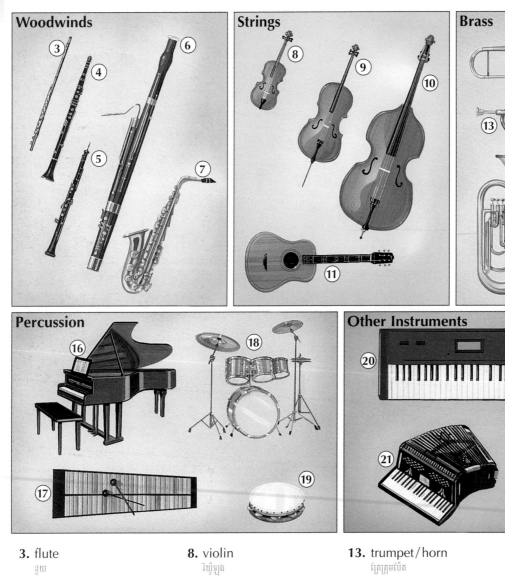

Woodwinds

Strings

Brass

Percussion

Other Instruments

3. flute
ខ្លុយ

4. clarinet
ក្លារីណែត

5. oboe
អ៊ូប

6. bassoon
បាស់ស៊ីន

7. saxophone
ស្រៃសាក់សូហ្វូន

8. violin
វីយ៉ូឡុង

9. cello
កែលឡូ

10. bass
បាស់

11. guitar
ហ្គីតា

12. trombone
ត្រុំបូន

13. trumpet / horn
ត្រែត្រុមប៉ែត

14. tuba
ត្រែសំលេងធំ

15. French horn
ត្រែបារាំង

16. piano
ព្យ៉ាណូ

17. xylophone
ស៊ីឡូហ្វូន

18. drums
ស្គរ

19. tambourine
តំប៊ូរីន

20. electric keyboard
ប៉្យាណូខ្សែភ្លើង

21. accordion
អាកកូដេអុង

22. organ
អរហ្គាន / ប៉្យាណូខ្យល់

120

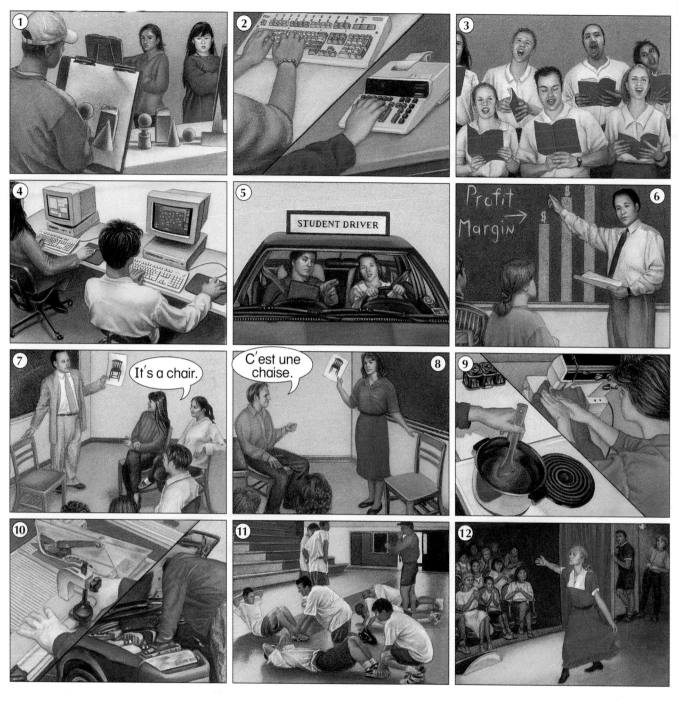

1. art
   សិល្បៈ

2. business education
   អប់រំផ្នែកពាណិជ្ជកម្ម

3. chorus
   ច្រៀងជាក្រុម

4. computer science
   វិទ្យាសាស្ត្រកុំព្យូទ័រ

5. driver's education
   ថ្នាក់រៀនបើកបរ

6. economics
   ថ្នាក់សេដ្ឋកិច្ច

7. English as a second language
   ភាសាអង់គ្លេសជាភាសាទីពីរ

8. foreign language
   ភាសាបរទេស

9. home economics
   វិជ្ជាមេផ្ទះ

10. industrial arts/shop
    សិល្បៈ, ឧស្សាហកម្ម/រោងជាង

11. PE (physical education)
    វិជ្ជាហាត់ប្រាណ

12. theater arts
    សិល្បៈល្ខោន

More vocabulary

core course: a subject students have to take

elective: a subject students choose to take

Share your answers.

1. What are your favorite subjects?

2. In your opinion, what subjects are most important? Why?

3. What foreign languages are taught in your school?

ATLANTIC OCEAN

BERMUDA

GREENLAND

Labrador Sea

Newfoundland ⑥

Gulf of St. Lawrence

Prince Edward Island

Nova Scotia

New Brunswick

Maine

⑪

Vermont
New Hampshire
Massachusetts
Rhode Island
Connecticut

New Jersey
Delaware
Maryland
WASHINGTON, D.C.

Baffin Bay

Québec

⑤

OTTAWA

New York

Pennsylvania

⑩

West Virginia

Virginia

North Carolina

South Carolina

Hudson Bay

Ontario

④

Michigan

Michigan

Ohio

Indiana

Kentucky

Tennessee

Wisconsin

Illinois

Queen Elizabeth Islands

Manitoba

Minnesota

⑨

Iowa

Missouri

Arkansas

Northwest Territories

①

Saskatchewan

③

North Dakota

South Dakota

Nebraska

Kansas

UNITED STATES OF AMERICA

Oklahoma

Beaufort Sea

Alberta

British Columbia

②

CANADA

Montana

⑧

Wyoming

Colorado

New Mexico

Yukon Territory

Washington

Idaho

Utah

Nevada

Arizona

ARCTIC OCEAN

Alaska (US)

Oregon

⑦

California

Gulf of Alaska

Hawaii (US)

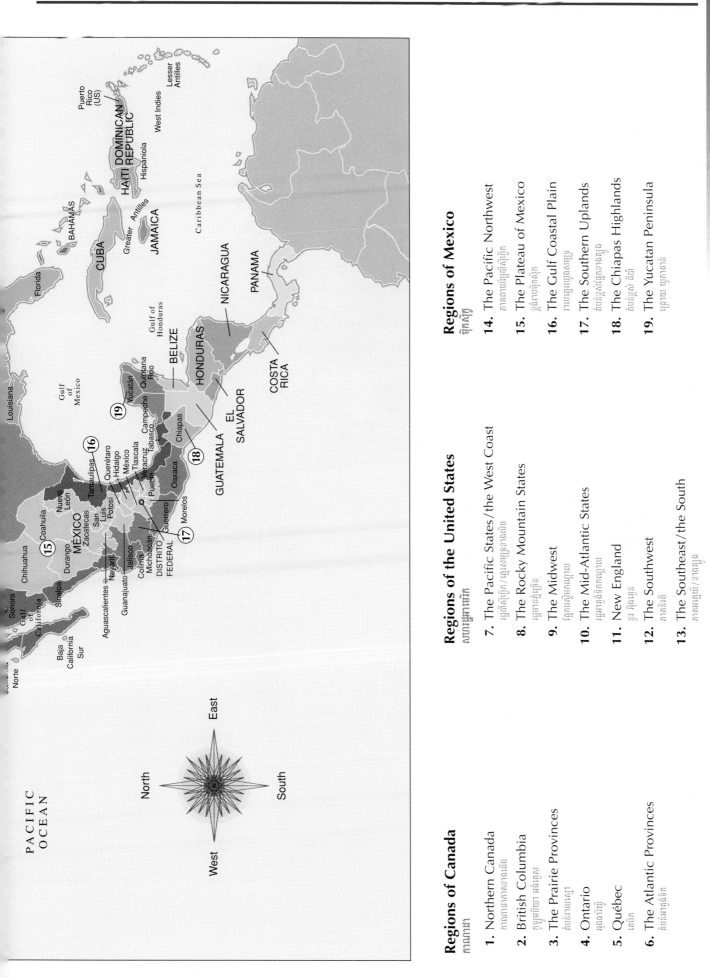

Regions of Canada
កោណដា

1. **Northern Canada** ការណាដាកាលខាងជើង
2. **British Columbia** ក្រុមប៊ីយ៉ា អង់គ្លេស
3. **The Prairie Provinces** ស៊ីវិរោលសូ៊ា
4. **Ontario** អូនតារីយ៉ូ
5. **Québec** កេបិក
6. **The Atlantic Provinces** ស៊ីអាត្លង់ទិក

Regions of the United States
សហរដ្ឋអាមេរិក

7. **The Pacific States/the West Coast** រដ្ឋប៉ាស៊ីហ្វិក/ឆ្នេរសមុទ្រខាងលិច
8. **The Rocky Mountain States** រដ្ឋភ្នំរ៉ុកគី
9. **The Midwest** ភ្នំកណ្ដាលខាងលិច
10. **The Mid-Atlantic States** រដ្ឋកណ្តាលអាត្លង់ទិក
11. **New England** ញូ អ៊ីងឡេន
12. **The Southwest** ភាគនិរតី
13. **The Southeast/the South** ភាគអាគ្នេយ៍/ខាងត្បូង

Regions of Mexico
ម៉ិកស៊ិកូ

14. **The Pacific Northwest** ភាគពាយ័ព្យប៉ាស៊ីហ្វិក
15. **The Plateau of Mexico** ខ្ពង់រាបម៉ិកស៊ិក
16. **The Gulf Coastal Plain** វាលទំនាបឆ្នេរឈូ៊ង
17. **The Southern Uplands** តំបន់ខ្ពស់ភាគខាងត្បូង
18. **The Chiapas Highlands** តំបន់ខ្ពស់ ឈៀប
19. **The Yucatan Peninsula** ឧបទ្វីប យូកាតាន់

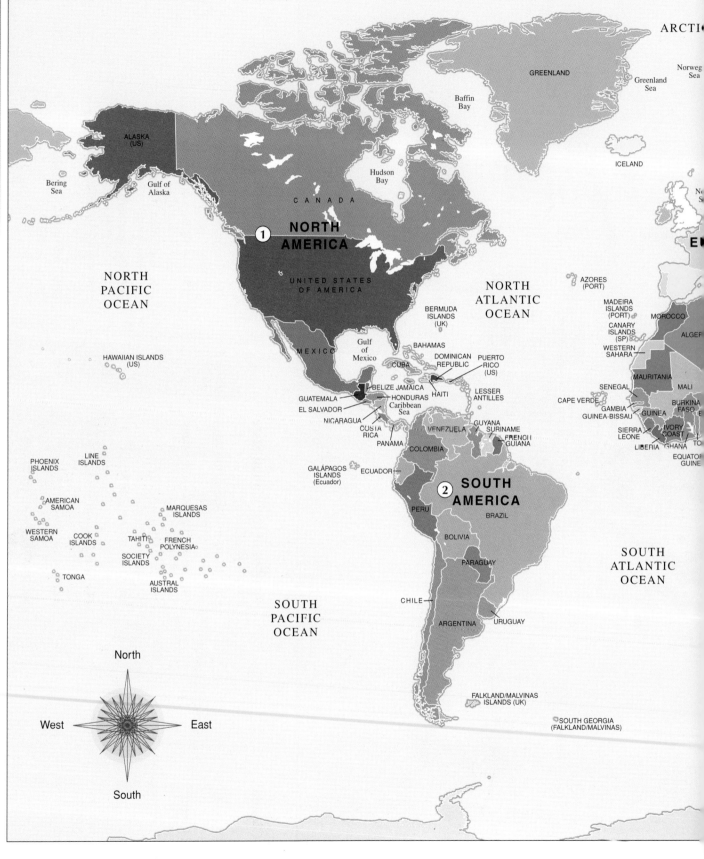

Continents
ទ្វីប

1. North America
អាមេរិកខាងជើង

2. South America
អាមេរិកខាងត្បូង

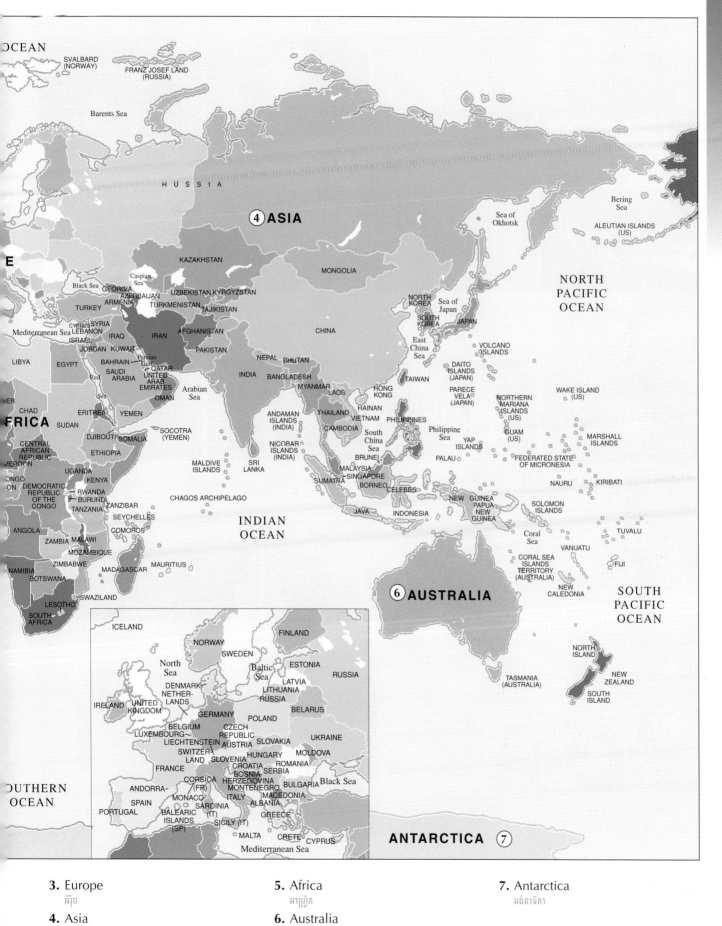

3. Europe
អឺរ៉ុប

4. Asia
អាស៊ី

5. Africa
អាហ្វ្រិក

6. Australia
អូស្ត្រាលី

7. Antarctica
អង់តាក់ទិកា

Energy resources ធនធានៃថាមពល

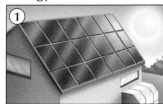

1. solar energy
ថាមពលព្រះអាទិត្យ

2. wind
ខ្យល់

3. natural gas
ឧស្ម័នធម្មជាតិ

4. coal
ធ្យូង

5. hydroelectric power
ថាមពលវារីអគ្គិសនី

6. oil / petroleum
ប្រេង / ប្រេងកាត

7. geothermal energy
ថាមពលចំហាយកំដៅផែនដី

8. nuclear energy
ថាមពលបរមាណូ

Pollution កញ្ច្រោលក្រខ្វក់

9. hazardous waste
កាកសំណល់គ្រោះថ្នាក់

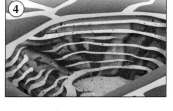

10. air pollution / smog
ខ្យល់ក្រខ្វក់ / ផ្សែងលាយអព្ទ

11. acid rain
ភ្លៀងមានជាតិអាស៊ីដ

12. water pollution
ទឹកក្រខ្វក់

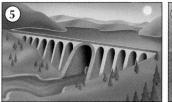

13. radiation
ចំហាយវិទ្យុសកម្ម

14. pesticide poisoning
ថ្នាំបំពុលសត្វល្អិត

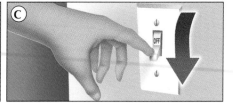

15. oil spill
កំពប់ហៀរប្រេង

Conservation ការរក្សាការពារ

A. recycle
ប្រើឡើងវិញ / យកមកប្រើឡើងវិញ

B. save water / conserve water
សន្សំ / រក្សាទឹក

C. save energy / conserve energy
សន្សំ / រក្សាថាមពល

Share your answers.

1. How do you heat your home?

2. Do you have a gas stove or an electric stove?

3. What are some ways you can save energy when it's cold?

4. Do you recycle? What products do you recycle?

5. Does your market have recycling bins?

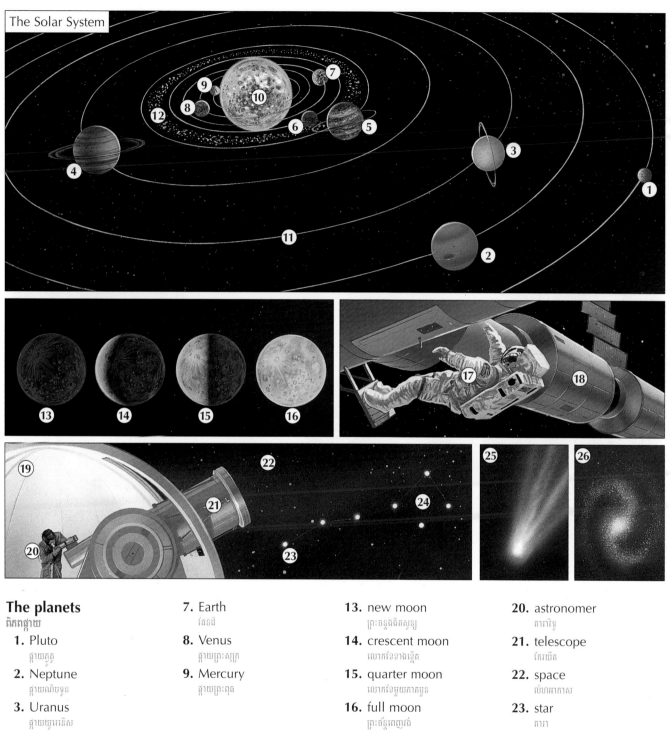

The Solar System

The planets
ពិភពផ្កាយ

1. Pluto
ផ្កាយភ្លុត

2. Neptune
ផ្កាយណិបទុន

3. Uranus
ផ្កាយឫរ៉េនិស

4. Saturn
ផ្កាយព្រះសៅរ៍

5. Jupiter
ផ្កាយព្រហស្បតី

6. Mars
ផ្កាយព្រះអង្គារ

7. Earth
ផែនដី

8. Venus
ផ្កាយព្រះសុក្រ

9. Mercury
ផ្កាយព្រះពុធ

10. sun
ព្រះអាទិត្យ

11. orbit
គាររវិថី

12. asteroid belt
កំទេចផ្កាយ

13. new moon
ព្រះចន្ទឧទ័យកសូន្យ

14. crescent moon
លោកខែខាងខ្ញើត

15. quarter moon
លោកខែមួយភាគបួន

16. full moon
ព្រះចន្ទ៍ពេញវង់

17. astronaut
អ្នកអវកាស

18. space station
ស្ថានីយអវកាស

19. observatory
កន្លែងឆ្លុះមើល / មន្ទីរសង្កេតពិភពផ្កាយ

20. astronomer
តារាវិទូ

21. telescope
កែវយឹត

22. space
លំហអាកាស

23. star
តារា

24. constellation
ក្រុមផ្កាយ

25. comet
ផ្កាយដុះកន្ទុយ

26. galaxy
កញ្ចុំផ្កាយ

More vocabulary

lunar eclipse: when the earth is between the sun and the moon

solar eclipse: when the moon is between the earth and the sun

Share your answers.

1. Do you know the names of any constellations?

2. How do you feel when you look up at the night sky?

3. Is the night sky in the U.S. the same as in your country?

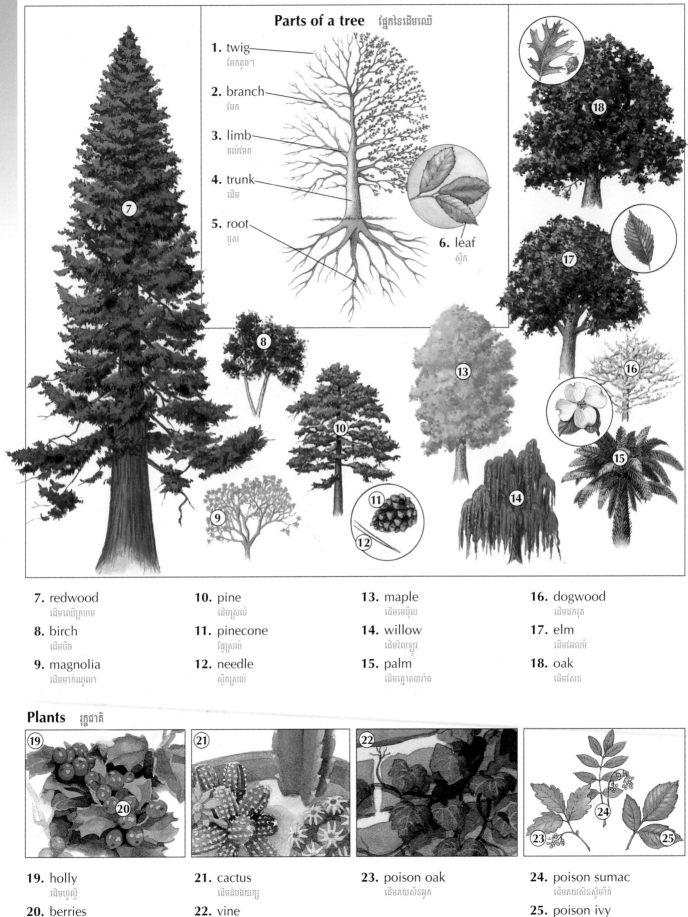

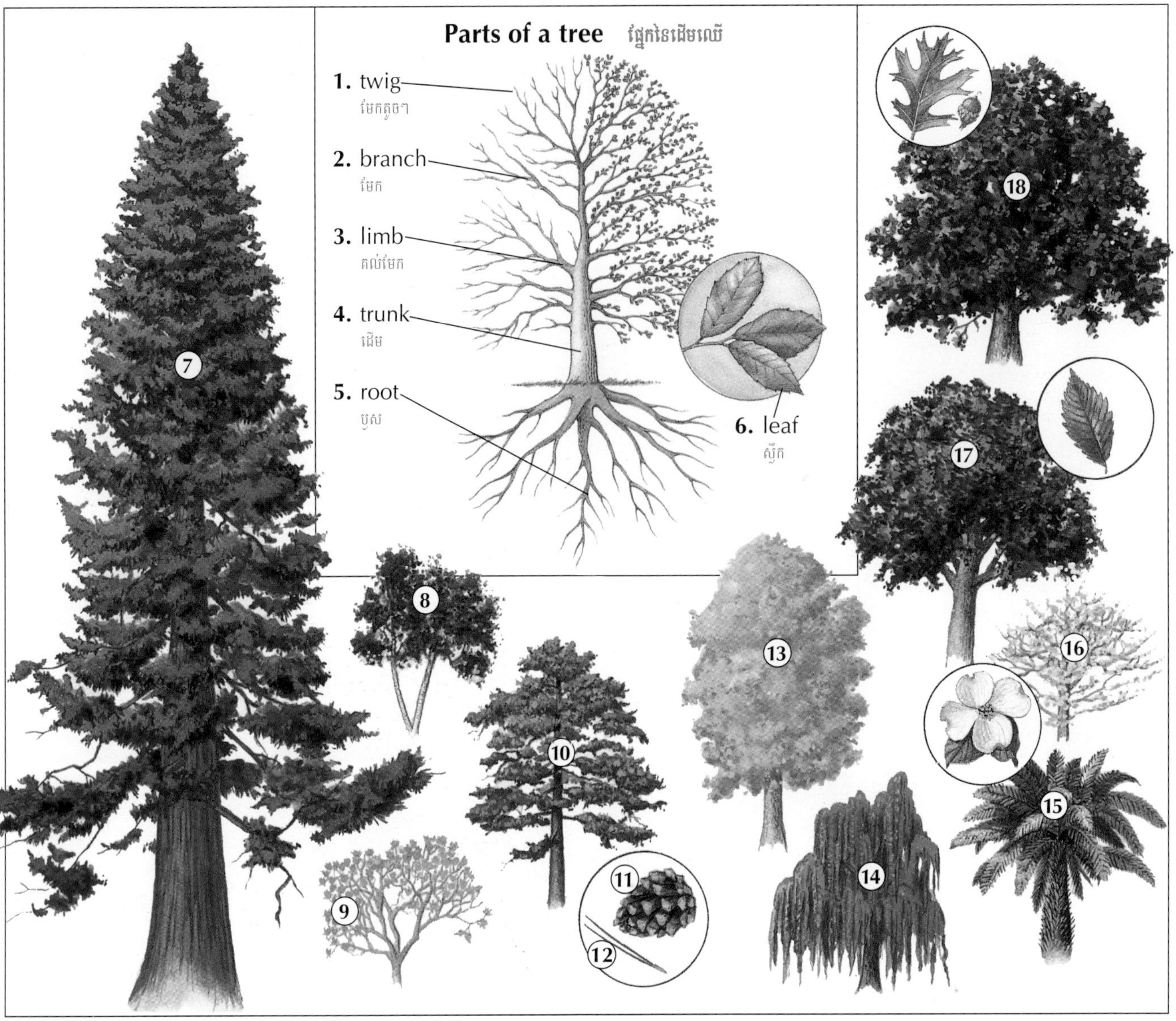
Parts of a tree ផ្នែកនៃដើមឈើ
1. twig
មែកតូចៗ
2. branch
មែក
3. limb
គល់មែក
4. trunk
ដើម
5. root
ឫស
6. leaf
ស្លឹក

7. redwood
ដើមឈើក្រហម

8. birch
ដើមប៊ីច

9. magnolia
ដើមមាក់ណូលា

10. pine
ដើមស្រល់

11. pinecone
ផ្លែស្រល់

12. needle
ស្លឹកស្រល់

13. maple
ដើមមេប៉ុល

14. willow
ដើមវិលឡូវ

15. palm
ដើមត្នោតបារាំង

16. dogwood
ដើមដកវុត

17. elm
ដើមអែលម៍

18. oak
ដើមសែន

Plants រុក្ខជាតិ

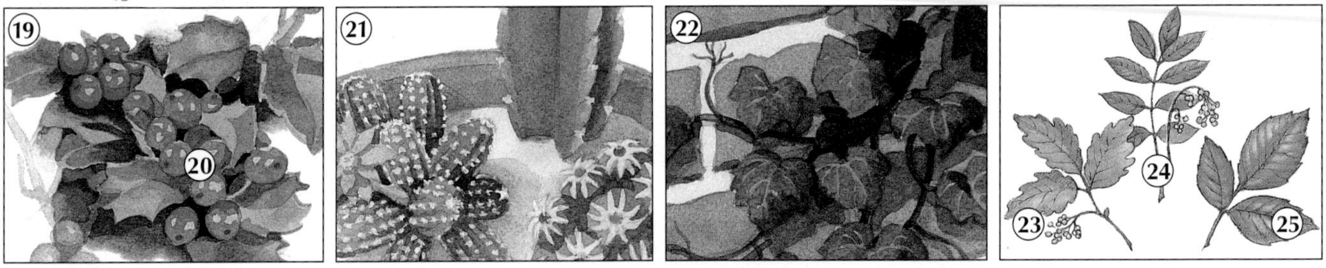

19. holly
ដើមហូល្លី

20. berries
ដើមប៊េរី

21. cactus
ដើមដំបងយក្ស

22. vine
វល្លិ

23. poison oak
ដើមភយសិនអូក

24. poison sumac
ដើមភយសិនស៊ូម៉ាក់

25. poison ivy
ដើមភយសិន អាយវី

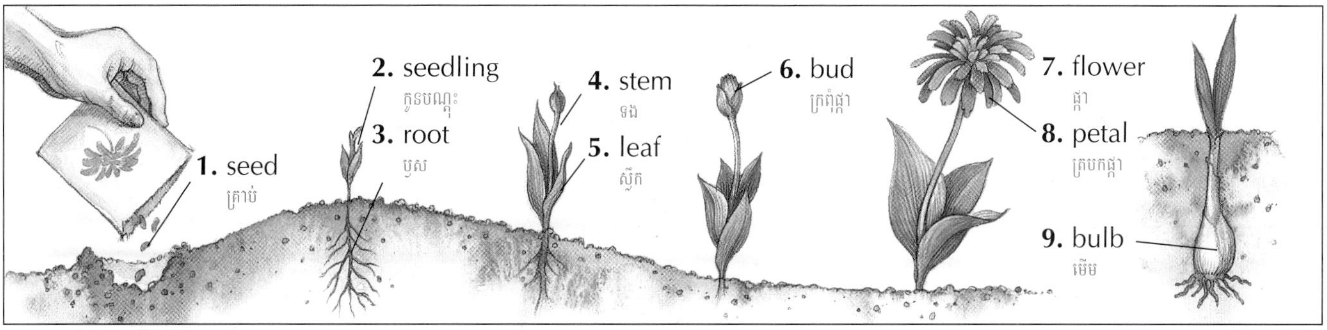
1. seed
គ្រាប់
2. seedling
កូនបណ្តុះ
3. root
ឫស
4. stem
ទង
5. leaf
ស្លឹក
6. bud
ក្រពុំផ្កា
7. flower
ផ្កា
8. petal
ត្របកផ្កា
9. bulb
មើម

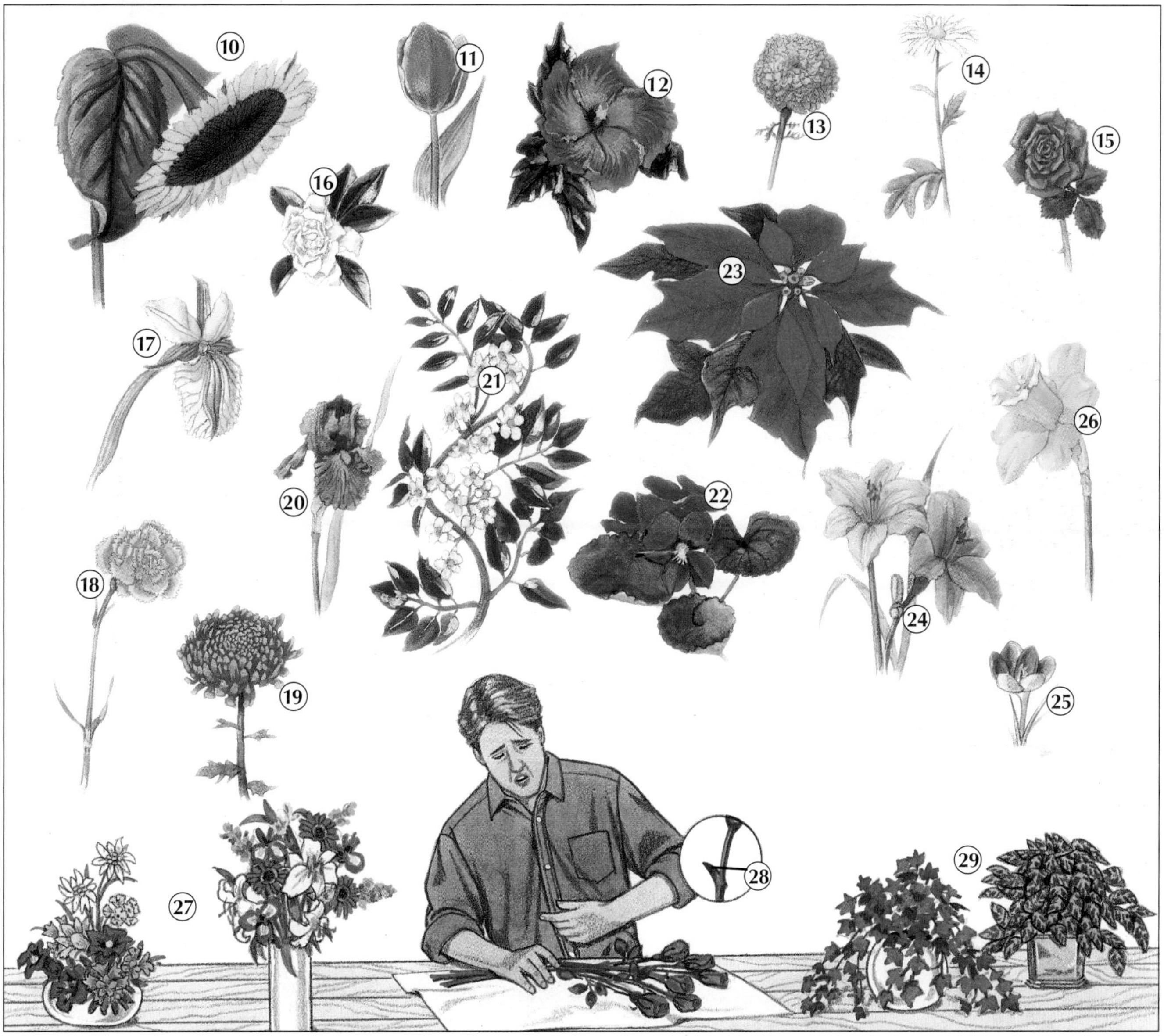
10
11
12
13
14
15
16
17
18
19
20
21
22
23
24
25
26
27
28
29

10. sunflower
ផ្កាឈូករ័ត្ន
11. tulip
ផ្កាទូលីប
12. hibiscus
ផ្ការំយោល
13. marigold
ផ្កាស្សៃរឿង
14. daisy
ផ្កាដេហ្ស៊ី
15. rose
ផ្កាកូឡាប
16. gardenia
ផ្កាទួនស្រី
17. orchid
ផ្កាអ័គីដេ
18. carnation
ផ្កាខានេស្យិន
19. chrysanthemum
ផ្កាគ្រីស្សង់តែម
20. iris
ផ្កាអៃរិះ
21. jasmine
ផ្កាម្លិះ
22. violet
ផ្កាវិយ៉ូឡេ
23. poinsettia
ផ្កាព័យសែតត្យា
24. lily
ផ្កាលីលី
25. crocus
ផ្កាក្រូកុស
26. daffodil
ផ្កាដាហ្វូឌិល
27. bouquet
បាច់ផ្កា
28. thorn
បន្លា
29. houseplant
កូនឈើដាំក្នុងផ្ទះ

Marine Life, Amphibians, and Reptiles សត្វសមុទ្រ, សត្វរស់ក្នុងទឹកនិងលើគោក, និង ឧរង្គសត្វ

Parts of a fish ផ្នែករបស់ត្រី

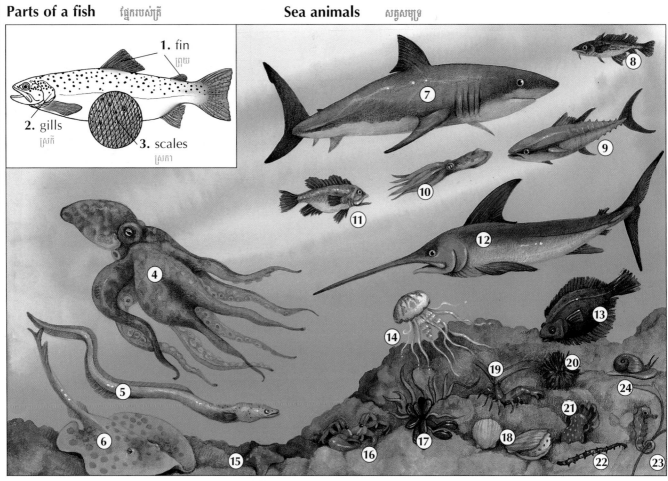

1. fin
ព្រុយ

2. gills
ស្រកី

3. scales
ស្រកា

Sea animals សត្វសមុទ្រ

4. octopus
ត្រីសមុទ្រដៃ8

5. eel
អន្ទង់

6. ray
ត្រីប្របែល

7. shark
ត្រីឆ្លាម

8. cod
ត្រីម៉ាវុយ

9. tuna
ត្រីធូណា

10. squid
ត្រីមឹក

11. bass
ត្រីបាស់

12. swordfish
ត្រីចំពុះស្នៀច

13. flounder
ត្រីអណ្ដាតឆ្កែ

14. jellyfish
ខ្ទើសមុទ្រ

15. starfish
ក្រចាប់សមុទ្រ

16. crab
ក្ដាម

17. mussel
ត្រីចំពុះទា

18. scallop
លាសសមុទ្រម្យ៉ាង/ខ្យងក្រែន

19. shrimp
ប្រហាន/កម្ពិស

20. sea urchin
ត្រីមានបន្លាដុំៗ

21. sea anemone
ត្រីអាន់មោន

22. worm
ជន្ធេន

23. sea horse
សេះសមុទ្រ

24. snail
ខ្យង

Amphibians ថដលិក

25. frog
កង្កែប

26. newt
សត្វត្រកួត

27. salamander
សត្វអន្ទង

28. toad
គីង្កក់

130

Sea mammals ថនិកសត្វសមុទ្រ

29. whale
ត្រីបាឡែន

30. dolphin
ត្រីផ្សោតហ្ស៊ីត/ផ្សោត

31. porpoise
ត្រីពពាយ

32. walrus
ភ្លូវីស/លោមមច្ឆា

33. seal
សត្វសេរ្សល/ឆ្មាទឹក

34. sea lion
គោសមុទ្រ/ស៊ីឡូអ៊ីន

35. otter
ភេ

Reptiles ឧរង្គសត្វ

36. alligator
ក្រពើ

37. crocodile
ក្រពើ

38. rattlesnake
ពស់ឥតពិស

39. garter snake
ពស់កណ្តឹង

40. cobra
ពស់វែក

41. lizard
ថ្លែន/បង្គួយ

42. turtle
អណ្តើក

Birds, Insects, and Arachnids សត្វស្លាប, សត្វល្អិត និង អដ្ឋបាទិកសត្

Parts of a bird ផ្នែកសត្វស្លាប

1. beak/bill
   ចំពុះ
2. wing
   ស្លាប
3. nest
   សំបុក
4. claw
   ក្រញ៉ាំ
5. feather
   រោម / ស្លាប

6. owl	**9.** woodpecker	**12.** penguin	**15.** peacock
ទិទុយ	ត្រសេះ	ភិនភ្លិន	ក្ងោក
7. blue jay	**10.** eagle	**13.** duck	**16.** pigeon
បូច	សត្វឥន្ទ្រី	ទា	ព្រាប
8. sparrow	**11.** hummingbird	**14.** goose	**17.** robin
ចាបស្រុក	ហ៊ាំមីញបើត	ក្ងាន	ចាបម្យ៉ាង

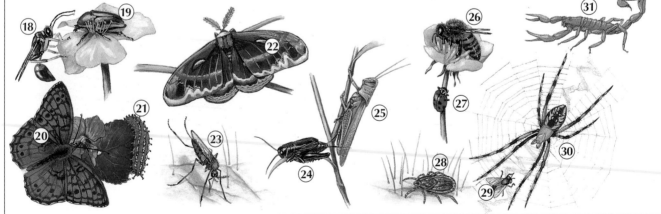

18. wasp	**22.** moth	**26.** honeybee	**30.** spider
ឪម៉ាល់	មេអំបៅយប់	ឃ្មុំ	ពីងពាង
19. beetle	**23.** mosquito	**27.** ladybug	**31.** scorpion
សត្វកញ្ចែ	មូស	អណ្ដើកមាស	ខ្យូ
20. butterfly	**24.** cricket	**28.** tick	
មេអំបៅ	ចង្រិត	ចៃឆ្កែ	
21. caterpillar	**25.** grasshopper	**29.** fly	
ដង្កូវមេអំបៅ	កណ្ដូប	រុយ	

Farm animals បសុសត្វ

1. goat
ពពែ

2. donkey
លា

3. cow
គោ

4. horse
សេះ

5. hen
មាន់ញី

6. rooster
មាន់ឈ្មោល/មាន់គក

7. sheep
ចៀម

8. pig
ជ្រូក

Pets សត្វចិញ្ចឹមក្នុងផ្ទះ

9. cat
ឆ្មា

10. kitten
កូនឆ្មា

11. dog
ឆ្កែ

12. puppy
កូនឆ្កែ

13. rabbit
ទន្សាយគាល់

14. guinea pig
កណ្ដុរសំពោ

15. parakeet
សេកភូច

16. goldfish
ត្រីក្រិមមាស

Rodents សត្វកកេរ

17. mouse
កណ្ដុរបង្ហុង

18. rat
កណ្ដុរប្រែង

19. gopher
សត្វហ្គោផ័រ

20. chipmunk
សត្វឈីបម៉ុង

21. squirrel
កំប្រុក

22. prairie dog
សត្វកកេរម្យ៉ាងសណ្ឋានដូចកំប្រុក ជាដើម

More vocabulary

Wild animals live, eat, and raise their young away from people, in the forests, mountains, plains, etc.

Domesticated animals work for people or live with them.

Share your answers.

1. Do you have any pets? any farm animals?

2. Which of these animals are in your neighborhood? Which are not?

1. **moose**
   ម៉ូស / ម៉ាងមួយបែប

2. **mountain lion**
   តោភ្នំ

3. **coyote**
   ឆ្កែចចក / ខ្យ៉ង់ច

4. **opossum**
   អាប៉ូស៊ុំ

5. **wolf**
   ឆ្កែព្រៃ

6. **buffalo/bison**
   គោព្រៃ / គោព្រៃផ្ទំ

7. **bat**
   ប្រជៀវ

8. **armadillo**
   ពពែធ្មល

9. **beaver**
   សត្វបីវ័រ

10. **porcupine**
    ប្រមា

11. **bear**
    ខ្លាឃ្មុំ

12. **skunk**
    ស្កុង

13. **raccoon**
    សំពោច

14. **deer**
    ក្ដាន់

15. **fox**
    កញ្ជ្រោង

16. **antler**
    ស្នែង (ប្រើស, ក្ដាន់)

17. **hoof**
    ក្រចក

18. **whiskers**
    ត្រយមាត់

19. **coat/fur**
    រោម

20. **paw**
    ក្រញ៉ា

21. **horn**
    ស្នែង (គោ, ក្របី)

22. **tail**
    កន្ទុយ

23. **quill**
    កាំប្រមា

24. anteater
សត្វពង្រូល / សត្វស៊ីស្រមោច

25. leopard
ខ្លាឃ្មុំ

26. llama
ឡាម៉ា (សត្វម្យ៉ាងដូចអូដ្ឋ)

27. monkey
ស្វា

28. chimpanzee
ស្វាស៊ី

29. rhinoceros
រមាស

30. gorilla
ស្វាធំ

31. hyena
សត្វស្វាន

32. baboon
ស្វាឆ្កែ

33. giraffe
សត្វរវែង / សត្វហ្សីរ៉ាហ្វ

34. zebra
សេះបង្កង់

35. antelope
សត្វអាន់ទីឡូប / សត្វស្រវៃងឈ្មោល

36. lion
តោ / សិង្ហ

37. tiger
ខ្លា

38. camel
អូដ្ឋ

39. panther
ខ្លាខ្មៅ

40. orangutan
ស្វាក្រហម

41. panda
សត្វផាន់ដា

42. elephant
ដំរី

43. hippopotamus
ដំរីទឹក

44. kangaroo
សត្វកង្ករូ

45. koala
សត្វកោឡា

46. platypus
សត្វផ្ដកធិតីស

47. trunk
ប្រមោយ

48. tusk
ភ្លុក

49. mane
សក់សិង្ហ

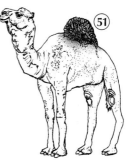

50. pouch
ថង់

51. hump
ថ្គម

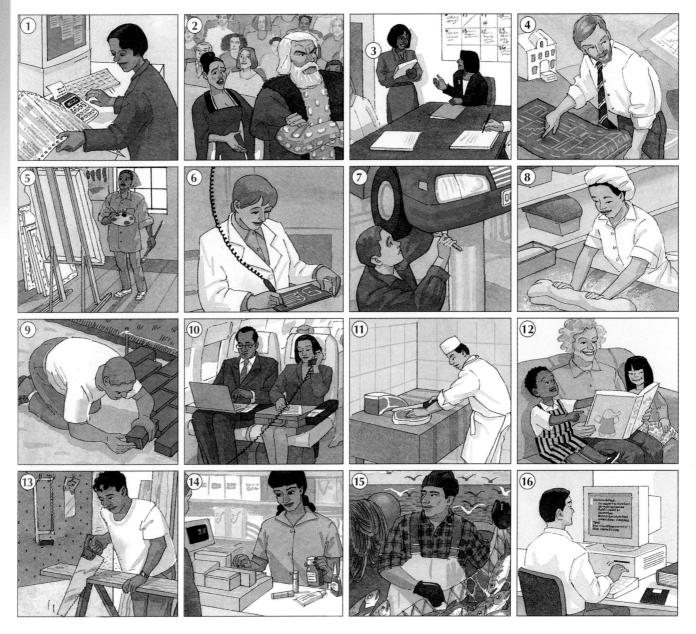

1. accountant
   គណនេយ្យករ

2. actor
   អ្នកសំដែង / អ្នកដើរតួ

3. administrative assistant
   អ្នកចាត់ការជំនួយ

4. architect
   និម្មាបនិក

5. artist
   វិចិត្រករ

6. assembler
   អ្នកផ្គុំគ្រឿង

7. auto mechanic
   ជាងឡាន

8. baker
   អ្នកធ្វើនំ

9. bricklayer
   ជាងកំបោរ

10. businessman / businesswoman
    អ្នកជំនួញប្រុស / ស្រី

11. butcher
    អ្នកកាត់សាច់

12. caregiver / baby-sitter
    អ្នកមើលក្មេង

13. carpenter
    ជាងឈើ

14. cashier
    អ្នកគិតលុយ

15. commercial fisher
    នេសាទពាណិជ្ជកម្ម

16. computer programmer
    អ្នករៀបរៀងកម្មវិធីកុំព្យូទ័រ

Use the new language.

1. Who works outside?

2. Who works inside?

3. Who makes things?

4. Who uses a computer?

5. Who wears a uniform?

6. Who sells things?

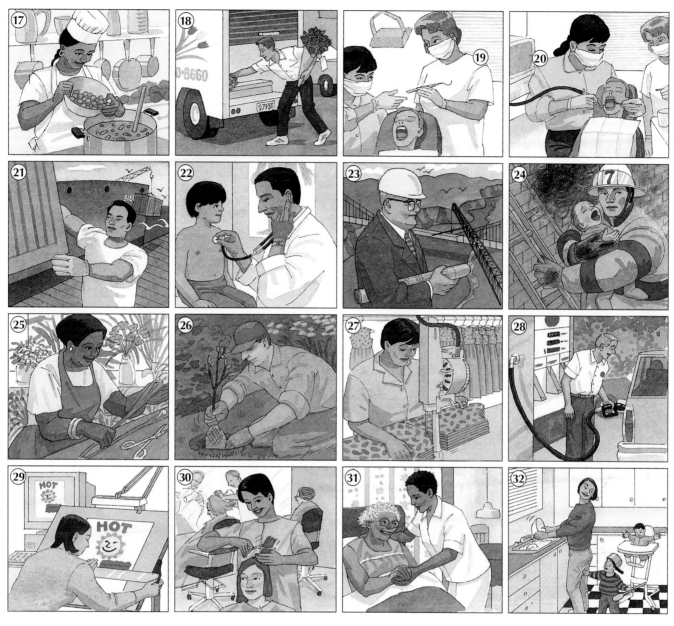

17. cook
ចុងភៅ

18. delivery person
អ្នកយក / ដឹកទំនិញរបស់អោយយកគេ

19. dental assistant
អ្នកជំនួយពេទ្យធ្មេញ

20. dentist
ពេទ្យធ្មេញ

21. dockworker
អ្នកធ្វើការនៅកំពង់ផែ

22. doctor
គ្រូពេទ្យ

23. engineer
វិស្វករ

24. firefighter
អ្នកពន្លត់ភ្លើង

25. florist
អ្នកលក់ផ្កា

26. gardener
អ្នកថែទាំសួនច្បារ

27. garment worker
អ្នកធ្វើការខាងសំលៀកបំពាក់

28. gas station attendant
អ្នកលក់សាំង

29. graphic artist
អ្នកគូរ

30. hairdresser
អ្នកធ្វើសក់

31. home attendant
អ្នកមើលថែទាំតាមផ្ទះ

32. homemaker
មេផ្ទះ

Share your answers.

1. Do you know people who have some of these jobs? What do they say about their work?

2. Which of these jobs are available in your city?

3. For which of these jobs do you need special training?

137

33. housekeeper
អ្នកថែទាំផ្ទះ

34. interpreter / translator
អ្នកបកប្រែភាសា

35. janitor / custodian
អ្នកបោសសំអាត / អ្នកថែទាំ

36. lawyer
មេធាវី

37. machine operator
អ្នកការ់ម៉ាស៊ីន

38. messenger / courier
អ្នកនាំសារ / អ្នកនាំសំបុត្រ

39. model
អ្នកបង្ហាញម៉ូដសំលៀកបំពាក់

40. mover
អ្នកផ្លាស់ប្តូរគេហដ្ឋាន / អ្នកផ្លាស់ប្តូរ

41. musician
ភ្លេងករ / អ្នកលេងភ្លេង

42. nurse
គិលានុបដ្ឋាយិកា

43. painter
អ្នកលាបថ្នាំ

44. police officer
នាយគ្រួត / ភ្នាក់ងារប៉ូលីស

45. postal worker
អ្នកធ្វើការប្រៃសណីយ

46. printer
អ្នកបោះពុម្ព

47. receptionist
អ្នកទទួលភ្ញៀវ

48. repair person
អ្នកផ្គុះសង្គ្រោះ

Talk about each of the jobs or occupations.

She's *a housekeeper*. She works in *a hotel*.

He's *an interpreter*. He works for *the government*.

She's *a nurse*. She works with *patients*.

138

49. reporter
អ្នករាយការណ៍

50. salesclerk / salesperson
អ្នកលក់

51. sanitation worker
អ្នកធ្វើការវៃផ្ទុកអនាម័យ

52. secretary
លេខាធិការ

53. server
អ្នកបំរើ

54. serviceman / servicewoman
យុទ្ធជន / យុទ្ធនារី

55. stock clerk
អ្នកលើករបស់ / អ្នកផ្ទុករបស់របរ

56. store owner
ម្ចាស់ហាង

57. student
សិស្ស

58. teacher / instructor
គ្រូបង្រៀន / អ្នកហ្វឹកហ្វឺន

59. telemarketer
អ្នកលក់តាមទូរស័ព្ទ

60. travel agent
អ្នកលក់សំបុត្រធ្វើដំណើរ

61. truck driver
អ្នកបើកឡានធំ

62. veterinarian
ពេទ្យសត្វ

63. welder
ជាងផ្សារ

64. writer / author
អ្នកសរសេរ / អ្នកនិពន្ធ

Talk about your job or the job you want.

What do you do?

  I'm a salesclerk. I work in a store.

What do you want to do?

  I want to be a veterinarian. I want to work with animals.

A. **assemble** components
ផ្គុំគ្រឿង / វៃផ្នែក

B. **assist** medical patients
ជួយមើលអ្នកជំងឺ

C. **cook**
ធ្វើម្ហូប

D. **do** manual labor
ធ្វើការដោយដៃ

E. **drive** a truck
បើកឡានធំ

F. **operate** heavy machinery
បើកឡាន ក្រៀងម៉ាស៊ីនធំៗ / ឡានស្ទូច

G. **repair** appliances
ផ្សះផ្សាគ្រឿងប្រើប្រាស់ក្នុងផ្ទះ

H. **sell** cars
លក់ឡាន

I. **sew** clothes
ដេរខោអាវ

J. **speak** another language
និយាយភាសាម្យ៉ាងទៀត

K. **supervise** people
មើលការខុសត្រូវ / ចាត់ចែងមនុស្ស

L. **take care** of children
ថែទាំក្មេង

M. **type**
វាយអក្សរ

N. **use** a cash register
ប្រើម៉ាស៊ីនគិតលុយ

O. **wait on** customers
រង់ចាំទទួលភ្ញៀវ

P. **work** on a computer
ប្រើកុំព្យូទ័រ

More vocabulary

act: to perform in a play, movie, or TV show

fly: to pilot an airplane

teach: to instruct, to show how to do something

Share your answers.

1. What job skills do you have? Where did you learn them?

2. What job skills do you want to learn?

A. **talk** to friends
និយាយទៅរកមិត្តភ័ក្ត្រ

B. **look** at a job board
មើលប្រកាសបិទផ្សាយការងារ

C. **look** for a help wanted sign
រកមើលសញ្ញាបិទប្រកាសរកអ្នកធ្វើការ

D. **look** in the classifieds
មើលក្នុងទំព័រផ្សាយពំណីង

E. **call** for information
ទូរស័ព្ទសួររកពិតមាន

F. **ask** about the hours
សួរពីម៉ោងធ្វើការ

G. **fill out** an application
បំពេញក្រដាសសុំធ្វើការងារ

H. **go** on an interview
ទៅសម្ភាសន៍

I. **talk** about your experience
និយាយពីបទពិសោធន៍របស់អ្នក

J. **ask** about benefits
សួរនាំអំពីតិន

K. **inquire** about the salary
សើបសួរពីប្រាក់បៀវត្ស

L. **get hired
បានធ្វើការ

1. desk
គុ

2. typewriter
ម៉ាស៊ីនរាយអក្សរលេខ

3. secretary
លេខាធិការ

4. microcassette transcriber
អ្នកចំឡុងពាក្យពិការសែតអាត់តួចៗ

5. stacking tray
ប្រអប់សំរាប់ដាក់តឹមានចូល និងឆ្ពោះចេញ

6. desk calendar
ស្បៀវភៅប្រក្រិតទិន

7. desk pad
ទ្រនាប់គុ

8. calculator
ប្រដាប់គិតលេខ

9. electric pencil sharpener
ម៉ាស៊ីនចិតខ្មៅដៃ

10. file cabinet
ទូដាក់សំណុំរឿង / ឯកសារ

11. file folder
ក្របដាក់បញ្ចូលឯកសារ

12. file clerk
អ្នករក្សាបញ្ជី

13. supply cabinet
ទូសម្ភារៈ

14. photocopier
ម៉ាស៊ីនថតរូបថត

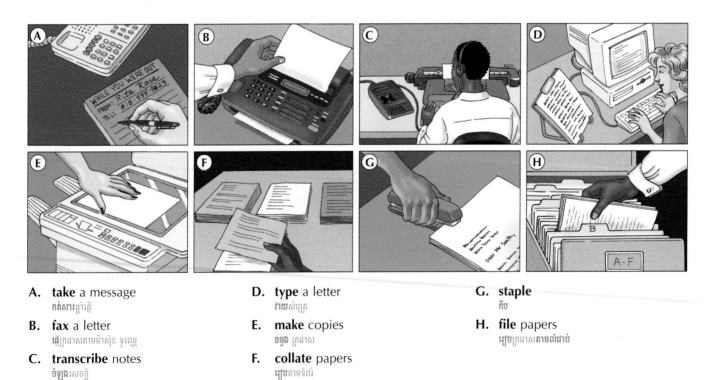

A. **take** a message
កត់សារឆ្នាំឆ្នើ

B. **fax** a letter
ផ្ញើក្រដាសតាមម៉ាស៊ីន ទូរក្រម

C. **transcribe** notes
ចំឡុងសេចក្ដី

D. **type** a letter
រាយសំបុត្រ

E. **make** copies
ថមង ក្រដាស

F. **collate** papers
រៀបតាមទំព័រ

G. **staple**
កីប

H. **file** papers
រៀបក្រដាសតាមលំដាប់

Practice taking messages.

Hello. My name is <u>Sara Scott</u>. Is <u>Mr. Lee</u> in?

   Not yet. Would you like to leave a message?

Yes. Please ask <u>him</u> to call me at <u>555-4859</u>.

Share your answers.

1. Which office equipment do you know how to use?
2. Which jobs does a file clerk do?
3. Which jobs does a secretary do?

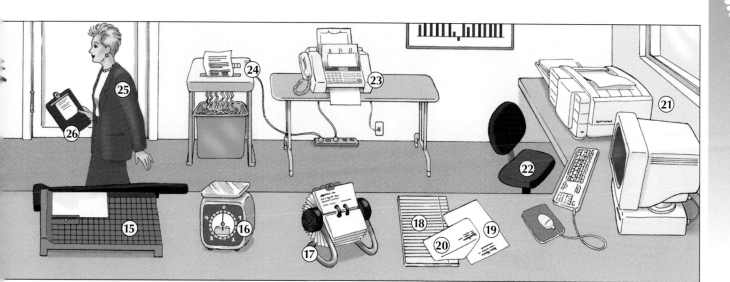

15. paper cutter
ប្រដាប់កាត់ក្រដាស

16. postal scale
ជញ្ជីងថ្លឹងតែម

17. rotary card file
ប្រដាប់ទុកកាតឈ្មោះ (បង្វិលបាន)

18. legal pad
ក្រដាសសរសេរផ្នែកធំ

19. letterhead paper
ក្រដាសមានឈ្មោះក្រុមហ៊ុន

20. envelope
ស្រោមសំបុត្រ

21. computer workstation
តុកុំព្យូទ័រ

22. swivel chair
កៅអីរិល

23. fax machine
ម៉ាស៊ីនទូរវាក្ស

24. paper shredder
ប្រដាប់ចិញ្ច្រាំក្រដាស

25. office manager
នាយការិយាល័យ

26. clipboard
ក្តារទ្រាប់សរសេរ

27. appointment book
សៀវភៅកំណត់ផ្សេ

28. stapler
ប្រដាប់ស្ទិប

29. staple
គ្រាប់ដែកស្ទិប

30. organizer
សៀវភៅរៀបសំរួល

31. typewriter cartridge
ដំហ្សិលអង្គុលីលេខ

32. mailer
ប្រដាប់ដាក់សំបុត្រ

33. correction fluid
ទឹកលប់

34. Post-it notes
ក្រដាសសរសេរស្អិតៗ

35. label
ផ្លាកបិទ

36. notepad
កូនសៀវភៅកត់ត្រា

37. glue
កាវ

38. rubber cement
កាវរំលាយ

39. clear tape
បង់ស្អិតថ្លា

40. rubber stamp
ត្រាកៅស៊ូ

41. ink pad
ប្រដាប់ផ្លិតត្រា

42. packing tape
បង់ប្រអប់ផ្នាៗ

43. pushpin
ម្ជុលបញ្ឈ/ដែកគោលបញ្ឈនឹងមេដៃ

44. paper clip
ដែកឃ្លៀបក្រដាស

45. rubber band
កៅស៊ូកង

Use the new language.

1. Which items keep things together?

2. Which items are used to mail packages?

3. Which items are made of paper?

Share your answers.

1. Which office supplies do students use?

2. Where can you buy them?

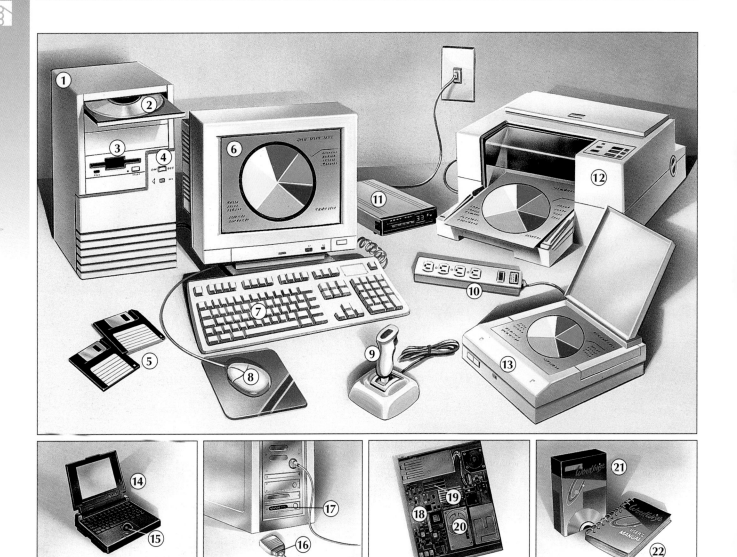

Hardware
ផ្នែកកុំព្យូទ័រ

1. CPU (central processing unit)
ផ្នែកបញ្ជា (ស៊ី.ភី.យូ)

2. CD-ROM disc
ថាស ស៊ីឌី រ៉ូម

3. disk drive
ឌិស ដ្រាយ

4. power switch
កុងតាក់ភ្លើង

5. disk / floppy
ឌិស / ផ្លុបពិ

6. monitor / screen
ម៉ូនីផ័រ / កញ្ចក់

7. keyboard
ប្រដាប់ចុចអក្សរ / លេខ

8. mouse
កូនកណ្ដុរ

9. joystick
បង្ហាលបញ្ជា

10. surge protector
ប្រដាប់ការពារភ្លើង

11. modem
ម៉ូដឹម

12. printer
ម៉ាស៊ីនព្រីន

13. scanner
ម៉ាស៊ីនស្កែន

14. laptop
កុំព្យូទ័រយួរចុះឡើងបាន

15. trackball
ត្រាកបល

16. cable
ខ្សែកាបអគ្គិសនី

17. port
ភាគ់

18. motherboard
ម៉ាដឺបត

19. slot
ចន្លោះ, ប្រហោង

20. hard disk drive
ហាត ឌិស ត្រាយ

Software
ប្រូក្រាម

21. program / application
ប្រូក្រាម / អាត្លិខេស្យិន

22. user's manual
ក្បួនវិណេន្ទ័

More vocabulary

data: information that a computer can read

memory: how much data a computer can hold

speed: how fast a computer can work with data

Share your answers.

1. Can you use a computer?

2. How did you learn? in school? from a book? by yourself?

1. valet parking
អ្នកបំរើចតឡានយន្ត

2. doorman
អ្នកយាមទ្វារ

3. lobby
កន្លែងទទួលភ្ញៀវក្នុងសណ្ឋាគារ

4. bell captain
អ្នកទទួលភ្ញៀវ

5. bellhop
អ្នកញញើសវ៉ាលី

6. luggage cart
រទេះដាក់វ៉ាលី

7. gift shop
ហាងលក់វត្ថុអនុស្សាវរីយ៍

8. front desk
តុទទួលខាងមុខ

9. desk clerk
អ្នកចាំតុខាងមុខ

10. guest room
បន្ទប់ភ្ញៀវ

11. guest
ភ្ញៀវ

12. room service
អ្នកបំរើអាហារបន្ទប់

13. hall
ផ្លូវដើរ

14. housekeeping cart
រទេះដាក់គ្រឿងសំអាត និងផ្លាស់កំណត់

15. housekeeper
អ្នកសំអាតបន្ទប់

16. pool
អាងទឹក

17. pool service
បំរើផ្នែកអាងទឹក

18. ice machine
ម៉ាស៊ីនទឹកកក

19. meeting room
បន្ទប់ប្រជុំ

20. ballroom
បន្ទប់រាំ

More vocabulary

concierge: the hotel worker who helps guests find restaurants and interesting places to go

service elevator: an elevator for hotel workers

Share your answers.

1. Does this look like a hotel in your city? Which one?

2. Which hotel job is the most difficult?

3. How much does it cost to stay in a hotel in your city?

1. front office
   ការិយាល័យខាងមុខ

2. factory owner
   ម្ចាស់រោងចក្រ

3. designer
   អ្នករចនា / អ្នកគូរប្លង់

4. time clock
   នាឡិការកត់ម៉ោង

5. line supervisor
   អ្នកទទួលខុសត្រូវផ្នែកបន្ទាញ

6. factory worker
   កម្មកររោងចក្រ

7. parts
   ផ្នែក / គ្រឿង

8. assembly line
   បន្ទាញផ្គុំគ្រឿង

9. warehouse
   ឃ្លាំង

10. order puller
    ម៉ាស៊ីនទាញ

11. hand truck
    រទេះផ្ទាញសម្ភារៈ

12. conveyor belt
    ខ្សែក្រវាត់ទាញ

13. packer
    អ្នកខ្ចប់

14. forklift
    ម៉ាស៊ីនលើក

15. shipping clerk
    អ្នកកាន់បញ្ជីដឹកជញ្ជូន

16. loading dock
    កន្លែងលើក / ដាក់ស្តុក

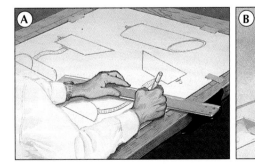

A. design
   រចនា / គូរប្លង់

B. manufacture
   ផលិត

C. ship
   ដឹកជញ្ជូន

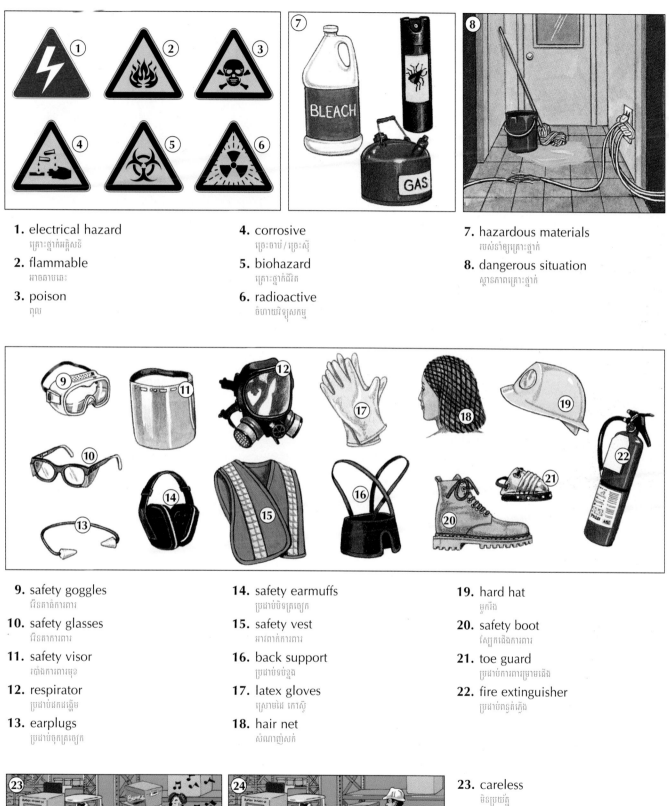

1. electrical hazard
គ្រោះថ្នាក់អគ្គិសនី

2. flammable
អាចឆាបឆេះ

3. poison
ពុល

4. corrosive
ច្រេះចាប់/ច្រេះស៊ី

5. biohazard
គ្រោះថ្នាក់ជីវិត

6. radioactive
ចំហាយវិទ្យុសកម្ម

7. hazardous materials
របស់នាំឱ្យគ្រោះថ្នាក់

8. dangerous situation
ស្ថានភាពគ្រោះថ្នាក់

9. safety goggles
វ៉ែនតាធំការពារ

10. safety glasses
វ៉ែនតាការពារ

11. safety visor
ថាំងការពារមុខ

12. respirator
ប្រដាប់ដកដង្ហើម

13. earplugs
ប្រដាប់ចុកត្រចៀក

14. safety earmuffs
ប្រដាប់បិទត្រចៀក

15. safety vest
អាវក្រៅការពារ

16. back support
ប្រដាប់ទប់ខ្នង

17. latex gloves
ស្រោមដៃ កៅស៊ូ

18. hair net
សំណាញ់សក់

19. hard hat
មួកវ៉ែង

20. safety boot
ស្បែកជើងការពារ

21. toe guard
ប្រដាប់ការពារម្រាមជើង

22. fire extinguisher
ប្រដាប់ពន្លត់ភ្លើង

23. careless
មិនប្រយ័ត្ន

24. careful
ប្រយ័ត្ន

Crops ផលដំណាំ

1. rice
ស្រូវ

2. wheat
ស្រូវសាឡី

3. soybeans
សណ្ដែកសៀង

4. corn
ពោត

5. alfalfa
ចំណីសត្វ / អាល់ហ្វាល់ហ្វា

6. cotton
កប្បាស

7. field
ចំការ

8. farmworker
អ្នកធ្វើការក្នុងចំការ

9. tractor
ត្រាក់ទ័រ

10. farm equipment
សម្ភារៈធ្វើចំការ

11. barn
ជង្រុកស្រូវ

12. vegetable garden
ច្បារដំណាំ

13. livestock
សត្វចិញ្ចឹមយកសាច់

14. vineyard
ចំការទំពាំងបាយជូរ

15. farmer / grower
កសិករ / អ្នកដាំដំណាំ

16. orchard
ចំការឈើស៊ីផ្លែ

17. corral
ក្រោល

18. hay
ចំបើង

19. fence
របង

20. hired hand
អ្នកស៊ីឈ្នួលធ្វើស្រែចំការ

21. steers / cattle
គោក្រៀវ / បសុសត្វ

22. rancher
ម្ចាស់វាលចិញ្ចឹមសត្វ

A. plant
ដាំ

B. harvest
ច្រូតកាត់ / ប្រមូលផល

C. milk
ប្រាថ់ទឹកដោះគោ

D. feed
បញ្ចុកចំណី / អោយចំណី

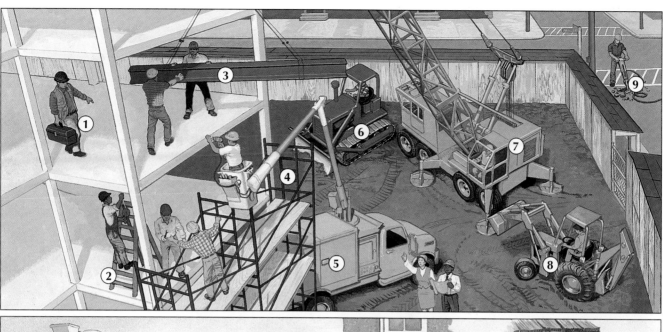

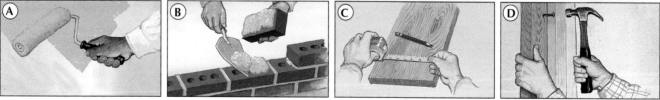

1. construction worker
កម្មករសំណង់

2. ladder
ជណ្តើរ

3. I beam / girder
ធ្នឹម / រវ

4. scaffolding
រង្វា

5. cherry picker
ប្រដាប់សំរាប់សួយទៅទីខ្ពស់

6. bulldozer
ត្រាក់ទ័រលុកសង្ហ

7. crane
ប្រដាប់សួច

8. backhoe
ត្រាក់ទ័រកាយដី

9. jackhammer / pneumatic drill
ម៉ាស៊ីនគាស់ថ្ម / ម៉ាស៊ីនខែនដី

10. concrete
ស៊ីម៉ង់

11. bricks
ឥដ្ឋ

12. trowel
ស្មាបប្រាបាយអរ

13. insulation
ទ្រនាប់កំដៅ

14. stucco
ស៊ីម៉ង់ក្រិតម៉ា

15. window pane
កញ្ចក់បង្អួច

16. plywood
ក្តារបន្ទះ

17. wood / lumber
ឈើអារ

18. drywall
ជញ្ជាំងក្រដាស

19. shingles
គ្រឿងប្រក់ដំបូល

20. pickax
ចបត្រសេះ

21. shovel
ប៉ែល

22. sledgehammer
ញញួរធំ

A. **paint**
ថ្នាំលាប

B. **lay** bricks
រៀប ឥដ្ឋ

C. **measure**
វាស់

D. **hammer**
ដំ

149

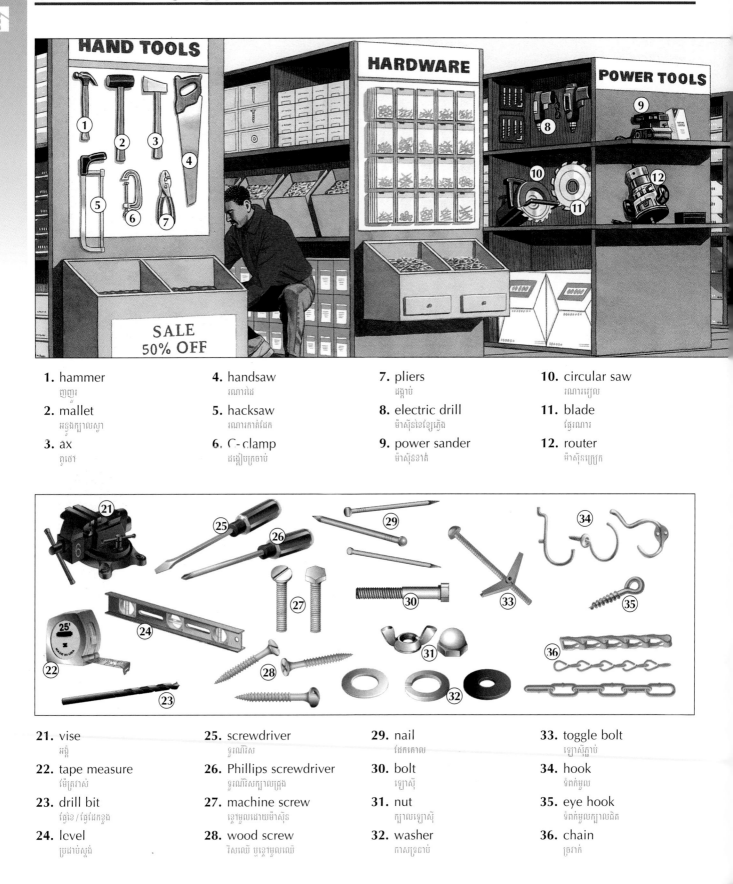

1. hammer
ញញួរ

2. mallet
អន្លង់ក្បាលស្វា

3. ax
ពូថៅ

4. handsaw
រណារដៃ

5. hacksaw
រណារកាត់ដែក

6. C-clamp
អង្គៀបគ្រាប់

7. pliers
អង្គាប់

8. electric drill
ម៉ាស៊ីនខ្វែខ្សែភ្លើង

9. power sander
ម៉ាស៊ីនខាត់

10. circular saw
រណារវៀល

11. blade
ផ្លែរណារ

12. router
ម៉ាស៊ីនឆ្នៀក

21. vise
អង្គៀ

22. tape measure
ម៉ែត្ររាស់

23. drill bit
ផ្លែខ្វែ / ផ្លែដែកខ្វែង

24. level
ប្រដាប់ស្ទង់

25. screwdriver
ទួណឺវីស

26. Phillips screwdriver
ទួណឺវីសកញ្ចាយត្រង

27. machine screw
ខ្ចៅមួលដោយម៉ាស៊ីន

28. wood screw
វីសឈើ ឬខ្ចៅមួលឈើ

29. nail
ដែកគោល

30. bolt
ខ្ចៅស៊ី

31. nut
ក្បាលខ្ចៅស៊ី

32. washer
កាសត្រូចាប់

33. toggle bolt
ខ្ចៅស៊ីឆ្នាប់

34. hook
ទំពក់មួប

35. eye hook
ទំពក់មួលក្បាលជិត

36. chain
ច្រវាក់

Use the new language.

1. Which tools are used for plumbing?

2. Which tools are used for painting?

3. Which tools are used for electrical work?

4. Which tools are used for working with wood?

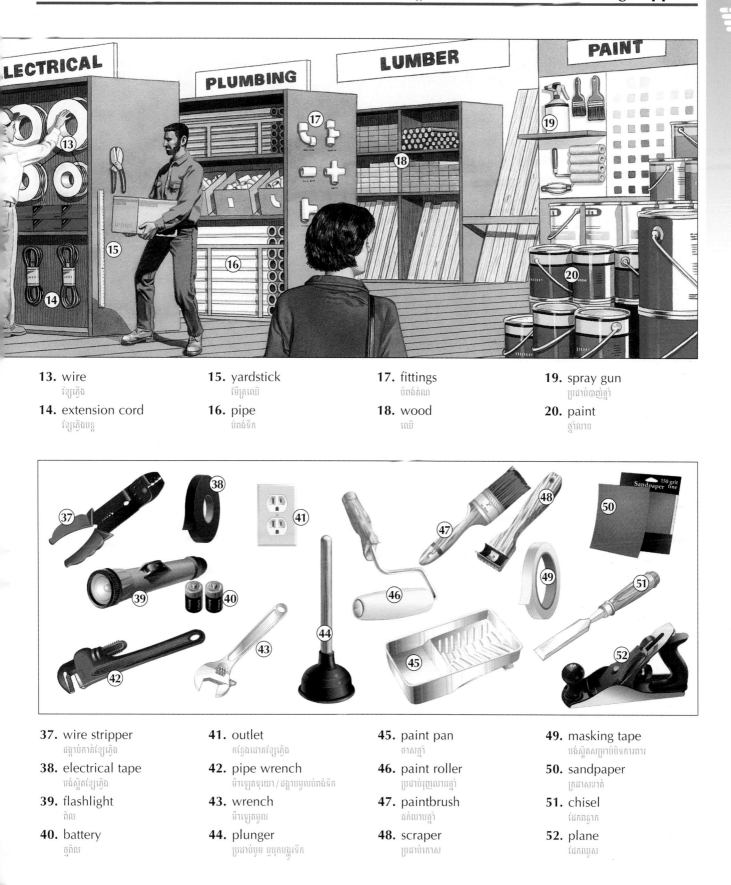

ELECTRICAL

PLUMBING

LUMBER

PAINT

13. wire
ខ្សែភ្លើង

14. extension cord
ខ្សែភ្លើងបន្ត

15. yardstick
ម៉ែត្រឈើ

16. pipe
បំពង់ទឹក

17. fittings
បំពង់តភ្ជាប់

18. wood
ឈើ

19. spray gun
ប្រដាប់បាញ់ថ្នាំ

20. paint
ថ្នាំលាប

37. wire stripper
ដង្កាប់កាត់ខ្សែភ្លើង

38. electrical tape
បង់ស្អិតខ្សែភ្លើង

39. flashlight
ពិល

40. battery
ថ្មពិល

41. outlet
កន្លែងដោតខ្សែភ្លើង

42. pipe wrench
ម៉ាឡេតទុរយោ/ដង្កាប់មូលបំពង់ទឹក

43. wrench
ម៉ាឡេតមូល

44. plunger
ប្រដាប់បូម ឬមុតបង្ហូរទឹក

45. paint pan
ថាសថ្នាំ

46. paint roller
ប្រដាប់រញ្ជាលាបថ្នាំ

47. paintbrush
ជក់លាបថ្នាំ

48. scraper
ប្រដាប់កោស

49. masking tape
បង់ស្អិតសម្រាប់បិទការពារ

50. sandpaper
ក្រដាសខាត់

51. chisel
ដែកពន្លាក

52. plane
ដែកឈូស

Use the new language.

Look at **Household Problems and Repairs,**
pages **48–49.**

Name the tools you use to fix the problems you see.

Share your answers.

1. Which tools do you have in your home?

2. Which tools can be dangerous to use?

1. zoo
សួនសត្វ

2. animals
សត្វ

3. zookeeper
អ្នករក្សាសួនសត្វ

4. botanical gardens
សួនច្បារដាំដើមឈើរុក្ខជាតិ

5. greenhouse
បន្ទប់ដាំដុះកូនឈើ / រុក្ខជាតិ

6. gardener
អ្នកថែសួនច្បារ

7. art museum
សារៈមន្ទីរសិល្បៈ

8. painting
គំនូរ

9. sculpture
រូបចម្លាក់

10. the movies
ភាពយន្ត

11. seat
កៅអី

12. screen
សំពត់បញ្ចាំងរូប

13. amusement park
សួនកំសាន្ត

14. puppet show
ល្បែង / កុនតុក្កតា

15. roller coaster
រទេះ ឆូស្សរ៍

16. carnival
បុណ្យលេងល្បែងកំសាន្ត

17. rides
ជិះ

18. game
ល្បែង

19. county fair
បុណ្យពិពណ៌តាមខោនធិ

20. first place / first prize
រង្វាន់ទី១

21. exhibition
តាំងពិពណ៌

22. swap meet / flea market
ផ្សារលក់របស់ចាស់ទោរខាងក្រៅ / ផ្សារមេម

23. booth
រោងតំណាំង / តូបលក់អីវ៉ាន់

24. merchandise
ទំនិញ

25. baseball game
កីឡាបាល់គប់ / ល្បែងបេសប្បល

26. stadium
កីឡដ្ឋាន

27. announcer
អ្នកប្រកាស

Talk about the places you like to go.

I like <u>animals</u>, so I go to <u>the zoo</u>.

I like <u>rides</u>, so I go to <u>carnivals</u>.

Share your answers.

1. Which of these places is interesting to you?
2. Which rides do you like at an amusement park?
3. What are some famous places to go to in your country?

1. **ball field**
   វាលលេងបាល់

2. **bike path**
   ផ្លូវជិះកង់

3. **cyclist**
   អ្នកជិះកង់

4. **bicycle/bike**
   កង់

5. **jump rope**
   ខ្សែលោតអន្ទាក់

6. **duck pond**
   ស្រះទឹកទាលេង

7. **tennis court**
   កន្លែងលេងតេននិស

8. **picnic table**
   តុបរិភោគអាហារ

9. **tricycle**
   ត្រីចក្រយាន

10. **bench**
    កៅអីវែង

11. **water fountain**
    ក្បាលម៉ាស៊ីនទឹក

12. **swings**
    ទោង

13. **slide**
    ក្តារអិល

14. **climbing apparatus**
    ឧបករណ៍សម្រាប់គោងឡើង

15. **sandbox**
    ធ្នាខ្សាច់សម្រាប់ក្មេងលេង

16. **seesaw**
    ក្តារធ្មើង

A. **pull** the wagon
   ទាញរទេះ

B. **push** the swing
   បោយទោង

C. **climb** on the bars
   ឡើងលើចំរឹង

D. **picnic/have** a picnic
   ភិចនិច/ញ៉ាំភិចនិច

1. camping
បោះជំរំ

2. boating
ជិះកាណូត

3. canoeing
ជិះទូកថែវ

4. rafting
ជិះទូកកោស៊ូ

5. fishing
ស្ទូចត្រី

6. hiking
ដើរកំសាន្ត

7. backpacking
ស្ពាយកាប៉ូប

8. mountain biking
ជិះកង់នៅភ្នំ

9. horseback riding
ជិះសេះ

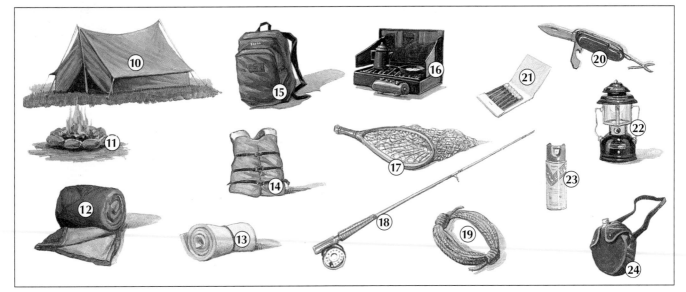

10. tent
តង់

11. campfire
ភ្លើងភ្លើង

12. sleeping bag
ថង់គេង

13. foam pad
ម្រទាប់កោស៊ូសំឡី

14. life vest
អាវសង្រ្គោះជីវិត / អាវបណ្តែតទឹក

15. backpack
កាប៉ូបស្ពាយ

16. camping stove
ចង្ក្រានសម្រាប់បោះជំរំ

17. fishing net
កន្ត្រងសំណាញ់ដងត្រី

18. fishing pole
ដងសន្ទូច

19. rope
ខ្សែព្វាត់

20. multi-use knife
កាំបិតមុខច្រើន

21. matches
ឈើគូស

22. lantern
ចង្កៀង

23. insect repellent
ថ្នាំបាញ់សត្វល្អិត

24. canteen
បិតង់ទឹកស្ពាយ

1. ocean/water	**9.** beach umbrella	**17.** sunbather
សមុទ្រ / ទឹក	ឆ័ត្រធំ	អ្នកដេកហាលថ្ងៃ
2. fins	**10.** sand castle	**18.** lifeguard
ជើងទាពាក់ហែលទឹក	កូនប្រាសាទដីខ្សាច់	អ្នកចាំសង្គ្រោះ
3. diving mask	**11.** cooler	**19.** lifesaving device
ស្រោមធាក់មុជទឹក	ធុងទឹកកក	គ្រឿងសង្គ្រោះជីវិត
4. sailboat	**12.** shade	**20.** lifeguard station
ទូកក្តោង	ម្លប់	បឹមអ្នកចាំសង្គ្រោះ
5. surfboard	**13.** sunscreen/sunblock	**21.** seashell
ក្តាជិះលើទឹករលក	ថ្នាំលាបស្បែក / ថ្នាំលាបការពារកំដៅ	សំបកលាស បខ្យង
6. wave	**14.** beach chair	**22.** pail/bucket
រលកទឹក	កៅអីសម្រាប់អង្គុយនៅមាត់សមុទ្រ	ធុង / ថាំង
7. wet suit	**15.** beach towel	**23.** sand
ខោអាវទឹក	កន្សែងក្រាល	ដីខ្សាច់
8. scuba tank	**16.** pier	**24.** rock
ធុងដាក់ខ្យល់សម្រាប់មុជទឹក	ផែ	ថ្ម

More vocabulary

seaweed: a plant that grows in the ocean

tide: the level of the ocean. The tide goes in and out every twelve hours.

Share your answers.

1. Are there any beaches near your home?

2. Do you prefer to spend more time on the sand or in the water?

3. Where are some of the world's best beaches?

A. **walk** ដើរ	E. **catch** ចាប់	I. **shoot** បោះបញ្ចូល	M. **tackle** ចាប់ផ្ដួល
B. **jog** រត់តិចៗ	F. **pitch** បោះ / ចោល	J. **jump** លោត	
C. **run** រត់	G. **hit** វាយ	K. **dribble / bounce** បណ្ដើរបាល់	
D. **throw** គប់ / គ្រវែង	H. **pass** ហុចទៅម្នាក់ទៀត	L. **kick** ទាត់	

Practice talking about what you can do.

I can <u>swim</u>, but I can't <u>dive</u>.

I can <u>pass the ball</u> well, but I can't <u>shoot</u> too well.

Use the new language.

Look at **Individual Sports**, page **159**.

Name the actions you see people doing.

The man in number 18 is riding a horse.

N. serve
ធ្វើមរាយបាល់

O. swing
រាយបាល់

P. exercise / work out
ហាត់ប្រាណ

Q. stretch
ពត់ខ្លួនប្រាណ

R. bend
បត់ខ្លួន

S. dive
លោតចោះទូរ

T. swim
ហែលទឹក

U. ski
ជិះស្គី

V. skate
ជិះស្គេត

W. ride
ជិះ

X. start
ចាប់ផ្ដើម

Y. race
ប្រណាំង

Z. finish
បញ្ចប់

Share your answers.

1. What do you like to do?

2. What do you have difficulty doing?

3. How often do you exercise? Once a week? Two or three times a week? More? Never?

4. Which is more difficult, throwing a ball or catching it?

1. score
ពិន្ទុ

2. coach
គ្រូកីឡា

3. team
ក្រុមកីឡា

4. fan
អ្នកមើលកីឡា

5. player
អ្នកលេងកីឡា

6. official/referee
អាជ្ញាកណ្ដាល

7. basketball court
កន្លែងលេងបាល់បោះ

8. basketball
បាល់បោះ

9. baseball
បាល់វាយដំបង

10. softball
សហ្វបល

11. football
បាល់អាប

12. soccer
បាល់ទាត់

13. ice hockey
កូនគោលពើទឹកកក

14. volleyball
បាល់ទះ

15. water polo
បាល់ទះក្នុងទឹក

More vocabulary

captain: the team leader

umpire: in baseball, the name for referee

Little League: a baseball league for children

win: to have the best score

lose: the opposite of win

tie: to have the same score as the other team

1. archery
   កីឡាបាញ់ធ្នូ

2. billiards/pool
   កីឡាប៊ីយ៉ា/ប៊ីយ៉ា

3. bowling
   កីឡាបោះប៊ូលីង

4. cycling/biking
   ជិះកង់

5. fencing
   កីឡាកាប់ដាវ

6. flying disc*
   ចោលចាន

7. golf
   ហ្គោល្វ

8. gymnastics
   កាយសម្ព័ន្ធ

9. inline skating
   ស្គេតតាមខ្សែ

10. martial arts
    ក្បាច់គុន

11. racquetball
    វាយតែសរាយសី

12. skateboarding
    ជិះក្តារស្គេត

13. table tennis/
    Ping-Pong™
    ក្រឹងបិុង

14. tennis
    តិន្នីស

15. weightlifting
    លើកទម្ងន់

16. wrestling
    បោកចំបាប់

17. track and field
    កន្ទ្រង និងលានកីឡា

18. horse racing
    ប្រណាំងសេះ

*Note: one brand is Frisbee®
(Mattel, Inc.)

Talk about sports.

Which sports do you like?

  I like <u>tennis</u> but I don't like <u>golf</u>.

Share your answers.

1. Which sports are good for children to learn? Why?
2. Which sport is the most difficult to learn? Why?
3. Which sport is the most dangerous? Why?

1. downhill skiing
លេងស្គីចុះដងរេល

2. snowboarding
ជិះក្តារទឹកកក

3. cross-country skiing
ស្គីកាត់ព្រៃភ្នំ

4. ice skating
លេងស្គេតលើទឹកកក

5. figure skating
លេងស្គេតលើទឹកកកធ្វើកាយវិការ

6. sledding
ការទឹកកក

7. waterskiing
លេងស្គីលើទឹក

8. sailing
ការបើកទូកក្តោង

9. surfing
ជិះក្តារលើរលក

10. sailboarding
ជិះទូកក្តោងសំបែតតូចៗ

11. snorkeling
មុជទឹកពាក់មុខ

12. scuba diving
មុជទឹក ពាក់ប្រដៀងដកដង្ហើម

Use the new language.

Look at **The Beach**, page **155**.

Name the sports you see.

Share your answers.

1. Which sports are in the Winter Olympics?

2. Which sports do you think are the most exciting to watch?

1. golf club
ដងវាយហ្គុលហ្វ៊ី

2. tennis racket
រ៉ាក្កែតវាយកីឡីស

3. volleyball
បាល់ទះ

4. basketball
បាល់បោះ

5. bowling ball
បាល់ប៊ូលិង

6. bow
ធ្នូ

7. arrow
ព្រួញ

8. target
ឆ្នូងទិដៅ

9. ice skates
ស្បែកជើងពាក់លេងស្គេត

10. inline skates
ស្បែកជើងមានកង់

11. hockey stick
ដំបងវាយកូនគោល

12. soccer ball
បាល់ទាត់

13. shin guards
ទ្រនាប់ស្មងជើង

14. baseball bat
ដំបងវាយបេស្បូល

15. catcher's mask
ម៉ាស់សម្រាប់អ្នកចាប់បាល់ពាក់ការពារ

16. uniform
ឯកសណ្ឋាន

17. glove
ស្រោមដៃ

18. baseball
បាល់វាយជំបង

19. weights
ទម្ងន់

20. football helmet
មួកបាល់អោម

21. shoulder pads
ទ្រនាប់ស្មា

22. football
បាល់អោម

23. snowboard
ក្តារៈអ៊ីលលើទឹកកក

24. skis
ប្រដាប់ស្គី / ក្តារស្គី

25. ski poles
ឆ្នុលស្គី

26. ski boots
ស្បែកជើងស្គី

27. flying disc*
ថាសរចោល

*Note: One brand is Frisbee®
(Mattel, Inc.)

Share your answers.

1. Which sports equipment is used for safety reasons?

2. Which sports equipment is heavy?

3. What sports equipment do you have at home?

Use the new language.

Look at **Individual Sports**, page **159**.

Name the sports equipment you see.

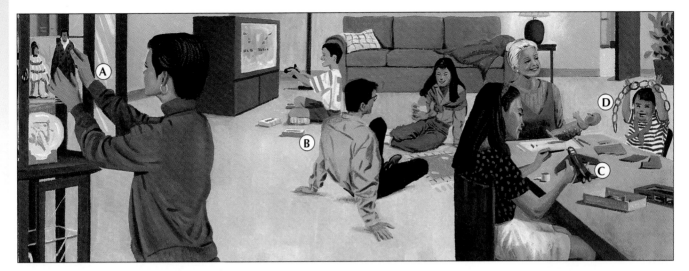

A. collect things	**B. play** games	**C. build** models	**D. do** crafts
សម្ព្យរភ្ក	លេងល្បែង	បង្កើតគំរូ	ធ្វើគ្រឿងសិប្បកម្ម

1. video game system
   ប្រព័ន្ធល្បែងវិដេអូ

2. cartridge
   អុំ (ចាសហ្គេម)

3. board game
   ក្តារល្បែង

4. dice
   គ្រាប់បង្វិល/គ្រាប់ឡូកឡាក់

5. checkers
   ចត្រង្គ

6. chess
   អុក

7. model kit
   គ្រឿងគំរូ

8. glue
   កាវ

9. acrylic paint
   ថ្នាំលាប អាគ្រីលិក

10. figurine
    រូបសូនតូច

11. baseball card
    ការ្តរបអ្នកលេងបាល់វាយដំបង

12. stamp collection
    ការសម្ព្យរតែម

13. coin collection
    ការសម្ព្យរកាក់

14. clay
    ដីឥដ្ឋដុណ្ណ

15. doll making kit
    គ្រឿងធ្វើកុនកុក្កុតា

16. woodworking kit
    ប្រដាប់សម្រាប់ប្រើធ្វើគ្រឿងឈើ

Talk about how much time you spend on your hobbies.

I *do crafts* all the time.

I *play chess* sometimes.

I never *build models*.

Share your answers.

1. How often do you play video games? Often? Sometimes? Never?

2. What board games do you know?

3. Do you collect anything? What?

E. paint
លាបពណ៌ / ផាត់គំនូរ

F. knit
ចាក់ / ប៉ាក់

G. pretend
ធ្វើប្រដូច

H. play cards
លេងបៀ

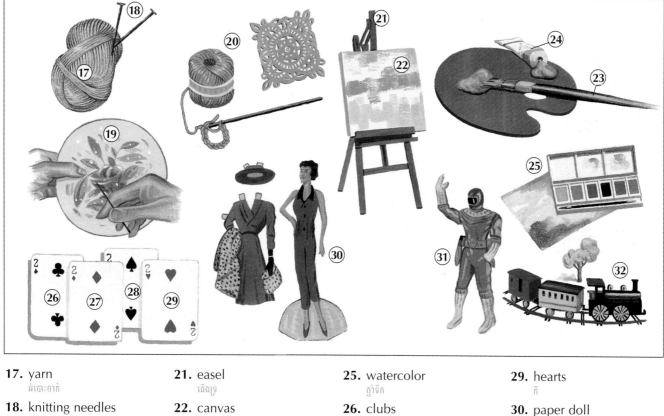

17. yarn
អំបោះចាក់

18. knitting needles
ម្ជុលចាក់

19. embroidery
ការប៉ាក់

20. crochet
ចាក់ក្សាច់

21. easel
ជើងទ្រ

22. canvas
ផ្ទាំងសំពត់សំរាប់គូរ

23. paintbrush
ជក់លាបថ្នាំ

24. oil paint
ថ្នាំប្រេង

25. watercolor
ថ្នាំទឹក

26. clubs
ផ្លូង

27. diamonds
ការ៉ូ

28. spades
ភិក

29. hearts
គឺ

30. paper doll
តុក្កតាក្រដាស

31. action figure
រូបតំណាង

32. model trains
កូនរទេះភ្លើងក្បួ

Share your answers.

1. Do you like to play cards? Which games?

2. Did you pretend a lot when you were a child? What did you pretend to be?

3. Is it important to have hobbies? Why or why not?

4. What's your favorite game?

5. What's your hobby?

1. clock radio
នាឡិកាវិទ្យុ

2. portable radio-cassette player
វិទ្យុយួរបាន / ម៉ាញ៉េ

3. cassette recorder
ម៉ាស៊ីនអាត់កាសែត

4. microphone
មីក្រូ

5. shortwave radio
វិទ្យុចាប់រលកធាតុអាកាសខ្លី

6. TV (television)
ទូរទស្សន៍

7. portable TV
ទូរទស្សន៍យួរបាន

8. VCR (videocassette recorder)
ម៉ាស៊ីនថតវីដេអូ / វីស្យអា

9. remote control
ប្រដាប់បើកពីចម្ងាយ

10. videocassette
កាសែតវីដេអូ

11. speakers
ប្រដាប់បំពងសំឡេង

12. turntable
ម៉ាស៊ីនចាក់ចាស

13. tuner
ប្រដាប់មួល

14. CD player
ម៉ាស៊ីនចាក់ស៊ីឌី

15. personal radio-cassette player
វិទ្យុតូច / ម៉ាស៊ីនចាក់កាសែត

16. headphones
ប្រដាប់ស្តាប់ដាក់ត្រចៀក

17. adapter
ប្រដាប់តម្រូវចរន្ត

18. plug
ក្បាលដោតខ្សែភ្លើង

19. video camera
ម៉ាស៊ីនថតកុន

20. tripod
ជើងម៉ាស៊ីនថត

21. camcorder
ម៉ាស៊ីនថត ខេមខតដ័រ

22. battery pack
អ៊ុំថ្មពិល

23. battery charger
ប្រដាប់បញ្ចូលថ្មើ

24. 35 mm camera
ម៉ាស៊ីនថត ទំហំ 35 មម

25. zoom lens
វែកទេញរូប

26. film
ហ្វីលថត

27. camera case
ស្រោមម៉ាស៊ីនថត

28. screen
ផ្ទាំងសំរាប់ស

29. carousel slide projector
ប្រដាប់ដាក់ហ្វីលរូបថតបញ្ចាំងដោយវិលជុំវិញ

30. slide tray
ថាសរូបបញ្ចាំង

31. slides
រូបថតបញ្ចាំង

32. photo album
សៀវភៅរូបថត

33. out of focus
ព្រិល

34. overexposed
ថតដោយប្រើភ្លើងផ្លុល

35. underexposed
ថតដោយប្រើភ្លើងតិច

A. record
អាត់ថំរៀង / ថត

B. play
ចាក់មើល / លេង

C. fast forward
ពន្លឿនទៅមុខ

D. rewind
ចាក់ថយក្រោយ

E. pause
សម្រាក

F. stop and eject
ឈប់ និងផ្លាក់ចេញ

Types of entertainment ប្រភេទនៃការកំសាន្ត

1. film/movie
កុន / ភាពយន្ត

2. play
ឆាកសម្ដែង

3. television program
កម្មវិធីទូរទស្សន៍

4. radio program
កម្មវិធីវិទ្យុ

5. stand-up comedy
អ្នកកំប្លែងម្នាក់ឯង

6. concert
មហោស្រព

7. ballet
ចាំបាឡេ

8. opera
ចាំអូប៉េរ៉ា / ល្ខោន

Types of stories ប្រភេទនៃរឿង

9. western
ភាពយន្តខោប៊យ

10. comedy
ឆាកកំប្លែង

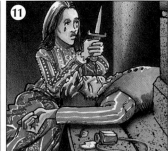

11. tragedy
សោកនាដកម្ម

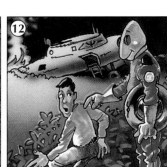

12. science fiction story
រឿងវិទ្យាសាស្ត្រប្រឌិត

13. action story/
adventure story
រឿងប្រយុទ្ធ / រឿងផ្សងព្រេង

14. horror story
រឿងខ្លាចរន្ធត់

15. mystery
រឿងអាថ៌កំបាំង

16. romance
រឿងស្នេហា

Types of TV programs ប្រភេទនៃកម្មវិធីទូរទស្សន៍

17. news
ពត៌មាន

18. sitcom (situation comedy)
ភាពកំប្លែងតាមកាលៈទេសៈ / ស៊ីដុងមេ

19. cartoon
របកំប្លែង

20. talk show
បង្ហាញការសន្ទនា និងវែកញែក

21. soap opera
ល្ខោនសម័យ

22. nature program
កម្មវិធីធម្មជាតិ

23. game show/quiz show
វែលវែង / ចំណោទសួរក្នុងវិទ្យុទូរទស្សន៍

24. children's program
កម្មវិធីកុមារាកុមារី

25. shopping program
កម្មវិធីលក់ដូរ

26. serious book
សៀវភៅរឿង**ពិត**

27. funny book
សៀវភៅរឿង**កំប្លែង**

28. sad book
សៀវភៅរឿង**កម្សត់**

29. boring book
សៀវភៅរឿង**គួរធុញទ្រាន់**

30. interesting book
សៀវភៅរឿង**គួរចាប់អារម្មណ៍**

1. New Year's Day
   ថ្ងៃបុណ្យចូលឆ្នាំ

2. parade
   ក្បួនហែរ

3. confetti
   ផ្កាក្រដាស

4. Valentine's Day
   ថ្ងៃវ៉ាឡិនថែន

5. card
   ក្រដាសជូនពរ

6. heart
   បេះដូង

7. Independence Day / 4th of July
   ថ្ងៃឯករាជ្យ / 4 កក្កដា

8. fireworks
   កាំជ្រួច

9. flag
   ទង់ជ័យ

10. Halloween
    បុណ្យហាឡូវីន

11. jack-o'-lantern
    ចង្កៀងគោមល្ពៅ

12. mask
    ក្បាំងមុខ

13. costume
    សំលៀកបំពាក់ហាឡូវីន

14. candy
    ស្ករគ្រាប់

15. Thanksgiving
    បុណ្យថ្ងៃឯណអំណរគុណព្រះ

16. feast
    ជប់លៀងអាហារ

17. turkey
    មាន់បារាំង

18. Christmas
    បុណ្យកំណើតព្រះយេស៊ូ

19. ornament
    គ្រឿងតុបតែងលំអ

20. Christmas tree
    ដើមស្រល់ណូអែល

168

A. **plan** a party
គ្រោងរៀបចំលៀ្ង

B. **invite** the guests
អញ្ជើញរៀ្វ

C. **decorate** the house
តុបតែងផ្ទះ

D. **wrap** a gift
ខ្ចប់អំណោយ

E. **hide**
លាក់ / ពួន

F. **answer** the door
ចាំបើ្វទ្វារ

G. **shout** "surprise!"
ស្រែក "ព្ញាក់!"

H. **light** the candles
អុតទៀន

I. **sing** "Happy Birthday"
ច្រៀងចំរៀង "ថ្ងៃកំណើត"

J. **make** a wish
នឹកស្មាន / បួងសួង / ប្រាថ្នា

K. **blow out** the candles
ផ្លុំកន្ទៀន

L. **open** the presents
បើកអំណោយ

Practice inviting friends to a party.

I'd love for you to come to my party <u>next week</u>.

Could <u>you and your friend</u> come to my party?

Would <u>your friend</u> like to come to a party I'm giving?

Share your answers.

1. Do you celebrate birthdays? What do you do?

2. Are there birthdays you celebrate in a special way?

3. Is there a special birthday song in your country?

Verb Guide

Verbs in English are either regular or irregular in the past tense and past participle forms.

Regular Verbs

The regular verbs below are marked 1, 2, 3, or 4 according to four different spelling patterns. (See page 172 for the **irregular verbs** which do not follow any of these patterns.)

Spelling Patterns for the Past and the Past Participle	*Example*		
1. Add **-ed** to the end of the verb.	**ASK**	→	**ASKED**
2. Add **-d** to the end of the verb.	**LIVE**	→	**LIVED**
3. Double the final consonant and add **-ed** to the end of the verb.	**DROP**	→	**DROPPED**
4. Drop the final y and add **-ied** to the end of the verb.	**CRY**	→	**CRIED**

The Oxford Picture Dictionary List of Regular Verbs

act (1)
add (1)
address (1)
answer (1)
apologize (2)
appear (1)
applaud (1)
arrange (2)
arrest (1)
arrive (2)
ask (1)
assemble (2)
assist (1)
bake (2)
barbecue (2)
bathe (2)
board (1)
boil (1)
borrow (1)
bounce (2)
brainstorm (1)
breathe (2)
broil (1)
brush (1)
burn (1)
call (1)
carry (4)
change (2)
check (1)
choke (2)
chop (3)
circle (2)
claim (1)
clap (3)
clean (1)
clear (1)
climb (1)
close (2)
collate (2)

collect (1)
color (1)
comb (1)
commit (3)
compliment (1)
conserve (2)
convert (1)
cook (1)
copy (4)
correct (1)
cough (1)
count (1)
cross (1)
cry (4)
dance (2)
design (1)
deposit (1)
deliver (1)
dial (1)
dictate (2)
die (2)
discuss (1)
dive (2)
dress (1)
dribble (2)
drill (1)
drop (3)
drown (1)
dry (4)
dust (1)
dye (2)
edit (1)
eject (1)
empty (4)
end (1)
enter (1)
erase (2)
examine (2)
exchange (2)

exercise (2)
experience (2)
exterminate (2)
fasten (1)
fax (1)
file (2)
fill (1)
finish (1)
fix (1)
floss (1)
fold (1)
fry (4)
gargle (2)
graduate (2)
grate (2)
grease (2)
greet (1)
grill (1)
hail (1)
hammer (1)
harvest (1)
help (1)
hire (2)
hug (3)
immigrate (2)
inquire (2)
insert (1)
introduce (2)
invite (2)
iron (1)
jog (3)
join (1)
jump (1)
kick (1)
kiss (1)
knit (3)
land (1)
laugh (1)
learn (1)

lengthen (1)
listen (1)
live (2)
load (1)
lock (1)
look (1)
mail (1)
manufacture (2)
mark (1)
match (1)
measure (2)
milk (1)
miss (1)
mix (1)
mop (3)
move (2)
mow (1)
need (1)
nurse (2)
obey (1)
observe (2)
open (1)
operate (2)
order (1)
overdose (2)
paint (1)
park (1)
pass (1)
pause (2)
peel (1)
perm (1)
pick (1)
pitch (1)
plan (3)
plant (1)
play (1)
point (1)
polish (1)
pour (1)
pretend (1)
print (1)
protect (1)

pull (1)
push (1)
race (2)
raise (2)
rake (2)
receive (2)
record (1)
recycle (2)
register (1)
relax (1)
remove (2)
rent (1)
repair (1)
repeat (1)
report (1)
request (1)
return (1)
rinse (2)
roast (1)
rock (1)
sauté (2)
save (2)
scrub (3)
seat (1)
sentence (2)
serve (2)
share (2)
shave (2)
ship (3)
shop (3)
shorten (1)
shout (1)
sign (1)
simmer (1)
skate (2)
ski (1)
slice (2)
smell (1)
sneeze (2)
sort (1)
spell (1)
staple (2)

start (1)
stay (1)
steam (1)
stir (3)
stir-fry (4)
stop (3)
stow (1)
stretch (1)
supervise (2)
swallow (1)
tackle (2)
talk (1)
taste (2)
thank (1)
tie (2)
touch (1)
transcribe (2)
transfer (3)
travel (1)
trim (3)
turn (1)
type (2)
underline (2)
unload (1)
unpack (1)
use (2)
vacuum (1)
vomit (1)
vote (2)
wait (1)
walk (1)
wash (1)
watch (1)
water (1)
weed (1)
weigh (1)
wipe (2)
work (1)
wrap (3)
yield (1)

Verb Guide

Irregular Verbs

These verbs have irregular endings in the past and/or the past participle.

The Oxford Picture Dictionary List of Irregular Verbs

simple	past	past participle	simple	past	past participle
be	was	been	leave	left	left
beat	beat	beaten	lend	lent	lent
become	became	become	let	let	let
begin	began	begun	light	lit	lit
bend	bent	bent	make	made	made
bleed	bled	bled	pay	paid	paid
blow	blew	blown	picnic	picnicked	picnicked
break	broke	broken	put	put	put
build	built	built	read	read	read
buy	bought	bought	rewind	rewound	rewound
catch	caught	caught	rewrite	rewrote	rewritten
come	came	come	ride	rode	ridden
cut	cut	cut	run	ran	run
do	did	done	say	said	said
draw	drew	drawn	see	saw	seen
drink	drank	drunk	sell	sold	sold
drive	drove	driven	send	sent	sent
eat	ate	eaten	set	set	set
fall	fell	fallen	sew	sewed	sewn
feed	fed	fed	shoot	shot	shot
feel	felt	felt	sing	sang	sung
find	found	found	sit	sat	sat
fly	flew	flown	speak	spoke	spoken
get	got	gotten	stand	stood	stood
give	gave	given	sweep	swept	swept
go	went	gone	swim	swam	swum
hang	hung	hung	swing	swung	swung
have	had	had	take	took	taken
hear	heard	heard	teach	taught	taught
hide	hid	hidden	throw	threw	thrown
hit	hit	hit	wake	woke	woken
hold	held	held	wear	wore	worn
keep	kept	kept	withdraw	withdrew	withdrawn
lay	laid	laid	write	wrote	written

Index

Two numbers are shown after words in the index: the first refers to the page where the word is illustrated and the second refers to the item number of the word on that page. For example, cool [kōōl] **10**-3 means that the word *cool* is item number 3 on page 10. If only the bold page number appears, then that word is part of the unit title or subtitle, or is found somewhere else on the page. A bold number followed by ◆ means the word can be found in the exercise space at the bottom of that page.

Words or combinations of words that appear in **bold** type are used as verbs or verb phrases. Words used as other parts of speech are shown in ordinary type. So, for example, **file** (in bold type) is the verb *file*, while file (in ordinary type) is the noun *file*. Words or phrases in small capital letters (for example, HOLIDAYS) form unit titles.

Phrases and other words that form combinations with an individual word entry are often listed underneath it. Rather than repeating the word each time it occurs in combination with what is listed under it, the word is replaced by three dots (...), called an ellipsis. For example, under the word *bus*, you will find ...driver and ...stop meaning *bus driver* and *bus stop*. Under the word *store* you will find shoe... and toy..., meaning *shoe store* and *toy store*.

Pronunciation Guide

The index includes a pronunciation guide for all the words and phrases illustrated in the book. This guide uses symbols commonly found in dictionaries for native speakers. These symbols, unlike those used in pronunciation systems such as the International Phonetic Alphabet, tend to use English spelling patterns and so should help you to become more aware of the connections between written English and spoken English.

Consonants

[b] as in back [băk]	[k] as in key [kē]	[sh] as in shoe [shōō]
[ch] as in cheek [chēk]	[l] as in leaf [lēf]	[t] as in tape [tāp]
[d] as in date [dāt]	[m] as in match [măch]	[th] as in three [thrē]
[dh] as in this [dhĭs]	[n] as in neck [něk]	[v] as in vine [vīn]
[f] as in face [fās]	[ng] as in ring [rĭng]	[w] as in wait [wāt]
[g] as in gas [găs]	[p] as in park [pärk]	[y] as in yams [yămz]
[h] as in half [hăf]	[r] as in rice [rīs]	[z] as in zoo [zōō]
[j] as in jam [jăm]	[s] as in sand [sănd]	[zh] as in measure [mĕzh′ər]

Vowels

[ā] as in bake [bāk]	[ĭ] as in lip [lĭp]	[ow] as in cow [kow]
[ă] as in back [băk]	[ï] as in near [nïr]	[oy] as in boy [boy]
[ä] as in car [kär] or box [bäks]	[ō] as in cold [kōld]	[ŭ] as in cut [kŭt]
[ē] as in beat [bēt]	[ö] as in short [shört]	[ü] as in curb [kürb]
[ĕ] as in bed [bĕd]	or claw [klö]	[ə] as in above [ə bŭv′]
[ë] as in bear [bër]	[ōō] as in cool [kōōl]	
[ī] as in line [līn]	[ŏŏ] as in cook [kŏŏk]	

All the pronunciation symbols used are alphabetical except for the schwa [ə]. The schwa is the most frequent vowel sound in English. If you use the schwa appropriately in unstressed syllables, your pronunciation will sound more natural.

Vowels before [r] are shown with the symbol [¨] to call attention to the special quality that vowels have before [r]. (Note that the symbols [ä] and [ö] are also used for vowels not followed by [r], as in *box* or *claw*.) You should listen carefully to native speakers to discover how these vowels actually sound.

Stress

This index follows the system for marking stress used in many dictionaries for native speakers.

1. Stress is not marked if a word consisting of a single syllable occurs by itself.

2. Where stress is marked, two levels are distinguished:

   a bold accent [′] is placed after each syllable with primary (or strong) stress, a light accent [′] is placed after each syllable with secondary (or weaker) stress.

In phrases and other combinations of words, stress is indicated for each word as it would be pronounced within the whole phrase or other unit. If a word consisting of a single syllable is stressed in the combinations listed below it, the accent mark indicating the degree of stress it has in the phrases (primary or secondary) is shown in parentheses. A hyphen replaces any part of a word or phrase that is omitted. For example, bus [bŭs(′–)] shows that the word *bus* is said with primary stress in the combinations shown below it. The word ...driver [–drī′vər], listed under bus, shows that *driver* has secondary stress in the combination *bus driver*: [bŭs′ drī′vər].

Syllable Boundaries

Syllable boundaries are indicated by a single space or by a stress mark.

Note: The pronunciations shown in this index are based on patterns of American English. There has been no attempt to represent all of the varieties of American English. Students should listen to native speakers to hear how the language actually sounds in a particular region.

abdomen [ăb/də mən] **74**–3
above [ə bŭv/] **13**–6
accelerator [ĭk sĕl/ə rā/tər] **109**–47
ACCESSORIES [ĭk sĕs/ə rēz] **68–69**
accident [ăk/sə dənt] **102**–2
accordion [ə kör/dē ən] **120**–21
accountant [ə kown/tnt] **136**–1
acid rain [ăs/əd rān/] **126**–11
across [ə krös/] **105**–3
acrylic paint [ə krĭl/ĭk pānt/] **162**–9
act [ăkt] **140** ✦
action [ăk/shən]
...figure [–fĭg/yər] **163**–31
...story [–stör/ē] **166**–13
actor [ăk/tər] **136**–2
acupuncture [ăk/yə pŭngk/chər] **81**–G
adapter [ə dăp/tər] **164**–17
add [ăd] **58**–Q, **72**–B
addition [ə dĭsh/ən] **118**–1
address [ə drĕs/] **96**–A
address [ə drĕs/, ă/drĕs] **4**–5, **96**–7,8
adhesive bandage [əd hē/sĭv băn/dĭj] **83**–3
administrative assistant [əd mĭn/ə strā/tĭv ə sĭs/tənt] **136**–3
administrator [əd mĭn/ə strā/tər] **5** ✦
adults [ə dŭlts/, ăd/ŭlts] **22**–9
adult school [ə dŭlt/ skool/, ăd/ŭlt–] **112**–8
adventure story [əd vĕn/chər stör/ē] **166**–13
aerogramme [ër/ə grăm/] **96**–13
afternoon [ăf/tər noon/] **17**–18
aftershave [ăf/tər shāv/] **77**–28
AGE AND PHYSICAL DESCRIPTION [āj/ ən fĭz/i kəl dĭ skrĭp/shən] **22**
AIDS (acquired immunodeficiency syndrome) [ādz] **79** ✦
air [ër(/–)] **109**–59
...bag [–băg/] **108**–16
...conditioner [–kən dĭsh/ə nər] **37**–19
...conditioning [–kən dĭsh/ə nĭng] **108**–28
...letter [–lĕt/ər] **96**–13
...pollution [–pə loo/shən] **126**–10
...purifier [–pyoor/ə fī ər] **80**–4
airline [ër/līn/]
...representative [–rĕp rĭ zĕn/tə tĭv] **110**–2
...terminal [–tür/mə nəl] **110**–1
airplane [ër/plān/] **110**–9
...crash [–krăsh/] **102**–3
AIRPORT [ër/pört/] **110**
airsickness bag [ër/sĭk/nəs băg/] **110**–15
aisle [īl] **54**–5
Alaska time [ə lăs/kə tīm/] **17**–25
alfalfa [ăl făl/fə] **148**–5
algebra [ăl/jə brə] **118**–25
allergies [ăl/ər jēz] **79**–8
alley [ăl/ē] **37**–21
alligator [ăl/ə gā/tər] **131**–36
alphabet [ăl/fə bĕt/] **3**–30
ALTERATIONS [öl/tə rā/shənz] **73**
aluminum foil [ə loo/mə nəm foyl/] **55**–55
a.m. [ā/ĕm/] **16** ✦
American cheese [ə mĕr/ə kən chēz/] **53**–9
AMPHIBIANS [ăm fĭb/ē ənz] **130–131**
amusement park [ə myooz/mənt pärk/] **152**–13
anesthesiologist [ăn/əs thē/zē äl/ə jĭst] **87**–35
angle [ăng/gəl] **118**–24
angry [ăng/grē] **31**–29
animals [ăn/ə məlz] **152**–2
ANIMALS, DOMESTIC [də mĕs/tĭk ăn/ə məlz] **133**

ankle [ăng/kəl] **75**–61, **78**–18
anniversary [ăn/ə vür/sə rē] **19**–42
announcer [ə nown/sər] **152**–27
answer [ăn/sər]
...a question [–ə kwĕs/chən] **6**–H
...the door [–dhə dör/] **169**–F
answering machine [ăn/sə rĭng mə shēn/] **9**–14
answer sheet [ăn/sər shēt/] **7**–T
antacid [ănt ăs/əd] **81**–18
anteater [ănt/ē/tər] **135**–24
antelope [ăn/tə lōp/] **135**–35
antibacterial ointment [ăn/tē băk tïr/ē əl oynt/mənt] **83**–9
antihistamine cream [ăn/tī hĭs/tə mēn krēm/] **83**–10
antler [ănt/lər] **134**–16
ants [ănts] **49**–24
apartment [ə pärt/mənt]
...building [–bĭl/dĭng] **34**–5
...number [–nŭm/bər] **4**–6
APARTMENTS [ə pärt/mənts] **36–37**
apologize [ə päl/ə jīz/] **8**–I
apostrophe [ə päs/trə fē] **113**–11
appear in court [ə pïr/ ĭn kört/] **99**–C
applaud [ə plöd/] **32**–B
apple juice [ăp/əl joos/] **55**–50, **57**–5
apples [ăp/əlz] **50**–4
application [ăp/lə kā/shən] **144**–21
appointment [ə poynt/mənt] **19**–45, **85**
...book [–book/] **143**–27
apricots [ăp/rə kăts/] **50**–7
April [ā/prəl] **19**–28
archery [är/chə rē] **159**–1
architect [är/kə tĕkt/] **136**–4
area [ër/ē ə] **34**–(1, 4)
area code [ër/ē ə kōd/] **4**–10
arm [ärm] **74**–9
armadillo [är/mə dĭl/ō] **134**–8
armchair [ärm/chër/] **42**–24
around [ə rownd/] **105**–10
arrange [ə rānj/] **35**–K
arrest [ə rĕst/] **99**–A
arrival and departure monitors [ə rī/vəl ən dĭ pär/chər män/ə tərz] **110**–4
arrival time [ə rī/vəl tīm/] **111** ✦
arrive [ə rīv/] **111**–O
arrow [ăr/ō] **161**–7
art [ärt] **121**–1
artery [är/tə rē] **75**–43
artichokes [är/tə chōks/] **51**–20
artist [är/tĭst] **136**–5
art museum [ärt/ myoo zē/əm] **152**–7
ask [ăsk(/–)]
...about benefits [–ə bowt/ bĕn/ə fĭts] **141**–J
...about the hours [–ə bowt/ dhē ow/ərz] **141**–F
...a question [–ə kwĕs/chən] **6**–G
asparagus [ə spăr/ə gəs] **51**–24
assault [ə sölt/] **100**–7
assemble [ə sĕm/bəl] **140**–A
assembler [ə sĕm/blər] **136**–6
assembly line [ə sĕm/blē līn/] **146**–8
assist [ə sĭst/] **140**–B
Associate of Arts (AA) [ə sō/shē ĭt əv ärts/, –sē ĭt–] / [ā/ā/] **112** ✦
asteroid belt [ăs/tə royd bĕlt/] **127**–12
asthma [ăz/mə] **79**–11
astronaut [ăs/trə nöt/] **127**–17
astronomer [ə strän/ə mər] **127**–20

athletic [ăth lĕt′ĭk]
...shoes [–shōōz′] **68**–23
...supporter [–sə pör′tər] **67**–14
Atlantic time [ət lăn′tĭk tīm′] **17**–30
atlas [ăt′ləs] **98**–3
ATM (automated teller machine) [ā′tē′ĕm′] **97**–3
ATM card [ā′tē′ĕm′ kärd′] **97**–9
atom [ăt′əm] **119**–17
attorney [ə tür′nē] **99**–4
attractive [ə trăk′tĭv] **22**–23
audience [ö′dē əns] **32**–10
audiocassette [ö′dē ō kə sĕt′] **98**–12
audiologist [ö′dē äl′ə jĭst] **81**–32
auditorium [ö′də tör′ē əm] **5**–3
August [ö′gəst] **19**–32
aunt [ănt] **24**–10
author [ö′thər] **98**–22, **139**–64
automatic transmission
 [ö′tə măt′ĭk trănz mĭsh′ən, –trăns–] **109**
auto mechanic [ö′tō mə kăn′ĭk] **136**–7
average [ăv′rĭj]
...height [–hīt′] **22**–17
...weight [–wāt′] **22**–21
avocadoes [ä′və kä′dōz, ăv′ə–] **50**–14
ax [ăks] **150**–3
baboon [bă bōōn′] **135**–32
baby [bā′bē] **22**–2
...backpack [–băk′păk′] **95**–15
...carrier [–kăr′ē ər] **95**–14
...food [–fōōd′] **95**–28
...monitor [–măn′ə tər] **45**–9
...powder [–pow′dər] **95**–18
baby-sitter [bā′bē sĭt′ər] **136**–12
Bachelor's degree [băch′lərz də grē′] **112** ✦
back [băk(′–)] **74**–11
...support [–sə pört′] **147**–16
backache [băk′āk′] **78**–5
backhoe [băk′hō′] **149**–8
backpack [băk′păk′] **69**–28, **95**–15, **154**–15
backpacking [băk′păk′ĭng] **154**–7
backseat [băk′sēt′] **109**–38
backyard [băk′yärd′] **38**–2
bacon [bā′kən] **52**–11, **61**–7
bad [băd] **11**–18
bag [băg] (market) **55**–22, 23, **56**–7, 19 (purse) **69**–27, 28, 29
baggage claim area [băg′ĭj klām′ ĕr′ē ə] **110**–17
bagger [băg′ər] **55**–21
baggy [băg′ē] **71**–42
bag of flour [băg′ əv flow′ər] **56**–19
bags (luggage) [băgz] **111**–B
bailiff [bā′ləf] **99**–13
bake [bāk] **58**–L
baked [bākt(′–)]
...goods [–gōōdz′] **54**–6
...potato [–pə tā′tō] **61**–14
baker [bā′kər] **136**–8
bakery [bā′kə rē] **89**–16
baking products [bā′kĭng prăd′ŭkts] **55**–13
balance [băl′əns] (bank) **97**–11, (science) **119**–11
balcony [băl′kə nē] **37**–17
bald [böld] **23**–12
ball [böl] **45**–16, **161**–3, 4, 5, 12, 18, 22
ballet [bă lā′] **166**–7
ball field [böl′ fēld′] **153**–1
ballroom [böl′rōōm′] **145**–20

bananas [bə năn′əz] **50**–3
bandage [băn′dĭj] **83**–3, 12
bangs [băngz] **23**–8
BANK [băngk] **97**
bank [băngk] **88**–3
banner [băn′ər] **33**–15
barbecue [bär′bĭ kyōō′] **58**–T
barbecue grill [bär′bĭ kyōō grĭl′] **39**–7
barber shop [bär′bər shäp′] **88**–15
bar code [bär′ kōd′] **21**–4
barn [bärn] **148**–11
barrette [bə rĕt′] **76**–18
baseball [bās′böl′] **158**–9, **161**–18
...bat [–băt′] **161**–14
...cap [–kăp′] **66**–27
...card [–kärd′] **162**–11
...game [–gām′] **152**–25
basement [bās′mənt] **36** ✦
basket [băs′kət] **42**–2
basketball [băs′kət böl′] **158**–8, **161**–4
...court [–kört′] **158**–7
bass (fish) [băs] **130**–11
bass (instrument) [bās] **120**–10
bassoon [bə sōōn′] **120**–6
bat [băt] (animal) **134**–7, (baseball) **161**–14
bath [băth(′–)]
...mat [–măt′] **43**–27
...powder [–pow′dər] **76**–3
...towel [–tow′əl] **43**–12
bathe [bādh] **76**–B
bathing suit [bā′dhĭng sōōt′] **66**–26
bathrobe [băth′rōb′] **67**–8
BATHROOM [băth′rōōm′] **43**
bathtub [băth′tŭb′] **43**–2
battery [băt′ə rē] (car) **109**–43, (flashlight) **151**–40
...charger [–chär′jər] **165**–23
...pack [–păk′] **165**–22
bay [bā] **117**–9
be [bē]
...18 years old [–ā′tēn′ yïrz′ ōld′] **116**–A
...**born** [–börn′] **28**–A
...**hurt** [–hürt′] **82**–A
...**injured** [–ĭn′jərd] **82**–A
...in school [–ĭn skōōl′] **26**–J
...in shock [–ĭn shäk′] **82**–C
...released [–rĭ lēst′] **99**–H
...unconscious [–ŭn kän′shəs] **82**–B
BEACH [bēch] **155**
beach [bēch(′–)] **117**–10
...chair [–chër′] **155**–14
...towel [–tow′əl] **155**–15
...umbrella [–ŭm brĕl′ə] **155**–9
beads [bēdz] **69**–32
beak [bēk] **132**–1
beaker [bē′kər] **119**–13
beam [bēm] **149**–3
beans [bēnz] **51**–25, **54**–26
bear [bër] **134**–11
beard [bïrd] **23**–6
beat [bēt] **58**–B
beautiful [byōō′tə fəl] **11**–21
beauty shop [byōō′tē shäp′] **92** ✦
beaver [bē′vər] **134**–9
become a citizen [bĭ kŭm′ ə sĭt′ə zən] **28**–H
bed [bĕd(′–)] **44**–8

Index

...control [–kən trōl/] **86**–12
...frame [–frām/] **44**–27
...table [–tā/bəl] **86**–9
bedpan [bĕd/păn/] **86**–13
BEDROOM [bĕd/rōōm/] **44**
bedspread [bĕd/sprĕd/] **44**–11
Beef [bēf] **52**
beef ribs [bēf/ rĭbz/] **52**–5
beetle [bēt/l] **132**–19
beets [bēts] **51**–6
begin [bĭ gĭn/] **8**–B
behind [bĭ hīnd/] **13**–3
beige [bāzh] **12**–9
bell captain [bĕl/ kăp/tən] **145**–4
bellhop [bĕl/hăp/] **145**–5
below [bĭ lō/] **13**–7
belt buckle [bĕlt/ bŭk/əl] **69**–41
belts [bĕlts] **69**–11
bench [bĕnch] **153**–10
bend [bĕnd] **157**–R
berries [bĕr/ēz] **128**–20
between [bĭ twēn/] **13**–10
beverages [bĕv/rə jəz] **55**–15, **61**
bib [bĭb] **95**–8
bicycle [bī/sĭ kəl] **153**–4
big [bĭg] **11**–2
bike [bīk(/–)] **153**–4
...path [–păth/] **153**–2
...shorts [–shörts/] **67**–3
biking [bī/kĭng] **159**–4
bikini panties [bə kē/nē păn/tēz] **67**–16
bill (bird) [bĭl] **132**–1
bill (invoice) [bĭl] **21** ✦
billiards [bĭl/yərdz] **159**–2
billion [bĭl/yən] **14**
bills (paper money) [bĭlz] **20, 20** ✦
bin [bĭn] **37**–20
binder [bīn/dər] **3**–24
biohazard [bī/ō hăz/ərd] **147**–5
biology [bī äl/ə jē] **119**–1
birch [bürch] **128**–8
BIRDS, INSECTS, AND ARACHNIDS
[bürdz/ ĭn/sĕkts ən ə răk/nĭdz] **132**
birth certificate [bürth/ sər tĭf/ə kət] **29**–1
birthday [bürth/dā/] **19**–41, **169**–I
bison [bī/sən] **134**–6
black [blăk(/–)] **12**–15
...hair [–hër/] **23**–15
bladder [blăd/ər] **75**–47
blade [blād] **150**–11
blanket [blăng/kət] **44**–12
...sleeper [–slē/pər] **67**–7
bleach [blēch] **72**–8
bleachers [blē/chərz] **5**–10
bleed [blēd] **82**–M
blender [blĕn/dər] **40**–12
blind [blīnd] **22**–26
blinds [blīndz] **43**–11
blister [blĭs/tər] **78**–15
blizzard [blĭz/ərd] **103**–11
block [blăk] **107**–2
blocks [blăks] **45**–15
blond [bländ] **23**–16
blood [blŭd(/–)] **79**–15
...pressure gauge [–prĕsh/ər gāj/] **84**–12

...test [–tĕst/] **86**–17
...work [–würk/] **86**–17
bloody nose [blŭd/ē nōz/] **78**–17
blouse [blows] **64**–9
blow dryer [blō/ drī/ər] **23**–20, **76**–16
blow out [blō/ owt/] **169**–K
blue [blōō] **12**–1
blueberries [blōō/bĕr/ēz] **50**–19
blue jay [blōō/ jā/] **132**–7
blush [blŭsh] **77**–36
board game [börd/ gām/] **162**–3
boarding area [bör/dĭng ër/ē ə] **110**–6
board the plane [börd/ dhə plān/] **111**–F
boating [bō/tĭng] **154**–2
bobby pins [bäb/ē pĭnz/] **76**–19
BODY [bäd/ē] **74**–75
body lotion [bäd/ē lō/shən] **76**–7
body of water [bäd/ē əv wö/tər] **117** ✦
boil [boyl] **58**–P
bolt [bōlt] **37**–29, **150**–30, 33
bone [bōn] (body) **75**–49, (broken) **82**–P
boneless [bōn/ləs] **52** ✦
bookbag [bōōk/băg/] **69**–28
bookcase [bōōk/kās/] **3**–8, **42**–1
bookstore [bōōk/stör/] **92**–4
booth [bōōth] **60**–19, **152**–23
boots [bōōts] **68**–18
bored [börd] **31**–26
boring [bör/ĭng] **167**–29
borrow [bär/ō, bör/ō] **20** ✦
botanical gardens [bə tăn/ĭ kəl gär/dnz] **152**–4
bottle [bät/l] **56**–1, **95**–26
...of soda [–əv sō/də] **56**–13
bottled water [bät/ld wö/tər] **55**–53
bottle return [bät/l rĭ türn/] **54**–1
bounce [bowns] **156**–K
bouquet [bō kā/, bōō–] **129**–27
bow [bō] **161**–6
bowl [bōl] **41**–25
bowling [bō/lĭng] **159**–3
...ball [–böl/] **161**–5
bow tie [bō/ tī/] **69**–40
box [bäks(/–)] **56**–6
...of cereal [–əv sĭr/ē əl] **56**–18
...spring [–sprĭng/] **44**–26
boxer shorts [bäk/sər shörts/] **67**–12
boy [boy] **22**–4, 7
bra [brä] **67**–20
brace [brās] **81**–31
bracelet [brās/lət] **69**–35, **83**–14
braces [brā/səz] **84**–24
brain [brān(/–)] **75**–35
...cancer [–kăn/sər] **79**–12
brainstorm [brān/störm/] **6**–K
brake [brāk(/–)]
...light [–līt/] **108**–13
...pedal [–pĕd/l] **109**–46
branch [brănch] **128**–2
Branches of government [brăn/chəz əv gŭv/ər mənt] **116**
Brass [brăs] **120**
bread [brĕd(/–)] **53**–1, 2, 3, **54**–29
...basket [–băs/kət] **63**–8
bread-and-butter plate [brĕd/ n bŭt/ər plāt/] **63**–16
break [brāk(/–)]
...a bone [–ə bōn/] **82**–P

...three eggs [–thrē′ ĕgz′] **58**–A
Breakfast [brĕk′fəst] **61**
breast (body) [brĕst] **74**–14
breasts (chicken) [brĕsts] **52**–19
bricklayer [brĭk′lā′ər] **136**–9
bricks [brĭks] **149**–11
bridge [brĭj] **105**–2
briefs [brēfs] **67**–13, 17
broccoli [bräk′ə lē] **51**–15, **58**–I
broil [broyl] **58**–V
broiler [broy′lər] **40**–21
broken [brō′kən] **48**–5, 6, 7, **49**–15, **70**–24
broom [bro͞om] **47**–10
brother [brŭdh′ər] / [–brŭdh′ər] **24**–9
  half... [hăf′–] **25**–29
brother-in-law [brŭdh′ər ĭn lö′] **24**–16
brown [brown(′–)] **12**–11
  ...hair [–hër′] **23**–17
bruise [bro͞oz] **78**–12
brush [brŭsh(′–)]
  ...hair [–hër′] **76**–I
  ...teeth [–tēth′] **77**–J
brush [(–)brŭsh(′)] **23**–18, **76**–14
  paint... [pānt′–] **151**–47, **163**–23
  scrub... [skrŭb′–] **47**–19
  toilet... [toy′lət–] **43**–16
bucket [bŭk′ət] **47**–20, **155**–22
buckle [bŭk′əl] **69**–41
bud [bŭd] **129**–6
buffalo [bŭf′ə lō] **134**–6
buffet [bə fā′] **33**–13
building [bĭl′dĭng] **34**–5
BUILDING SUPPLIES [bĭl′dĭng sə plīz′] **150–151**
build models [bĭld′ mäd′lz] **162**–C
bulb [bŭlb] **129**–9
bulldozer [bool′dō′zər] **149**–6
bulletin board [bool′ə tn börd′] **3**–14
bumper [bŭm′pər] **108**–7
bumper pad [bŭm′pər păd′] **45**–7
bunk [bŭngk] **45**–1
Bunsen burner [bŭn′sən bür′nər] **119**–9
bureau [byoor′ō] **44**–2
burglary [bür′glə rē] **100**–6
burner [bür′nər] **40**–19
burn (your)self [bürn′ (yər)sĕlf′] **82**–H
bus [bŭs(′–)] **90**–15, **104**–4
  ...driver [–drī′vər] **104**–8
  ...stop [–stäp′] **91**–16, **104**–1
bush [boosh] **39**–20
business education [bĭz′nəs ĕj ə kā′shən] **121**–2
businessman [bĭz′nəs măn′] **136**–10
businesswoman [bĭz′nəs woom′ən] **136**–10
busperson [bŭs′pür′sən] **63**–9
butcher [booch′ər] **136**–11
butter [bŭt′ər] **54**–36
butterfly [bŭt′ər flī′] **132**–20
buttocks [bŭt′əks] **74**–12
button [bŭt′n] **73**–21
buttonhole [bŭt′n hōl′] **73**–12
buy [bī(′–)] **21**–C
  ...a house [–ə hows′] **29**–O
  ...your ticket [–yər tĭk′ət] **111**–A
Buying a house [bī′ĭng ə hows′] **35**
cab [kăb] **104**–18, **106**–16
cabbage [kăb′ĭj] **51**–2

cabinet [kăb′ə nət] **40**–1
cable [kā′bəl] **144**–16
cactus [kăk′təs] **128**–21
cafeteria [kăf′ə tĭr′ē ə] **5**–4
cake [kāk(′–)] **54**–32, **61**–19
  ...mix [–mĭks′] **55**–47
  ...pan [–păn′] **59**–26
calculator [kăl′kyə lā′tər] **142**–8
calculus [kăl′kyə ləs] **118**–28
CALENDAR [kăl′ən dər] **18–19**
calf [kăf] **74**–18
call [köl] **141**–E
call button [köl′ bŭt′n] **86**–10
calm [käm] **30**–10
camcorder [kăm′kör′dər] **165**–21
camel [kăm′əl] **135**–38
camera [kăm′rə] **165**–19, 24, 27
  ...case [–kās′] **165**–27
camisole [kăm′ə sōl′] **67**–21
camper [kăm′pər] **106**–11
campfire [kămp′fīr′] **154**–11
camping [kăm′pĭng] **154**–1
  ...stove [–stōv′] **154**–16
can [kăn(′–)] **56**–3
  ...of soup [–əv so͞op′] **56**–15
  ...opener [–ō′pə nər] **40**–14, **59**–1
cancer [kăn′sər] **79**–12
candle [kăn′dl] **41**–7
candles [kăn′dlz] **169**–H, K
candlestick [kăn′dl stĭk′] **41**–8
candy [kăn′dē] **55**–41, **168**–14
  ...bar [–bär′] **55**–41
  ...store [–stör′] **92**–3
cane [kān] **80**–7
canned goods [kănd′ go͞odz′] **54**–4
canoeing [kə no͞o′ĭng] **154**–3
cantaloupes [kăn′tə lōps′] **50**–15
can't breathe [kănt′ brēdh′] **82**–N
canteen [kăn tēn′] **154**–24
canvas [kăn′vəs] **163**–22
canyon [kăn′yən] **117**–17
cap [kăp] (graduation) **32**–3, (clothing) **66**–6
capsule [kăp′səl] **81**–27
captain [kăp′tən] **158** ✦
car [kär(′–)]
  ...accident [–ăk′sə dənt] **102**–2
  ...dealership [–dē′lər shĭp] **88**–4
  ...safety seat [–sāf′tē sēt′] **95**–13
card [kärd(′–)] **96**–4, **168**–5
  ...catalog [–kăt′l ög, –äg] **98**–10
  ...store [–stör′] **92**–7
cardigan sweater [kär′də gən swĕt′ər] **65**–27
Cardinals [kärd′nəlz] **14**
cardiologist [kär′dē äl′ə jĭst] **86**–3
cards [kärdz] **163**–H
careful [kër′fəl] **147**–24
caregiver [kër′gĭv′ər] **136**–12
careless [kër′ləs] **147**–23
CAR MAINTENANCE [kär′ mān′tn əns] **108–109**
carnation [kär nā′shən] **129**–18
carnival [kär′nə vəl] **152**–16
carousel [kăr′ə sĕl′] **110**–18
carousel slide projector [kăr′ə sĕl′ slīd′ prə jĕk′tər] **165**–29
carpenter [kär′pən tər] **48**–12, **136**–13
carpet [kär′pət] **42**–27

Index

carriage [kăr/ĭj] **95**–16
carrots [kăr/əts] **51**–3
carry [kăr/ē] **62**–H
carry-on bag [kăr/ē än băg/, –ön–] **111**–H
CARS AND TRUCKS [kärz/ ən trŭks/] **106**
cart [kärt] **54**–3, **91**–31
carton [kär/tn] **56**–4
  ...of eggs [–əv ĕgz/] **56**–16
cartoon [kär tōōn/] **167**–19
cartridge [kär/trĭj] / [–kär/trĭj] **162**–2
  typewriter... [tīp/rī/tər–] **143**–31
carving knife [kär/vĭng nīf/] **59**–12
cash [kăsh(/–)] **20**–13, **97**–D
  ...register [–rĕj/ə stər] **55**–18, **140**–N
cashier [kă shïr/] **136**–14
casserole dish [kăs/ə rōl dĭsh/] **59**–11
cassette [kə sĕt/]
  ...player [–plā/ər] **3**–11, **164**–2, 15
  ...recorder [–rĭ kör/dər] **164**–3
cast [kăst] **81**–29
casual [kăzh/ōō əl] **71**–37
cat [kăt] **133**–9
catch [kăch] **156**–E
catcher's mask [kăch/ərz măsk/] **161**–15
caterer [kā/tər ər] **33**–12
caterpillar [kăt/ə pĭl/ər, kăt/ər–] **132**–21
catfish [kăt/fĭsh/] **53**–17
cattle [kăt/l] **148**–21
cauliflower [kö/lĭ flow/ər, kä/–] **51**–16
cavity [kăv/ə te] **84**–20
C-clamp [sē/klămp/] **150**–6
CD (compact disc) [sē/dē/] **98**–14
  ...player [–plā/ər] **164**–14
  ...ROM disc [–räm/ dĭsk/] **144**–2
ceiling [sē/lĭng] **42**–5
  ...fan [–făn/] **41**–4
celery [sĕl/ə rē] **51**–9
cello [chĕl/ō] **120**–9
cellular phone [sĕl/yə lər fōn/] **9**–13
Celsius [sĕl/sē əs] **10**
cent [sĕnt] **20**–1
centimeter (cm) [sĕn/tə mē/tər] **15**–12
CENTRAL AMERICA [sĕn/trəl ə mĕr/ə kə] **122**–**123**
central time [sĕn/trəl tīm/] **17**–28
cents [sĕnts] **20**–2, 3, 4
cereal [sïr/ē əl] **56**–18
Ceremony [sĕr/ə mō/nē] **32**
Certificate of Naturalization
  [sər tĭf/ə kət əv năch/rə lə zā/shən] **29**–6
certified mail [sür/tə fīd/ māl/] **96**–11
chain [chān] (hardware) **37**–28, **150**–36, (jewelry) **69**–31
chair [(–)chër(/)] **2**–7
  dining room... [dī/nĭng rōōm/–] **41**–16
  easy... [ē/zē–] **42**–24
  high... [hī/–] **95**–7
  rocking... [räk/ĭng–] **94**–6
  swivel... [swĭv/əl–] **143**–22
chalk [chök] **3**–16
chalkboard [chök/börd/] **2**–1
  ...eraser [–ĭ rā/sər] **3**–17
change [chānj(/–)] **21**–9
  ...purse [–pürs/] **69**–25
change [chānj(/–)]
  ...diapers [–dī/pərz] **94**–E
  ...the sheets [–dhə shēts/] **46**–P

...your diet [–yər dī/ət] **80**–C
changing table [chān/jĭng tā/bəl] **45**–12, **95**–9
cheap [chēp] **11**–20
check [chĕk(/–)]
  ...blood pressure [–blŭd/ prĕsh/ər] **85**–B
  ...your bags [–yər băgz/] **111**–B
  ...your work [–yər würk/] **7**–Y
checkbook [chĕk/bŏŏk/] **97**–7
checked [chĕkt] **70**–11
checker [chĕk/ər] **55**–19
checkers [chĕk/ərz] **162**–5
check in [chĕk/ ĭn/] **111**–D
check-in counter [chĕk/ĭn kown/tər] **110**–3
checking account number [chĕk/ĭng ə kownt/ nŭm/bər] **97**–8
check out [chĕk/ owt/] **98** ✦
checkout desk [chĕk/owt dĕsk/] **98**–16
checkstand [chĕk/stănd/] **55**–17
cheddar cheese [chĕd/ər chēz/] **53**–10
cheek [chēk] **74**–29
cheese [chēz] **53**–9, 10, 11, 12, **54**–38
cheeseburger [chēz/bür/gər] **60**–3
chef [shĕf] **63**–11
chef's salad [shĕfs/ săl/əd] **61**–9
chemistry [kĕm/ə strē] **119**–2
cherries [chĕr/ēz] **50**–16
cherry picker [chĕr/ē pĭk/ər] **149**–5
chess [chĕs] **162**–6
chest (body) [chĕst] **74**–13
chest of drawers [chĕst/ əv drörz/] **45**–8
chicken [chĭk/ən] **52**–16, **61**–12
  ...soup [sōōp/] **58**
chicken pox [chĭk/ən päks/] **79**–6
Chief Justice [chēf/ jŭs/təs] **116**–9
CHILDCARE CENTER [chīld/kër sĕn/tər] **94**–**95**
childcare worker [chīld/kër wür/kər] **94**–3
Childhood diseases [chīld/hŏŏd dĭ zē/zəz] **79**
children [chĭl/drən] **11**–11, 12, **22**–1
CHILDREN'S BEDROOM [chĭl/drənz bĕd/rōōm] **45**
children's program [chĭl/drənz prō/grăm] **167**–24
child safety seat [chīld/ sāf/tē sēt/] **109**–39
chili peppers [chĭl/ē pĕp/ərz] **51**–8
chills [chĭlz] **78**–9
chimney [chĭm/nē] **38**–21
chimpanzee [chĭm/păn zē/] **135**–28
chin [chĭn] **74**–31
china cabinet [chī/nə kăb/ə nət] **41**–1
chipmunk [chĭp/mŭngk/] **133**–20
chiropractor [kī/rə prăk/tər] **81**–H
chisel [chĭz/əl] **151**–51
choke [chōk] **82**–L
chop [chäp] **58**–G
chorus [kör/əs] **121**–3
Christmas [krĭs/məs] **168**–18
  ...tree [–trē/] **168**–20
chrysanthemum [krĭ săn/thə məm] **129**–19
church [chürch] **88**–6
cigarette lighter [sĭg/ə rĕt/ lī/tər, sĭg/ə rĕt–] **108**–32
circle [sür/kəl] **7**–5
circle [sür/kəl] **118**–5
circular saw [sür/kyə lər sö/] **150**–10
circumference [sər kŭm/frəns] **118**–15
Citizen application requirements
  [sĭt/ə zən ăp/lə kā/shən rĭ kwīr/mənts] **116**
CITIZENSHIP [sĭt/ə zən shĭp/] **116**
city [sĭt/ē] **4**–7, **34**–1

...center [–sĕn/tər] **88** ✦
...hall [–höl/] **89**–17
CITY STREETS [sĭt/ē strēts/] **88–89**
claim your baggage [klām/ yər băg/ĭj] **111**–P
clams [klămz] **53**–28
clap [klăp] **32**–B
clarinet [klăr/ə nĕt/] **120**–4
CLASSROOM [klăs/rōōm/] **2–3**
classroom [klăs/rōōm/] **5**–1
Class work [klăs/ würk/] **7**
claw [klö] **132**–4
clay [klā] **162**–14
clean [klēn] (household) **27**–N, **46**–C, **72**–D, (teeth) **85**–I
clean [klēn] **72**–16
CLEANING SUPPLIES [klē/nĭng sə plīz/] **47**
cleanser [klĕn/zər] **47**–23
clear [klĭr(/–)] **10**–6
...tape [–tāp/] **143**–39
clear [klĭr] **62**–G
clear [klĭr] **10**–6
clerk [(–)klürk(/)] **5**–18
desk... [dĕsk/–] **145**–8
file... [fīl/–] **142**–12
library... [lī/brër ē–] **98**–17
shipping... [shĭp/ĭng–] **146**–15
stock... [stäk/–] **139**–55
climb [klīm] **153**–C
climbing apparatus [klī/mĭng ăp ə răt/əs] **153**–14
CLINICS [klĭn/ĭks] **84**
clipboard [klĭp/börd/] **143**–26
clip-on earrings [klĭp/än ïr/ĭngz, –ön–] **69**–38
clock [kläk(/–)] **3**–10
...radio [–rā/dē ō] **44**–16, **164**–1
close [klōz] **2**–J
closet [kläz/ət] **11**–15, 16, **43** ✦, **44**–4
cloth diapers [klöth/ dī/pərz] **95**–21
clothesline [klōz/līn/] **72**–9
clothespin [klōz/pĭn/] **72**–10
CLOTHING I, II, III [klō/dhĭng] **64–67**
cloudy [klow/dē] **10**–7
clubs [klŭbz] **163**–26
clutch [klŭch] **109**–45
coach [kōch] **5** ✦, **158**–2
coal [kōl] **126**–4
coat [kōt] (clothing) **66**, (animal) **134**–19
cobra [kō/brə] **131**–40
cockpit [käk/pĭt/] **110**–11
cockroaches [käk/rō/chəz] **49**–25
coconuts [kō/kə nŭts/] **50**–22
cod [käd] **130**–8
coffee [kö/fē] **55**–51, **61**–22
...cup [–kŭp/] **41**–27
...shop [–shäp/] **88**–2
...table [–tā/bəl] **42**–23
instant... [ĭn/stənt–] **55**–51
coffeemaker [kö/fē mā/kər] **40**–11
COFFEE SHOP MENU [kö/fē shäp/ mĕn/yōō] **61**
coin collection [koyn/ kə lĕk/shən] **162**–13
Coins [koynz] **20**
colander [käl/ən dər] **59**–17
cold [kōld] (weather) **10**–4, (feeling) **30**–4
cold (illness) [kōld(/–)] **79**–1
...tablets [–tăb/ləts] **81**–17
cold water [kōld/ wö/tər] **43**–7
coleslaw [kōl/slö/] **53**–14

collar [käl/ər] **73**–7
collate [kō/lāt/, kə lāt/] **142**–F
collect [kə lĕkt/]
...the papers [–dhə pā/pərz] **7**–Q
...things [–thĭngz/] **162**–A
collection [kə lĕk/shən] **162**–12, 13
college [käl/ĭj] **112**–10
...degree [–də grē/] **29**–7
...dormitory [–dör/mə tör/ē] **34**–9
community... [kə myōō/nə tē–] **112** ✦
cologne [kə lōn/] **76**–5
colon [kō/lən] **113**–12
color hair [kŭl/ər hër/] **23**–D
coloring book [kŭl/ə rĭng bōōk/] **45**–20
COLORS [kŭl/ərz] **12**
comb...hair [kōm/ hër/] **76**–G
comb [kōm] **23**–22, **76**–13
comedy [käm/ə dē] **166**–10
come home [kŭm/ hōm/] **27**–Q
comet [käm/ət] **127**–25
comfortable [kŭmf/tə bəl, –tər–] **30**–7
comforter [kŭm/fər tər] **45**–2
comma [käm/ə] **113**–10
commercial fisher [kə mür/shəl fĭsh/ər] **136**–15
commit a crime [kə mĭt/ ə krīm/] **100** ✦
Common illnesses and childhood diseases
[käm/ən ĭl/nə səz ən chīld/hōōd dĭ zē/zəz] **79**
community college [kə myōō/nə tē käl/ĭj] **112** ✦
compact [käm/păkt] **106**–2
compact disc (CD) [käm/păkt dĭsk/] **98**–14
compliment [käm/plə mĕnt/] **8**–G
components [kəm pō/nənts] **140**–A
composition [käm/pə zĭsh/ən] **113**–2
compost pile [käm/pōst pīl/] **39**–10
computer [kəm pyōō/tər] **3**–15
...programmer [–prō/grăm ər] **136**–16
...science [–sī/əns] **121**–4
...workstation [–würk/stā/shən] **143**–21
COMPUTERS [kəm pyōō/tərz] **144**
concert [kän/sərt] **166**–6
concierge [kän/sē ërzh/, kōn/–] **145** ✦
concrete [käng/krēt, kän krēt/] **149**–10
condiments [kän/də mənts] **60** ✦
conditioner [kən dĭsh/ə nər] **76**–10
condominium [kän/də mĭn/ē əm] **34** ✦
conductor [kən dŭk/tər] **104**–16
cone [kōn] **118**–11
confetti [kən fĕt/ē] **168**–3
confused [kən fyōōzd/] **31**–27
congestion [kən jĕs/chən] **78**–7
Congressman [käng/grəs mən] **116**–2
Congresswoman [käng/grəs wōōm/ən] **116**–2
Conservation [kän/sər vā/shən] **126**
conserve [kən sürv/] **126**–B, C
constellation [kän/stə lā/shən] **127**–24
CONSTRUCTION [kən strŭk/shən] **149**
construction worker [kən strŭk/shən wür/kər] **149**–1
contact lenses [kän/tăkt lĕn/zəz] **81**–36
container [kən tā/nər] **56**–5, **59**–3
...of cottage cheese [–əv kät/ĭj chēz/] **56**–17
CONTAINERS AND PACKAGED FOODS
[kən tā/nərz ən păk/ĭjd fōōdz/] **56**
Continents [kän/tə nənts] **124**
control tower [kən trōl/ tow/ər] **110**–7
convenience store [kən vēn/yəns stör/] **90**–3

Index

CONVERSATION, EVERYDAY [ĕv′rē dā′ kän′vər sā′shən] **8**
convertible [kən vür′tə bəl] **106**–5
convert the measurements
   [kən vürt′ dhə mĕzh′ər mənts] **57**–C
conveyor belt [kən vā′ər bĕlt′] **146**–12
convict [kən vĭkt′] **99**–14
cook [kook] **27**–P, **58**–F, **140**–C
cook [kook] **137**–17
cooked chicken [kookt′ chĭk′ən] **52**–25
cookies [kook′ēz] **54**–31, **56**–20
cookie sheet [kook′ē shēt′] **59**–27
cool [kool] **10**–3
coolant [koo′lənt] **109**–56
cooler [koo′lər] **155**–11
co-op [kō′äp′] **34** ✦
copy [käp′ē] **6**–F
copy center [käp′ē sĕn′tər] **91**–22
cord [körd] **9**–3, **151**–14
cordless phone [körd′ləs fōn′] **9**–12
core course [kör′ körs′] **121** ✦
corn [körn] **51**–27, **148**–4
corned beef [körnd′ bēf′] **53**–8
corner [kör′nər] **91**–17, **105**–10, **107**–1
corral [kə răl′] **148**–17
correct [kə rĕkt′] **7**–Z
correction fluid [kə rĕk′shən floo′əd] **143**–33
corrosive [kə rō′sĭv] **147**–4
cost [köst] **21**–6
costume [käs′toom] **168**–13
cottage cheese [kät′ĭj chēz′] **56**–17
cotton [kät′n] **70**–16, **148**–6
couch [kowch] **42**–19
cough [köf] **78**–A
cough syrup [köf′ sĭr′əp, –sür′–] **81**–20
counselor [kown′slər] **5**–16
counselor's office [kown′slərz ö′fəs] **5**–15
count [kownt] **15** ✦
counter [kown′tər] **40**–22, **46**–O, **60**–13, **80**–12, **110**–3
country [kŭn′trē] **34**–4
county fair [kown′tē fër′] **152**–19
courier [kür′ē ər, koor′–] **138**–38
court [kört(′–)] **99**–C
   ...reporter [–rĭ pör′tər] **99**–12
courthouse [kört′hows′] **89**–18
courtroom [kört′room′] **99**–7
courtyard [kört′yärd′] **37**–18
cousin [kŭz′ən] **24**–12
cover-up [kŭv′ər ŭp′] **66**–25
cow [kow] **133**–3
coyote [kī ō′tē, kī′ōt′] **134**–3
CPR (cardiopulmonary resuscitation) [sē′pē′är′] **83**–17
CPU (central processing unit) [sē′pē′yoo′] **144**–1
crab [krăb] **53**–22, **130**–16
cracked [krăkt] **48**–4
cradle [krād′l] **45**–19
crane [krān] **149**–7
crash [krăsh] **102**–3
crayons [krā′änz] **45**–21
creamer [krē′mər] **41**–13
credit card [krĕd′ət kärd′] **20**–15
creek [krēk, krĭk] **117** ✦
crescent moon [krĕs′ənt moon′] **127**–14
crewneck sweater [kroo′nĕk′ swĕt′ər] **71**–26
crib [krĭb] **45**–6
cricket [krĭk′ət] **132**–24

CRIME [krīm] **100**
criminal [krĭm′ə nəl] **100** ✦
crochet [krō shā′] **163**–20
crocodile [kräk′ə dīl′] **131**–37
crocus [krō′kəs] **129**–25
Crops [kräps] **148**
cross-country skiing [krös′kŭn′trē skē′ĭng] **160**–3
cross out [krös′ owt′] **7**–U
cross the street [krös′ dhə strēt′] **90**–A
crosswalk [krös′wök′] **90**–8
crucible tongs [kroo′sə bəl tängz′, –töngz′] **119**–15
crutches [krŭch′əz] **80**–1
cry [krī] **32**–C
cubby [kŭb′ē] **94**–4
cube [kyoob] **118**–10
cucumbers [kyoo′kŭm bərz] **51**–12
cuff [kŭf] **73**–5
cup [kŭp(′–)] **63**–21
   ...of flour [–əv flow′ər] **57**–10
   ...of oil [–əv oyl′] **57**–2
curb [kürb] **90**–10
curling iron [kür′lĭng ī′ərn] **76**–15
curly [kür′lē] **23**–11
curtains [kür′tnz] **44**–5
curved [kürvd] **118**–19
custodian [kŭ stō′dē ən] **138**–35
customs [kŭs′təmz] **110**–20
   ...officer [–ö′fə sər] **110**–21
cut [kŭt] **23**–A, **77**–N
cut [kŭt] **78**–13
cute [kyoot] **22**–24
cutting board [kŭt′ĭng börd′] **40**–27
cut up [kŭt′ ŭp′] **58**–M
cycling [sī′klĭng] **159**–4
cyclist [sī′klĭst] **153**–3
cylinder [sĭl′ən dər] **118**–12
daffodil [dăf′ə dĭl] **129**–26
DAILY ROUTINES [dā′lē roo tēnz′] **26**–**27**
dairy section [dër′ē sĕk′shən] **54**–9
daisy [dā′zē] **129**–14
dance [dăns] **33**–J
dance floor [dăns′ flör′] **33**–16
dangerous situation [dān′jər əs sĭch′oo ā′shən] **147**–8
dark blue [därk′ bloo′] **12**–2
dashboard [dăsh′börd′] **108**–17
data [dā′tə, dăt′ə] **144** ✦
date [dāt(′–)] **18**–14
   ...of birth [–əv bürth′] **4**–16
dates (fruit) [dāts] **50**–25
daughter [dö′tər] **24**–21
daughter-in-law [dö′tər ĭn lö′] **24** ✦
day [dā] **18**–10
daylight saving time [dā′līt′ sā′vĭng tīm′] **17**–33
Days of the week [dāz′ əv dhə wēk′] **18**
dead-bolt lock [dĕd′bōlt′ läk′] **37**–29
dead end [dĕd′ĕnd′] **107**–8
deaf [dĕf] **22**–27
decaf coffee [dē′kăf′ kö′fē] **61**–23
December [dĭ sĕm′bər] **19**–36
deck [dĕk] **38**–16
declaration form [dĕk′lə rā′shən förm′] **110**–22
decorate [dĕk′ə rāt′] **169**–C
deer [dïr] **134**–14
defendant [dĭ fĕn′dənt] **99**–5
defense attorney [dĭ fĕns′ ə tür′nē] **99**–4

degree [də grē/] **29**–7, **112** ✦
degrees [də grēz/]
...Celsius [–sĕl/sē əs] **10**
...Fahrenheit [–făr/ən hīt/] **10**
DELI AND SEAFOOD [dĕl/ē ən sē/fōōd/] **53**
deliver [də lĭv/ər] **96**–C
delivery person [də lĭv/ə rē pür/sən] **137**–18
dental [dĕn/təl]
...assistant [–ə sĭs/tənt] **84**–19, **137**–19
...floss [–flös/, –fläs/] **77**–22
...hygienist [–hī jē/nĭst, –jĕn/ĭst] **84**–16
Dental clinic [dĕn/təl klĭn/ĭk] **84**
DENTAL EXAMS [dĕn/təl ĭg zămz/] **85**
dentist [dĕn/tĭst] **84**–18, **137**–20
deodorant [dē ō/dər ənt] **76**–4
department store [dĭ pärt/mənt stör/] **93**–13
departure time [dĭ pär/chər tīm/] **111** ✦
deposit [dĭ päz/ət] **9**–C
deposit [dĭ päz/ət] **97**–C
...slip [–slĭp/] **97**–12
depth [dĕpth] **15**–15
DESCRIBING CLOTHES [dĭ skrī/bĭng klōz/] **70**–**71**
DESCRIBING HAIR [dĭ skrī/bĭng hĕr/] **23**
DESCRIBING THINGS [dĭ skrī/bĭng thĭngz/] **11**
desert [dĕz/ərt] **117**–4
design [dĭ zīn/] **146**–A
designated drivers [dĕz/ĭg nā/təd drī/vərz] **101** ✦
designer [dĭ zī/nər] **146**–3
desk [dĕsk(/–)] **2**–6, **142**–1
...calendar [–kăl/ən dər] **142**–6
...clerk [–klürk/] **145**–9
...pad [–păd/] **142**–7
dessert tray [dĭ zürt/ trā/] **63**–7
destination [dĕs/tə nā/shən] **111** ✦
diabetes [dī/ə bē/tēz, –təs] **79**–9
diagonal [dī ăg/ə nəl, –ăg/nəl] **118**–23
dial [dī/əl] **9**–D
dial tone [dī/əl tōn/] **9**–B
diameter [dī ăm/ə tər] **118**–17
diamonds [dī/məndz] **163**–27
diaper [dī/pər]
...pail [–pāl/] **45**–13, **95**–23
...pins [–pĭnz/] **95**–22
dice [dīs] **162**–4
dictate [dĭk/tāt] **6**–N
dictionary [dĭk/shə nër/ē] **3**–28
Dictionary work [dĭk/shə nër ē würk/] **6**
die [dī] **29**–R
dietician [dī/ə tĭsh/ən] **87**–25
difference [dĭf/rəns] **118** ✦
difficult [dĭf/ĭ kŭlt/] **11**–24
dime [dīm] **20**–3
Dimensions [də mĕn/shənz] **15**
diner [dī/nər] **62**–5
DINING AREA [dī/nĭng ër/ē ə] **41**
dining room [dī/nĭng rōōm/] **62**–2
...chair [–chër/] **41**–16
...table [–tā/bəl] **41**–17
dinner [dĭn/ər]
...fork [–förk/] **63**–25
...plate [–plāt/] **63**–15
diploma [də plō/mə] **29**–2, **32**–7
direct flight [də rĕkt/ flīt/, dī–] **111** ✦
Directions [də rĕk/shənz, dī–] **107**

DIRECTIONS AND TRAFFIC SIGNS
[də rĕk/shənz ən trăf/ĭk sīnz/, dī–] **107**
directory [də rĕk/tə rē, dī–] **9**–8, **93**–19
directory assistance (411) [də rĕk/tə rē ə sĭs/təns, dī–] **9**–8
dirty [dür/tē] **72**–15
discuss [dĭ skŭs/] **6**–L
disgusted [dĭ skŭs/təd] **30**–9
dish [dĭsh(/–)]
...drainer [–drā/nər] **40**–3
...towel [–tow/əl] **47**–22
dishroom [dĭsh/rōōm/] **63**–12
dishwasher [dĭsh/wä/shər, –wö/–] (machine) **40**–4,
(person) **63**–13
dishwashing liquid [dĭsh/wä/shĭng lĭk/wəd, –wö/–] **47**–21
disinfectant [dĭs/ən fĕk/tənt] **95**–19
disk [dĭsk(/–)] **144**–5
...drive [–drīv/] **144**–3
display case [dĭ splā/ kās/] **69**–7
disposable diapers [dĭ spō/zə bəl dī/pərz] **95**–20
dissection kit [dĭ sĕk/shən kĭt/, dī–] **119**–7
dive [dīv] **157**–5
diving mask [dī/vĭng măsk/] **155**–3
division [də vĭzh/ən] **118**–4
divorced [də vörst/] **25**–24
DJ (disc jockey) [dē/jā/] / [dĭsk/ jäk/ē] **33**–17
do [dōō(/–)]
...an experiment [–ən ĭk spër/ə mənt] **119**–A
...crafts [–krăfts/] **162**–A
...errands [–ër/əndz] **90** ✦
...homework [–hōm/würk/] **27**–T
...manual labor [–măn/yōō əl lā/bər] **140**–D
dockworker [däk/wür/kər] **137**–21
doctor [däk/tər] **84**–6, **137**–22
Doctorate [däk/tər ət] **112** ✦
dog [dög] **11**–17, 18, **133**–11
dogwood [dög/wōōd/] **128**–16
DOING THE LAUNDRY [dōō/ĭng dhə lön/drē] **72**–2
doll [däl] **45**–18
dollar [däl/ər] **20**–7
dollhouse [däl/hows/] **45**–14
doll making kit [däl/ mā/kĭng kĭt/] **162**–15
dolphin [däl/fən, döl/–] **131**–30
DOMESTIC ANIMALS AND RODENTS
[də mĕs/tĭk ăn/ə məlz ən rōd/nts] **133**
domesticated animals [də mĕs/tə kā/təd ăn/ə məlz] **133** ✦
donkey [däng/kē, dŭng/–, döng/–] **133**–2
do not enter [dōō/ nät/ ĕn/tər] **107**–4
do not wash [dōō/ nät/ wäsh/, –wösh/] **72** ✦
don't [dōnt(/–)]
...**drink** and **drive** [–drĭngk/ ən drīv/] **101**–G
...**open** [–ō/pən] **101**–F
donut shop [dō/nŭt shäp/] **91**–20
doorbell [dör/bĕl/] **38**–10
door chain [dör/ chān/] **37**–28
doorknob [dör/näb/] **37**–30
doorman [dör/măn/] **36**–10, **145**–2
dosage [dō/sĭj] **80** ✦
double boiler [dŭb/əl boy/lər] **59**–8
doughnut [dō/nŭt] **60**–15, **60** ✦
down (feathers) [down(/–)]
...jacket [–jăk/ət] **66**–15
...vest [–vĕst/] **66**–13
down (preposition) [down] **105**–8
downhill skiing [down/hĭl/ skē/ĭng] **160**–1
downstairs [down/stërz/] **38** ✦

Index

downtown [down/town/] **88** ✦
drain [drān] **43**–4
drapes [drāps] **42**–16
draw a picture [drö/ ə pĭk/chər] **6**–M
draw blood [drö/ blŭd/] **85**–G
drawer [drör] **40**–23, **44**–3
dress [(–)drĕs(/)] **64**–3
   maternity… [mə tür/nə tē–] **65**–19
dress [drĕs] **94**–J
dresser [drĕs/ər] **44**–2
dressmaker [drĕs/mā/kər] **73**–2
dress shop [drĕs/ shäp/] **92** ✦
dribble [drĭb/əl] **156**–K
drill [drĭl(/–)] **84**–21, **150**–8, 23
   …bit [–bĭt/] **150**–23
drill a tooth [drĭl/ ə tōōth/] **85**–K
drink [drĭngk(/–)] / [–drĭngk/] **60**–B
   …fluids [–flōō/ədz] **80**–B
   don't… [dōnt/–] **101**–G
dripping [drĭp/ĭng] **49**–16
drive [drīv] **26**–I, **90**–C, **140**–E
drive (computer) [drīv] **144**–3, 20
driver's [drī/vərz]
   …education [–ĕj/ə kā/shən] **121**–5
   …license [–lī/səns] **29**–4
drive-thru window [drīv/thrōō/ wĭn/dō] **90**–13
driveway [drīv/wā/] **38**–5
drop off [dräp/ öf/] **94**–A
dropper [dräp/ər] **119**–14
drought [drowt] **103**–10
drown [drown] **82**–I
drugs [drŭgz] **100**–4
drugstore [drŭg/stör/] **90**–2
drums [drŭmz] **120**–18
drumsticks [drŭm/stĭks/] **52**–22
drunk driving [drŭngk/ drī/vĭng] **100**–3
dry [drī(/–)]
   …hair [–hër/] **76**–H
   …the dishes [–dhə dĭsh/əz] **46**–N
dry [drī] **72**–18
dry-clean [drī/klēn/] **72** ✦
dry cleaners [drī/ klē/nərz] **72** ✦, **91**–24
dryer [drī/ər] **72**–4
   …sheets [–shēts/] **72**–5
Dry measures [drī/ mĕzh/ərz] **57**
drywall [drī/wöl/] **149**–18
duck [dŭk(/–)] **52**–18, **132**–13
   …pond [–pänd/] **153**–6
dump truck [dŭmp/ trŭk/] **106**–12
duplex house [dōō/plĕks hows/] **34** ✦
dust [dŭst] **46**–A
dust [dŭst(/–)]
   …mop [–mäp/] **47**–17
   …ruffle [–rŭf/əl] **44**–22
   …storm [–störm/] **10**–21
dustpan [dŭst/păn/] **47**–11
dye hair [dī/ hër/] **23**–D
eagle [ē/gəl] **132**–10
ear [ïr(/–)] **74**–28
   …infection [–ĭn fĕk/shən] **79**–3
earache [ïr/āk/] **78**–3
early [ür/lē] **17**–22
earmuffs [ïr/mŭfs/] (outdoor) **66**–12, (safety) **147**–14
earplugs [ïr/plŭgz/] **147**–13
earrings [ïr/ĭngz] **69**–37

Earth [ürth] **127**–7
earthquake [ürth/kwāk/] **102**–5
easel [ē/zəl] **163**–21
east [ēst] **107, 123, 124**
eastern time [ē/stərn tīm/] **17**–29
easy [ē/zē] **11**–23
   …chair [–chër/] **42**–24
eat [ēt(/–)] **60**–B
   …breakfast [–brĕk/fəst] **26**–E
eat out [ēt/ owt/] **62** ✦
eclipse [ĭ klĭps/]
   lunar… [lōō/nər–] **127** ✦
   solar… [sō/lər–] **127** ✦
economics [ĕk/ə näm/ĭks, ē/kə–] **121**–6
edit [ĕd/ət] **113**–B
eel [ēl] **130**–5
eggbeater [ĕg/bē/tər] **59**–20
eggplants [ĕg/plănts/] **51**–18
eggs [(–)ĕgz(/)] **54**–34
   scrambled… [skrăm/bəld–] **61**–1
eight [āt] **14**
eighteen [ā/tēn/] **14**
eighteenth [ā/tēnth/] **14**
eighth [ātth, āth] **14, 15**–1
eighty [ā/tē] **14, 15**–10
eject [ĭ jĕkt/] **165**–F
elastic bandage [ĭ lăs/tĭk băn/dĭj] **83**–12
elbow [ĕl/bō] **74**–15
elderly [ĕl/dər lē] **22**–15
Election [ĭ lĕk/shən] **115**
elective [ĭ lĕk/tĭv] **121** ✦
electric [ĭ lĕk/trĭk]
   …can opener [–kăn ō/pə nər] **40**–14
   …drill [–drĭl/] **150**–8
   …keyboard [–kē/börd/] **120**–20
   …mixer [–mĭk/sər] **40**–25
   …pencil sharpener [–pĕn/səl shär/pə nər] **142**–9
   …shaver [–shā/vər] **77**–24
electrical [ĭ lĕk/trĭ kəl] **151**–38
   …hazard [–hăz/ərd] **147**–1
   …tape [–tāp/] **151**–38
electrician [ĭ lĕk trĭsh/ən] **48**–9
ELECTRONICS AND PHOTOGRAPHY
   [ĭ lĕk trän/ĭks ən fə täg/rə fē] **164–165**
electronics store [ĭ lĕk trän/ĭks stör/] **93**–18
elementary school [ĕl/ə mĕn/trē skōōl/] **112**–5
elephant [ĕl/ə fənt] **135**–42
elevator [ĕl/ə vā/tər] **37**–34, **145** ✦
eleven [ĭ lĕv/ən] **14**
eleventh [ĭ lĕv/ənth] **14**
ellipse [ĭ lĭps/] **118**–9
elm [ĕlm] **128**–17
embarrassed [ĭm băr/əst] **31**–25
embroidery [ĭm broy/də rē] **163**–19
EMERGENCIES AND NATURAL DISASTERS [ĭ mür/jən sēz ən
   năch/rəl dĭ zăs/tərz, –năch/ər əl–] **102–103**
emergency [ĭ mür/jən sē]
   …brake [–brāk/] **109**–44
   …card [–kärd/] **111**–K
   …exit [–ĕg/zət, –ĕk/sət] **111**–J
   …medical technician (EMT)
     [–mĕd/ĭ kəl tĕk nĭsh/ən] / [ē/ĕm/tē/] **87**–26
   …service (911) [–sür/vəs] **9**–9
Emergency room [ĭ mür/jən sē rōōm/] **87**
emery board [ĕm/ə rē börd/, ĕm/rē–] **77**–30

empty [ĕmp/tē] **46**–F
empty [ĕmp/tē] **11**–10
encyclopedia [ĭn sī/klə pē/dē ə] **98**–18
end table [ĕnd/ tā/bəl] **42**–21
end the conversation [ĕnd/ dhə kän/vər sā/shən] **8**–C
ENERGY AND THE ENVIRONMENT
  [ĕn/ər jē ən dhē ĭn vī/rən mənt, –vī/ərn–] **126**
Energy resources [ĕn/ər jē rē/sör səz, –rī sör/səz] **126**
engine [ĕn/jən] **109**–41
engineer [ĕn/jə nïr/] **137**–23
English as a second language
  [ĭng/glĭsh əz ə sĕk/ənd lăng/gwĭj] **121** 7
ENGLISH COMPOSITION [ĭng/glĭsh käm/pə zĭsh/ən] **113**
ENTERTAINMENT [ĕn/tər tān/mənt] **166**–167
enter your PIN number [ĕn/tər yər pĭn/ nŭm/bər] **97**–B
entrance [ĕn/trəns] **36** ✦
Entryway [ĕn/trē wā/] **37**
envelope [ĕn/və lōp/] **96**–1, **143**–20
ENVIRONMENT [ĭn vī/rən mənt, –vī/ərn–] **126**
Equivalents [ĭ kwĭv/ə lənts] **15**
erase [ĭ rās/] **2**–H
eraser [ĭ rā/sər] **3**–21
escalator [ĕs/kə lā/tər] **93**–21
evening [ēv/nĭng] **17**–19
  ...gown [–gown/] **65**–29
every day [ĕv/rē dā/] **18**–21
EVERYDAY CONVERSATION [ĕv/rē dā/ kän/vər sā/shən] **8**
evidence [ĕv/ə dəns] **99**–9
examination table [ĭg zăm/ə nā/shən tā/bəl] **84**–13
examine [ĭg zăm/ən] **85**–F
examining room [ĭg zăm/ə nĭng rōōm/] **84**–9
exchange [ĭks chānj/] **21**–G
excited [ĭk sī/təd] **31**–23
exclamation mark [ĕk/sklə mā/shən märk/] **113**–8
Excuse me. [ĭk skyōōz/ mē] **8**
Executive [ĭg zĕk/yə tĭv] **116**
exercise [ĕk/sər sīz/] **27**–W, **80**–D, **157**–P
exhausted [ĭg zö/stəd] **30** ✦
exhibition [ĕk/sə bĭsh/ən] **152**–21
expensive [ĭk spĕn/sĭv] **11**–19
experience turbulence [ĭk spïr/ē əns tür/byə ləns] **111**–N
expiration date [ĕk/spə rā/shən dāt/] **80** ✦
Exploration [ĕk/splə rā/shən] **114**
explosion [ĭk splō/zhən] **102**–4
Express Mail [ĭk sprĕs/ māl/] **96**–15
extension cord [ĭk stĕn/shən körd/] **151**–14
exterminate [ĭk stür/mə nāt/] **49** ✦
exterminator [ĭk stür/mə nā/tər] **49**–21
extra [ĕk/strə]
  ...large [–lärj/] **70**–5
  ...small [–smöl/] **70**–1
extract a tooth [ĭk străkt/ ə tōōth/] **85** ✦
eye [ī(/–)] / [–ī/] **73**–23, **74**–27
  ...chart [–chärt/] **84**–11
  ...glasses [–glăs/əz] **81**–35
  ...hook [–hōōk/] **150**–35
  ...shadow [–shăd/ō] **77**–34
  hook and... [hōōk/ ən–] **73**–23
eyebrow [ī/brow/] **74**–32
  ...pencil [–pĕn/səl] **77**–33
eyedrops [ī/dräps/] **81**–22
eyelashes [ī/lăsh/əz] **74**–34
eyelid [ī/lĭd/] **74**–33
eyeliner [ī/lī/nər] **77**–35
fabric softener [făb/rĭk sö/fə nər] **72**–6

Face [fās] **74, 77**
face powder [fās/ pow/dər] **77**–39
FACTORY [făk/tə rē, –trē] **146**
factory [făk/tə rē, –trē]
  ...owner [–ō/nər] **146**–2
  ...worker [–wür/kər] **146**–6
fall [föl] **82**–O
fall [föl] **19**–39
fall in love [föl/ ĭn lŭv/] **28**–K
FAMILY [făm/lē, făm/ə lē] **24**–25
fan [făn] (appliance) **41**–4, (person) **158**–4
fancy [făn/sē] **71**–39
fare [fër(/–)] **104**–5
  ...card [–kärd/] **104**–12
far from [fär/ frŭm/, –frəm] **13** ✦
farm [färm(/–)] **34**–13
  ...equipment [–ĭ kwĭp/mənt] **148**–10
Farm animals [färm/ ăn/ə məlz] **133**
farmer [fär/mər] **148**–15
FARMING AND RANCHING [fär/mĭng ən răn/chĭng] **148**
farmworker [färm/wür/kər] **148**–8
fashion designer [făsh/ən dĭ zī/nər] **73** ✦
fast [făst] **11**–3
fasten your seat belt [făs/ən yər sēt/ bĕlt/] **111**–I
FAST FOOD [făst/ fōōd/] **60**
fast food restaurant [făst/ fōōd/ rĕs/tə rənt, –ränt] **90**–14
fast forward [făst/ för/wərd] **165**–C
fat [făt] **11**–7
father [fä/dhər] **24**–6, **25**–26
father-in-law [fä/dhər ĭn lö/] **24**–14
faucet [fö/sət] **43**–6, **49**–16
fax [făks] **142**–B
fax machine [făks/ mə shēn/] **143**–23
feast [fēst] **168**–16
feather [fĕdh/ər] **132**–5
  ...duster [–dŭs/tər] **47**–1
February [fĕb/yōō ër/ē, fĕb/rōō–] **19**–26
feed [fēd] **94**–D, **148**–D
feel [fēl(/–)]
  ...dizzy [–dĭz/ē] **78**–C
  ...nauseous [–nö/shəs, –zē əs] **78**–D
FEELINGS [fē/lĭngz] **30**–31
feet [fēt] **15** ✦
female [fē/māl/] **4**–14
fence [fĕns] **38**–3, **148**–19
fencing [fĕn/sĭng] **159**–5
ferry [fĕr/ē] **104**–23
fever [fē/vər] **78**–8
fiction [fĭk/shən] **98, 166**
field [fēld] (school) **5**–12, (farm) **148**–7, (sports) **159**–17
fifteen [fĭf/tēn/] **14**
fifteenth [fĭf/tēnth/] **14**
fifth [fĭfth] **14**
fifty [fĭf/tē] **14**
  ...dollars [–däl/ərz] **20**–11
  ...percent [–pər sĕnt/] **15**–9
figure skating [fĭg/yər skā/tĭng] **160**–5
figurine [fĭg/yə rēn/] **162**–10
file [fīl] **142**–H
file [fīl(/–)]
  ...cabinet [–kăb/ə nət] **142**–10
  ...clerk [–klürk/] **142**–12
  ...folder [–fōl/dər] **142**–11
filet of sole [fĭ lā/ əv sōl/] **53**–21
fill a cavity [fĭl/ ə kăv/ə tē] **85**–L

Index

fill in the blank [fĭl′ ĭn dhə blăngk′] **7**–R
fill out [fĭl′ owt′] / [fĭl′ owt′–]
...a form [–ə förm′] **4**–B
...an application [–ən ăp′lə kā′shən] **141**–G
filling [fĭl′ĭng] **84**–22
film [fĭlm] (camera) **165**–26, (movie) **166**–1
fin [fĭn] **130**–1
find your seat [fīnd′ yər sēt′] **111**–G
FINDING A HOME [fīn′dĭng ə hōm′] **35**
fingernail [fĭng′gər nāl′] **75**–58
fingers [fĭng′gərz] **75**–57
finish [fĭn′ĭsh] **157**–Z
fins [fĭnz] **155**–2
fire [fīr(′–)] **42**–10, **102**–7
...escape [–ī skāp′] **36**–7
...exit [–ĕg/zət, –ĕk/sət] **37**–23
...extinguisher [–ĭk stĭng′gwĭ shər] **147**–22
...hydrant [–hī′drənt] **91**–28
...screen [–skrēn′] **42**–11
...station [–stā′shən] **88**–1
...truck [–trŭk′] **102**–9
firefighter [fīr′fī′tər] **102**–8, **137**–24
fireplace [fīr′plās′] **42**–9
fireworks [fīr′würks′] **168**–8
first [fürst(′–)] **14**
...draft [–drăft′] **113**–A
...floor [–flör′] **36**–1
...name [–nām′] **4**–2
...place [–plās′] **152**–20
...prize [–prīz′] **152**–20
FIRST AID [fürst′ ād′] **83**
first aid [fürst′ ād′]
...kit [–kĭt′] **83**–1
...manual [–măn′yōō əl] **83**–7
Fish [fĭsh] **53**
fish [fĭsh] **61**–17, **130**–12, 14, 15
fishing [fĭsh′ĭng] **154**–5
...net [–nĕt′] **154**–17
...pole [–pōl′] **154**–18
fitted sheet [fĭt′əd shēt′] **44**–14
fittings [fĭt′ĭngz] **151**–17
five [fīv(′–)] **14**–5, 20
...after one [–ăf′tər wŭn′] **16**–5
...to two [tə tōō′] **16**–15
Five ways to cook chicken [fīv′ wāz′ tə kōōk′ chĭk′ən] **58**
fix [fĭks] **49** ✦
flag [flăg] **168**–9
flammable [flăm′ə bəl] **147**–2
flashlight [flăsh′līt′] **151**–39
flat sheet [flăt′ shēt′] **44**–13
flea market [flē′ mär/kət] **152**–22
fleas [flēz] **49**–23
flight attendant [flīt′ ə tĕn/dənt] **110**–13
flood [flŭd] **103**–16
floor [flör(′–)] / [–flör′] **44**–24
...lamp [–lămp′] **42**–15
...plan [–plăn′] **38**–1
dance... [dăns′–] **33**–16
floppy [flăp′ē] **144**–5
floral [flör′əl] **70**–12
florist [flör′ĭst] **92**–12, **137**–25
floss [flös, fläs] **77**–K
flounder [flown′dər] **130**–13
flour [flow′ər] **55**–45, **57**–10
flower [flow′ər] **39**–19, **129**–7

...bed [–bĕd′] **39**–A
...pot [–pät′] **39**–18
Parts of a... [pärts′ əv ə–] **129**
FLOWERS [flow′ərz] **129**
flu [flōō] **79**–2
fluid ounce [flōō′əd owns′] **57**–1
flute [flōōt] **120**–3
fly [flī] **140** ✦
fly [flī] **132**–29
flying disc [flī′ĭng dĭsk′] **159**–6, **161**–27
foam pad [fōm′ păd′] **154**–13
foggy [fö′gē, fäg′ē–] **10**–11
fold [fōld] **72**–F
Follow directions [fäl′ō də rek′shənz, –dī–] **7**
food [fōōd(′–)]
...court [–kört′] **93**–14
...processor [–prä′sĕ sər] **40**–26
FOOD PREPARATION [fōōd′ prĕp ə rā′shən] **58**
Foot [fōōt] **75**
foot [fōōt] (measurement) **15** ✦, (body) **74**–7
football [fōōt′böl′] **158**–11, **161**–22
...helmet [–hĕl′mət] **161**–20
forceps [för′səps, –sĕps] **119**–8
forehead [för′əd, –hĕd′, fär′–] **74**–20
foreign language [för′ən lăng′gwĭj, fär′–] **121**–8
forest [för′əst, fär′–] **117**–11
fork [förk] **41**–21, **63**–24, 25, ✦
forklift [förk′lĭft′] **146**–14
form [(–)förm(′)]
declaration... [dĕk′lə rā′shən–] **110**–22
registration... [rĕj′ə strā′shən–] **4**
formal [för′məl] **71**–36
former husband [för′mər hŭz′bənd] **25** ✦
former wife [för′mər wīf′] **25** ✦
formula [för′myə lə] **95**–25, **119**–19
forty [för′tē] **14**, **16**–12
foundation [fown dā′shən] **77**–40
fountain [fown′tn] / [–fown′tn] **92**–11
water... [wö′tər–] **153**–11
four [för] **14**
fourteen [för′tēn′] **14**
fourteenth [för′tēnth′] **14**
fourth [förth(′–)] **14**, **15**–2
...floor [–flör′] **36**–4
fox [fäks] **134**–15
Fractions [frăk′shənz] **15**
freezer [frē′zər] **40**–10
freezing [frē′zĭng] **10**–5
french fries [frĕnch′ frīz′] **60**–2
French horn [frĕnch′ hörn′] **120**–15
fresh [frĕsh] **53**–29
Friday [frī′dā, –dē] **18**–6
fried [frīd] **61**–17
frog [frög, fräg] **130**–25
front... [frŭnt(′–)]
...desk [–dĕsk′] **145**–8
...door [–dör′] **38**–11
...office [–ö′fəs] **146**–1
...seat [–sēt′] **109**–35
...walk [–wök′] **38**–14
...yard [–yärd′] **38**–15
frozen [frō′zən]
...fish [–fĭsh′] **53**–30
...foods [–fōōdz′] **55**–12
...vegetables [–vĕj′tə bəlz] **55**–43

...yogurt [–yō/gərt] **60**–11
FRUIT [frōot] **50**
frustrated [frŭs/trā/təd] **31**–28
fry [frī] **58**–5
frying pan [frī/ĭng păn/] **59**–5
fuel injection system [fyōo/əl ĭn jĕk/shən sĭs/təm] **109**–40
full [fŏol] (not empty) **11**–9, (satisfied) **30**–6
full [fŏol(/–)]
...moon [–mōon/] **127**–16
...slip [–slĭp/] **67**–22
full-size car [fŏol/sīz/ kär/] **106**–4
funnel [fŭn/əl] **119**–12
funny [fŭn/ē] **167**–27
fur [für] **134**–19
furious [fyŏor/ē əs] **30** ✦
furniture [für/nĭ chər] / [–für/nĭ chər] **35**–K
...polish [–päl/ĭsh] **47**–18
...store [–stör/] **88**–13
patio... [păt/ē ō–] **39**–5
fuse box [fyōoz/ bäks/] **48**–13
galaxy [găl/ək sē] **127**–26
gallbladder [göl/blăd/ər] **75**–40
gallon [găl/ən] **57**–5
game [gām(/–)] **152**–18
...show [–shō/] **167**–23
GAMES [gām(/–)] **162**–163
gang violence [găng/ vī/ə ləns] **100**–2
garage [gə räzh/, –räj/] / [–gə räzh/, –räj/] **36, 38**–6
...door [–dör/] **38**–7
garbage [gär/bĭj] **46**–Q
...can [–kăn/] **39**–3
...disposal [–dĭ spō/zəl] **40**–5
...truck [–trŭk/] **91**–27
garden [gär/dn] (vegetable) **148**–12, (botanical) **152**–4
gardener [gärd/nər, gär/dn ər] **137**–26, **152**–6
gardenia [gär dēn/yə] **129**–16
gargle [gär/gəl] **77**–L
garlic [gär/lĭk] **51**–29
...bread [–brĕd/] **61**–16
...press [–prĕs/] **59**–10
garment worker [gär/mənt wür/kər] **73** ✦, **137**–27
garter belt [gär/tər bĕlt/] **67**–19
garter snake [gär/tər snāk/] **131**–39
gas [găs(/–)] / [–găs/] **109**–54
...gauge [–gāj/] **108**–22
...meter [–mē/tər] **48**–14
...pedal [–pĕd/l] **109**–47
...station [–stā/shən] **88**–12, **137**–28
...station attendant [–stā/shən ə tĕn/dənt] **137**–28
...tank [–tăngk/] **108**–12
natural... [năch/rəl–, năch/ər əl–] **126**–3
gate [gāt] (garage) **36**, (airport) **110**–5, **111**–D
gauge [gāj] **84**–12, **108**–19, 22, 23
gauze [göz] **83**–6
gearshift [gïr/shĭft/] **108**–27
GEOGRAPHY [jē äg/rə fē] **117**
geometry [jē äm/ə trē] **118**–26
geothermal energy [jē/ō thür/məl ĕn/ər jē] **126**–7
get [gĕt(/–)]
...a checkup [–ə chĕk/ŭp/] **85** ✦
...acupuncture [–ăk/yə pŭngk/chər] **81**–G
...a job [–ə jäb/] **28**–G
...a loan [–ə lōn/] **35**–I
...an electric shock [–ən ĭ lĕk/trĭk shäk/] **82**–F
...an injection [–ən ĭn jĕk/shən] **80**–E
...an X ray [–ən ĕks/ rā/] **85**–H
...bed rest [–bĕd/ rĕst/] **80**–A
...feedback [–fēd/băk/] **113**–C
...frostbite [–fröst/bīt/] **82**–G
...home [–hōm/] **27**–Q
...your boarding pass [–yər bör/dĭng păs/] **111**–E
get dressed [gĕt/ drĕst/] **26**–D
get hired [gĕt/ hīrd/] **141**–L
get married [gĕt/ măr/ēd] **28**–L
get up [gĕt/ ŭp/] **26**–B
gift [gĭft(/–)] **169**–D
...shop [–shäp/] **145**–7
gifts [gĭfts] **33**–18
gills [gĭlz] **130**–2
giraffe [jə răf/] **135**–33
girder [gür/dər] **149**–3
girdle [gür/dl] **67**–18
girl [gürl] **22**–5, 8
give [gĭv(/–)] **21**–D
...a shot of anesthetic [–ə shät/ əv ăn/əs thet/ĭk] **85**–J
...a speech [–ə spēch/] **32**–E
...the verdict [–dhə vür/dĭkt] **99**–E
gizzards [gĭz/ərdz] **52**–23
glass [glăs(/–)] **11**–9, 10, **41**–26, **63**–19, 20, ✦
...cleaner [–klē/nər] **47**–8
glasses [glăs/əz] **81**–35
globe [glōb] **3**–9
glove [glŭv(/–)] **161**–17
...compartment [–kəm pärt/mənt] **108**–33
gloves [glŭvz] **66**–5
glue [glōo] **143**–37, **162**–8
go [gō(/–)]
...on an interview [–än ən ĭn/tər vyōo/, –ön–] **141**–H
...straight [–strāt/] **107**–A
...through security [–thrōo sĭ kyŏor/ə tē] **111**–C
...to a chiropractor [–tōo ə kī/rə prăk/tər] **81**–H
...to bed [–tə bĕd/] **27**–X
...to college [–tə käl/ĭj] **28**–J
...to jail [–tə jāl/] **99**–G
...to prison [–tə prĭz/ən] **99**–G
...to sleep [–tə slēp/] **27**–Y
...to the market [–tə dhə mär/kət] **26**–L
...to work [–tə würk/] **26**–I
goat [gōt] **133**–1
goggles [gäg/əlz] **147**–9
goldfish [gōld/fĭsh/] **133**–16
golf [gälf(/–), gölf(/–)] **159**–7
...club [–klŭb/] **161**–1
good [gŏod] **11**–17
good-bye [gŏod bī/, gə–] **8**
goose [gōos] **132**–14
gopher [gō/fər] **133**–19
gorilla [gə rĭl/ə] **135**–30
gown [gown] **32**–2, **65**–29
graduate [grăj/ōo āt/] **28**–D, **32**–A
graduate [grăj/ōo ət] **32**–6
...school [–skōol/] **112** ✦
graduated cylinder [grăj/ōo ā/təd sĭl/ən dər] **119**–10
graduating class [grăj/ōo ā/tĭng klăs/] **32**–1
GRADUATION [grăj/ōo ā/shən] **32**–33
grams [grămz] **57** ✦
grandchild [grăn/chīld/, grănd/–] **29**–Q
granddaughters [grăn/dö/tərz] **24** ✦
grandfather [grăn/fä/dhər, grănd/–] **24**–3
grandmother [grăn/mŭdh/ər, grănd/–] **24**–2

grandparents [grăn/për/ənts, grănd/–] **24**–1
grandson [grăn/sŭn/, grănd/–] **24**–7
grapefruit [grāp/frōot/] **50**–9
grapes [grāps] **50**–1
graphic artist [grăf/ĭk är/tĭst] **137**–29
grasshopper [grăs/häp/ər] **132**–25
grate [grāt] **58**–J
grater [grā/tər] **59**–2
gray [grā(/–)] **12**–5
...hair [–hër/] **23**–13
grease [grēs] **58**–C
green [grēn] **12**–8
greenhouse [grēn/hows/] **152**–5
green salad [grēn/ săl/əd] **60**–8
greeting card [grē/tĭng kärd/] **96**–4
greet someone [grēt/ sŭm/wŭn] **8**–A
grill [grĭl] **58**–T
grilled cheese sandwich [grĭld/ chēz/ săn/wĭch, –sănd/–] **61**–8
ground beef [grownd/ bēf/] **52**–4
ground post [grownd/ pōst/] **96**–14
grower [grō/ər] **148**–15
guard [gärd] **97**–4, **99**–3
guest [gĕst(/–)] **32**–9, **145**–11
...room [–rōom/] **145**–10
...speaker [–spē/kər] **32**–9
guests [gĕsts] **33**–14, **169**–B
guilty [gĭl/tē] **99**
guinea pig [gĭn/ē pĭg/] **133**–14
guitar [gĭ tär/] **120**–11
gum [gŭm] **55**–42
gums [gŭmz] **74**–24
gun [gŭn] **100**–9
gurney [gür/nē] **87**–28
gutter [gŭt/ər] **38**–19
gym [jĭm] **5**–9
gymnastics [jĭm năs/tĭks] **159**–8
gynecologist [gī/nə käl/ə jĭst] **86** ✦
hacksaw [hăk/sö/] **150**–5
hail [hāl] **10**–19
hail a taxi [hāl/ ə tăk/sē] **104** ✦
hailstorm [hāl/störm/] **10**–18
hair [hër(/–)] **23**, **74**–19
...clip [–klĭp/] **76**–17
...gel [–jĕl/] **76**–11
...net [–nĕt/] **147**–18
...salon [–sə län/] **23** ✦, **93**–16
...spray [–sprā/] **76**–12
...stylist [–stī/lĭst] **23** ✦
hairdresser [hër/drĕs/ər] **137**–30
half [hăf(/–)] **15**–4, **16**–10, **20**–5
...bath [–băth/] **43** ✦
...brother [–brŭdh/ər] **25**–29
...cup of raisins [–kŭp/ əv rā/zənz] **57**–9
...past one [–păst/ wŭn/] **16**
...sister [–sĭs/tər] **25**–30
...slip [–slĭp/] **67**–23
halibut [hăl/ə bət] **53**–20
hall [höl] **89**–17, **145**–13
Halloween [hăl/ə wēn/, häl/–] **168**–10
Hallway [höl/wā/] **37**
ham [hăm] **52**–9
hamburger [hăm/bür/gər] **60**–1
hammer [hăm/ər] **149**–D
hammer [hăm/ər] **150**–1
hammock [hăm/ək] **39**–2

hamper [hăm/pər] **43**–1
Hand [hănd] **75**
hand [hănd(/–)] **2**, **11**, **74**–8
...towel [–tow/əl] **43**–13
...truck [–trŭk/] **146**–11
handbags [hănd/băgz/] **69**–6
handcuffs [hănd/kŭfs/] **99**–2
handicapped parking [hăn/dē kăpt pär/kĭng] **107**–14
handkerchief [hăng/kər chĭf, –chēf/] **69**–42
handsaw [hănd/sö/] **150**–4
hanger [hăng/ər] **72**–11
hang up [hăng/ ŭp/] / [hăng/ ŭp/–]
...the clothes [–dhə klōz/] **72**–H
...the receiver [–dhə rĭ sē/vər] **9**–F
happy [hăp/ē] **31**–32
Happy Birthday [hăp/ē bürth/dā] **169**
hard [härd] (surface) **11**–5, (difficult) **11**–24
hard [härd(/–)]
...disk drive [–dĭsk/ drīv/] **144**–20
...hat [–hăt/] **147**–19
Hardware [härd/wër/] **144**
hardware [härd/wër/] **150**
...store [–stör/] **88**–14
harvest [här/vəst] **148**–B
hat [hăt] **66**–1
hats [hăts] **68**–5
have [hăv(/–)]
...a baby [–ə bā/bē] **29**–M
...a grandchild [–ə grăn/chīld/, grănd/–] **29**–Q
...a heart attack [–ə härt/ ə tăk/] **82**–D
...an allergic reaction [–ən ə lür/jĭk rē ăk/shən] **82**–E
...a picnic [–ə pĭk/nĭk] **153**–D
...dinner [–dĭn/ər] **27**–R
Hawaii-Aleutian time [hə wī/ē ə lōo/shən tīm/] **17**–24
hay [hā] **148**–18
hazardous [hăz/ər dəs]
...materials [–mə tïr/ē əlz] **147**–7
...waste [–wāst/] **126**–9
head [hĕd] **74**–1
headache [hĕd/āk/] **78**–1
headboard [hĕd/börd/] **44**–15
headlight [hĕd/līt/] **108**–5
headphones [hĕd/fōnz/] **164**–16
HEALTH CARE [hĕlth/ kër/] **80**–81
health [hĕlth(/–)]
...club [–klŭb/] **89**–21
...insurance card [–ĭn shōor/əns kärd/] **84**
hear [hïr] **75**–B
hearing aid [hïr/ĭng ād/] **81**–33
hearing impaired [hïr/ĭng ĭm përd/] **22**–27
heart (symbol) [härt] **168**–6
heart (body) [härt(/–)] **75**–38, **79**–14
...disease [–dĭ zēz/] **79**–14
listen to... [lĭs/ən tə–] **85**–D
hearts [härts] **163**–29
heater [hē/tər] **48**–1, **108**–29
heating pad [hē/tĭng păd/] **80**–3
heat wave [hēt/ wāv/] **10**–15
heavy [hĕv/ē] **11**–13, **71**–41
...machinery [–mə she/nə rē] **140**–F
heavyset [hĕv/ē sĕt/] **22**–20
hedge [hĕj(/–)] **39**–1
...clippers [–klĭp/ərz] **39**–12
heel [hēl] (shoe) **68**–13, (foot) **75**–62
height [hīt] **15**–14, **22**

Heimlich maneuver [hīm/lĭk mə noo/vər] **83**–18
helicopter [hĕl/ə kăp/tər] **110**–8
hello [hə lō/, hĕ–] **8**
help [hĕlp] **6**–J
help wanted sign [hĕlp/ wän/təd sīn/, –wön/–] **141**–C
hemline [hĕm/līn/] **73**–1
hen [hĕn] **133**–5
Hi! [hī] **8**
hibiscus [hī bĭs/kəs, hĭ–] **129**–12
hide [hīd] **169**–E
high [hī(/–)]
   …chair [–chër/] **95**–7
   …heels [–hēlz/] **68**–17, **71**–47
high blood pressure [hī/ blŭd/ prĕsh/ər] **79**–15
high-rise building [hī/rīz/ bĭl/dĭng] **89**–25
high school [hī/ skool/] **112**–7
hiking [hī/kĭng] **154**–6
   …boots [–boots/] **68**–21
hills [hĭlz] **117**–16
hip [hĭp] **74**–5
hippopotamus [hĭp/ə pät/ə məs] **135**–43
hire [hīr] **99**–B
hired hand [hīrd/ hănd/] **148**–20
hit [hĭt] **156**–G
HIV (human immunodeficiency virus) [ăch/ī/vē/]
   [hyoo/mən ĭm/yə nō dĭ fĭsh/ən sē vī/rəs] **79**–10
HOBBIES AND GAMES [häb/ēz ən gāmz/] **162**–163
hockey stick [häk/ē stĭk/] **161**–11
hold [hōld] **94**–B, **101**–C
holiday [häl/ə dā/] **19**–43, 44
HOLIDAYS [häl/ə dāz/] **168**
holly [häl/ē] **128**–19
home [hōm(/–)]
   …attendant [–ə tĕn/dənt] **137**–31
   …economics [–ĕk/ə näm/ĭks, –ē/kə–] **121**–9
homemaker [hōm/mā/kər] **137**–32
homesick [hōm/sĭk/] **31**–21
honeybee [hŭn/ē bē/] **132**–26
hood [hood] **108**–6
hoof [hoof] **134**–17
hook [hook(/–)] **150**–34, 35
   …and eye [–ən ī/] **73**–23
horn [hörn] (car) **108**–24, (music) **120**–13, (animal) **134**–21
horror story [hör/ər stör/ē, här/–] **166**–14
horse [hörs(/–)] **133**–4
   …racing [–rā/sĭng] **159**–18
horseback riding [hörs/băk rī/dĭng] **154**–9
hose [hōz] **39**–9
HOSPITAL [häs/pĭ tl] **86**–87
hospital [häs/pĭ tl] **88**–7
   …bed [–bĕd/] **86**–11
   …gown [–gown/] **86**–15
Hospital staff [häs/pĭ tl stăf/] **86**
hostess [hō/stəs] **62**–1
hot [hät] (weather) **10**–1, (feeling) **30**–1
hot dog [hät/ dög/] **60**–6
HOTEL [hō tĕl/] **145**
hotel [hō tĕl/] **88**–5
hot water [hät/ wö/tər] **43**–5
hour [ow/ər] **16**–3
HOUSE [hows] **38**
house [(–)hows(/)] **34**–6
   buy a… [bī/ ə–] **29**–O
   clean the… [klēn/ dhə–] **27**–N
Household Pests [hows/hōld/ pĕsts/] **49**

HOUSEHOLD PROBLEMS AND REPAIRS
   [hows/hōld/ präb/ləmz ən rĭ përz/] **48**–49
housekeeper [hows/kē/pər] **138**–33, **145**–15
housekeeping cart [hows/kē/pĭng kärt/] **145**–14
House of Representatives [hows/ əv rĕp/rĭ zĕn/tə tĭvz] **116**–1
houseplant [hows/plănt/] **129**–29
HOUSEWORK [hows/würk/] **46**
hubcap [hŭb/kăp/] **108**–9
hug [hŭg] **33**–G
humid [hyoo/məd] **10**–12
humidifier [hyoo mĭd/ə fī/ər] **80**–2
humiliated [hyoo mĭl/ē ā/təd] **30** ✦
hummingbird [hŭm/ĭng bürd/] **132**–11
hump [hŭmp] **135**–51
hundred [hŭn/drəd] **14**
hungry [hŭng/grē] **30**–5
hurricane [hür/ə kān/] **103**–12
hurt [hürt] (feeling) **30**–17, (medical) **82**–A
husband [hŭz/bənd] **24**–19
hydrant [hī/drənt] **91**–28
hydroelectric power [hī/drō ĭ lĕk/trĭk pow/ər] **126**–5
hydrogen peroxide [hī/drə jən pə räk/sīd] **83**–8
hyena [hī ē/nə] **135**–31
hygienist [hī jē/nĭst, –jĕn/ĭst] **84**–16
hypertension [hī/pər tĕn/shən] **79** ✦
hypoallergenic [hī/pō ăl/ər jĕn/ĭk] **77** ✦
I beam [ī/ bēm/] **149**–3
ice [īs(/–)]
   …hockey [–häk/ē] **158**–13
   …machine [–mə shēn/] **145**–18
   …pack [–păk/] **83**–13
   …skates [–skāts/] **161**–9
   …skating [–skā/tĭng] **160**–4
ice cream [īs/ krēm/] **55**–44
ice cream stand [īs/ krēm stănd/] **93**–20
iced tea [īst/ tē/] **60**–5
icy [ī/sē] **10**–13
ignition [ĭg nĭsh/ən] **108**–25
illegal drugs [ĭ lē/gəl drŭgz/] **100**–4
ILLNESSES AND MEDICAL CONDITIONS
   [ĭl/nə səz ən mĕd/ĭ kəl kən dĭsh/ənz] **79**
immigrate [ĭm/ə grāt/] **28**–C
Immigration [ĭm/ə grā/shən] **114**
immunization [ĭm/yə nə zā/shən] **80** ✦
in [ĭn] **13**–5
   …fashion [–făsh/ən] **64** ✦
   …front of [–frŭnt/ əv] **13**–4
   …love [–lŭv/] **28**–K, **30**–19
   …pain [–pān/] **30**–12
   …shock [–shäk/] **82**
inch (in.) [ĭnch] **15**–13
Independence Day [ĭn/də pĕn/dəns dā/] **168**–7
INDIVIDUAL SPORTS [ĭn/də vĭj/oo əl spörts/] **159**
industrial arts [ĭn dŭs/trē əl ärts/] **121**–10
infectious disease [ĭn fĕk/shəs dĭ zēz/] **79** ✦
influenza [ĭn/floo ĕn/zə] **79** ✦
information booth [ĭn/fər mā/shən booth/] **93**–22
ingredients [ĭn grē/dē ənts] **58**–K
INJURIES [ĭn/jə rēz] **78**
ink pad [ĭngk/ păd/] **143**–41
inline [ĭn/līn/]
   …skates [–skāts/] **161**–10
   …skating [–skā/tĭng] **159**–9
inquire about the salary [ĭn kwīr/ ə bowt/ dhə săl/ə rē] **141**–K
insect [ĭn/sĕkt]

Index

...bite [–bīt/] **78**–11
...repellent [–rĭ pĕl/ənt] **154**–23
INSECTS [ĭn/sĕkts] **132**
insert [ĭn sürt/] **97**–A
Inside the body [ĭn/sīd/ dhə bäd/ē] **75**
instant coffee [ĭn/stənt kö/fē] **55**–51
instructor [ĭn strŭk/tər] **5** ✦, **139**–58
instrument [ĭn/strə mənt] **120**–A
insulation [ĭn/sə lā/shən] **149**–13
insurance [ĭn shoor/əns]
...card [–kärd/] **84**–4
...form [–förm/] **84**–5
intercom [ĭn/tər käm/] **36**–8
interesting [ĭn/trə stĭng, ĭn/tə rĕs/tĭng] **167**–30
international call [ĭn/tər năsh/ə nəl köl/] **9**–6
internist [ĭn/tür/nĭst] **86**–2
interpreter [ĭn tür/prə tər] **138**–34
INTERSECTION [ĭn/tər sĕk/shən] **90–91**
interview [ĭn/tər vyoo/] **141**–H
intestinal parasites [ĭn tĕs/tə nəl pär/ə sīts/] **79**–16
intestines [ĭn tĕs/tənz] **75**–42
into [ĭn/too, –tə] **105**–4
introduce [ĭn/trə doos/] **8**–D, F
Invention [ĭn vĕn/shən] **115**
invite [ĭn vīt/] **169**–B
iris [ī/rəs] **129**–20
iron [ī/ərn] **72**–G
iron [ī/ərn] **72**–13
ironed shirt [ī/ərnd shürt/] **72**–20
ironing board [ī/ər nĭng börd/] **72**–14
island [ī/lənd] **117**–8
IV (intravenous drip) [ī/vē/] / [ĭn/trə vē/nəs drĭp/] **87**–27
jack [jăk] **109**–51
jack cheese [jăk/ chēz/] **53**–12
jacket [jăk/ət] **66**–7
jack hammer [jăk/ hăm/ər] **149**–9
jack-o'-lantern [jăk/ə lăn/tərn] **168**–11
jam [jăm] **56**–14
janitor [jăn/ə tər] **138**–35
January [jăn/yoo ër/ē] **19**–25
jar [jär(/–)] **56**–2
...of jam [–əv jăm/] **56**–14
jasmine [jăz/mən] **129**–21
jaw [jö] **74**–23
jeans [jēnz] **64**–5
jellyfish [jĕl/ē fĭsh/] **130**–14
jewelry [joo/əl rē] **69**–8
...store [–stör/] **92**–2
job [jäb(/–)] / [–jäb/]
...board [–börd/] **141**–B
get a... [gĕt/ ə–] **28**–G
JOB SAFETY [jäb/ sāf/tē] **147**
JOB SEARCH [jäb/ sürch/] **141**
JOB SKILLS [jäb/ skĭlz/] **140**
JOBS AND OCCUPATIONS A–H [jäbz/ ən äk/yə pā/shənz]
136–137
JOBS AND OCCUPATIONS H–W [jäbz/ ən äk/yə pā/shənz]
138–139
jockstrap [jäk/străp/] **67**–14
jog [jäg] **156**–B
join the army [joyn/ dhē är/mē] **28**–F
joystick [joy/stĭk/] **144**–9
judge [jŭj] **99**–6
Judicial [joo dĭsh/əl] **116**
July [joo lī/] **19**–31, **168**–7
jump [jŭmp] **156**–J

jumper [jŭm/pər] **65**–18
jumper cables [jŭm/pər kā/bəlz] **109**–52
jump rope [jŭmp/ rōp/] **153**–5
jumpsuit [jŭmp/soot/] **65**–16
June [joon] **19**–30
junior high school [joon/yər hī/ skool] **112**–6
Jupiter [joo/pə tər] **127**–5
jury [joor/ē] **99**–8, **116**
Justices [jŭs/tə səz] **116**–10
kangaroo [kăng/gə roo/] **135**–44
keep [kēp] **21**–E
ketchup [kĕch/əp, kăch/–] **60**–23
key [kē(/–)] **37**–31
...chain [–chān/] **69**–43
keyboard [kē/börd/] **120**–20, **144**–7
kick [kĭk] **156**–L
kidney [kĭd/nē] **75**–45
kilometers [kĭ läm/ə tərz, kĭl/ə mē/tərz] **15** ✦
kiss [kĭs] **33**–F
KITCHEN [kĭch/ən] **40**
kitchen [kĭch/ən] **63**–10
...timer [–tī/mər] **59**–18
KITCHEN UTENSILS [kĭch/ən yoo tĕn/səlz] **59**
kitten [kĭt/n] **133**–10
knee [nē(/–)] **74**–17
...socks [–säks/] **67**–25
knee-highs [nē/hīz/] **67**–24
knife [(–)nīf(/)] **41**–22, **63**–27
carving... [kär/vĭng–] **59**–12
multi-use... [mŭl/tē yoos/–, mŭl/tī–] **154**–20
paring... [për/ĭng–] **59**–16
knit [nĭt] **163**–F
knit shirt [nĭt/ shürt/] **65**–20
knitting needles [nĭt/ĭng nēd/lz] **163**–18
koala [kō ä/lə] **135**–45
label [lā/bəl] / [–lā/bəl] **143**–35
prescription... [prĭ skrĭ/shən–] **80**–14
lab technician [lăb/ tĕk nĭsh/ən] **86**–16
ladder [lăd/ər] **149**–2
ladle [lād/l] **59**–7
ladybug [lā/dē bŭg/] **132**–27
lake [lāk] **117**–13
lamb [lăm(/–)] **52**–13, 14, 15
...chops [–chäps/] **52**–15
...shanks [–shăngks/] **52**–13
lamp [lămp] **42**–15, **44**–17
lampshade [lămp/shād/] **44**–18
land [lănd] **111**–O
landlord [lănd/lörd/] **37**–32
language [lăng/gwĭj]
English as a second... [ĭng/glĭsh əz ə sĕk/ənd–] **141**–7
foreign... [för/ən–, fär/–] **141**–8
speak another... [spēk/ ə nä/thər] **140**–J
use the new... [yooz/ thə noo/–] **143** ✦
lantern [lăn/tərn] **154**–22
laptop [lăp/täp/] **144**–14
large [lärj] **70**–4
last [lăst(/–)]
...name [–nām/] **4**–4
...week [–wek/] **18**–18
late [lāt] **17**–23
latex gloves [lā/tĕks glŭvz/] **87**–33, **147**–17
laugh [lăf] **33**–H
Laundromat [lön/drə măt/] **90**–1
laundry [lön/drē] **72**–1

...basket [–băs/kət] **72**–2
...detergent [–dĭ tür/jənt] **72**–7
...room [–rōōm/] **36**
lawn [lön(/–)] **39**–21
...mower [–mō/ər] **39**–22
lawyer [lö/yər] **99**–B, **138**–36
lay bricks [lā/ brĭks/] **149**–B
leaf [lēf(/–)] **128**–6, **129**–5
...blower [–blō/ər] **39**–4
leaking [lē/kĭng] **48**–3
learn to drive [lürn/ tə drīv/] **28**–E
lease [lēs] **35** ✦
leather [lĕdh/ər]
...boots [–bōōts/] **70**–18
...jacket [–jăk/ət] **66**–3
leave [lēv(/–)] **111**–L
...a message [–ə mĕs/ĭj] **9**–E
...a tip [–ə tĭp/] **62**–J
...work [–würk/] **26**–M
left [lĕft] **13**–1
leg [lĕg(/–)] **74**–6
...of lamb [–əv lăm/] **52**–14
legal [lē/gəl]
...holiday [–häl/ə dā/] **19**–43
...pad [–păd/] **143**–18
LEGAL SYSTEM [lē/gəl sĭs/təm] **99**
leggings [lĕg/ĭngz] **65**–23
Legislative [lĕj/əs lā/tĭv] **116**
lemons [lĕm/ənz] **50**–11
lend [lĕnd] **20** ✦
length [lĕngkth] **15**–16
lengthen [lĕngk/thən] **73**–C
leopard [lĕp/ərd] **135**–25
leotard [lē/ə tärd/] **67**–1
let out [lĕt/ owt/] **73**–F
letter [lĕt/ər] / [–lĕt/ər] **96**–2, **142**–B, D
...carrier [–kăr/ē ər] **96**–6
air... [ër/–] **96**–13
letterhead paper [lĕt/ər hĕd pā/pər] **143**–19
lettuce [lĕt/əs] **51**–1, **60**–17
level [lĕv/əl] **150**–24
librarian [lī brër/ē ən] **98**–1
LIBRARY [lī/brër ē] **98**
library [lī/brër ē] **5**–6, **89**–28, **98**–17, 19, 20
...book [–bōōk/] **98**–20
...card [–kärd/] **98**–19
...clerk [–klürk/] **98**–17
license plate [lī/səns plāt/] **108**–15
lid [lĭd] **59**–24
LIFE EVENTS [līf/ ĭ vĕnts/] **28**–29
lifeguard [līf/gärd/] **155**–18
...station [–stā/shən] **155**–20
lifesaving device [līf/sā/vĭng dĭ vīs/] **155**–19
life vest [līf/ vĕst/] **154**–14
light [līt] **169**–H
light [līt] (weight) **11**–14, **71**–40, (color) **12**–3
light (appliance) [līt(/–)] / [–līt/]
...fixture [–fĭks/chər] **41**–5
...switch [–swĭch/] **44**–19
porch... [pörch/–] **38**–9
lightbulb [līt/bŭlb/] **42**–4
lightning [līt/nĭng] **10**–17
lily [lĭl/ē] **129**–24
limb [lĭm] **128**–3
limes [līmz] **50**–12

line [līn(/–)] / [–līn/] **55**–20
...supervisor [–sōō/pər vī zər] **146**–5
assembly... [ə sĕm/blē–] **146**–8
line dry [līn/ drī/] **72** ✦
linen [lĭn/ən] **70**–17
linen closet [lĭn/ən kläz/ət] **43** ✦
Lines [līnz] **118**
lingerie [län/zhə rā/, –jə–] **67** ✦
lion [lī/ən] **135**–36
lip [lĭp] **74**–30
lipstick [lĭp/stĭk/] **77**–37
Liquid measures [lĭk/wəd mĕzh/ərz] **57**
list [lĭst] **6**–L
listen [lĭs/ən] **2**–C, **85**–D
listen for the dial tone [lĭs/ən fər dhə dī/əl tōn/] **9**–B
liters [lē/tərz] **57** ✦
little [lĭt/l] **11**–1
Little League [lĭt/l lēg/] **158** ✦
live [lĭv] **116**–B
liver [lĭv/ər] (food) **52**–7, (body) **75**–39
livestock [līv/stäk/] **148**–13
LIVING ROOM [lĭv/ĭng rōōm/] **42**
lizard [lĭz/ərd] **131**–41
llama [lä/mə] **135**–26
loading dock [lō/dĭng däk/] **146**–16
load the washer [lōd/ dhə wä/shər, –wö/–] **72**–C
loaf [lōf(/–)] **56**–10
...of bread [–əv brĕd/] **56**–22
loafers [lō/fərz] **68**–19
loan [lōn] **35**–I
Lobby [läb/ē] **37**
lobby [läb/ē] **145**–3
lobster [läb/stər] **53**–23
local call [lō/kəl köl/] **9**–4
lock [läk] **101**–E
lock [läk] (house) **37**–29, **48**–6, (car) **109**–34
lockers [läk/ərz] **5**–7
locket [läk/ət] **69**–33
locksmith [läk/smĭth/] **48**–11
logs [lögz, lägz] **42**–12
lonely [lōn/lē] **30**–18
long [löng(/–)] **23**–3, **71**–34
...underwear [–ŭn/dər wër/] **67**–11
long-distance call [löng/dĭs/təns köl/] **9**–5
long-sleeved shirt [löng/slēvd/ shürt/] **71**–31
look at [lōōk/ ăt/, –ət] **111**–K, **141**–B
look for [lōōk/ för/] / [lōōk/ fər]
...a help wanted sign [–ə hĕlp/ wän/təd sīn/, –wön–] **141**–C
...a new apartment [–ə nōō/ ə pärt/mənt] **35**–A
...the emergency exit
[–dhē ĭ mür/jən sē ĕg/zət, –ĕk/sət] **111**–J
look in [lōōk/ ĭn]
...the classifieds [–dhə klăs/ə fīdz/] **141**–D
...throat [–thrōt/] **85**–E
look up a word [lōōk/ ŭp ə würd/] **6**–A
loose [lōōs] **71**–42
lose [lōōz] **158** ✦
lost child [löst/ chīld/] **102**–1
loud [lowd] **11**–11
loungewear [lownj/wër/] **67** ✦
love [lŭv(/–)] **30**–19
...seat [–sēt/] **42**–25
low [lō] **71**–46
LPN (licensed practical nurse)
[ĕl/pē/ĕn/] / [lī/sənst prăk/tĭ kəl nürs/] **87**–24

Index

luggage [lŭg/ĭj]
…carrier [–kăr/ē ər] **110**–19
…cart [–kärt/] **145**–6
lug wrench [lŭg/ rĕnch/] **109**–50
lumber [lŭm/bər] **149**–17, **151**
lunar eclipse [loo/nər ī klĭps/] **127** ✦
lunch [lŭnch(/–)] **61**
…benches [–bĕn/chəz] **5**–5
lung [lŭng] **75**–37
LVN (licensed vocational nurse)
  [ĕl/vē/ĕn] / [lī/sənst vō kā/shə nəl nürs/] **87**–24
machine [mə shēn/]
…operator [–äp/ə rā tər] **138**–37
…screw [–skroo/] **150**–27
magazine [măg/ə zēn/, măg/ə zēn/] **98**–7
…holder [–hōl/dər] **42**–22
magnet [măg/nət] **119**–21
magnolia [măg nōl/yə] **128**–9
mailbox [māl/bäks/] **38**–4, **90**–12
mailboxes [māl/bäk/səz] **37**–36
mailer [mā/lər] **143**–32
mailing address [mā/lĭng ə drĕs/, –ă/drĕs/] **96**–8
mail [māl/ ĭt] **96**–B
main office [mān/ ö/fəs] **5**–17
make [māk] **106** ✦
make [māk(/–)]
…a deposit [–ə dĭ päz/ət] **97**–C
…an appointment [–ən ə poynt/mənt] **85**–A
…an offer [–ən ö/fər] **35**–H
…a toast [ə tōst/] **33**–I
…a wish [–ə wĭsh/] **169**–J
…copies [–käp/ēz] **142**–E
…lunch [–lŭnch/] **26**–F
…the bed [–dhə bĕd/] **46**–G
make sure you understand
  [māk/ shoor/ yoo ŭn/dər stănd/] **8**–E
male [māl] **4**–13
MALL [möl] **92**–93
mallet [măl/ət] **150**–2
MAMMALS [măm/əlz] **134**–135
Mammals, Sea [sē/ măm/əlz] **131**
man [măn] **22**–11
manager [măn/ĭ jər] **35**–B, **36**–12, **54**–8, **143**–25
mane [mān] **135**–49
mangoes [măng/gōz] **50**–21
mantel [măn/təl] **42**–8
manual [măn/yoo əl] **144**–22
manual labor [măn/yoo əl lā/bər] **140**–D
manufacture [măn/yə făk/chər] **146**–B
map [măp] **3**–12
maple [mā/pəl] **128**–13
March [märch] **19**–27
margarine [mär/jər ən] **54**–39
marigold [mär/ə gōld/] **129**–13
MARINE LIFE, AMPHIBIANS, AND REPTILES
  [mə rēn/ līf/ ăm fĭb/ē ənz ən rĕp/tīlz] **130**–131
mark [märk] **7**–T
marker [mär/kər] **3**–19
MARKET [mär/kət] **54**–55
market [mär/kət] **89**–20
marriage license [măr/ĭj lī/səns] **29**–8
married [măr/ēd] **25**–23, **28**–L
Mars [märz] **127**–6
martial arts [mär/shəl ärts/] **159**–10
mascara [mă skăr/ə] **77**–38

mashed potatoes [măsht/ pə tā/tōz] **61**–11
mask [măsk] **168**–12
masking tape [măs/kĭng tāp/] **151**–49
Master's degree [măs/tərz də grē/] **112** ✦
match [măch] **7**–X
matches [măch/əz] **154**–21
maternity dress [mə tür/nə tē drĕs/] **65**–19
maternity shop [mə tür/nə tē shäp/] **93**–17
MATHEMATICS [măth/ə măt/ĭks] **118**
mattress [mă/trəs] **44**–25
May [mā] **19**–29
mayonnaise [mā/ə nāz/, mā/ə nāz/] **60**–25
meadow [mĕd/ō] **117**–20
measles [mē/zəlz] **79**–5
measure [mĕzh/ər] **15** ✦, **149**–C
Measurement [mĕzh/ər mənt] **15**
MEASUREMENTS [mĕzh/ər mənts] **14**–15
MEASURES [mĕzh/ərz] **57**
measure the ingredients [mĕzh/ər dhē ĭn grē/dē ənts] **57**–A
MEAT AND POULTRY [mēt/ n pōl/trē] **52**
meat and poultry section [mēt/ n pōl/trē sĕk/shən] **54**–2
media section [mē/dē ə sĕk/shən] **98**–11
medical [mĕd/ĭ kəl]
…charts [–chärts/] **87**–20
…emergency bracelet [–ī mür/jən sē brās/lət] **83**–14
…waste disposal [–wāst/ dĭ spō/zəl] **86**–14
MEDICAL AND DENTAL EXAMS
  [mĕd/ĭ kəl ən dĕn/təl ĭg zămz/] **85**
Medical clinic [mĕd/ĭ kəl klĭn/ĭk] **84**
MEDICAL CONDITIONS [mĕd/ĭ kəl kən dĭsh/ənz] **79**
Medical conditions and serious diseases
  [mĕd/ĭ kəl kən dĭsh/ənz ən sĭr/ē əs dĭ zē/zəz] **79**
MEDICAL EMERGENCIES [mĕd/ĭ kəl ĭ mür/jən sēz] **82**
medication [mĕd/ə kā/shən] **80**–11, 12
…tray [–trā/] **87**–23
medicine cabinet [mĕd/ə sən kăb/ə nət] **43**–19
medium [mē/dē əm] **70**–3
meeting room [mē/tĭng room/] **145**–19
memory [mĕm/ə rē] **144** ✦
men's store [mĕnz/ stör/] **90** ✦
menu [mĕn/yoo] **62**–3
MENU, COFFEE SHOP [kö/fē shäp/ mĕn/yoo] **61**
merchandise [mür/chən dīz/, –dīs/] **152**–24
Mercury [mür/kyə rē] **127**–9
messenger [mĕs/ən jər] **138**–38
messy [mĕs/ē] **11**–16
meter [mē/tər] (measurement) **15**, (taxi) **104**–21
meter [mē/tər] / [–mē/tər]
  gas… [găs/–] **48**–14
  parking… [pär/kĭng–] **91**–18
mice [mīs] **49**–26
microcassette transcriber [mī/krō kə sĕt/ trăn skrī/bər] **142**–4
microfilm [mī/krə fĭlm/] **98**–5
microfilm reader [mī/krə fĭlm rē/dər] **98**–4
microphone [mī/krə fōn/] **164**–4
microscope [mī/krə skōp/] **119**–4
microwave oven [mī/krə wāv/ ŭv/ən] **40**–13
middle-aged [mĭd/l ājd/] **22**–14
middle initial [mĭd/l ĭ nĭsh/əl] **4**–3
middle school [mĭd/l skool/] **112**–6
midnight [mĭd/nīt/] **17**–21
midsize car [mĭd/sīz/ kär/] **106**–3
mile [mīl] **15** ✦
milk [mĭlk] **148**–C
milk [mĭlk(/–)] **54**–35

...shake [–shāk/] **60**–12
milliliters [mĭl/ə lē/tərz] **57** ✦
million [mĭl/yən] **14**
miniblinds [mĭn/ē blīndz/] **43**–11
minivan [mĭn/ē văn/] **106**–10
minute [mĭn/ət] **16**–2
mirror [mĭr/ər] **43**–18, **44**–1
    rearview... [rĭr/vyoo/–] **108**–1
    sideview... [sīd/vyoo/–] **108**–8
missing [mĭs/ĭng] **70**–25
miss the bus [mĭs/ dhə bŭs/] **104** ✦
mistake [mĭ stāk/] **7**–2
mittens [mĭt/nz] **66**–9
mix [mĭks] **58**–K
mixing bowl [mĭk/sĭng bōl/] **59**–31
mobile [mō/bēl] **45**–4
mobile home [mō/bəl hōm/] **34**–8
model (occupation) [mäd/l] **138**–39
model (hobby) [mäd/l] **106** ✦
    ...kit [–kĭt/] **162**–7
    ...trains [–trānz/] **163**–32
models [mäd/lz] **162**–C
modem [mō/dəm, –dĕm] **144**–11
moisturizer [moys/chə rī/zər] **76**–8
molecule [mäl/ĭ kyool/] **119**–18
Monday [mŭn/dā, –dē] **18**–2
MONEY [mŭn/ē] **20**
money order [mŭn/e ör/dər] **20**–16
monitor [män/ə tər] **144**–6
monitors [män/ə tərs] **110**–4
monkey [mŭng/kē] **135**–27
month [mŭnth] **4**–16, **18**–9
monthly statement [mŭnth/lē stāt/mənt] **97**–10
Months of the year [mŭnths/ əv dhə yïr/] **19**
moon [moon] **127**–13, 14, 15, 16
moose [moos] **134**–1
mop [mäp] **46**–J
mop [(–)mäp(/)]
    dust... [dŭst/–] **47**–17
    wet... [wĕt/–] **47**–16
MORE SCHOOL SUBJECTS [mör/ skool/ sŭb/jĭkts] **121**
morning [mör/nĭng] **17**–16
mosque [mäsk] **89**–23
mosquito [mə skē/tō] **132**–23
motel [mō tĕl/] **89**–22
moth [möth] **132**–22
mother [mŭdh/ər] **24**–5, **25**–25
motherboard [mŭdh/ər börd/] **144**–18
mother-in-law [mŭdh/ər ĭn lö/] **24**–13
motorcycle [mō/tər sī/kəl] **91**–19
mountain [mown/tn]
    ...biking [–bī/kĭng] **154**–8
    ...lion [lī/ən] **134**–2
    ...peak [–pēk/] **117**–14
    ...range [–rānj/] **117**–15
    ...time [–tīm/] **17**–27
mouse [mows] (animal) **133**–17, (computer) **144**–8
mouth [mowth] **74**–22
mouthwash [mowth/wäsh/, –wösh/] **77**–23
move [moov] **29**–P
move in [moov/ ĭn/] **35**–D
Movement [moov/mənt] **115**
mover [moo/vər] **138**–40
movie [moo/vē] **166**–1
movies [moo/vēz] **152**–10

movie theater [moo/vē thē/ə tər] **88**–11
moving van [moo/vĭng văn/] **106**–14
mow [mō] **39**–C
mudslide [mŭd/slīd/] **102**–6
muffin [mŭf/ən] **60**–14
muffler [mŭf/lər] (clothing) **66**–4, (car part) **108**–11
mug [mŭg] **41**–28
mugging [mŭg/ĭng] **100**–5
multiplication [mŭl/tə plə kā/shən] **118**–3
multi-use knife [mŭl/tē yoos/ nīf/, mŭl/tī–] **154**–20
mumps [mŭmps] **79**–7
murder [mür/dər] **100**–8
muscle [mŭs/əl] **75**–48
mushrooms [mŭsh/roomz/] **51**–26
MUSIC [myoo/zĭk] **120**
musician [myoo zĭsh/ən] **138**–41
music store [myoo/zĭk stör/] **92**–1
mussel [mŭs/əl] **130**–17
mussels [mŭs/əlz] **53**–26
mustache [mŭs/tăsh] **23**–5
mustard [mŭs/tərd] **60**–24
mystery [mĭs/tə rē] **166**–15
nachos [nä/chōz] **60**–10
nail (hardware) [nāl] **150**–29
nail (body) [nāl(/–)]
    ...clipper [–klĭp/ər] **77**–29
    ...polish [–päl/ĭsh] **77**–31
    ...polish remover [–päl/ĭsh rĭ moo/vər] **77**–32
    ...salon [–sə län/] **91**–25
name [nām] **4**–1, 2, 3, 4, A, C, D
napkin [năp/kĭn] **41**–19, **63**–23
narrow [năr/ō] **71**–45
nasal congestion [nā/zəl kən jĕs/chən] **78**–7
nasal spray [nā/zəl sprā/] **81**–23
NATURAL DISASTERS
    [năch/rəl dĭ zăs/tərz, năch/ər əl–] **102**–**103**
natural gas [năch/rəl găs/, năch/ər əl–] **126**–3
nature program [nā/chər prō/grăm] **167**–22
near [nïr] **13** ✦
neat [nēt] **11**–15
neck [nĕk] **74**–2
necklaces [nĕk/lə səz] **69**–9
need [nēd] **109**–(54–59)
needle [nēd/l] (sewing) **73**–22, (pine) **128**–12
neighbor [nā/bər] **37**–22
neighborhood [nā/bər hood/] **90** ✦
Neighborhood Watch
    [nā/bər hood/ wäch/, –wöch/] **101** ✦
nephew [nĕf/yoo] **24**–18
Neptune [nĕp/toon] **127**–2
nerve [nürv] **75**–50
nervous [nür/vəs] **30**–11
nest [nĕst] **132**–5
new [noo(/–)] **71**–32
    ...moon [–moon/] **127**–13
Newfoundland time [noo/fən lənd tīm/, –fənd–] **17**–31
news [nooz] **167**–17
newspaper [nooz/pā/pər] **98**–8
newsstand [nooz/stănd/] **90**–11
newt [noot] **130**–26
New Year's Day [noo/ yïrz/ dā/] **168**–1
next to [nĕkst/ too, –tə] **13**–1, 2
next week [nĕkst/ wēk/] **18**–20
nickel [nĭk/əl] **20**–2
niece [nēs] **24**–17

Index

night [nīt] **17**–20
nightgown [nīt/gown/] **67**–5
night-light [nīt/līt/] **45**–3
nightshirt [nīt/shürt/] **67**–9
night table [nīt/ tā/bəl] **44**–21
nine [nīn] **14**
nineteen [nīn/tēn/] **14**
nineteenth [nīn/tēnth/] **14**
nineteen-year-old [nīn/tēn/yïr ōld/] **22**–8
ninety [nīn/tē] **14**
ninth [nīnth] **14**
nipple [nĭp/əl] **95**–27
noisy children [noy/zē chĭl/drən] **11**–11
nonfiction [nän/fĭk/shən] **98** ✦
noon [nōōn] **17**–17
no outlet [nō/ owt/lĕt, –lət] **107**–8
no parking [nō/ pär/kĭng] **107**–12
north [nörth] **107, 123, 124**
NORTH AMERICA AND CENTRAL AMERICA
[nörth/ ə mĕr/ə kə ən sĕn/trəl ə mĕr/ə kə] **122**–123
nose [nōz] **74**–21
not [nät(/–)]
...guilty [–gĭl/tē] **99**
...ripe [–rīp] **50**–28
notebook [nōt/bŏŏk/] **3**–24
...paper [–pā/pər] **3**–25
note pad [nōt/ păd/] **143**–36
November [nō vĕm/bər] **19**–35
nuclear energy [nōō/klē ər ĕn/ər jē] **126**–8
numbers [nŭm/bərz] **3**–31
NUMBERS AND MEASUREMENTS
[nŭm/bərz ən mĕzh/ər mənts] **14**–15
nurse [nürs] **94**–C
nurse [nürs(/–)] **84**–10, **87**–22, 24, 29, ✦, **138**–42, ✦
...midwife [–mĭd/wīf/] **86** ✦
...practitioner [–prăk tĭsh/ə nər] **86** ✦
Nurse's station [nür/səz stā/shən] **87**
nursing home [nür/sĭng hōm/] **34**–11
nut (hardware) [nŭt] **150**–31
nuts (food) [nŭts] **50**–23
nylon [nī/län] **70**–19
oak [ōk] **128**–18
obey the law [ō bā/ dhə lö/] **116**–H
oboe [ō/bō] **120**–5
observatory [əb zür/və tör/ē] **127**–19
observe [əb zürv/] **119**–B
obstetrician [äb/stə trĭsh/ən] **86**–1
OCCUPATIONS (A-H) [äk/yə pā/shənz] **136**–137
OCCUPATIONS (H-W) [äk/yə pā/shənz] **138**–139
ocean [ō/shən] **117**–6, **155**–1
o'clock [ə kläk/] **16**–4
October [äk tō/bər] **19**–34
octopus [äk/tə pəs] **130**–4
odometer [ō däm/ə tər] **108**–21
off [öf] **105**–7
OFFICE [ö/fəs] **142**–143
Office [ö/fəs] **37**
office [ö/fəs] **5**–13, 15, 17, **146**–1
...building [–bĭl/dĭng] **89**–24
...manager [–măn/ĭ jər] **143**–25
official [ə fĭsh/əl] **158**–6
oil (cooking) [oyl] **55**–49, **57**–2
oil (petroleum) [oyl(/–)] **109**–55, **126**–6
...gauge [–gāj/] **108**–19
...paint [–pānt/] **163**–24

...spill [–spĭl/] **126**–15
ointment [oynt/mənt] **81**–24, **83**–9
old [ōld] **71**–33
on [än, ön] **13**–8
...the left [–dhə lĕft/] **13**–1
...the right [–dhə rīt/] **13**–2
once a week [wŭns/ə wēk/] **18**–22
one [wŭn(/–)] **14, 15**–1, 2, 3, 4, 5, 11, **16**–4, 15, **20**–1, 12
...o'clock [–ə kläk/] **16**–4
...way [–wā/] **107**–6
one billion [wŭn/ bĭl/yən] **14**
one-eighth [wŭn/ ātth/, –āth/] **15**–1
one-fifteen [wŭn/ fĭf/tēn/] **16**–7
one-fifty [wŭn/ fĭf/tē] **16**–14
one-forty [wŭn/ för/tē] **16**–12
one-fourth [wŭn/ förth/] **15**–2
one-half [wŭn/ hăf/] **15**–4
one-hundred percent [wŭn/ hŭn/drəd pər sĕnt/] **15**–11
one-oh-five [wŭn/ ō fīv/] **16**–5
one-ten [wŭn/ tĕn/] **16**–6
one-third [wŭn/ thürd/] **15**–3
one-thirty [wŭn/ thür/tē] **16**–10
one-twenty [wŭn/ twĕn/tē] **16**–8
onions [ŭn/yənz] **51**–28, **58**–G, H
online catalog [än/līn/ kăt/l ög/, –äg/, ön/–] **98**–9
on time [än/ tīm/, ön/–] **17** ✦
onto [än/tōō, –tə, ön/–] **105**–6
open [ō/pən] **2**–I
...the presents [–dhə prĕz/ənts] **169**–L
don't... [dōnt/–] **101**–F
opera [äp/rə] **166**–8
operate heavy machinery
[äp/ə rāt/ hĕv/ē mə shē/nə rē] **140**–F
Operating room [äp/ə rā/tĭng rōōm/] **87**
operating table [äp/ə rā/tĭng tā/bəl] **87**–34
Operations (math) [äp/ə rā/shənz] **118**
operator [äp/ə rā/tər] **9**–7
ophthalmologist [äf/thəl mäl/ə jĭst, –thə mäl/–, äp/–] **86**–7
opossum [ə päs/əm, päs/əm] **134**–4
optician [äp tĭsh/ən] **92**–8
optometrist [äp täm/ə trĭst] **81**–34
orange [ör/ənj, är/–] **12**–6
oranges [ör/ən jəz, är/–] **50**–10
orangutan [ə răng/ə tăng/, –tăn/] **135**–40
orbit [ör/bət] **127**–11
orchard [ör/chərd] **148**–16
orchestra [ör/kə strə] **120**–1
orchid [ör/kĭd] **129**–17
order [ör/dər] **62**–D
orderly [ör/dər lē] **87**–18
order puller [ör/dər pŏŏl/ər] **146**–10
Ordinals [ör/dn əlz, örd/nəlz] **14**
organ [ör/gən] **120**–22
organizer [ör/gə nī/zər] **143**–30
ornament [ör/nə mənt] **168**–19
orthodontist [ör/thə dän/tĭst] **84**–23
orthopedist [ör/thə pē/dĭst] **81**–28
Other instruments [ŭdh/ər ĭn/strə mənts] **120**
otter [ät/ər] **131**–35
ounce [owns] **57**–11
out [owt(/–)] **48**–2
...of focus [–əv fō/kəs] **165**–33
...of the taxi [–əv dhə tăk/sē] **105**–5
OUTDOOR RECREATION [owt/dör rĕk/rē ā/shən] **154**
outfit [owt/fĭt] **64** ✦

outlet [owt/lĕt, –lət] **44**–20, **107**–8, **151**–41

oval [ō/vəl] **118**–9

oven [ŭv/ən] **40**–20, **46**–C, **47**–3

...cleaner [–klē/nər] **47**–3

microwave...[mī/krə wāv/–] **40**–13

over [ō/vər] **105**–2

overalls [ō/vər ölz/] **65**–21

overcoat [ō/vər kōt/] **66**–2

overdose [ō/vər dōs/, ō/vər dōs/] **82**–K

overdrawn account [ō/vər drön/ ə kownt/] **97** ✦

overexposed [ō/vər ĭk spōzd/] **165**–34

overflowing [ō/vər flō/ĭng] **49**–17

overhead [ō/vər hĕd/]

...compartment [–kəm pärt/mənt] **110**–10

...projector [–prə jĕk/tər] **2**–4

overjoyed [ō/vər joyd/] **30** ✦

overnight mail [ō/vər nīt/ māl/] **96**–15

over-the-counter medication
[ō/vər dhə kown/tər mĕd/ə kā/shən] **80**–12

owl [owl] **132**–6

owner [ō/nər] **139**–56

oxfords [äks/fərdz] **68**–20

oxygen mask [äk/sĭ jən mäsk/] **110**–14

oysters [oy/stərz] **53**–27

Pacific time [pə sĭf/ĭk tīm/] **17**–26

pacifier [päs/ə fī/ər] **95**–29

package [päk/ĭj] **56**–8, **96**–5

...of cookies [–əv kŏok/ēz] **56**–20

PACKAGED FOODS [päk/ĭjd fŏodz/] **56**

packer [päk/ər] **146**–13

packing tape [päk/ĭng tāp/] **143**–42

pager [pā/jər] **9**–16

pail [pāl] **45**–13, **47**–20, **155**–22

pain [pān(/–)]

...reliever [–rĭ lē/vər] **81**–16

paint [pānt] **149**–A, **163**–E

paint [pānt(/–)] / [–pānt] **151**–20

...pan [–păn/] **151**–45

...roller [–rō/lər] **151**–46

acrylic... [ə krĭl/ĭk–] **162**–47

paintbrush [pānt/brŭsh/] **151**–9, **163**–23

painter [pān/tər] **138**–43

painting [pān/tĭng] **42**–7, **152**–8

pair of scissors [për/ əv sĭz/ərz] **73**–18

paisley [pāz/lē] **70**–13

pajamas [pə jä/məz, –jä/–] **67**–4

palm [päm] (hand) **75**–59, (tree) **128**–15

pan [păn] **40**–24, **59**–5, 13, 26, 28

pancakes [păn/kāks/] **61**–6

pancreas [păng/krē əs] **75**–46

panda [păn/də] **135**–41

panther [păn/thər] **135**–39

panties [păn/tēz] **67**–16

pants [pănts] **64**–8

pantyhose [păn/tē hōz/] **67**–27

papayas [pə pī/əz] **50**–20

paper [pā/pər] (composition) **113**–2

paper [pā/pər] / [–pā/pər]

...bag [–băg/] **55**–22

...clip [–klĭp/] **143**–44

...cutter [–kŭt/ər] **143**–15

...doll [–däl/] **163**–30

...products [–präd/ŭkts] **55**–14

...shredder [–shrĕd/ər] **143**–24

...towels [–tow/əlz] **40**–2, **56**–23

notebook... [nōt/bŏok/–] **3**–24, 25, 26

parade [pə rād/] **168**–2

paragraph [păr/ə grăf/] **113**–5

parakeet [păr/ə kēt/] **133**–15

parallel [păr/ə lĕl/] **118**–21

parcel post [pär/səl pōst/] **96**–14

parent [për/ənt] **94**–1

parents [për/ənts] **24**–4

paring knife [për/ĭng nīf/] **59**–16

park [pärk] **91**–D

park [pärk] **88**–8

parka [pär/kə] **66**–8

PARK AND PLAYGROUND [pärk/ ən plā/grownd/] **153**

parking [pär/kĭng]

...garage [–gə räzh/, –räj/] **89**–26

...meter [–mē/tər] **91**–18

...space [–spās/] **36**–15, **90**–5

parochial school [pə rō/kē əl skŏol/] **112**–3

parsley [pär/slē] **51**–10

part [pärt] **23**–4

partner [pärt/nər] **6**–J

parts [pärts] **146**–7

Parts of a bird [pärts/ əv ə bürd/] **132**

PARTS OF A CAR AND CAR MAINTENANCE
[pärts/ əv ə kär/ ən kär/ mān/tn əns] **108**–**109**

Parts of a circle [pärts/ əv ə sür/kəl] **118**

Parts of a fish [pärts/ əv ə fĭsh/] **130**

Parts of a flower [pärts/ əv ə flow/ər] **129**

Parts of a square [pärts/ əv ə skwër/] **118**

Parts of a tree [pärts/ əv ə trē/] **128**

PARTY [pär/tē] **169**

Party [pär/tē] **33**

pass [păs] **156**–H

passbook [păs/bŏok/] **97**–5

passenger [păs/ən jər] **104**–7, **110**–23

pass out [păs/ owt/] **7**–O

passport [păs/pört/] **29**–9

pasta [päs/tə] **61**–15

...salad [–săl/əd] **53**–15

pastrami [pə strä/mē] **53**–6

patient [pā/shənt] **84**–3

Patient's room [pā/shənts rŏom/] **86**

patio [păt/ē ō] **39**–6

...furniture [–für/nĭ chər] **39**–5

patron [pā/trən] **62**–5

pattern (clothes) [păt/ərn] **73**–8

pattern maker [păt/ərn mā/kər] **73** ✦

Patterns (fabric) [păt/ərnz] **70**

pause [pöz] **165**–E

paw [pö] **134**–42

pay [pā(/–)]

...taxes [–tăk/səz] **116**–E

...the check [–dhə chĕk/] **62**–I

...the mortgage [–dhə mör/gĭj] **35**–L

...the rent [–dhə rĕnt/] **35**–F

pay phone [pā/ fōn] **9**–11

pay back [pā/ băk/] **20** ✦

pay for [pā/ för/, –fər] **21**–C

PE (physical education) [pē/ē/] / [fĭz/ĭ kəl ĕj/ə kā/shən]
121–11

peaches [pē/chəz] **50**–5

peacock [pē/käk/] **132**–15

peak [pēk] **117**–14

pearls [pürlz] **69**–30

pears [përz] **50**–6

Index

peas [pēz] **51**–19
pedestrian [pə dĕs/trē ən] **90**–7
...crossing [–krö/sĭng] **107**–10
pediatrician [pē/dē ə trĭsh/ən] **86**–4
peel [pēl] **58**–N
peephole [pēp/hōl/] **37**–27
pelvis [pĕl/vəs] **75**–55
pen [pĕn] **3**–18
pencil [pĕn/səl] **3**–20
...eraser [–ī rā/sər] **3**–21
...sharpener [–shär/pə nər] **3**–13, **142**–9
penguin [pĕng/wĭn] **132**–12
peninsula [pə nĭn/sə lə] **117**–7
penny [pĕn/ē] **20**–1
peppers [pĕp/ərz] **51**–7
pepper shaker [pĕp/ər shā/kər] **41**–15
Percents [pər sĕnts/] **15**
Percussion [pər kŭsh/ən] **120**
perfume [pür/fyoōm/, pər fyoōm/] **76**–5
period [pïr/ē əd] **113**–6
periodical section [pïr/ē äd/ĭ kəl sĕk/shən] **98**–6
perm hair [pürm/ hër/] **23**–B
perpendicular [pür/pən dĭk/yə lər] **118**–20
personal check [pür/sə nəl chĕk/] **20**–14
PERSONAL HYGIENE [pür/sə nəl hī/jēn] **76–77**
personal identification number (PIN)
  [pür/sə nəl ī dĕn/tə fə kā/shən nŭm/bər] **97**–B
PERSONAL INFORMATION [pür/sə nəl ĭn/fər mā/shən] **4**
personal radio-cassette player
  [pür/sə nəl rā/dē ō kə sĕt/ plā/ər] **164**–15
pesticide [pĕs/tə sīd/] **49**✦
...poisoning [–poy/zə nĭng] **126**–14
pet [pĕt(/–)]
...food [–foōd/] **54**–10
...store [–stör/] **92**–6
petal [pĕt/l] **129**–8
petri dish [pē/trē dĭsh/] **119**–6
petroleum [pə trō/lē əm] **126**–6
Pets [pĕts] **133**
pharmacist [fär/mə sĭst] **80**–10
pharmacy [fär/mə sē] **80**–9, **90**–2
Phillips screwdriver [fĭl/ĭps skroō/drī/vər] **150**–26
phone [fōn(/–)] **9**–1
...card [–kärd/] **9**–10
photo [fō/tō]
...album [–ăl/bəm] **165**–32
...shop [–shäp/] **90**–4
photocopier [fō/tə käp/ē ər] **142**–14
photograph [fō/tə grăf/] **44**–7
photographer [fə täg/rə fər] **32**–11
PHOTOGRAPHY [fə täg/rə fē] **164-165**
PHYSICAL DESCRIPTION [fĭz/ĭ kəl dĭ skrĭp/shən] **22**
physically challenged [fĭz/ĭ klē chăl/ənjd] **22**–25
physical therapist [fĭz/ĭ kəl thĕr/ə pĭst] **81**–30
physics [fĭz/ĭks] **119**–3
pi (π) [pī] **118**✦
piano [pē ăn/ō] **120**–16
pickax [pĭk/ăks/] **149**–20
pick up [pĭk/ ŭp/] / [pĭk/ ŭp/–] **94**–G
...the children [–dhə chĭl/drən] **27**–O
...the receiver [–dhə rĭ sē/vər] **9**–A
pickup truck [pĭk/ŭp trŭk/] **106**–7
picnic [pĭk/nĭk] **153**–D
picnic table [pĭk/nĭk tā/bəl] **153**–8
picture [pĭk/chər]

...book [–boōk/] **45**–17
...dictionary [–dĭk/shə nër ē] **3**–29
pie [pī(/–)] **61**–21
...pan [–păn/] **59**–28
pier [pïr] **155**–16
pierced earrings [pïrst/ ïr/ĭng] **69**–37
pig [pĭg] **133**–8
pigeon [pĭj/ən] **132**–16
pill [pĭl] **81**–26
pillow [pĭl/ō] **42**–20, **44**–9
pillowcase [pĭl/ō kās/] **44**–10
pilot [pī/lət] **110**–12
PIN (personal identification number) [pĭn] **97**–B
pin [pĭn] (jewelry) **69**–36, (sewing) **73**–14
pin [pĭn(/–)] / [–pĭn/]
...cushion [–koōsh/ən] **73**–15
push... [poōsh/–] **143**–43
pine [pīn] **128**–10
pinecone [pīn/kōn/] **128**–11
pineapples [pī/năp/əlz] **50**–2
Ping-Pong [pĭng/päng/, –pöng/] **159**–13
pink [pĭngk] **12**–10
pint [pīnt] **57**–3
pipe [pīp(/–)] **151**–16
...wrench [–rĕnch/] **151**–43
pipes [pīps] **49**–19
pitch [pĭch] **156**–F
pizza [pēt/sə] **60**–7
place [plās(/–)]
...mat [–măt/] **41**–20
...setting [–sĕt/ĭng] **63**–14
place of birth [plās/ əv bürth/] **4**–17
PLACES TO GO [plā/səz tə gō/] **152**
PLACES TO LIVE [plā/səz tə lĭv/] **34**
plaid [plăd] **70**–9
plain [plān] **71**–38
plains [plānz] **117**–19
plan [plăn] **169**–A
plane (tool) [plān] **151**–52
PLANE TRIP [plān/ trĭp/] **111**
Planets [plăn/əts] **127**
plant [plănt] **39**–D, **148**–A
plant [plănt] **39**–B, **42**–18
PLANTS [plănts] **128**
plastic [plăs/tĭk] **70**
...bag [–băg/] **55**–23
...storage container [–stör/ĭj kən tā/nər] **59**–3
...wrap [–răp/] **55**–54
plate [plāt] **41**–24, **63**–15, 16, 17
platform [plăt/förm/] **104**–15
platter [plăt/ər] **41**–3
platypus [plăt/ĭ pəs, –poōs/] **135**–46
play [plā(/–)] **94**–K, **165**–B
...an instrument [–ən ĭn/strə mənt] **120**–A
...cards [–kärdz/] **163**–H
...games [–gāmz/] **162**–C
play [plā] **166**–2
player [plā/ər] **158**–5, **164**–2, 14, 15
PLAYGROUND [plā/grownd/] **153**
playground [plā/grownd/] **36**–6
playpen [plā/pĕn/] **95**–11
pliers [plī/ərz] **150**–7
plug [plŭg] **164**–18
plumber [plŭm/ər] **49**–20
plums [plŭmz] **50**–8

plunger [plŭn′jər] **151**–44
Pluto [plōō′tō] **127**–1
plywood [plī′wŏŏd′] **149**–16
p.m. [pē′ĕm′] **16**
pneumatic drill [nŏŏ măt′ĭk drĭl′] **149**–9
pocket [päk′ət] **73**–4
podium [pō′dē əm] **32**–5
poinsettia [poyn sĕt′ē ə, –sĕt′ə] **129**–23
point [poynt] **2**–F
poison [poy′zən] **82**–J, **147**–3
   ...ivy [–ī′vē] **128**–25
   ...oak [–ōk′]**128**–23
   ...sumac [–sōō′măk, –shōō′–] **128**–24
police [pə lēs′]
   ...officer [–ö′fə sər] **99**–1, **138**–44
   ...station [–stā′shən] **89**–19
polish [päl′ĭsh]
   ...nails [–nālz′] **77**–O
   ...the furniture [–dhə für′nĭ chər] **46**–K
polka-dotted [pō′kə dät′əd] **70**–8
Pollution [pə lōō′shən] **126**
polyester [päl′ē ĕs′tər, päl′ē ĕs′tər] **70**
poncho [pän′chō] **66**–18
pond [pänd] **117**–21, **153**–6
pool (game) [pōōl] **159**–2
pool (swimming) [pōōl(′–)] **37**–16, **145**–16
   ...service [–sür′vəs] **145**–17
porch light [pörch′ līt′] **38**–9
porcupine [pör′kyə pīn′] **134**–10
Pork [pörk] **52**
pork chops [pörk′ chäps′] **52**–10
porpoise [pör′pəs] **131**–31
port [pört] **144**–17
portable [pör′tə bəl]
   ...radio-cassette player [–rā′dē ō kə sĕt′ plā′ər] **164**–2
   ...TV [–tē′vē′] **164**–7
postage [pō′stĭj] **96**–10
postal [pō′stəl]
   ...scale [–skāl′] **143**–16
   ...worker [–wür′kər] **138**–45
postcard [pōst′kärd′] **96**–3
Post-it notes [pōst′ĭt nōts′] **143**–34
postmark [pōst′märk′] **96**–9
post office [pōst′ ö′fəs] **89**–29
pot [pät(′–)] **40**–16, **59**–6
   ...holders [–hōl′dərz] **59**–29
potato [pə tā′tō]
   ...chips [–chĭps′] **55**–40
   ...salad [–sāl′əd] **53**–13
potatoes [pə tā′tōz] **51**–21, **61**–11
potty seat [pät′ē sēt′] **95**–10
pouch [powch] **135**–50
POULTRY [pōl′trē] **52**
poultry section [pōl′trē sĕk′shən] **54**–2
pound [pownd] **57**–12
pour [pör(′–)]
   ...the eggs into the pan [–dhē ĕgz′ ĭn′tə dhə păn′] **58**–D
   ...the water [–dhə wö′tər] **62**–C
power [pow′ər] **48**–2
   ...sander [–săn′dər] **150**–9
   ...switch [–swĭch′] **144**–4
prairie dog [prër′ē dög′] **133**–22
pregnant [prĕg′nənt] **22**–19
PREPOSITIONS [prĕp′ə zĭsh′ənz] **13**
PREPOSITIONS OF MOTION [prĕp′ə zĭsh′ənz əv mō′shən] **105**

preschool [prē′skōōl′] **112**–4
prescription [prĭ skrĭp′shən] **80**–13
   ...label [–lā′bəl] **80**–14
   ...medication [–mĕd′ə kā′shən] **80**–11
President [prĕz′ə dənt] **116**–6
pretend [prĭ tĕnd′] **163**–G
price [prīs(′–)] **21**–6
   ...tag [–tăg′] **21**–1
principal [prĭn′sə pəl] **5**–14
principal's office [prĭn′sə pəlz ö′fəs] **5**–13
print [prĭnt] **4**–C
print [prĭnt] **70**–10
printer [prĭn′tər] (occupation) **138**–46, (computer) **144**–12
print shop [prĭnt′ shäp′] **91**–22
priority mail [prī ör′ə tē māl′, –är′–] **96**–12
prism [prĭz′əm] **119**–20
prison [prĭz′ən] **99**–G
private school [prī′vət skōōl′] **112**–2
Problems (clothing) [präb′ləmz] **70**
PROBLEMS, HOUSEHOLD [hows′hōld′ präb′ləmz] **48**–**49**
produce section [prō′dōōs sĕk′shən] **54**–11
product [präd′ŭkt] **118** ✦
program (computer) [prō′grăm] **144**–21
Programs (TV) [prō′grămz] **167**
projector [prə jĕk′tər] / [–prə jĕk′tər]
   carousel slide... [kăr′ə sĕl′ slīd′–] **165**–29
   overhead... [ō′vər hĕd′–] **2**–4
prosecuting attorney [präs′ĭ kyōō′tĭng ə tür′nē] **99**–10
protect your wallet [prə tĕkt′ yər wä′lət, –wö′–] **101**–D
proud [prowd] **31**–22
prunes [prōōnz] **50**–26
pruning shears [prōō′nĭng shïrz′] **39**–15
psychiatrist [sī kī′ə trĭst, sə–] **86**–6
PUBLIC SAFETY [pŭb′lĭk sāf′tē] **101**
public school [pŭb′lĭk skōōl′] **112**–1
public telephone [pŭb′lĭk tĕl′ə fōn′] **91**–21
PUBLIC TRANSPORTATION
   [pŭb′lĭk trăns′pər tā′shən] **104**
pudding [pŏŏd′ĭng] **61**–20
pull [pŏŏl(′–)]
   ...a tooth [–ə tōōth′] **85**–M
   ...the wagon [–dhə wăg′ən] **153**–A
pullover sweater [pŏŏl′ō′vər swĕt′ər] **64**–11
pumps [pŭmps] **68**–16
Punctuation [pŭngk′chōō ā′shən] **113**
puppet show [pŭp′ət shō′] **152**–14
puppy [pŭp′ē] **133**–12
purple [pür′pəl] **12**–7
purses [pür′səz] **69**–6
push [pŏŏsh] **153**–B
pushpin [pŏŏsh′pĭn′] **143**–43
put away [pŏŏt′ə wā′] / [pŏŏt′ə wā′–]
   ...the toys [–dhə toyz′] **46**–H
   ...your pencil [–yər pĕn′səl] **2**–L
put in order [pŏŏt′ ĭn ör′dər] **7**–W
put on [pŏŏt′ än′, –ön′] / [pŏŏt′ än–, –ön–]
   ...makeup [–māk′ŭp′] **77**–P
   ...sunscreen [–sŭn′skrēn′] **76**–D
puzzle [pŭz′əl] **45**–22
pyramid [pïr′ə mĭd] **118**–13
quart [kwört] **57**–4
quarter [kwör′tər] (time) **16,** (money) **20**–4
quarter cup [kwör′tər kŭp′] **57**–8
quarter moon [kwör′tər mōōn′] **127**–15
question mark [kwĕs′chən märk′] **113**–7

Index

quiet [kwī/ət] **11**–12
quill [kwĭl] **134**–23
quiz show [kwĭz/ shō/] **167**–23
quotation marks [kwō tā/shən märks/] **113**–9
quotient [kwō/shənt] **118** ✦
rabbit [răb/ət] **133**–13
raccoon [ră kōōn/] **134**–13
race [rās] **157**–Y
racquetball [răk/ət böl/] **159**–11
radiation [rā/dē ā/shən] **126**–13
radiator [rā/dē ā/tər] **109**–42, 56
radio [rā/dē ō] **44**–16, **108**–31
   ...program [-prō/grăm] **166**–4
radioactive [rā/dē ō ăk/tĭv] **147**–6
radiologist [rā/dē äl/ə jĭst] **86**–5
radishes [răd/ĭ shəz] **51**–5
radius [rā/dē əs] **118**–16
rafting [răf/tĭng] **154**–4
rags [răgz] **47**–6
railroad crossing [rāl/rōd krö/sĭng] **107**–11
rain boots [rān/ bōōts/] **66**–19
raincoat [rān/kōt/] **66**–17
rain forest [rān/ för/əst, fär/–] **117**–1
raining [rā/nĭng] **10**–8
raise [rāz] **2**–A
raisins [rā/zənz] **50**–27
rake [rāk] **39**–F
rake [rāk] **39**–11
ranch [rănch] **34**–12
rancher [răn/chər] **148**–22
RANCHING [răn/chĭng] **148**
rash [răsh] **78**–10
raspberries [răz/bĕr/ēz] **50**–18
rat [răt] **133**–18
rats [răts] **49**–27
rattle [răt/l] **95**–31
rattlesnake [răt/l snāk/] **131**–38
raw [rö] **52**–24
ray [rā] **130**–6
rayon [rā/än] **70**
razor [rā/zər] **77**–25
   ...blade [-blād/] **77**–26
read [rēd] **6**–B, **27**–V, **94**–F
Realtor [rē/əl tər] **35**
rearview mirror [rĭr/vyōō/ mĭr/ər] **108**–1
receipt [rĭ sēt/] **21**–5
receive [rĭ sēv/] **96**–D
receiver [rĭ sē/vər] **9**–2
receptionist [rĭ sĕp/shə nĭst] **84**–2, **138**–47
recharging [rē chär/jĭng] **109**–58
record [rĕk/ərd] **98**–15
record [rĭ körd/] (science) **119**–C, (cassette player) **165**–A
Recreation room [rĕk/rē ā/shən rōōm/] **36**
rec room [rĕk/ rōōm/] **36** ✦
rectangle [rĕk/tăng/gəl] **118**–8
recycle [rē sī/kəl] **46**–B, **126**–A
recycling bin [rē sī/klĭng bĭn/] **47**–2
red [rĕd(/–)] **12**–13
   ...hair [-hĕr/] **23**–14
redwood [rĕd/wŏŏd/] **128**–1
referee [rĕf/ə rē/] **158**–6
reference [rĕf/rəns]
   ...desk [-dĕsk/] **98**–2
   ...librarian [lī brĕr/ē ən] **98**–1
refrigerator [rĭ frĭj/ə rā/tər] **40**–9

register [rĕj/ə stər] **116**–F
registered [rĕj/ə stərd]
   ...nurse (RN) [–nürs/] **87**–22
regular price [rĕg/yə lər prīs/] **21**–2
relax [rĭ lăks/] **27**–U
relieved [rĭ lēvd/] **30**–16
religious holiday [rĭ lĭj/əs häl/ə dā/] **19**–44
relish [rĕl/ĭsh] **60**–26
remarried [rē măr/ēd] **25**–27
remote control [rĭ mōt/ kən trōl/] **164**–9
remove [rĭ mōōv/] **97**–F
rent [rĕnt] **28**–I
Renting an apartment [rĕn/tĭng ən ə pärt/mənt] **35**
repair [rĭ për/] **140**–G
repair person [rĭ për/ pür/sən] **48**–10, **138**–48
REPAIRS [rĭ përz/] **48–49**
repeat [rĭ pēt/] **6**–D
report crimes [rĭ pört/ krīmz/] **101**–H
reporter [rĭ pör/tər] **99**–12, **139**–49
Reptiles [rĕp/tīlz] **131**
request [rĭ kwĕst/] **111**–M
rescue breathing [rĕs/kyōō brē/dhĭng] **83**–16
Resident Alien card [rĕz/ə dənt ā/lē ən kärd/] **29**–3
respirator [rĕs/pə rā/tər] **147**–12
Responsibilities (of citizenship)
   [rĭ spän/sə bĭl/ə tēz əv sĭt/ə zən shĭp/] **116**
RESTAURANT [rĕs/tə rənt, –ränt/] **62–63**
restaurant [rĕs/tə rənt, –ränt/] **90**–14
rest rooms [rĕst/ rōōmz/] **5**–8
retire [rĭ tīr/] **29** ✦
return [rĭ türn/] **21**–F
return address [rĭ türn/ ə drĕs/, –ā/drĕs] **96**–7
rewind [rē wīnd/] **165**–D
rewrite [rē rīt/] **113**–D
rhinoceros [rī näs/ər əs] **135**–29
rib cage [rĭb/ kāj/] **75**–53
rice [rīs(/–)] **54**–28, **148**–1
   ...pilaf [–pē/läf, –pĭ läf/] **61**–18
ride [rīd] **91**–E, **157**–W
rides [rīdz] **152**–17
right [rīt(/–)] / [–rīt/]
   ...turn only [–türn/ ōn/lē] **107**–9
   on the... [än dhə–, ön–] **13**–2
right-of-way [rīt/əv wā/] **107** ✦
Rights and responsibilities [rīts/ ən rĭ spän/sə bĭl/ə tēz] **116**
ring [rĭng] **69**–39
rinse [rĭns] **76**–F
rip [rĭp] **70**–23
ripe [rīp] **50**–29
river [rĭv/ər] **117**–3
RN (registered nurse) [är/ĕn/] **87**–22
roast [rōst] **58**–U
roast [rōst(/–)]
   ...beef [–bēf/] **52**–1, **53**–7, **57**–12
   ...chicken [–chĭk/ən] **61**–12
roasting [rō/stĭng]
   ...pan [–păn/] **59**–13
   ...rack [–răk/] **59**–14
robin [räb/ən] **132**–17
rock [räk] **94**–H
rock [räk(/–)] **155**–24
rock band [räk/ bănd/] **120**–2
rocking chair [räk/ĭng chĕr/] **94**–6
RODENTS [rōd/nts] **133**
roll [rōl(/–)] **56**–11

...of paper towels [–əv pā/pər tow/əlz] **56**–23
roller coaster [rō/lər kō/stər] **152**–15
rollers [rō/lərz] **23**–21
rolling pin [rō/lĭng pĭn/] **59**–30
rolls [rōlz] **54**–30
romance [rō măns/, rō/măns] **166**–16
Roman numerals [rō/mən nōō/mər əlz] **14**
roof [rōōf] **38**–20, **48**–3
roofer [rōō/fər] **48**–8
roof garden [rōōf/ gär/dn] **36**–5
room service [rōōm/ sür/vəs] **145**–12
rooster [rōō/stər] **133**–6
root [rōōt] **128**–5, **129**–3
rope [rōp] **154**–19
rose [rōz] **129**–15
rotary card file [rō/tə rē kärd/ fīl/] **143**–17
rotten [rät/n] **50**–30
rouge [rōōzh] **77**–36
route [rōōt, rowt] **104**–2
router [row/tər] **150**–12
rubber [rŭb/ər]
   ...band [–bănd/] **143**–45
   ...cement [–sə mĕnt/] **143**–38
   ...gloves [–glŭvz/] **47**–4
   ...mat [–măt/] **43**–3
   ...stamp [–stămp/] **143**–40
rug [rŭg] **44**–23
ruler [rōō/lər] **3**–27
run [rŭn] **156**–C
rural area [rōōr/əl ër/ē ə] **34**–4
rye bread [rī/ brĕd/] **53**–3
sad [săd] **31**–20, **167**–28
safe-deposit box [sāf/dĭ päz/ət bäks/] **97**–13
safety [sāf/tē]
   ...boot [–bōōt/] **147**–20
   ...earmuffs [–ïr/mŭfs] **147**–14
   ...glasses [–glăs/əz] **147**–10
   ...goggles [–gäg/əlz] **147**–9
   ...pin [–pĭn/] **73**–24
   ...seat [–sēt/] **109**–39
   ...vest [–vĕst/] **147**–15
   ...visor [–vī/zər] **147**–11
SAFETY, PUBLIC [pŭb/lĭk sāf/tē] **101**
sailboarding [sāl/bör/dĭng] **160**–10
sailboat [sāl/bōt/] **155**–4
sailing [sā/lĭng] **160**–8
salad [săl/əd]
   ...bar [–bär/] **60**–16
   ...dressing [–drĕs/ĭng] **60**–18
   ...fork [–förk/] **63**–24
   ...plate [–plāt/] **63**–17
salamander [săl/ə măn/dər] **130**–27
salami [sə lä/mē] **53**–5
sale price [sāl/ prīs/] **21**–3
salesclerk [sālz/klürk/] **68**–1, **139**–50
salesperson [sālz/pür/sən] **139**–50
sales tax [sālz/ tăks/] **21**–7
salmon steak [săm/ən stāk/] **53**–19
saltshaker [sölt/shā/kər] **41**–14
sand [sănd(/–)] **155**–23
   ...castle [–kăs/əl] **155**–10
   ...dune [–dōōn/] **117**–5
sandals [săn/dlz] **68**–24
sandbox [sănd/bäks/] **153**–15
sandpaper [sănd/pā/pər] **151**–50

sanitation worker [săn/ə tā/shən wür/kər] **139**–51
Saturday [săt/ər dā/, –dē] **18**–7
Saturn [săt/ərn] **127**–4
saucepan [sös/păn/] **59**–25
saucer [sö/sər] **63**–22
sausage [sö/sĭj] **52**–12, **61**–2
sauté [sö tā/, sö–] **58**–H
save [sāv] **126**–B, C
savings account number [sā/vĭngz ə kownt/ nŭm/bər] **97**–6
saxophone [săk/sə fōn/] **120**–7
say [sā] **6**–C
scaffolding [skăf/əl dĭng] **149**–4
scale (weight) [skāl] **43**–26, **84**–7
scales (fish) [skālz] **130**–3
scallions [skăl/yənz] **51**–17
scallop [skăl/əp, skäl/–] **130**–18
scallops [skăl/əps, skäl/–] **53**–25
scanner [skăn/ər] **144**–13
scared [skërd] **31**–24
scarf [skärf] **66**–4, **70**–15
schedule [skĕj/ōōl, –ōō əl] **104**–3
SCHOOL [skōōl] **5**
school **89**–27
   ...crossing [–krö/sĭng] **107**–13
   adult... [ə dŭlt/–, ăd/ŭlt–] **112**–8
   elementary... [ĕl/ə mĕn/trē–] **112**–5
   high... [hī/–] **112**–7
   junior high... [jōōn/yər hī/–] **112**–6
   middle... [mĭd/l–] **112**–6
   parochial... [pə rō/kē əl–] **112**–3
   private... [prī/vət–] **112**–2
   trade... [trād/–] **112**–9
   vocational... [vō kā/shə nəl–] **112**–9
School Registration Form [skōōl/ rĕj/ə strā/shən förm/] **4**
SCHOOLS, TYPES OF [tīps/ əv skōōlz/] **112**
SCHOOL SUBJECTS, MORE [mör/ skōōl/ sŭb/jĭkts] **121**
SCIENCE [sī/əns] **119**
science fiction story [sī/əns fĭk/shən stör/ē] **166**–12
scissors [sĭz/ərz] **23**–19, **73**–18
score [skör] **158**–1
scorpion [skör/pē ən] **132**–31
scrambled eggs [skrăm/bəld ĕgz/] **58**, **61**–1
scraper [skrā/pər] **151**–48
screen [skrēn] **2**–2, **144**–6, **152**–12, **165**–28
screen door [skrēn/ dör/] **38**–8
screwdriver [skrōō/drī/vər] **150**–25
   Phillips... [fĭl/ĭps–] **150**–26
scrub [skrŭb] **46**–L
scrub brush [skrŭb/ brŭsh/] **47**–19
scuba [skōō/bə]
   ...diving [–dī/vĭng] **160**–12
   ...tank [–tăngk/] **155**–8
sculpture [skŭlp/chər] **152**–9
sea [sē(/–)]
   ...anemone [–ə nĕm/ə nē] **130**–21
   ...horse [–hörs/] **130**–23
   ...lion [–lī/ən] **131**–34
   ...urchin [–ür/chən] **130**–20
Sea animals [sē/ ăn/ə məlz] **130**
SEAFOOD [sē/fōōd/] **53**
seal [sēl] **131**–33
seam [sēm(/–)] **73**–11
   ...ripper [–rĭp/ər] **73**–19
Sea mammals [sē/ măm/əlz] **131**
search and rescue team [sürch/ ən rĕs/kyōō tēm/] **103**–17

Index

seashell [sē/shĕl/] **155**–21
Seasons [sē/zənz] **19**
seat [sēt(/–)] **2**–E, **152**–11
...belt [–bĕlt/] **109**–36
seat [sēt] **62**–B
seaweed [sē/wēd/] **155** ✦
second [sĕk/ənd] **14, 16**–1
...floor [–flör/] **36**–2
secretary [sĕk/rə tër/ē] **139**–52, **142**–3
section [sĕk/shən] / [–sĕk/shən]
dairy... [dër/ē–] **54**–9
produce... [prō/dōōs–] **54**–11
security [sĭ kyŏŏr/ə tē] **111**–C
...gate [–gāt/] **36**–13
...guard [–gärd/] **97**–4
...system [–sĭs/təm] **36**–9
see [sē] **75**–A
seed [sēd] **129**–1
seedling [sēd/lĭng] **129**–2
seesaw [sē/sö/] **153**–16
See you [sē/ yə] **8**
Selective Service [sə lĕk/tĭv sür/vəs] **116**–F
sell [sĕl] **21**–B, **140**–H
semi [sĕm/ī] **106**–15
semicolon [sĕm/ē kō/lən] **113**–13
Senate [sĕn/ət] **116**–3
Senator [sĕn/ə tər] **116**–4
send [sĕnd] **96**–B
senior citizen [sēn/yər sĭt/ə zən] **22**–12
Senses [sĕn/səz] **75**
sentence [sĕn/tns] **113**–4
sentence the defendant [sĕn/tns dhə dĭ fĕn/dənt] **99**–F
September [sĕp tĕm/bər] **19**–33
serious [sïr/ē əs] **167**–26
Serious Diseases [sïr/ē əs dĭ zē/zəz] **79**
serve (sports) [sürv] **157**–N
serve on a jury [sürv/ än ə jŏŏr/ē, –ön–] **116**–G
server [sür/vər] **62**–4, **63**–6, **139**–53
serve the meal [sürv/ dhə mēl/] **62**–F
service elevator [sür/vəs ĕl/ə vā tər] **145** ✦
serviceman [sür/vəs măn/, –mən] **139**–54
servicewoman [sür/vəs wŏŏm/ən] **139**–54
serving dish [sür/vĭng dĭsh/] **41**–6
set [sēt(/–)]
...hair [–hër/] **23**–C
...the table [–dhə tā/bəl] **62**–A
set of dishes [sĕt/ əv dĭsh/əz] **41**–2
seven [sĕv/ən] **14**
seventeen [sĕv/ən tēn/] **14**
seventeenth [sĕv/ən tēnth/] **14**
seventh [sĕv/ənth] **14**
seventy [sĕv/ən tē] **14**
sew [sō(/–)]
...by hand [–bī hănd/] **73**–A
...by machine [–bī mə shēn/] **73**–B
...clothes [–klōz/] **140**–L
SEWING AND ALTERATIONS [sō/ĭng ən öl/tə rā/shənz] **73**
sewing machine [sō/ĭng mə shēn/] **73**–10
sex [sĕks] **4**–12
shade [shād] **155**–11
shampoo [shăm pōō/] **76**–9
Shapes [shāps] **118**
share [shër] **6**–I
shark [shärk] **130**–7
shave [shāv] **77**–M

shaving cream [shā/vĭng krēm/] **77**–27
shears [shïrz] **39**–15
sheep [shēp] **133**–7
sheet [shēt] **44**–13, 14
shelf [shĕlf] **40**–8
Shellfish [shĕl/fĭsh/] **53**
shelter [shĕl/tər] **34**–10
shingles [shĭng/gəlz] **149**–19
shin guards [shĭn/ gärdz/] **161**–13
ship [shĭp] **146**–C
shipping clerk [shĭp/ĭng klürk/] **146**–15
shirt [shürt] **64**–4, **65**–20
shock [shäk] **82**–C
shoe [shōō(/–)]
...department [–dĭ pärt/mənt] **68**–3
...store [–stör/] **92**–10
shoelace [shōō/lās/] **68**–14
SHOES AND ACCESSORIES [shōōz/ ən ĭk sĕs/ə rēz] **68–69**
shoot [shōōt] **156**–I
shop [shäp] **21**–A
shop [shäp] **121**–10
SHOPPING [shäp/ĭng] **21**
shopping [shäp/ĭng]
...basket [–băs/kət] **54**–7
...cart [–kärt/] **54**–3
...program [–prō/grăm] **167**–25
shore [shör] **117**–12
short [shört] **22**–18, **23**–1, **71**–35
shorten [shör/tn] **73**–D
short-sleeved [shört/slēvd/] **71**–30
shorts [shörts] **64**–13, **67**–3, 12
shortwave radio [shört/wāv/ rā/dē ō] **164**–5
shoulder [shōl/dər] **74**–10
...bag [–băg/] **69**–27
...harness [–här/nəs] **109**–37
...pads [–pădz/] **161**–21
shoulder-length [shōl/dər lĕngkth/] **23**–2
shout [showt] **169**–G
shovel [shŭv/əl] **39**–13, **149**–21
show (puppet) [shō] **152**–14
shower cap [show/ər kăp/] **76**–1
showerhead [show/ər hĕd/] **43**–10
shrimp [shrĭmp] **53**–24, **130**–19
shutter [shŭt/ər] **38**–18
sick [sĭk] **30**–14
side [sīd] **118**–22
sideburns [sīd/bürnz/] **23**–7
sideview mirror [sīd/vyōō/ mïr/ər] **108**–8
sidewalk [sīd/wök/] **91**–26
sight impaired [sīt/ ĭm përd/] **22**–26
sign [sīn(/–)]
...a rental agreement [–ə rĕn/təl ə grē/mənt] **35**–C
...your name [–yər nām/] **4**–D
sign [sīn] **91**–29
signature [sĭg/nə chər] **4**–18
Signs [sīnz] **107**
silk [sĭlk] **70**–15
silk scarves [sĭlk/ skärvz/] **68**–4
silver dollar [sĭl/vər däl/ər] **20**–6
simmer [sĭm/ər] **58**–R
sing [sĭng] **120**–B, **169**–I
single [sĭng/gəl]
...father [–fä/dhər] **25**–25
...mother [–mŭdh/ər] **25**–26
sink [sĭngk] **40**–6, **43**–22, **49**–17

sister [sĭs/tər] **24**–8, **25**–30, 32
sister-in-law [sĭs/tər ĭn lö/] **24**–15
sitcom [sĭt/käm/] **167**–18
sit down [sĭt/ down/] **2**–E
situation comedy [sĭch/ōō ā/shən käm/ə dē] **167**–18
six [sĭks] **14**
six-pack [sĭks/păk/] **56**–9
six-pack of soda [sĭks/păk/ əv sō/də] **56**–21
sixteen [sĭks/tēn/] **14**
sixteenth [sĭks/tēnth/] **14**
sixth [sĭksth] **14**
sixty [sĭks/tē] **14**
six-year-old [sĭks/yïr ōld/] **22**–4
Sizes [sī/zəz] **70**
skate [skāt] **157**–V
skateboarding [skāt/bör/dĭng] **159**–12
skating [skā/tĭng] **160**–4, 5
Skeleton [skĕl/ə tn] **75**
ski [skē] **157**–V
ski [skē(/–)]
...boots [–bōōts/] **161**–26
...cap [–kăp/] **66**–10
...mask [–măsk/] **66**–14
...poles [–pōlz/] **161**–25
skiing [skē/ĭng] **160**–1, 3, 7
skin [skĭn] **75**–51
skinless [skĭn/ləs] **52** ✦
skirt [skürt] **64**–10, **65**–25
skis [skēz] **161**–24
skull [skŭl] **75**–52
skunk [skŭngk] **134**–12
skyscraper [skī/skrā/pər] **88** ✦
slacks [slăks] **64**–8
sledding [slĕd/ĭng] **160**–6
sledgehammer [slĕj/hăm/ər] **149**–22
sleeping bag [slē/pĭng băg/] **154**–12
sleepy [slē/pē] **30**–3
sleeve [slēv] **73**–6
sleeveless [slēv/ləs] **71**–29
slice [slīs] **58**–O
slide [slīd] (science) **119**–5, (park) **153**–13
slides [slīdz] **165**–31
slide tray [slīd/ trā/] **165**–30
slim [slĭm] **22**–22
sling [slĭng] **80**–8
slippers [slĭp/ərz] **67**–6
slot [slät] **144**–19
slow [slō] **11**–4
small [smöl(/–)] **70**–2
...town [–town/] **34**–3
smell [smĕl] **75**–C
smog [smäg(/–), smög(/–)] **126**–10
...check [–chĕk/] **109**–57
smoggy [smä/gē, smö/–] **10**–14
smoke detector [smōk/ dĭ tĕk/tər] **37**–25, **45**–11
smoked turkey [smōkt/ tür/kē] **53**–4
snack foods [snăk/ fōōdz/] **55**–16
snail [snāl] **130**–24
snake [snāk] **131**–38, 39
sneeze [snēz] **78**–B
snorkeling [snör/kə lĭng] **160**–11
snowboard [snō/börd/] **161**–23
snowboarding [snō/bör/dĭng] **160**–2
snowing [snō/ĭng] **10**–9
snowstorm [snō/störm/] **10**–20

soap [sōp(/–)] **43**–23, **76**–2
...dish [–dĭsh/] **43**–24
...pads [–pădz/] **47**–5
soap opera [sōp/ äp/rə] **167**–21
soccer [säk/ər] **158**–12
...ball [–böl/] **161**–12
Social Security card [sō/shəl sĭ kyoor/ə tē kärd/] **29**–5
Social Security number [sō/shəl sĭ kyoor/ə tē nŭm/bər] **4**–15
socks [säks] **67**–15
soda [sō/də] **55**–52, **60**–4
sofa [sō/fə] **42**–19
soft [söft] **11**–6
softball [söft/böl/] **158**–10
Software [söft/wër/] **144**
solar [sō/lər]
...eclipse [–ī klĭps/] **127** ✦
...energy [–ĕn/ər jē] **126**–1
...system [–sĭs/təm] **127**
sole [sōl] (fish) **53**–21, (shoe) **68**–12
solid [säl/əd] **70**–6
Solids [säl/ədz] **118**
son [sŭn] **24**–22
son-in-law [sŭn/ĭn lö/] **24** ✦
sore throat [sör/ thrōt/] **78**–6
Sorry. [sär/ē, sör/ē] **8**
sort [sört] **72**–A
soup [sōōp(/–)] **54**–24
...bowl [–bol/] **63**–18
...of the day [–əv dhə dā/] **61**–10
soupspoon [sōōp/spōōn/] **63**–29
sour cream [sow/ər krēm/] **54**–37
south [sowth] **107, 123, 124**
soybeans [soy/bēnz/] **148**–3
space [spās(/–)] **127**–22
...station [–stā/shən] **127**–18
spades [spādz] **163**–28
spaghetti [spə gĕt/ē] **54**–27
spare tire [spër/ tīr/] **109**–53
sparrow [spär/ō] **132**–8
spatula [spăch/ə lə] **59**–19
speak [spēk] **140**–J
speaker [spē/kər] **36**–8
speakers [spē/kərz] **164**–11
specialist [spĕsh/ə lĭst] **86** ✦
speed [spēd(/–)] **144** ✦
...limit [–lĭm/ət] **107**–5
speedometer [spĭ däm/ə tər] **108**–20
spell [spĕl] **4**–A, **6**–E
sphere [sfïr] **118**–14
spices [spī/səz] **55**–46
spider [spī/dər] **132**–30
spinach [spĭn/ĭch] **51**–11
spinal column [spī/nəl käl/əm] **75**–54
spiral notebook [spī/rəl nōt/bōōk/] **3**–26
splint [splĭnt] **83**–11
split skirt [splĭt/ skürt/] **65**–25
sponge [spŭnj] **47**–24
spool of thread [spōōl/ əv thrĕd/] **73**–17
spoon [spōōn] **41**–23, **59**–9
SPORTS [spörts] **158–160**
sports [spörts(/–)]
...car [–kär/] **106**–6
...coat [–kōt/] **64**–6
...shirt [–shürt/] **65**–26
SPORTS EQUIPMENT [spörts/ ĭ kwĭp/mənt] **161**

Index

SPORTS VERBS [spörts/ vürbz/] **156–157**
sprained ankle [spränd/ ăng/kəl] **78**–18
spray [sprā(/–)]
...gun [–gŭn/] **151**– 19
...starch [–stärch/] **72**–12
spring [sprĭng] **19**–37
sprinkler [sprĭng/klər] **39**–8
square [skwër] **118**–6
squash [skwäsh, skwösh] **51**–13
squeegee [skwē/jē] **47**–9
squid [skwĭd] **130**–10
squirrel [skwür/əl] **133**–21
stacking tray [stăk/ĭng trā/] **142**–5
stadium [stā/dē əm] **152**–26
stage [stāj] **32**–4
stain [stān] **70**–22
stairs [stërz] **37**–35, **105**–8, 9
stairway [stër/wā/] **37**–26
stall shower [stöl/ show/ər] **43** ✦
stamp [stămp(/–)] **96**–10
...collection [–kə lĕk/shən] **162**–12
standard [stăn/dərd]
...time [–tīm/] **17**–32
...transmission [–trănz mĭsh/ən, –trăns–] **109**
stand trial [stănd/ trī/əl, –trīl/] **99**–D
stand up [stănd/ ŭp/] **2**–D
stand-up comedy [stănd/ŭp/ kăm/ə dē] **166**–5
staple [stā/pəl] **142**–G
staple [stā/pəl] **143**–29
stapler [stā/plər] **143**–28
star [stär] **127**–23
starfish [stär/fĭsh/] **130**–15
start [stärt(/–)] **157**–X
...school [–skool/] **28**–B
starving [stär/vĭng] **30** ✦
state [stāt] **4**–8
station wagon [stā/shən wăg/ən] **106**–8
stay [stā] **101**–B
steak [stāk(/–)] **52**–2, **61**–13
...knife [–nīf/] **63**–26
steam [stēm] **58**–I
steamer [stē/mər] **59**–4
steel-wool soap pads [stēl/wool/ sōp/ pădz/] **47**–5
steering wheel [stïr/ĭng wēl/] **108**–26
steers [stïrz] **148**–21
stem [stěm] **129**–4
stepbrother [stĕp/brŭdh/ər] **25**–33
stepdaughter [stĕp/dö/tər] **25** ✦
stepfather [stĕp/fä/dhər] **25**–28
stepladder [stĕp/lăd/ər] **47**–7
stepmother [stĕp/mŭdh/ər] **25**–31
steps [stĕps] **38**–13, **48**–7
stepsister [stĕp/sĭs/tər] **25**–32
stereo system [stĕr/ē ō sĭs/təm] **42**–14
sterile pad [stĕr/əl păd/] **83**–4
stethoscope [stĕth/ə skōp/] **84**–8
stewing beef [stoo/ĭng bēf/] **52**–3
stick shift [stĭk/ shĭft/] **109**–48
stir [stür] **58**–E
stir-fry [stür/frī/] **58**–W
stitches [stĭch/əz] **83**–15
stock clerk [stäk/ klürk/] **139**–55
stockings [stäk/ĭngz] **67**–26
stomach [stŭm/ək] **75**–41
stomachache [stŭm/ək āk/] **78**–4

stop [stäp] **165**–F
stop [stäp] **107**–3
stopover [stäp/ō/vər] **111** ✦
stopped up [stäpt/ ŭp/] **49**–18
storage locker [stör/ĭj läk/ər] **36**–14
store [stör(/–)] / [–stör/]
...owner [–ō/nər] **139**–56
candy... [kăn/dē–] **92**–3
card... [kärd/–] **92**–7
convenience... [kən vēn/yəns–] **90**–3
department... [dĭ pärt/mənt–] **93**–13
electronics... [ĭ lĕk trän/ĭks–] **93**–18
jewelry... [joo/əl rē–] **92**–2
music... [myoo/zĭk–] **92**–1
pet... [pĕt/–] **92**–6
shoe... [shoo/–] **92**–10
toy... [toy/–] **92**–5
video... [vĭd/ē ō–] **93**–15
storm [störm] **10**–16, 18, 20, 21
storm door [störm/ dör/] **38**–12
stove [stōv] **40**–18, **154**–16
stow [stō] **111**–H
straight [strāt(/–)]
...hair [–hër/] **23**–9
...line [–līn/] **118**–18
strainer [strā/nər] **59**–22
stranger [strān/jər] **101**–F
straw [strö] **60**–20
strawberries [strö/bĕr/ēz] **50**–17
straw hat [strö/ hăt/] **66**–23
stream [strēm] **117** ✦
street [strēt(/–)] **90**–9
...vendor [–vĕn/dər] **91**–30
streetlight [strēt/līt/] **91**–23
strep throat [strĕp/ thrōt/] **79**–4
stretch [strĕch] **157**–Q
stretcher [strĕch/ər] **87**–28
string beans [strĭng/ bēnz/] **51**–25
string of pearls [strĭng/ əv pürlz/] **69**–30
Strings [strĭngz] **120**
striped [strīpt] **70**–7
stroller [strō/lər] **94**–2
stucco [stŭk/ō] **149**–14
student [stood/nt] **2**–3, **139**–57
STUDYING [stŭd/ē ĭng] **6**–7
stuffed animals [stŭft/ ăn/ə məlz] **45**–23
subcompact [sŭb/käm/păkt] **106**–1
subtraction [səb trăk/shən] **118**–2
suburbs [sŭb/ürbz] **34**–2
subway [sŭb/wā/] **104**–9
sugar [shoog/ər] **55**–48, **60**–21
...bowl [–bōl/] **41**–12
...substitute [–sŭb/stə toot/] **60**–22
suit [soot] (clothing) **64**–2, (diving) **155**–7
summer [sŭm/ər] **19**–38
sun [sŭn] **127**–10
sunbather [sŭn/bā/dhər] **155**–17
sunblock [sŭn/bläk/] **155**–13
sunburn [sŭn/bürn/] **78**–14
Sunday [sŭn/dā, –dē] **18**–1
sunflower [sŭn/flow/ər] **129**–10
sunglasses [sŭn/glăs/əz] **66**–21
sunny [sŭn/ē] **10**–6
sunscreen [sŭn/skrēn/] **76**–6, **155**–13
superintendent [soo/prĭn tĕn/dənt, soo/pər ĭn–] **36**–12

supervise people [soo/pər vīz pē/pəl] **140**–K

supply cabinet [sə plī/ kăb/ə nət] **142**–13

Supreme Court [sə prēm/ kört/] **116**–8

surfboard [sürf/börd/] **155**–5

surfing [sür/fīng] **160**–9

surgeon [sür/jən] **87**–30

surge protector [sürj/ prə tĕk/tər] **144**–10

surgical [sür/jĭ kəl]

...cap [–kăp/] **87**–31

...gown [–gown/] **87**–32

...nurse [–nürs/] **87**–29

surprised [sər prīzd/, sə–] **31**–31

suspect [sŭs/pĕkt] **99**–A

suspenders [sə spĕn/dərz] **68**–2

SUV (sports utility vehicle)
[ĕs/yoo/vē/] / [spörts/ yoo tĭl/ə tē vē/ĭ kəl] **106**–9

swallow [swäl/ō] **82**–J

swap meet [swäp/ mēt/] **152**–22

sweater [swĕt/ər]

cardigan... [kär/də gən–] **65**–27

crewneck... [kroo/nĕk/–] **71**–26

pullover... [pool/ō/vər–] **64**–11

turtleneck... [tür/tl nĕk/–] **71**–28

V-neck... [vē/nĕk/–] **71**–27

sweatpants [swĕt/pănts/] **64**–15

sweatshirt [swĕt/shürt/] **64**–14

sweep [swēp] **46**–E

sweet peppers [swēt/ pĕp/ərz] **51**–7

swim [swĭm] **157**–T

swimming [swĭm/ĭng]

...pool [–pool/] **37**–16

...trunks [–trŭngks/] **66**–22

swimsuit [swĭm/soot/] **66**–26

swing [swĭng] **157**–O

swings [swĭngz] **153**–12

Swiss cheese [swĭs/ chēz/] **53**–11

swivel chair [swĭv/əl chër/] **143**–22

swollen [swō/lən] **78**–16

swordfish [sörd/fĭsh/] **130**–12

SYMPTOMS AND INJURIES [sĭmp/təmz ən ĭn/jə rēz] **78**

synagogue [sĭn/ə gäg/] **88**–9

synthetic materials [sĭn thĕt/ĭk mə tïr/ē əlz] **70**

syringe [sə rĭnj/] **84**–14

syrup [sĭr/əp, sür/–] **61**–5

table [tā/bəl] / [–tā/bəl]

dining room... [dī/nĭng room/–] **41**–17

night... [nīt/–] **44**–21

picnic... [pĭk/nĭk–] **153**–8

tablecloth [tā/bəl klöth/] **41**–18

tablespoon [tā/bəl spoon/] **57**–7

tablet [tăb/lət] **81**–25

table tennis [tā/bəl tĕn/əs] **159**–13

tackle [tăk/əl] **156**–M

taco [tä/kō] **60**–9

tail [tāl] **134**–22

taillight [tāl/līt/] **108**–14

tailor [tā/lər] **73**–9

take [tāk(/–)]

...a bath [–ə băth/] **76**–B

...a citizenship test [–ə sĭt/ə zən shĭp tĕst/] **116**–C

...a message [–ə mĕs/ĭj] **142**–A

...a nap [–ə năp/] **94**–L

...a picture [–ə pĭk/chər] **32**–D

...a seat [–ə sēt/] **2**–E

...a shower [–ə show/ər] **26**–C, **76**–A

...medicine [–mĕd/ə sən] **80**–F

...ownership [–ō/nər shĭp/] **35**–J

...the bus [–dhə bŭs/] **26**–H, **104** ✦

...the children to school [–dhə chĭl/drən tə skool/] **26**–G

...the order [–dhē ör/dər] **62**–E

...(your) temperature [–yər tĕm/prə chər] **85**–C

take care of [tāk/ kër/ əv] **140**–L

take in [tāk/ ĭn/] **73**–E

take off [tāk/ öf/] **111**–L

take out [tāk/ owt/] **2**–K, **46**–Q

take out (food) [tāk/ owt/] **62** ✦

talcum powder [tăl/kəm pow/dər] **76**–3

talk [tök] **2**–B, **7**–P, **35**–B, G, **141**–A, I

talk show [tök/ shō/] **167**–20

tall [töl] **22**–16

tambourine [tăm/bə rēn/] **120**–19

tangerines [tăn/jə rēnz/] **50**–13

tank top [tăngk/ täp/] **67**–2

tape [tāp(/–)] **83**–5, **143**–39, 42

...deck [–dĕk/] **108**–30

...measure [–mĕzh/ər] **73**–13, **150**–22

target [tär/gət] **161**–8

tartar [tär/tər] **84**–17

taste [tāst] **75**–D

taxi [tăk/sē] **104**–18

...driver [–drī/vər] **104**–20

...license [–lī/səns] **104**–22

...stand [–stănd/] **104**–19

TB (tuberculosis) [tē/bē/] / [too bür/kyə lō/səs] **79**–13

tea [tē] **60**–5, **61**–24

teach [tēch] **140** ✦

teacher [tē/chər] **2**–5, **5**–2, **139**–58

teakettle [tē/kĕt/l] **40**–17

team [tēm] **103**–17, **158**–3

TEAM SPORTS [tēm/ spörts/] **158**

teapot [tē/pät/] **41**–11

tear [tër] **70**–23

teaspoon [tē/spoon/] **57**–6, **63**–28

technician [tĕk nĭsh/ən] **86**–8, 16

teddy bear [tĕd/ē bër/] **45**–10

teenagers [tē/nā/jərz] **22**–6

teeth [tēth] **74**–25, **77**–J, K, **85**–I

teething ring [tē/dhĭng rĭng/] **95**–30

telemarketer [tĕl/ə mär/kə tər] **139**–59

TELEPHONE [tĕl/ə fōn/] **9**

telephone [tĕl/ə fōn/] **9**–1, 15

...book [–book/] **9**–15

...card [–kärd/] **9**–10

...number [–nŭm/bər] **4**–11

telescope [tĕl/ə skōp/] **127**–21

television (TV) [tĕl/ə vĭzh/ən] **42**–26, **164**–6

...program [–prō/grăm] **166**–3

teller [tĕl/ər] **97**–1

Temperature (weather) [tĕm/prə chər] **10**

temperature (fever) [tĕm/prə chər] **78**–8

temperature gauge [tĕm/prə chər gāj/] **108**–23

ten [tĕn] **14**, **15**–7, **16**–6, **20**–9

tenant [tĕn/ənt] **37**–33

tennis [tĕn/əs] **159**–14

...court [–kört/] **153**–7

...racket [–răk/ət] **161**–2

...shoes [–shooz/] **68**–22

tent [tĕnt] **154**–10

tenth [tĕnth] **14**

ten-year-old [tĕn/yïr ōld/] **22**–5

Index

termites [tür/mīts] **49**–22
terrified [tĕr/ə fīd/] **30** ✦
test tube [tĕst/ toob/] **119**–16
textbook [tĕkst/book/, tĕks/–] **3**–22
thank [thăngk] **8**–H
Thanksgiving [thăngks gĭv/ĭng] **168**–15
Thank you [thăngk/ yoo] **8**
theater [thē/ə tər] / [thē/ə tər] **88**–10
   ...arts [–ärts/] **121**–12
   movie... [–moo/vē–] **88**–11
thermometer [thər măm/ə tər] **84**–15
thick book [thĭk/ book/] **11**–7
thigh [thī] **74**–16
thighs [thīz] **52**–21
thimble [thĭm/bəl] **73**–20
thin [thĭn] **11**–8, **22**–22
third [thürd(/–)] **14**
   ...floor [–flör/] **36**–3
thirsty [thür/stē] **30**–2
thirteen [thür/tēn/] **14**
thirteenth [thür/tēnth/] **14**
thirteen-year-old [thür/tēn/yïr ōld/] **22**–7
thirty [thür/tē] **14**
this week [dhĭs/ wēk/] **18**–19
thorn [thörn] **129**–28
thousand [thow/zənd] **14**
thread [thrĕd] **73**–17
three [thrē(/–)] **14**
   ...times a week [–tīmz/ ə wēk/] **18**–24
three-fourths [thrē/förths/] **15**–5
three-piece suit [thrē/pēs/ soot/] **64**–1
throat [thrōt(/–)] **75**–36
   ...lozenges [–lăz/ən jəz] **81**–21
through [throo] **105**–11
throw [thrō] **156**–D
throw pillow [thrō/ pĭl/ō] **42**–20
throw up [thrō/ ŭp/] **78**–E
thumb [thŭm] **75**–56
thunderstorm [thŭn/dər störm/] **10**–16
Thursday [thürz/dā, –dē] **18**–5
tick [tĭk] **132**–28
ticket [tĭk/ət] **104**–14
tidal wave [tīd/l wāv/] **103**–15
tide [tīd] **155** ✦
tie [tī] **94**–I
tie [tī] (clothing) **69**–40, (sports) **158** ✦
ties [tīz] (clothing) **69**–10
tiger [tī/gər] **135**–37
tight [tīt] **71**–43
tights [tīts] **66**–11
tile [tīl] **43**–9
TIME [tīm] **16–17**
time clock [tīm/ kläk/] **146**–4
Time zones [tīm/ zōnz/] **17**
tire [tīr] **108**–10, **109**–53
tired [tīrd] **31**–33
tires [tīrz] **109**–59
title [tīt/l] **98**–21, **113**–3
toad [tōd] **130**–28
toast [tōst] **33, 61**–3
toaster [tō/stər] **40**–7
   ...oven [–ŭv/ən] **40**–15
today [tə dā/] **18**–15
toddler [täd/lər] **22**–3
toe [tō(/–)] **68**–15, **75**–63

...guard [–gärd/] **147**–21
toenail [tō/nāl/] **75**–64
toggle bolt [täg/əl bōlt/] **150**–33
toilet [toy/lət] **43**–17, **49**–18
   ...brush [–brŭsh/] **43**–16
   ...paper [–pā/pər] **43**–15
token [tō/kən] **104**–11
tomatoes [tə mā/tōz] **51**–23
tomorrow [tə mär/ō, –mör/ō] **18**–16
tongs [tängz, töngz] **59**–23, **119**–15
tongue [tŭng] **74**–26
too big [too/ bĭg/] **70**–21
TOOLS AND BUILDING SUPPLIES
   [toolz/ ən bĭl/dĭng sə plīz/] **150–151**
too small [too/ smöl/] **70**–20
toothache [tooth/āk/] **78**–2
toothbrush [tooth/brŭsh/] **43**–20, **77**–20
   ...holder [–hōl/dər] **43**–21
toothpaste [tooth/pāst/] **77**–21
tornado [tör nā/dō] **103**–13
total [tōt/l] **21**–8, **118** ✦
tote bag [tōt/ băg/] **69**–29
touch [tŭch] **75**–E
towel [tow/əl] **43**–8, 12, 13
   ...rack [–răk/] **43**–8
townhouse [town/hows/] **34**–7
tow truck [tō/ trŭk/] **106**–13
toy [toy(/–)]
   ...chest [–chĕst/] **45**–24
   ...store [–stör/] **92**–5
toys [toyz] **46**–II, **94**–5
track [trăk] (athletic) **5**–11, (train) **104**–10
track and field [trăk/ ən fēld/] **159**–17
trackball [trăk/böl/] **144**–15
track lighting [trăk/ lī/tĭng] **42**–3
tractor [trăk/tər] **148**–9
   ...trailer [–trā/lər] **106**–15
trade school [trād/ skool/] **112**–9
traffic light [trăf/ĭk līt/] **90**–6
TRAFFIC SIGNS [trăf/ĭk sīnz/] **107**
tragedy [trăj/ə dē] **166**–11
trailer [trā/lər] **106**–17
train [trān(/–)] **104**–17
   ...station [–stā/shən] **104**–13
training pants [trā/nĭng pănts/] **95**–24
transcribe [trăn skrīb/] **142**–C
transcriber (medical) [trăn skrī/bər] **142**–4
transfer [trăns für/, trăns/fər] **97**–E
transfer [trăns/fər] **104**–6
translator [trănz/lā/tər, trăns/–] **138**–34
transmission [trănz mĭsh/ən, trăns–]
   automatic... [ö/tə măt/ĭk–] **109**
   standard... [stăn/dərd–] **109**
TRANSPORTATION, PUBLIC [pŭb/lĭk trăns/pər tā/shən] **104**
trash [trăsh(/–)]
   ...bags [–băgz/] **47**–12
   ...bin [–bĭn/] **37**–20
   ...chute [–shoot/] **37**–24
travel [trăv/əl] **29**–N
travel [trăv/əl]
   ...agency [–ā/jən sē] **92**–9
   ...agent [–ā/jənt] **139**–60
traveler's check [trăv/lərz chĕk/] **20**–17
tray [trā(/–)] **41**–10, **62**–H, **63**–7
   ...table [–tā/bəl] **110**–16

treatment [trēt/mənt] **80** ✦
TREES AND PLANTS [trēz/ ən plănts/] **128**
trench coat [trĕnch/ kōt/] **66**–20
triangle [trī/ăng/gəl] **118**–7
tricycle [trī/sĭ kəl] **153**–9
trigonometry [trĭg/ə năm/ə trē] **118**–27
trim [trĭm] **39**–E
tripe [trīp] **52**–8
tripod [trī/päd] **165**–20
trombone [träm bōn/] **120**–12
trout [trowt] **53**–16
trowel [trow/əl] **39**–14, **149**–12
truck driver [trŭk/ drī/vər] **139**–61
TRUCKS [trŭks] **106**
trumpet [trŭm/pət] **120**–13
trunk [trŭngk] (car) **109**–49, (tree) **128**–4, (animal) **135**–47
T-shirt [tē/shürt/] **64**–12, **70**–16, **72**–15, 16, 17, 18
tuba [tōō/bə] **120**–14
tube [tōōb(/–)] **56**–12
    ...of toothpaste [–əv tōōth/pāst/] **56**–24
Tuesday [tōōz/dā, –dē] **18**–3
tulip [tōō/ləp] **129**–11
tuna [tōō/nə] **54**–25, **130**–9
tuner [tōō/nər] **164**–13
tunic [tōō/nĭk] **65**–22
tunnel [tŭn/əl] **105**–11
turbulence [tür/byə ləns] **111**–N
turkey [tür/kē] **52**–17, **53**–4, **168**–17
turn [türn(/–)]
    ...left [–lĕft/] **107**–C
    ...right [–rīt/] **107**–B
turn in [türn/ ĭn/] **113**–E
turnips [tür/nəps] **51**–14
turn signal [türn/ sĭg/nəl] **108**–4
turntable [türn/tā/bəl] **164**–12
turquoise [tür/koyz, –kwoyz] **12**–4
turtle [tür/tl] **131**–42
turtleneck [tür/tl nĕk/] **64**–7
    ...sweater [–swĕt/ər] **71**–28
tusk [tŭsk] **135**–48
tuxedo [tŭk sē/dō] **65**–28
TV (television) [tē/vē/] **42**–26, **164**–6
    ...antenna [–ăn tĕn/ə] **38**–22
tweezers [twē/zərz] **83**–2
twelfth [twĕlfth] **14**
twelve [twĕlv] **14**
twentieth [twĕn/tē əth] **14**
twenty [twĕn/tē] **14**, **16**–8, 9, **20**–10
twenty-five after one [twĕn/tē fīv/ ăf/tər wŭn/] **16**–9
twenty-five to two [twĕn/tē fīv/ tə tōō/] **16**–11
twenty percent [twĕn/tē pər sĕnt/] **15**–8
twenty to two [twĕn/tē tə tōō/] **16**–12
twice a week [twīs/ ə wēk/] **18**–23
twig [twĭg] **128**–1
two [tōō] **14**
two-story house [tōō/stör/ē hows/] **38** ✦
type [tīp] **140**–M, **142**–D
Types of entertainment [tīps/ əv ĕn/tər tān/mənt] **166**
Types of material [tīps/ əv mə tïr/ē əl] **70**
Types of math [tīps/ əv măth/] **118**
TYPES OF SCHOOLS [tīps/ əv skōōlz/] **112**
Types of stories [tīps/ əv stör/ēz] **166**
Types of TV programs [tīps/ əv tē/vē/ prō/grămz] **167**
typewriter [tīp/rī/tər] **142**–2
    ...cartridge [–kär/trĭj] **143**–31

ugly [ŭg/lē] **11**–22
umbrella [ŭm brĕl/ə] **66**–16, **155**–9
umpire [ŭm/pīr] **158** ✦
uncle [ŭng/kəl] **24**–11
uncomfortable [ŭn kŭmf/tə bəl, –tər–] **30**–8
under [ŭn/dər] **13**–9, **105**–1
underexposed [ŭn/dər ĭk spōzd/] **165**–35
underline [ŭn/dər līn/] **7**–V
underpants [ŭn/dər pănts/] **67**–17
undershirt [ŭn/dər shürt/] **67**–10
uniform [yōō/nə förm/] **65**–17, **161**–16
UNIVERSE [yōō/nə vürs/] **127**
university [yōō/nə vür/sə tē] **112**–10
unload [ŭn lōd/] **72**–E
unpack [ŭn păk/] **35**–E
unscented [ŭn sĕn/təd] **77** ✦
up [ŭp] **105**–9
upset [ŭp sĕt/] **31**–30
upstairs [ŭp/stërz/] **38** ✦
Uranus [yŏŏr/ə nəs, yŏŏ rā/nəs] **127**–3
urban area [ür/bən ër/ē ə] **34**–1
use [yōōz(/–)] **140**–N
    ...deodorant [–dē ō/dər ənt] **76**–C
user's manual [yōō/zərz măn/yōō əl] **144**–22
U.S. GOVERNMENT AND CITIZENSHIP
    [yōō/ĕs/ gŭv/ər mənt ən sĭt/ə zən shĭp/] **116**
U.S. HISTORY [yōō/ĕs/ hĭs/tə rē] **114**–**115**
Using a pay phone [yōō/zĭng ə pā/ fōn/] **9**
Using the ATM machine [yōō/zĭng dhē ā/tē/ĕm/ mə shēn/] **97**
U.S. MAIL [yōō/ĕs/ māl/] **96**
utilities [yōō tĭl/ə tēz] **35** ✦
U-turn OK (sign) [yōō/türn/ ō kā/] **107**–7
vacancy sign [vā/kən sē sīn/] **36**–11
vacation [vā kā/shən] **19**–46
vaccination [văk/sə nā/shən] **80** ✦
vacuum [văk/yōōm] **46**–I
vacuum cleaner [văk/yōōm klē/nər] **47**–13
    ...attachments [–ə tăch/mənts] **47**–14
    ...bag [–băg/] **47**–15
valedictorian [văl/ə dīk tör/ē ən] **32**–8
Valentine's Day [văl/ən tīnz dā/] **168**–4
valet parking [văl/ā pär/kĭng] **145**–1
valley [văl/ē] **117**–18
van [văn] **106**–10, 14
vandalism [văn/də lĭz/əm] **100**–1
vase [vās, văz, väz] **41**–9
vault [völt] **97**–2
VCR (videocassette recorder)
    [vē/sē/är/] / [vĭd/ē ō kə sĕt/ rĭ kör/dər] **164**–8
veal cutlets [vēl/ kŭt/ləts] **52**–6
vegetable [vĕj/tə bəl]
    ...casserole [–kăs/ə rōl/] **58**
    ...garden [–gär/dn] **148**–12
    ...peeler [–pē/lər] **59**–15
VEGETABLES [vĕj/tə bəlz] **51**
vegetables [vĕj/tə bəlz] **55**–43
vegetarian [vĕj/ə tër/ē ən] **52** ✦
vein [vān] **75**–44
vendor [vĕn/dər] **91**–30
Venus [vē/nəs] **127**–8
vest [vĕst] **65**–24, **66**–13
veterinarian [vĕt/ər ə nër/ē ən] **139**–62
Vice President [vīs/ prĕz/ə dənt] **116**–7
victim [vĭk/təm] **100** ✦
video [vĭd/ē ō]

...camera [–kăm/rə] **165**–19
...game system [–gām/ sĭs/təm] **162**–1
...store [–stör/] **93**–15
videocassette [vĭd/ē ō kə sĕt/] **98**–13, **164**–8, 10
view [vyoō] **11**–21, 22
vine [vīn] **128**–22
vineyard [vĭn/yərd] **148**–14
violet [vī/ə lət, vī/lət] **129**–22
violin [vī/ə lĭn/] **120**–8
vise [vīs] **150**–21
visor [vī/zər] **147**–11
vital signs monitor [vīt/l sīnz/ män/ə tər] **87**–21
vitamins [vī/tə mənz] **81**–19
V-neck sweater [vē/nĕk/ swĕt/ər] **71**–27
vocational school [vō kā/shə nəl skoōl/] **112**–9
volcanic eruption [väl kăn/ĭk ĭ rŭp/shən] **103**–14
volleyball [väl/ē böl/] (sport) **158**–14, (equipment) **161**–3
Volume [väl/yəm, –yoōm] **57**
volunteer [väl/ən tïr/] **87**–19
vomit [väm/ət] **78**–E
vote [vōt] **116**–D
waffles [wä/fəlz, wö/–] **61**–4
waist [wāst] **74**–4
waistband [wāst/bănd/] **73**–3
wait [wāt] **90**–B
waiter [wā/tər] **62**–4
waiting room [wā/tĭng roōm/] **84**–1
wait on customers [wāt/ än kŭs/tə mərz, –ön–] **140**–O
waitress [wā/trəs] **63**–6
wake up [wāk/ ŭp/] **26**–A
walk [wok] **101**–A, **156**–A
walker [wö/kər] **80**–5, **95**–12
wall [wöl(/–)] **42**–6, **48**–4
...unit [–yoō/nət] **42**–13
wallet [wä/lət, wö/–] **69**–26
wallpaper [wöl/pā/pər] **45**–5
walrus [wöl/rəs] **131**–32
War [wör] **114**
warehouse [wër/hows/] **146**–9
warm [wörm] **10**–2
warning label [wör/nĭng lā/bəl] **80**–15
wash [wäsh(/–), wösh(/–)]
...hair [–hër/] **76**–E
...the dishes [–dhə dĭsh/əz] **46**–M
...the windows [–dhə wĭn/doz] **46**–D
washcloth [wäsh/klöth/, wösh/–] **43**–14
washer [wä/shər, wö/–] **72**–3, **150**–32
wasp [wäsp, wösp] **132**–18
wastebasket [wāst/băs/kət] **43**–25, **46**–F
watch [wäch, wöch] **69**–34
watch TV [wäch/ tē/vē/, wöch/–] **27**–5
water [wö/tər] **39**–B
water [wö/tər] **117**, **155**–1
...fountain [–fown/tn] **153**–11
...glass [–glăs/] **63**–19
...pollution [–pə loō/shən] **126**–12
...polo [–pō/lō] **158**–15
watercolor [wö/tər kŭl/ər] **163**–25
waterfall [wä/tər föl/] **117**–2
watering can [wö/tər ĭng kăn/] **39**–17
watermelons [wö/tər mĕl/ənz] **50**–24
waterskiing [wö/tər skē/ĭng] **160**–7
WATER SPORTS [wö/tər spörts/] **160**
wave [wāv] **155**–6
wavy [wā/vē] **23**–10

Ways to pay [wāz/ tə pā/] **20**
WEATHER [wĕdh/ər] **10**
Wednesday [wĕnz/dā, –dē] **18**–4
weed [wēd] **39**–A
week [wēk] **18**–11
weekdays [wēk/dāz/] **18**–12
weekend [wēk/ĕnd/] **18**–13
weigh [wā] **57**–B
weight [wāt] **22**–21, **57**
weightlifting [wāt/lĭf/tĭng] **159**–15
weights [wāts] **161**–19
WEIGHTS AND MEASURES [wāts/ ən mĕzh/ərz] **57**
welder [wĕl/dər] **139**–63
well [wĕl] **30**–15
west [wĕst] **107**, **123**, **124**
western [wĕs/tərn] **166**–9
wet [wĕt(/–)] **72**–17
...mop [–mäp/] **47**–16
...suit [–soōt/] **155**–7
whale [wāl] **131**–29
wheat [wēt(/–)] **148**–2
...bread [–brĕd/] **53**–2
wheelbarrow [wēl/băr/ō] **39**–16
wheelchair [wēl/chër/] **80**–6
whisk [wĭsk] **59**–21
whiskers [wĭs/kərz] **134**–18
white [wīt(/–)] **12**–14
...bread [–brĕd/] **53**–1
White House [wīt/ hows/] **116**–5
whole [hōl(/–)] **15**–6
...salmon [–săm/ən] **53**–18
wide [wīd] **71**–44
widow [wĭd/ō] **29** ✦
widower [wĭd/ō ər] **29** ✦
width [wĭdth, wĭtth] **15**–17
wife [wīf] **24**–20, **25** ✦
wild animals [wīld/ ăn/ə məlz] **133** ✦
willow [wĭl/ō] **128**–14
win [wĭn] **158** ✦
wind [wĭnd] **126**–2
windbreaker [wĭnd/brā/kər] **66**–24
window [wĭn/dō] **38**–17, **42**–17
...pane [–pān/] **149**–15
...shade [–shād/] **44**–6
windshield [wĭnd/shēld/] **108**–2
...wipers [–wī/pərz] **108**–3
windy [wĭn/dē] **10**–10
wine glass [wīn/ glăs/] **63**–20
wing [wĭng] **132**–2
wings [wĭngz] **52**–20
winter [wĭn/tər] **19**–40
WINTER SPORTS AND WATER SPORTS
  [wĭn/tər spörts/ ən wö/tər spörts/] **160**
wipes [wīps] **95**–17
wipe the counter [wīp/ dhə kown/tər] **46**–O
wire [wīr(/–)] **151**–13
...stripper [–strĭp/ər] **151**–37
wish [wĭsh] **169**–J
withdraw cash [wĭdh drö/ kăsh/, wĭth–] **97**–D
witness [wĭt/nəs] **99**–11
wolf [woŏlf] **134**–5
woman [woŏm/ən] **22**–10
wood [woŏd(/–)] **149**–17, **151**–18
...screw [–skroō/] **150**–28
wooden spoon [woŏd/n spoōn/] **59**–9

woodpecker [wŏŏd/pĕk/ər] **132**–9
Woodwinds [wŏŏd/wĭndz/] **120**
woodworking kit [wŏŏd/wûr/kĭng kĭt/] **162**–16
wool [wŏŏl(/–)] **70**–14
  ...scarf [–skärf/] **66**–4
work [wûrk/] **26**–K, **140**–P
workbook [wûrk/bŏŏk/] **3**–23
Work in a group [wûrk/ ĭn ə grŏŏp/] **6**
working [wûr/kĭng] **48**–1
work out [wûrk/ owt/] **157**–P
Work with a partner [wûrk/wĭdh/ ə pärt/nər, –wĭth/–] **6**
WORLD [wûrld] **124–125**
worm [wûrm] **130**–22
worried [wûr/ēd] **30**–13
wrap [răp] **169**–D
wrench [rĕnch] **109**–50, **151**–42, 43
wrestling [rĕs/lĭng] **159**–16
wrinkled [rĭng/kəld] **72**–19
wrist [rĭst] **69**–34, **75**–60
wristwatch [rĭst/wäch/, –wöch/] **69**–34
write [rīt] **2**–G, **113**–A
writer [rī/tər] **139**–64
writing assignment [rī/tĭng ə sīn/mənt] **113**–1
wrong [röng(/–)]
  ...number [–nŭm/bər] **9** ✦
  ...way [–wā/] **107**–4
X-ray [ĕks/rā/]
  ...technician [–tĕk nĭsh/ən] **86**–8
xylophone [zī/lə fōn/] **120**–17
yams [yămz] **51**–22
YARD [yärd] **39**
yard [(–)yärd(/)]
  front... [frŭnt/–] **38**–15
yard (measurement) [yärd] **15** ✦
yardstick [yärd/stĭk/] **151**–15
yarn [yärn] **163**–17
year [yïr] **4**–16, **18**–8
yellow [yĕl/ō] **12**–12
yesterday [yĕs/tər dā/, –dē] **18**–17
yield [yēld] **107** ✦
yogurt [yō/gərt] **54**–33, **60**–11
young [yŭng] **22**–13
zebra [zē/brə] **135**–34
zero [zïr/ō] **14**
ZIP code [zĭp/ kōd/] **4**–9
zipper [zĭp/ər] **73**–16
zoo [zŏŏ] **152**–1
zookeeper [zŏŏ/kē/pər] **152**–3
zoom lens [zŏŏm/ lĕnz/] **165**–25
zucchini [zŏŏ kē/nē] **51**–4

Geographical Index

Continents

Africa [ăf/rĭ kə] **125**–5
Antarctica [ănt ärk/tĭ kə, –är/tĭ–] **125**–7
Asia [ā/zhə] **125**–4
Australia [ö strāl/yə] **125**–6
Europe [yŏŏr/əp] **125**–3
North America [nörth/ ə mĕr/ə kə] **124**–1
South America [sowth/ ə mĕr/ə kə] **124**–2

Countries and other locations

Afghanistan [ăf găn/ə stän/] **124**–**125**
Albania [ăl bā/nē ə] **124**–**125**
Algeria [ăl jïr/ē ə] **124**–**125125**
American Samoa [ə mĕr/ə kən sə mō/ə] **124**–**125**
Andorra [ăn dör/ə] **124**–**125**
Angola [ăng gō/lə] **124**–**125**
Argentina [är/jən tē/nə] **124**–**125**
Armenia [är mē/nē ə] **124**–**125**
Australia [ö strāl/yə] **124**–**125**
Austria [ö/strē ə] **124**–**125**
Azerbaijan [ăz/ər bī jän/] **124**–**125**
Bahamas [bə hä/məz] **122**–**125**
Bahrain [bä rän/] **124**–**125**
Bangladesh [băng/glə dĕsh/, băng/–] **124**–**125**
Barbados [bär bā/dōs] **124**–**125**
Belarus [bē/lə rōōs/, byĕl/ə–] **124**–**125**
Belgium [bĕl/jəm] **124**–**125**
Belize [bə lēz/] **124**–**125**
Benin [bə nĭn/, –nēn/] **124**–**125**
Bermuda [bər myōō/də] **122**–**125**
Bhutan [bōō tän/] **124**-**125**
Bolivia [bə lĭv/ē ə] **124**–**125**
Borneo [bör/nē ō] **124**–**125**
Bosnia-Herzegovina [băz/nē ə hër/tsə gō vē/nə] **124**–**125**
Botswana [bät swä/nə] **124**–**125**
Brazil [brə zĭl/] **124**–**125**
Brunei [brōō nī/] **124**–**125**
Bulgaria [bŭl gër/ē ə] **124**–**125**
Burkina Faso [bər kē/nə fä/sō] **124**–**125**
Burundi [bōō rōōn/dē] **124**–**125**
Cambodia [kăm bō/dē ə] **124**–**125**
Cameroon [kăm/ə rōōn/] **124**–**125**
Canada [kăn/ə də] **122**–**125**
Cape Verde [kāp/ vürd/] **124**–**125**
Central African Republic [sĕn/trəl ăf/rĭ kən rĭ pŭb/lĭk]
    124–**125**
Chad [chăd] **124**–**125**
Chile [chĭl/ē] **124**–**125**
China [chī/nə] **124**–**125**
Colombia [kə lŭm/bē ə] **124**–**125**
Comoros [kăm/ə rōz] **124**–**125**
Congo [käng/gō] **124**–**125**
Costa Rica [kōs/tə rē/kə, käs/–] **122**–**125**
Croatia [krō ā/shə] **124**–**125**
Cuba [kyōō/bə] **122**–**125**
Cyprus [sī/prəs] **124**–**125**
Czech Republic [chĕk/ rĭ pŭb/lĭk] **124**–**125**
Democratic Republic of the Congo [dĕm/ə krăt/ĭk rĭ pŭb/lĭk
    əv dhə käng/gō] **124**–**125**
Denmark [dĕn/märk] **124**–**125**
Djibouti [jĭ bōō/tē] **124**–**125**
Dominica [däm/ə nē/kə] **124**–**125**
Dominican Republic [də mĭn/ĭ kən rĭ pŭb/lĭk] **122**–**125**
Ecuador [ĕk/wə dör/] **124**–**125**
Egypt [ē/jĭpt] **124**–**125**
El Salvador [ĕl săl/və dör/] **122**–**125**
Equatorial Guinea [ē/kwə tör/ē əl gĭn/ē, ĕk/wə–] **124**–**125**
Eritrea [ĕr/ə trē/ə] **124**–**125**
Estonia [ĕ stō/nē ə] **124**–**125**
Ethiopia [ē/thē ō/pē ə] **124**–**125**
Fiji [fē/jē] **124**–**125**
Finland [fĭn/lənd] **124**–**125**
France [frăns] **124**–**125**
French Guiana [frĕnch/ gē ăn/ə, –ä/nə] **124**–**125**
French Polynesia [frĕnch/ päl/ə nē/zhə] **124**–**125**
Gabon [gă bōn/] **124**–**125**
Georgia [jör/jə] **124**–**125**
Germany [jür/mə nē] **124**–**125**
Ghana [gä/nə] **124**–**125**
Greece [grēs] **124**–**125**
Greenland [grēn/lənd, –lănd/] **122**–**125**
Grenada [grə nā/də] **124**–**125**
Guatemala [gwä/tə mä/lə] **122**–**125**
Guinea [gĭn/ē] **124**–**125**
Guinea-Bissau [gĭn/ē bĭ sow/] **124**–**125**
Guyana [gī ăn/ə] **124**–**125**
Haiti [hā/tē] **122**–**125**
Honduras [hän dŏŏr/əs] **122**–**125**
Hong Kong [häng/ käng/] **124**–**125**
Hungary [hŭng/gə rē] **124**–**125**
Iceland [īs/lənd] **124**–**125**
India [ĭn/dē ə] **124**–**125**
Indonesia [ĭn/də nē/zhə] **124**–**125**
Iran [ĭ rän/, ĭ răn/] **124**–**125**
Iraq [ĭ räk/, ĭ răk/] **124**–**125**
Ireland [īr/lənd] **124**–**125**
Israel [ĭz/rē əl, –rā–] **124**–**125**
Italy [ĭt/l ē] **124**–**125**
Ivory Coast [īv/rē kōst/] **124**–**125**
Jamaica [jə mā/kə] **122**–**125**
Japan [jə păn/] **124**–**125**
Java [jä/və] **124**–**125**
Jordan [jör/dn] **124**–**125**
Kazakhstan [kä/zäk stän/] **124**–**125**
Kenya [kĕn/yə, kēn/–] **124**–**125**
Kiribati [kïr/ə bäs/] **124**–**125**
Kuwait [kōō wāt/] **124**–**125**
Kyrgyzstan [kïr/gĭ stän/, –stän/] **124**–**125**
Laos [lows, lä/ōs] **124**–**125**
Latvia [lăt/vē ə] **124**–**125**
Lebanon [lĕb/ə nən, –nän/] **124**–**125**
Lesotho [lə sō/tō, –sōō/tōō] **124**–**125**
Liberia [lī bïr/ē ə] **124**–**125**
Libya [lĭb/ē ə] **124**–**125**
Liechtenstein [lĭk/tən stīn/] **124**–**125**
Lithuania [lĭth/ōō ā/nē ə] **124**–**125**
Luxembourg [lŭk/səm bürg/] **124**–**125**
Macedonia [măs/ə dō/nē ə] **124**–**125**
Madagascar [măd/ə gäs/kər] **124**–**125**
Malawi [mə lä/wē] **124**–**125**
Malaysia [mə lā/zhə] **124**–**125**
Maldives [möl/dēvz, –dīvz] **124**–**125**
Mali [mä/lē] **124**–**125**
Malta [möl/tə] **124**–**125**
Marshall Islands [mär/shəl ī/ləndz] **124**–**125**
Mauritania [mör/ə tā/nē ə] **124**–**125**
Mauritius [mö rĭsh/əs] **124**–**125**
Mexico [mĕk/sĭ kō/] **122**–**125**
Micronesia [mī/krə nē/zhə] **124**–**125**
Moldova [mäl dō/və, möl–] **124**–**125**
Monaco [män/ə kō/] **124**–**125**

Mongolia [mäng gō/lē ə] **124–125**
Montenegro [män/tə nē/grō, –nĕ/–] **124–125**
Morocco [mə räk/ō] **124–125**
Mozambique [mō/zəm bēk/] **124–125**
Myanmar [myän/mär] **124–125**
Namibia [nə mĭb/ē ə] **124–125**
Nauru [nä ōō/rōō] **124–125**
Nepal [nə pöl/, –päl/] **124–125**
Netherlands [nĕdh/ər ləndz] **124–125**
New Guinea [nōō/ gĭn/ē] **124–125**
New Zealand [nōō/ zē/lənd] **124–125**
Nicaragua [nĭk/ə rä/gwə] **122–125**
Niger [nī/jər, nē zhër/] **124–125**
Nigeria [nī jïr/ē ə] **124–125**
North Korea [nörth/ kə rē/ə] **124–125**
Norway [nör/wā] **124–125**
Oman [ō män/] **124–125**
Pakistan [păk/ə stän/] **124–125**
Palau [pə low/] **124–125**
Panama [păn/ə mä/] **122–125**
Papua New Guinea [păp/yōō ə nōō/ gĭn/ē] **124–125**
Paraguay [păr/ə gwī/, –gwä/] **124–125**
Peru [pə rōō/] **124–125**
Philippines [fĭl/ə pēnz/, fĭl/ə pēnz/] **124–125**
Poland [pō/lənd] **124–125**
Portugal [pör/chə gəl] **124–125**
Puerto Rico [pwër/tə rē/kō, pör/tə–] **122–125**
Qatar [kä/tär, kə tär/] **124–125**
Romania [rō mā/nē ə, rōō–] **124–125**
Russia [rŭsh/ə] **124–125**
Rwanda [rōō än/də] **124–125**
Saudi Arabia [sow/dē ə rā/bē ə, sö/dē–] **124–125**
Senegal [sĕn/ə göl/, –gäl/] **124–125**
Serbia [sür/bē ə] **124–125**
Seychelles [sā shĕlz/, –shĕl/] **124–125**
Sierra Leone [sē ĕr/ə lē ōn/, –lē ō/nē] **124–125**
Singapore [sĭng/ə pör/] **124–125**
Slovakia [slō vä/kē ə] **124–125**
Slovenia [slō vē/nē ə] **124–125**
Solomon Islands [säl/ə mən ī/ləndz] **124–125**
Somalia [sə mä/lē ə] **124–125**
South Africa [sowth/ ăf/rĭ kə] **124–125**
South Korea [sowth/ kə rē/ə] **124–125**
Spain [spān] **124–125**
Sri Lanka [srē/ läng/kə, shrē/–] **124–125**
Sudan [sōō dän/] **124–125**
Sumatra [sōō mä/trə] **124–125**
Suriname [sōōr/ə nä/mə] **124–125**
Swaziland [swä/zē lănd/] **124–125**
Sweden [swēd/n] **124–125**
Switzerland [swĭt/sər lənd] **124–125**
Syria [sïr/ē ə] **124–125**
Tahiti [tə hē/tē] **124–125**
Taiwan [tī/wän/] **124–125**
Tajikistan [tä jĭk/ə stän/, –stăn/] **124–125**
Tanzania [tăn/zə nē/ə] **124–125**
Tasmania [tăz mā/nē ə] **124–125**
Thailand [tī/lănd/, –lənd] **124–125**
The Gambia [dhə găm/bē ə] **124–125**
Togo [tō/gō] **124–125**
Tonga [täng/gə] **124–125**
Tunisia [tōō nē/zhə] **124–125**
Turkey [tür/kē] **124–125**
Turkmenistan [türk mĕn/ə stän/, –stăn/] **124–125**
Uganda [yōō găn/də] **124–125**

Ukraine [yōō/krān, yōō krān/] **124–125**
United Arab Emirates [yōō nī/təd ăr/əb ĕm/ər əts] **124–125**
United Kingdom [yōō nī/təd kĭng/dəm] **124–125**
United States of America [yōō nī/təd stāts/ əv ə mĕr/ə kə]
　　122–125
Uruguay [yōōr/ə gwī/, –gwā/] **124–125**
Uzbekistan [ōōz bĕk/ə stän/, –stăn/] **124–125**
Venezuela [vĕn/ə zwā/lə] **124–125**
Vietnam [vē/ĕt näm/, –năm/] **124–125**
Western Sahara [wĕs/tərn sə hăr/ə] **124–125**
Western Samoa [wĕs/tərn sə mō/ə] **124–125**
Yemen [yĕm/ən] **124–125**
Zambia [zăm/bē ə] **124–125**
Zimbabwe [zĭm bäb/wā] **124–125**

Bodies of water

Arabian Sea [ə rā/bē ən sē/] **124–125**
Arctic Ocean [ärk/tĭk ō/shən] **122–125**
Baffin Bay [băf/ən bā/] **122–125**
Baltic Sea [böl/tĭk sē/] **124–125**
Barents Sea [băr/ənts sē/] **124–125**
Beaufort Sea [bō/fərt sē/] **122–125**
Bering Sea [bër/ĭng sē/, bïr/–] **122–125**
Black Sea [blăk/ sē/] **124–125**
Caribbean Sea [kăr/ə bē/ən sē/, kə rĭb/ē ən–] **122–125**
Caspian Sea [kăs/pē ən sē/] **124–125**
Coral Sea [kör/əl sē/] **124–125**
East China Sea [ēst/ chī/nə sē/] **124–125**
Greenland Sea [grēn/lənd sē/, –lănd/–] **124–125**
Gulf of Alaska [gŭlf/ əv ə lăs/kə] **122–125**
Gulf of California [gŭlf/ əv kăl/ə förn/yə] **122–125**
Gulf of Honduras [gŭlf/ əv hän dōōr/əs] **122–125**
Gulf of Mexico [gŭlf/ əv mĕk/sĭ kō/] **122–125**
Gulf of St. Lawrence [gŭlf/ əv sānt/ lör/əns, –lär/–] **122–125**
Hudson Bay [hŭd/sən bā/] **122–125**
Indian Ocean [ĭn/dē ən ō/shən] **124–125**
Labrador Sea [lăb/rə dör/ sē/] **122–125**
Mediterranean Sea [mĕd/ə tə rā/nē ən sē/] **124–125**
North Atlantic Ocean [nörth/ ət lăn/tĭk ō/shən] **122–125**
North Pacific Ocean [nörth/ pə sĭf/ĭk ō/shən] **122–125**
North Sea [nörth/ sē/] **124–125**
Norwegian Sea [nör wē/jən sē/] **124–125**
Persian Gulf [pür/zhən gŭlf/] **124–125**
Philippine Sea [fĭl/ə pēn/ sē/] **124–125**
Red Sea [rĕd/ sē/] **124–125**
Sea of Japan [sē/ əv jə păn/] **124–125**
Sea of Okhotsk [sē/ əv ō kätsk/] **124–125**
South Atlantic Ocean [sowth/ ət lăn/tĭk ō/shən] **124–125**
South China Sea [sowth/ chī/nə sē/] **124–125**
Southern Ocean [sŭdh/ərn ō/shən] **124–125**
South Pacific Ocean [sowth/ pə sĭf/ĭk ō/shən] **124–125**

The United States of America

Capital: Washington, D.C. (District Of Columbia)
　　[wä/shĭng tən dē/sē/, wö/–]

Regions of the United States

Mid-Atlantic States [mĭd/ət lăn/tĭk stāts/] **123–10**
Midwest [mĭd/wĕst/] **123–9**
New England [nōō/ ĭng/glənd] **123–11**
Pacific States [pə sĭf/ĭk stāts/] **123–7**
Rocky Mountain States [räk/ē mown/tn stāts/] **123–8**
South [sowth] **123–13**
Southeast [sowth/ēst/] **123–13**
Southwest [sowth/wĕst/] **123–12**
West Coast [wĕst/ kōst/] **123–7**

Geographical Index

States of the United States

Alabama [ăl/ə băm/ə] **122–123**
Alaska [ə lăs/kə] **122–125**
Arizona [ăr/ə zō/nə] **122–123**
Arkansas [är/kən sö/] **122–123**
California [kăl/ə förn/yə] **122–123**
Colorado [kăl/ə răd/ō, –ra/dō] **122–123**
Connecticut [kə nĕt/ĭ kət] **122–123**
Delaware [dĕl/ə wër/] **122–123**
Florida [flör/ə də, flär/–] **122–123**
Georgia [jör/jə] **122–123**
Hawaii [hə wī/ē] **122–123**
Idaho [ī/də hō/] **122–123**
Illinois [ĭl/ə noy/] **122–123**
Indiana [ĭn/dē ăn/ə] **122–123**
Iowa [ī/ə wə] **122–123**
Kansas [kăn/zəs] **122–123**
Kentucky [kən tŭk/ē] **122–123**
Louisiana [lōō ē/zē ăn/ə] **122–123**
Maine [mān] **122–123**
Maryland [mër/ə lənd] **122–123**
Massachusetts [măs/ə chōō/səts] **122–123**
Michigan [mĭsh/ĭ gən] **122–123**
Minnesota [mĭn/ə sō/tə] **122–123**
Mississippi [mĭs/ə sĭp/ē] **122–123**
Missouri [mə zŏŏr/ē, –zŏŏr/ə] **122–123**
Montana [män tăn/ə] **122–123**
Nebraska [nə brăs/kə] **122–123**
Nevada [nə văd/ə, –vä/də] **122–123**
New Hampshire [nōō/ hămp/shər] **122–123**
New Jersey [nōō/ jŭr/zē] **122–123**
New Mexico [nōō/ mĕk/sĭ kō/] **122–123**
New York [nōō/ yörk/] **122–123**
North Carolina [nörth/ kăr/ə lī/nə] **122–123**
North Dakota [nörth/ də kō/tə] **122–123**
Ohio [ō hī/ō] **122–123**
Oklahoma [ō/klə hō/mə] **122–123**
Oregon [ör/ĭ gən, –găn/, är/–] **122–123**
Pennsylvania [pĕn/səl vān/yə] **122–123**
Rhode Island [rōd/ ī/lənd] **122–123**
South Carolina [sowth/ kăr/ə lī/nə] **122–123**
South Dakota [sowth/ də kō/tə] **122–123**
Tennessee [tĕn/ə sē/] **122–123**
Texas [tĕk/səs] **122–123**
Utah [yōō/tö, –tä] **122–123**
Vermont [vər mänt/] **122–123**
Virginia [vər jĭn/yə] **122–123**
Washington [wä/shĭng tən, wö/–] **122–123**
West Virginia [wĕst/ vər jĭn/yə] **122–123**
Wisconsin [wĭs kän/sən] **122–123**
Wyoming [wī ō/mĭng] **122–123**

Canada

Capital: Ottawa [ät/ə wə]

Regions of Canada

Atlantic Provinces [ət lăn/tĭk prăv/ən səz] **123–6**
British Columbia [brĭt/ĭsh kə lŭm/bē ə] **123–2**
Northern Canada [nör/dhərn kăn/ə də] **123–1**
Ontario [än tër/ē ō/] **123–4**
Prairie Provinces [prë/ē prăv/ən səz] **123–3**
Quebec [kwĭ bĕk/] **123–5**

Provinces of Canada

Alberta [ăl bür/tə] **122–123**
British Columbia [brĭt/ĭsh kə lŭm/bē ə] **122–123**
Manitoba [măn/ə tō/bə] **122–123**

New Brunswick [nōō/ brŭnz/wĭk] **122–123**
Newfoundland [nōō/fən lənd] **122–123**
Northwest Territories [nörth/wĕst/ tër/ə tör/ēz] **122–123**
Nova Scotia [nō/və skō/shə] **122–123**
Ontario [än tër/ē ō/] **122–123**
Prince Edward Island [prĭns/ ĕd/wərd ī/lənd] **122–123**
Quebec [kwĭ bĕk/] **122–123**
Saskatchewan [să skăch/ə wən, –wän/] **122–123**
Yukon Territory [yōō/kän tër/ə tör/ē] **122–123**

Mexico

Capital: Mexico (City) [mĕk/sĭ kō/ (sĭt/ē)]

Regions of Mexico

Chiapas Highlands [chē ä/pəs hī/ləndz] **123–18**
Gulf Coastal Plain [gŭlf/ kō/stəl plān/] **123–16**
Pacific Northwest [pə sĭf/ĭk nörth/wĕst] **123–14**
Plateau of Mexico [plă tō/ əv mĕk/sĭ kō/] **123–15**
Southern Uplands [sŭdh/ərn ŭp/ləndz] **123–17**
Yucatan Peninsula [yōō/kə tăn/ pə nĭn/sə lə, yōō/kə tän/–]
 123–19

States of Mexico

Aguascalientes [ä/gwəs käl yĕn/täs] **122–123**
Baja California Norte [bä/hä kăl/ə förn/yə nör/tä] **122–123**
Baja California Sur [bä/hä kăl/ə förn/yə sŏŏr/] **122–123**
Campeche [käm pā/chä, käm pē/chē] **122–123**
Chiapas [chē ä/pəs] **122–123**
Chihuahua [chĭ wä/wä, –wə] **122–123**
Coahuila [kō/ə wē/lə] **122–123**
Colima [kə lē/mə] **122–123**
Distrito Federal [dĭ strē/tō fĕd/ə räl/] **122–123**
Durango [dŏŏ räng/go, –räng/–] **122–123**
Guanajuato [gwä/nə hwä/tō] **122–123**
Guerrero [gə rër/ō] **122–123**
Hidalgo [hĭ dăl/gō, ē dhäl/gō] **122–123**
Jalisco [hə lĭs/kō, –lēs/–] **122–123**
México [mĕk/sĭ kō/, mĕ/hē kō] **122–123**
Michoacán [mē/chō ä kän/] **122–123**
Morelos [mö rĕl/ōs] **122–123**
Nayarit [nä/yə rēt/] **122–123**
Nuevo León [nwā/vō lā ōn/] **122–123**
Oaxaca [wə hä/kə, wä–] **122–123**
Puebla [pwĕb/lä] **122–123**
Querétaro [kə rĕt/ə rō/] **122–123**
Quintana Roo [kēn tä/nə rō/] **122–123**
San Luis Potosí [sän/ loo ēs/ po/tə sē/] **122–123**
Sinaloa [sē/nə lō/ə] **122–123**
Sonora [sə nör/ə] **122–123**
Tabasco [tə băs/kō] **122–123**
Tamaulipas [tä/mow lē/pəs] **122–123**
Tlaxcala [tlä skä/lə] **122–123**
Veracruz [vĕr/ə krōōz/, –krōōs/] **122–123**
Yucatán [yōō/kə tän/, –tän/] **122–123**
Zacatecas [zä/kə tä/kəs, sä/–] **122–123**

ក **74**–2
កក់...សក់ **76**–E
កក្កដា **19**–31
4 កក្កដា **168**–7
កងករ **95**–30
កងដៃ **69**–35
កង់ **153**–4
កង់ត្រូវការខ្យល់ **109**–59
កង់បង្វារ/សាគ្នូវ **109**–53
កង់ឡាន **108**–10
កង្កែប **130**–25
កញ្ចាល់ពិដាន **41**–4
កជើង **75**–61
កញ្ជក់ **43**–18, **44**–1, **144**–6
កញ្ចក់ចំហៀង **108**–8
កញ្ចក់បង្អួច **149**–1
កញ្ចក់មុខ **108**–2
កញ្ចក់មើលក្រោយ **108**–1
កញ្ចប់ **56, 56**–8, **96**–5
កញ្ចុំផ្លោយ **127**–26
កញ្ចុំក្រខូ **126**
កំប្រោងដាក់ខោអាវបោកគក់ **72**–2
កំប្រោងដំបុង **63**–8
កញ្ញើដាក់ខោអាវប្រឡាក់ **43**–1
កញ្ជ្រិល **79**–5
កប្រៀង **134**–15
កញ្ញា **19**–33
កំដៃ **75**–60
កណ្ដាល **70**–3
កណ្ដាស់ **78**–B
កណ្ដឹងទ្វារ **38**–10
កណ្ដុរ **49**–26
កណ្ដុរបង្គង **133**–17
កណ្ដុរប្រែង **49**–27, **133**–18
កណ្ដុរសំពោរ **133**–14
កណ្ដប **132**–25
កណ្ដៀរ **49**–22
កត់ត្រាវាលខ្នួផល **119**–C
កត់សារផ្លាវគ្នេ **142**–A
កញ្រែកដាក់ឥវ៉ាន់ **54**–7
កញ្រែងសំណាញ់ដងត្រី **154**–17
កញ្រែ **23**–19, **73**–18
កញ្រែកាត់កូនលើ **39**–12
កញ្រែកាត់ក្រចក **77**–29
កញ្រែកាត់មែកលើ **39**–15
កញ្ញារអ្នកជំងឺ **86**–13
កញ្ចបក្រឡាក់ **95**–21
កញ្ចបជ្រើសហើយបោះចោល **95**–20
កញ្ចុយ **134**–22
កញ្ជាត **49**–25
កញ្ញាស់ (អហង្ការ) **69**–36
កញ្ញៃតិកល្យ **55**–17
កញ្ញៃសិលានុបដ្ឋាកិគ **87**
កញ្ញៃចតឡ្យាត **36**–15, **89**–26
កញ្ញៃចូលយន្តហោះ **110**–6
កញ្ញៃចាំ **104**–15

កញ្ញៃចាំងៈរថយន្តឈ្នួល **91**–16
កញ្ញៃដែកយកស្បែរគោរចេញ **98**–16
កញ្ញៃដែកសំប្រុត **110**–3
កញ្ញៃភ្លុមើល **127**–19
កញ្ញៃដាក់ទស្សនាវដ្ដី **98**–6
កញ្ញៃដាក់សាឡ្យាត់ **60**–16
កញ្ញៃដែលគួរទៅ **152**
កញ្ញៃដោតខ្យល់ភ្លឹង **151**–41
កញ្ញៃដោតភ្លឹង **44**–20
កញ្ញៃទូលវៀវក្នុងសណ្ឋាគារ **145**–3
កញ្ញៃធំសំរាប់អគ្គុយមើល **5**–3
កញ្ញៃបង្អេកទឹក **43**–4
កញ្ញៃថ្ងៃផ្ទៃលើ **54**–11
កញ្ញៃបោកខោអាវ **90**–1
កញ្ញៃបុរុងទុករបស់ឥណ្ណោន លើកទី១ នៅ វិជិវញ្ញា **114**
កញ្ញៃផ្តុកឥវ៉ាន់មានចាក់សោ **36**–14
កញ្ញៃផតិមានប្រចាំថ្ងៃ **98**–11
កញ្ញៃផ្សេខោអាវ **44**–4
កញ្ញៃយកឥវ៉ាន់ **110**–17
កញ្ញៃរស់នៅ **34**
កញ្ញៃលក់គ្រឿងទឹកដោះ **54**–9
កញ្ញៃលក់សាច់ និងសាច់បសុបក្សី **54**–2
កញ្ញៃលក់ស្បែកជើង **68**–3
កញ្ញៃលក់សំគ្រឿងផ្ទៃដំណើរ **92**–9
កញ្ញៃលក់ឱាហារដែលអ្នកចិញ្ចាំរិសយកខ្លួនឯង **5**–4
កញ្ញៃលេបិក/ដាក់ឥវ៉ាន់ **146**–16
កញ្ញៃលេងតេខ្វិស **153**–7
កញ្ញៃលេងបាល់បោះ **158**–7
កញ្ញៃសំរាប់ពតិមាន **93**–22
កញ្ញៃអគ្គុយញ្ញា **60**–19
កញ្ញៃអគ្គុយមើលការប្រកួត **5**–10
កញ្ញៃអ្នកបើកយន្តហោះ **110**–11
កញ្ញៃក្រាល **155**–15
កញ្ញៃផ្ទកខូន **43**–12
កញ្ញៃផ្ទកចាន **47**–22
កញ្ញៃផ្ទកដៃ **43**–13
កញ្ញៃដៃ **69**–42
កញ្ញៃអុក **66**–4
កញ្ញៃស្ងូត្រ **70**–15
កញ្ចាល់រោរៈផ្ទាក់ **102**–3
កម្ចាស **148**–6
កម្ពីស **53**–24, **130**–19
កម្មករនោងចក្រ **146**–6
កម្មករសំណណ **149**–1
កម្មវិធីកុមារាកុមារី **167**–24
កម្មវិជិវទេស្សន៍ **166**–3
កម្មវិធិធម្មជាត **167**–22
កម្មវិធិលក់ដូរ **167**–25
កម្មវិធីវិទ្យ **166**–4
កម្មង-ក **95**–8
កម្មងសិទ្ធិកជន **115**
កម្រោលផ្ទកជើង **43**–27
កម្រោលដាក់ក្នុងអាងទឹកកុំអោយអិលល **43**–3
កម្រោលតុ **41**–18
កម្រោលពុក **44**–11
កម្រោលពុកខាងក្រោម **44**–14

កម្រោលពុកខាងលើ **44**–13
កម្រោលគ្រ **42**–27
កម្រោលរវេលចជោយ **44**–22
កម្រោលវា **33**–16
កម្រោលតង្គ **44**–24
កម្រៃកល្បៀន **107**–5
កសិករ **148**–15
កអាវ **73**–7
កាកសំណល់គ្រោះថ្នាក់ **126**–9
កាក់ **20**
កាក់ជៈឡ្យាន **104**–11
កាចម្រៃង **91**–17, **107**–1
កាណាជា **123**
កាណាជាភាគខាងជើង **123**–1
កាតគ្រេឌិត **20**–15
កាតទូរស័ព្ទ **9**–10
កាតប៉ុស្ដិស្ដាល់ **96**–3
កាតផ្គល់សិទ្ធិរស់នៅ **29**–3
កាតាយឈ្មោះរបស់ **98**–10
កាតរូបអ្នកលេងបាល់រាយដំបង **162**–11
កាតសន្ដិសុខសង្គម **29**–5
កាតសំរាប់ដលលុយពតិម៉ាស៊ុន **97**–9
កាត់...ក្រចក **77**–N
កាត់ទោសអ្នកចុងចោទ **99**–F
កាត់សក់ **23**–A
កាត់សក់សៈ **23**–8
កាត់ស្មៅ **39**–C
កាត់អោយជាប់ទោស **99**–14
កាតុង **56**–4
កាន់ **94**–B
កាន់ចាស **62**–H
កាប់សាច់មាន់ **58**–M
កាប្ប **69**–6
កាប្បបៃ **69**–25
កាប្បដៃប្យូ **69**–6
កាប្ប (ប្រុស) **69**–26
កាប្បស្បែរគោ **69**–28
កាប្បស្មោយ **69**–27, **154**–15
កាប្បឥវ៉ាន់ **69**–29
កាយសម្ថន្ត **159**–8
ការកាត់ក្ដី **99**–D
ការកំសាន្ត **166**–167
ការកំសាន្តនៅក្រោផ្ទៃ **154**
ការប្ជៃនជាតិជប់ុង **114**
ការងារ **136**–139
ការចិញ្ចឹមសត្ត **148**
ការចូលបុង **100**–6
ការចូលសញ្ញាត **116**
ការជប់លេ្យង **169**–1
ការជួសជុល **48**–49
ការជួសសង្រ្គោះជាបឋាន់ **83**
ការជីកវាសាធារណៈ **104**
ការដេរចាក់ **73**
ការតែឥណសេចក្ដីជាភាសាសាមង់គេស **113**
ការចរូប **164**–165
ការថែទាំ **108**–109

ការវេចទាំងួខភាព **80–81**
ការទិញអូរ **21**
ការធ្វើយាគនៃលោកកិណ្ណាធិ **115**
ការធ្វើយាគនៃលោក លិនកិច **115**
ការធ្វើដំណើរតាមយន្តហោះ **111**
ការធ្វើស្រែចំការ **148**
ការនិយមនៃកុំព្យូទ័រ **115**
ការបញ្ចប់កម្មវិធីសិក្សា **32–33**
ការប៉ាក់ **163–19**
ការបើកទូកក្តោង **160–8**
ការបំផ្លាញទ្រព្យរងកជន ឬសាធារណៈ **100–1**
ការបំពាធបំពារ **100–7**
ការប្រមើស្ទូងដាក់កាសដកល្លយ **97**
ការពារគ្រោះថ្នាក់នៅក្នុងផ្ទើការ **147**
ការពិនិត្យផ្ទេញ **85**
ការរក្សាការពារ **126**
ការរៀបចំម្ហូប **58**
ការវាយបន្តិ **100–5**
ការសន្ទនាប្រចាំថ្ងៃ **8**
ការសង្ស័កាត់ **162–13**
ការសង្ស័រតែម **162–12**
ការិយាល័យ **142–143**
ការិយាល័យខាងមុខ **146–1**
ការិយាល័យចាងហ្វាង **5–13**
ការិយាល័យធំ **5–17**
ការិយាល័យអ្នកពេរាឪឆវាគ **5–15**
ការុត **51–3**
ការ៉ូ **163–27**
ការអ៊ីយ៉ូហ្ស៊ិត **60–11**
ការ៉ីមេក **55–44**
ការ **143–37, 162–8**
ការជំរេវរូប **143–38**
កាសទ្រនាប់ **150–32**
កាសេតចាក់ស្តាប់ **98–12**
កាសេតវីឌីអូ **98–13, 164–10**
ការហ្ល **61–22**
ការហ្ល៊កករស្រេច **55–51**
ការហ្ល ឌិកាហ្ល **61–23**
កិច្ចការក្នុងផ្ទះ **46**
កិច្ចការធ្វើតាមថ្នាក់ **7**
កិច្ចការប្រចាំថ្ងៃ **26–27**
កិច្ចការរៀបនានុក្រម **6**
កិច្ចប្រមច្រៀង មិស្ស៊ី **114**
កិរិយាសព្ទ្ធទាក់ទងពាក្យកិច្ឆា **156–157**
កិ **163–29**
កិទ្យាកាប់ដារ **159–5**
កិឡ្យាក្នុងទឹក **160**
កិឡ្យាជាក្រុម **158**
កិឡ្យាដ្ឋាន **152–26**
កិឡ្យានៅវេដរុក្រុជាក់ **160**
កិឡ្យាបាញ់ផ្គ **159–1**
កិឡ្យាបាល់តប់ **152–25**
កិឡ្យាបុកគួស **159–2**
កិឡ្យាបោះបួលិង **159–3**
កិឡ្យាម្ការ **159–1**

កីប **142–G**
កុងតាក់ភ្លើង **44–19, 144–4**
កុងទំរដាក់កាក់ចតឡ្យាន **91–18**
កុន **166–1**
កុនមានសំលេងលើកទី១ **114**
កម្ម្រៃ **19–26**
កុលស្ត្រ **53–14**
កូឆកលបិស្ស្រម្មយកំប៉ុង **56–17**
កូនកណ្ណុ **144–8**
កូនកន្ទ្រងដុតមុខ **43–14**
កូនគាំបិត **59–16**
កូនក្មេង **22–1**
កូនក្មេង (អាយុពីពីរទៅបីឆ្នាំ) **22–3**
កូនខ្មើយ **42–20**
កូនខ្វាញ្ញាក់សំប៉ូ **45–10**
កូនគោលលេីទីកកក **158–13**
កូនភ្គ **133–12**
កូនភ្ការ **59–25**
កូនថ្ត **133–10**
កូនណើរផៅក្នុងផ្ដៈ **129–29**
កូនគុ **42–21**
កូនគុក្តា **45–18**
កូនគុក្តាក់ជិតក្សាលព្រែ **44–21**
កូនបណ្ណុ **129–2**
កូនប្រាសាទដើខ្លាថ់ **155–10**
កូនព្រែស **24–22**
កូនភ្ត **117–16**
កូនរទេះភ្លើងគ៌ុរ **163–32**
កូនស្សេវរគៅរកក់គ្រា **143–36**
កូនស្ត្រ **24–21**
កូនឡ្យកឡ្យក់ **162–4**
កូរ **58–E**
កូឡ្មបិយ៉ា អង់គ្រេស **123–2**
កេិត **28–A**
កេិតទុក **31–20**
ក្សែត **95–12**
កែកហុស **7–Z**
កែង **118–20**
កែងចោរ **71–47**
កែងជើង **75–62**
កែងដៃ **74–15**
កែងទាប **71–46**
កែងស្សែកដើង **68–13**
កែវ **41–26, 56–2**
កែវកិត **119–10**
កែវចំពួយ **119–13**
កែវធ្នូយវភ្កេ **81–36**
កែវទេទេ **11–10**
កែវទាញរូប **165–25**
កែវទឹក **63–19**
កែវរិតសោផធ៌ **119–16**
កែវពេញ **11–9**
កែវយើត **127–21**
កែវស្រោ **63–20**
កែវប្ផែងធំ **41–28**

កែសំ្យរលអគ្លូបធអ្នក **113–B**
កែឡ្យាក់ **60–24**
កោង **118–19**
កោរ **77–M**
កោសបួឡ្យសលយិស្ស្រ **58–J**
កោសិប **14**
កោស្ស្រិកង **143–45**
កោស្ស្រ្យាលដោះ **95–29**
កោអិ **2–7, 152–11**
កោអិក្មេង **109–39**
កោអិក្មេងក្នុងឡ្យាន **95–13**
កោអិក្រោយ **109–38**
កោអិខ្ទស់ **95–7**
កោអិញ្ញាប៉ាយ **41–16**
កោអិទទិ **11–6**
កោអិបៈបេិក **94–6**
កោអិមានភ្នាក់ដៃ **42–24**
កោអិមុខ **109–35**
កោអិរិង **11–5**
កោអិរិល **143–22**
កោអិរិវេង **42–19, 153–10**
កោអិរិវេងសម្រាប់អង្គុយញុំៈបាយ **5–5**
កោអិសម្រាប់ទារកវេអ្ស្រៈ **95–10**
កោអិសម្រាប់អង្គុយនៅមាត់សមុទ្រ **155–14**
កោអិអង្គុយក្ភ្ការតិទាក់ **42–25**
កៅអិ៉ម្ការ៉ិការ **80–6**
កុបើក្ឆ្ការអោយមនុស្សចម្មកចូល **101–F**
កុំឌីកហ្លើយបើកបរ **101–G**
កុំព្យូទ័រ **3–15, 144**
កុំព្យូទ័របង្ក្លាញពិពេលចេញ និងពេលមកដល់ **110–4**
កុំព្យូទ័រយ៉្រច:ឡ្ជឹងបាន **144–14**
កំណត់ពេល **104–3**
កំទេចផ្ការ **127–12**
កំប៉ុង **56–3**
កំបៈគួទ **74–12**
កំប្រែក **133–21**
កំលប់ហ្ល្រប្រេង **126–15**
កំពស់មធ្យម **22–17**
កំពស់ **15–14**
កំពុលភ្ត **117–14**
កំភ្ជនជើង **74–18**
កំភ្ជនជើងមាន៍ **52–22**
កំស្ស្រវតែ **40–17**
កា **118–16**
កាជណ្ណ៉ុរ **38–13**
កាំជ្ជត **168–8**
កាំបិត **41–22, 63–27**
កាំបិតកាត់សាថ **59–12, 63–26**
កាំបិតមុខឧ្គ្រិត **154–20**
កាំប្រមា **134–23**
កាំភ្លិង **100–9**
កោះ **117–8**
កោះមាត៌ **52–23**
ក្ភារ **132–14**
ក្ភាក **132–15**

ក្លាន់ **134**–14
ក្លាម **53**–22, **130**–16
ក្លារខ្សែន **2**–1
ក្លារ�ជញ្ជីង **153**–16
ក្លារឆេលើទឹករលេក **155**–5
ក្លារឆះអំលលើទឹកកក **161**–23
ក្លារទ្រាប់សរសេរ **143**–26
ក្លារបន្ទះ **149**–16
ក្លារបិទប្រកាស **3**–14
ក្លារអំពិល **153**–13
ក្លារល្បែង **162**–3
ក្លារស្គី **161**–24
ក្លារអុិតខោអាវ **72**–14
ក្ដៅ **10**–1, **30**–1
ក្ដៅល្មម **10**–2
ក្បាច់គុន **159**–10
ក្បាល **74**–1
ក្បាលខ្សែក្រវាត់ **69**–41
ក្បាលត្រែ **44**–15
ក្បាលចង្ក្រានដុតឧស្ម័ន **40**–19
ក្បាលជោតខ្សែក្បិង **164**–18
ក្បាលជោះ **95**–27
ក្បាលទឹកផ្កាឈូក **43**–10
ក្បាលបំពង់បាញ់ទឹកលប្ម **92**–11
ក្បាលម៉ាស៊ីនទឹក **43**–6, **153**–11
ក្បាលម៉ាស៊ីនទឹកពន្លត់ភ្លើង **91**–28
ក្បាលរុឺបឺណេស្រក់ទឹក **49**–16
ក្បាលឃ្លាន **106**–16
ក្បាលឡ្បាស្ប៊ុ **150**–31
ក្បួនណែនាំ **144**–22
ក្បួនហែរ **168**–2
ក្រៀស **113**–10
ក្បាំងមុខ **168**–12
កុយប្រុស **24**–18
កុយស្រី **24**–17
ក្បែង **22**–13
ក្បែងជំងំ **22**–6
ក្បែងប្រុសអាយុ ៦ ឆ្នាំ **22**–4
ក្បែងប្រុសអាយុ ១៣ ឆ្នាំ **22**–7
ក្បែងមាត់ច្រើន **11**–11
ក្បែងស្ងាត់ស្ងៀម **11**–12
ក្បែងស្រីអាយុ ១០ ឆ្នាំ **22**–5
ក្បែងស្រីអាយុ ១៩ ឆ្នាំ **22**–8
ក្រុងសក់ **23**–C
ក្រចក **134**–17
ក្រចកជើង **75**–64
ក្រចកដៃ **75**–58
ក្រចាប់សមុទ្រ **130**–15
ក្រញាំ **132**–4, **134**–20
ក្រដាសកាសែតយកទៅធ្វើម្ដងទៀត **46**–B
ក្រដាសក្រុបអូបធ្វើអាយខោអាវទទ់ **72**–5
ក្រដាសខាត់ **151**–50
ក្រដាសចះឈ្មោះចូលរៀន **4**
ក្រដាសជូតតំដៃ **40**–2, **41**–19, **63**–23
ក្រដាសជូតដៃមួយរបរ **56**–23
ក្រដាសជូតពារ **168**–5

ក្រដាសទ្រនាប់ទំ **59**–27
ក្រដាសធានាប៉ាប់រង **84**–5
ក្រដាសបង្កាន់ដៃ **21**–5
ក្រដាសបង្គន់ **43**–15
ក្រដាសប្រកាសបញ្ជាក់ **110**–22
ក្រដាសប្រាក់ **20**
ក្រដាសមានឈ្មោះក្រុមហ៊ុន **143**–19
ក្រដាសសរសេរផ្ទធំ **143**–18
ក្រដាសសរសេរស្ដើៗ **143**–34
ក្រដាសអាលុមីញ៉ូម **55**–55
ក្រណាត់ការពារការរៀង **66**–18
ក្រណាត់ផ្កា **70**–12
ក្រណាត់ផ្កាបត្ូរ **70**–10
ក្រណាត់យឺតសម្រាប់រុ **83**–12
ក្រណាត់សំរាប់ផ្ទតធ្មលិ **47**–6
ក្រណាត់អុចា **70**–8
ក្របត្រែ **44**–27
ក្របដាក់បញ្ជីងកសារ **142**–11
ក្រពា **131**–36
ក្រពិ **131**–37
ក្រពុំផ្កា **129**–6
ក្រពៈ **75**–41
ក្រមឆ្មេញ **84**–17
ក្រមាស្ប្រ **68**–4
ក្រវាត់ក **69**–10
ក្រវាត់ក្ភុថ **71**–45
ក្រវាត់កណិ **71**–44
ក្រវិល **69**–37
ក្រវិលកឹប **69**–38
ក្រវិលសោ **69**–43
ក្រហម **12**–13
ក្រឡ្បាឈើត្រង់ **70**–11
ក្រាស់ **23**–22, **76**–13
ក្រុងភ្ភចា **34**–3
ក្រុមកីឡ្យា **158**–3
ក្រុមផ្នាយ **127**–24
ក្រុមវិទ្យុផ្ម័យ **99**–8
ក្រុមស្ដេរក និងសង្គ្រោះ **103**–17
ក្រុមអង្គគេសទិម្ផុយ នៅ វ៉ជិនញ៉ា **114**
ក្រចឈ្ប្ុួ **50**–13
ក្រចឆ្ការ **50**–12
ក្រចឆ្ការលៀង **50**–11
ក្រចប្រុង **50**–9
ក្រចជោពផ័សាត់ **50**–10
ក្រមេកោរ **77**–27
ក្រមេផ្ស្រ **54**–37
ក្រមេបចូរមាត់ **77**–37
ក្រោកលណៈ **2**–D
ក្រោកឡ្ើង **26**–B
ក្រោមស្ដាន **105**–1
ក្រោល **148**–17
ក្រោលសត្ **34**–12
ករីវ័រណែណ **120**–4
ក្ថិន **75**–C
កិបហាត់ព្រាណ **89**–21
ក្ថក **78**–A, **78**–E

ខាណ្ឌ **113**–6
ខាងក្ុងវាងកាយ **75**
ខាងក្ុខ **123**–13
ខាត់ណាមេរិកាំង **51**–15
ខឹង **31**–29
ឧសផ្ **107**–4
ខ្យ៉ឺ **134**–3
ខ្វក្យាល **75**–35
ខ្យូវ **12**–1
ខ្យូវក្រម៉ៅ **12**–2
ខ្យូវថ្ម **12**–3
ខ្យូវ-បែកង **12**–4
ខែ **4, 18**–9
ខៃថ្ងកំណើត **4**–16
ខៃប្រចាំឆ្នាំ **19**
ខៃធ្នញ **85**–K
ខៅកញ្ក្រាកា **71**–42
ខៅកឹឡ្បារជើងរៃង **64**–15
ខៅខូវបៃយ **64**–5
ខៅឡិធិះកង់ **67**–3
ខៅងួតទឹក **66**–22
ខៅជើងខ្ទី **64**–13
ខៅជើងរៃង **64**–8
ខៅតីង **71**–43
ខៅទារកអ្យេងស្ៀក **95**–24
ខៅទ្រនាប់ខ្ទី **67**–12
ខៅទ្រនាប់បីយ័ធិ **67**–16
ខៅទ្រនាប់ប្រស **67**–13
ខៅត្រនាប់ស្រី **67**–17
ខៅទ្រនាប់អ្នកកីឡ្យា **67**–14
ខៅយឺតរៃង **66**–11
ខៅរលុច **71**–42
ខៅរៃតក្រ្បក **67**–18
ខៅរ័បជើង **65**–23
ខៅសំវត់ **65**–25
ខៅស្ញ្បប្រស **67**–13
ខៅស្ញ្បស្រី **67**–17
ខៅអាវទឹក **155**–7
ខៅអាវបោកកត់ **72**–1
ខៅអាវពាក់ក្ុង **67**–11
ខៅអាវពាក់ៈកាត់ **87**–32
ខៅអាវម្ម្យសំរាប **64**–2
ខៅអ្ម្រម **65**–21
ខ្ចប់អំណោយ **169**–D
ខ្ចីប្រាក់ **35**–I
ខ្ទ្មួលដោយម៉ាស៊ីន **150**–27
ខ្ទិសម្ម្ប **130**–14
ខ្ទិមបារាំង **51**–28
ខ្ទិមស **51**–29
ខ្ទយ **132**–31
ខ្ទ **40**–24
ខ្ទៈឆ្ប្យ/ផា **59**–5
ខ្ទង **74**–11
ខ្ទាតទំហិ **15**
ខៃម **44**–9
ខ្ទាៈដៃ **99**–2

ចង្កៀងពេលយប់ **45**–3
ចង្កៀងមុខ **108**–5
ចង្កុះ **74**–4
ចង្កេះខៅ **73**–3
ចង្អោរដុត **119**–9
ចង្អានដុតអុស **42**–9
ចង្អានដាវ្ស **40**–18
ចង្អានបាយ **63**–10
ចង្អានសម្រាប់បោះជំរ **154**–16
ចង្អានអាំង **39**–7
ចង្អានអាំងសាច់ **40**–21
ចម្រិត **132**–24
ចងុលទេវរូបភាព **2**–F
ចង្អោរ **78**–E
ចតឡ្បាន **91**–D
ចតុវង្គ **162**–5
ចាំថ្ល **18**–2
ចន្ធាសអាំង **59**–14
ចន្លោះ, ប្រហោង **144**–19
ចបត្រសេ **149**–20
ចប់ការសិក្សា **28**–D, **32**–A
ចម្មុង ក្រដាស **142**–E
គណនាទាមទារសំឡិត្ថិមនុស្ស **115**
ចាកចេញពីប្រទេស **28**–C
ចាក់ **163**–F
ចាក់ក្បាច់ **163**–20
ចាក់ថយក្រោយ **165**–D
ចាក់ថ្មា **80**–E
ចាក់...ថ្នាំស្តឹក/សន្លប់ **85**–J
ចាក់ទឹក **62**–C
ចាក់តងទាចូលខ្ទះ **58**–D
ចាក់មេល **165**–B
ចាក់មូលវិទ្យាសាស្ត្រ **81**–G
ចាងហ្វាង **5**–14
ចាត់ចែងមនុស្ស **140**–K
ចានកាសីរ៉ូល **59**–11
ចានកោម **41**–25
ចានចម្រុះ **41**–2
ចានរ៉ៅ **41**–25
ចានត្រូវដាក់ម្លូប **41**–6
ចានទាប **41**–24
ចានទៀប **63**–15
ចាន/ចុងបាញ់ស្តឹក **59**–3
ចាននំប៉័ង-បីរ **63**–16
ចានពិសោធមេរោគ **119**–6
ចានលាយគ្រឿង **59**–31
ចានសាថ្វ **43**–24
ចានសាឡ្បាត់ **63**–17
ចានស៊ុប **63**–18
ចានសំប៉ិត **41**–24
ចានសំប៉ិតធំ **41**–3
ចានស្ករ **41**–12
ចាបម្យ៉ាង **132**–17
ចាបស្រុក **132**–8
ចាប **156**–E

ចាប់ជនដែលគេសង្ស័យ **99**–A
ចាប់ផ្តួល **156**–M
ចាប់ផ្តើម **157**–X
ចាប់ផ្តើមចូលរៀន **28**–B
ចាប់រាវ **73**–8
ចារអាសយដ្ឋានលើប៊ុស្ត៍កាត **96**–A
ចិត្កើម **74**–32
ចិត្កើមថ្ងូល **90**–10, **91**–26
ចិញ្ជៀន **69**–39
ចិញ្ជៀនចោក **11**–20
ចិញ្ជៀនថ្ងៃ **11**–19
ចិក្រ្តាំខ្មែបារាំង **58**–G
ចិតករុំគដាចំណិត **58**–O
ចិតសប **14**
ចិតសំបកការុំត **58**–N
ចុកចាប់ **30**–12
ចុងចោម **99**–5
ចុងជើងខៅ **73**–5
ចុងគោ **63**–11, **137**–17
ចុងសថ្ចហ៊ី **18**–13
ចុចលេខសំគាល់ខ្លួន **97**–B
ចូលភ្លុងតាក់ស៊ី **105**–4
ចូលភ្លើងទៀហារ **28**–F
ចូលនៅ **35**–D
ចូលមហាវិថី **105**–6
ប្រុលសព្ញាតិ **28**–H
ឆ្យេន **58**–S
ឆ្យេនខ្មែបារាំង **58**–H
ឆ្យេម **133**–7
ចេក **50**–3
ចេញណាម **82**–M
ចេញពិធ្មិការ **26**–M
ចេញពិមហាវិថី **105**–7
ចេញសាលាក្រម **99**–E
ចែកក្រដាស **7**–O
ចែកស្បូវភៅគ្នាមើល **6**–I
ចែកសំប៉ុត្រ **96**–C
ថែវត្ត **49**–23, **132**–28
ចោល **156**–F
ចោលចាស **159**–6
ចោលសំរាម **46**–F
ចេញក្រម **99**–6, **116**–10
ចេញក្រមកំពូល **116**–9
ចេញប្រស **24**–7
ចំការ **148**–7
ចំការលើស៊ីវ័ផ្ទៃ **148**–16
ចំការទីព័ងបាយដូរ **148**–14
ចំឡងជើង **98**–21, **113**–3
ចំឡតជនពិការ **107**–14
ចំឡតតាក់ស៊ី **104**–19
ចំឡតរថយន្ត **90**–5
ចំឡតឡ្បានឈ្នួល **104**–1
ចំឡតអាកាសយាន **110**–1
ចំពិរ្តត **148**–5
ចំណិស្រស់ស្រួច **55**–16

ចំណុចក្បៀស **113**–13
ចំណុចតិរ **113**–12
ចិន្តនប្រជាធន **114**
ចិន្តនប្រាក់នៅសល់ **97**–11
ចំបិង **148**–18
ចំពុះ **132**–1
ចំហាយវិទ្យុសកម្ម **126**–13, **147**–6
ចំហុយប្រកលិ **58**–I
ចំឡ្បតាមអានប្រយោគមួយ **6**–N
ចំឡ្បុជាក្យ **6**–F
ចំឡ្បសេចក្ត **142**–C
ចំអិនទាល់តែឆ្អិនល្អ **58**–F
ចំអិនបៃធ្មតាមបែប កាស៍រ៉ូល **58**
ចាំផ្ញើយទ្វារ **169**–F
ចុះ **111**–O
ចុះជណ្តើរ **105**–8
ចុះឈ្មោះក្នុងកងទ័ព **116**–F
ចុះពិតភាក់ស៊ី **105**–5
ចុះហត្ថលេខាឈ្មោះអ្នក **4**–D
ចុះហត្ថលេខាលើកិច្ចក្រមត្រៀងផ្តល់លក្ខ **35**–C
ចុះអ៊ិ្ត **10**–11
ឆ្វាប់គម្រៃចូលសញ្ញាតិ **116**
ឆ្វាប់បណ្ណញ្ញត្តផ្ទាន **114**
ឆ្វានដំណា **148**–12
ច្រកចូល **110**–5
ច្រកដៃរ **54**–5
ច្របាច់ទឹកដោះគោ **148**–C
ច្រមុះ **74**–21
ច្រវាត់ **150**–36
ច្រវាត់ទ្វារ **37**–28
ច្រាសដុស **47**–19
ច្រាសដុសធ្មេញ **43**–20, **77**–20
ច្រាសបន្ថុំ **43**–16
ច្រាសសិតសក់ **23**–18, **76**–14
ច្រតកាគ់ **148**–B
ច្រ្រែងចំរៀន **120**–B
ច្រ្រែងចំរៀន "ខ្មែកណិត" **169**–I
ច្រ្រែងជាក្រម **121**–3
ច្រាងសមុទ្រ **117**–12
ច្រេះចាប់ **147**–4
ច្រេះស៊ុ **147**–4
ឆត្រ **66**–16
ឆត្រតំ **155**–9
ឆា **58**–W
ឆាកក់ប្បង **166**–10
ឆាកក់ប្បងតាមកាលៈទេស: **167**–18
ឆាកសម្ដែង **166**–2
ឆាប់ **17**–22
ឆែលទ្យ **120**–9
ឆែថាមូល **51**–14
ឆ្ក **133**–11
ឆ្កចចក **134**–3
ឆ្កព្រៃ **134**–5
ឆ្កល្ល **11**–17
ឆ្កែអាក្រក់ **11**–18

ឆ្នូត **70**–7
ឆ្នូតខ្មៅស្កាគ្នា **70**–9
ឆ្នេរសមុទ្រ **117**–10
ឆ្នេរសមុទ្រខាងលិច **123**–7
ឆ្នាំ **4, 18**–8
ឆ្នាំង **40**–16, **59**–6
ឆ្នាំងដាំពិរជាធ់ **59**–8
ឆ្នាំងឡ្បាស្ទីង **59**–8
ឆ្នាំងអុក **72**–13
ឆ្នា **133**–9
ឆ្នាំទីក **131**–33
ឆុងកាត់ម៉ាស៊ីនត្រួតពិនិត្យ **111**–C
ឆុងថ្ងូល **90**–A
ឆុងទីក **105**–3
ឆ្លើយសំណួរ **6**–H
ឆូខ្លួនដោយស្ទឺ X **85**–H
ឆ្អឹង **75**–49
ឆ្អឹងខ្នង **75**–54
ឆ្អឹងជំនិរគោ **52**–5
ឆ្អឹងត្រគាក **75**–55
ឆ្អឹងលលាដ៍ក្បាល **75**–52
ឆ្អឹម **30**–9
ឆ្អែត **30**–6
ជក់លាបច្ឆ្នាំ **151**–47, **163**–23
ជង្គង់ **74**–17
ជម្រុកស្ករ **148**–11
ជញ្ជីង **84**–7, **119**–11
ជញ្ជីងថ្លឹង **43**–26
ជញ្ជីងថ្លឹងតែម **143**–16
ជញ្ជាំង **42**–6
ជញ្ជាំងក្រដាស **45**–5, **149**–18
ជញ្ជាំងច្រេះវែក **48**–4
ជញ្ជាំងដុតក្នុងចន្លុះបន្ទុកទីក **43**–9
ជណ្ដើរ **37**–26, **37**–35, **47**–7, **149**–2
ជណ្ដើរបោក **48**–7
ជណ្ដើរយន្ត **37**–34, **93**–21
ជនជាតិកូរ៉េ **115**
ជនជាតិកុយបា **115**
ជនជាតិចិន, ស្ពាង់ឬណារី **115**
ជនជាតិជប៉ុន **115**
ជនជាតិដើមអាមេរិកាំង **114, 115**
ជនជាតិ ព័រតូរីកិន **114**
ជនជាតិម៉្បិរមប្ប៉ិកា **115**
ជនជាតិមុីកស៊ិកកិន **114**
ជនជាតិរុស្ស៉ី **115**
ជនជាតិហុងគ្រ **115**
ជនជាតិហេទី **115**
ជនជាតិហ្ប៉ិល្ស៉ីពិន **115**
ជនជាតិអាេនាន, អ៊ីរុបភាគខាងត្បូង និងភាគខាងកេីត **115**
ជនជាតិអាមេរិកកណ្ដាល **115**
ជនជាតិអាស៊ីអគ្នេយ៍ **115**
ជនជាតិអ៊ីអិស **114**
ជបេទ **34**–4
ជនរគ្បុសខ្លួនសម្ងាមលោកលេីកទិ២ ចូលមក **114**
ជន្ទន **130**–22

ជប់លៀងអាហារ **168**–16
ជម្ពួ **79**
ជម្ពួទីកទេនាមផ្អែម **79**–9
ជម្ពួឥម្មតា និងជម្ពួក្មេងៗ **79**
ជម្ពួបេះដូង **79**–14
ជម្ពួរបេង **79**–13
ជម្រក **34**–10
ជម្រោ **15**–15
ជា **30**–15
ជាងកំបោរ **136**–9
ជាងលេី **48**–12, **136**–13
ជាងផ្ញើសា **48**–11
ជាងជំបង់ **49**–20
ជាងផ្លា **139**–63
ជាងគ្រឹត **48**–9
ជាងឌ្ឋាន **136**–7
ជាន់ទីបិ **36**–3
ជាន់ទីបួន **36**–4
ជាន់ទីពិរ **36**–2
ជាន់ទីមួយ **36**–1
ជាប់គុក / ពន្ធនាគារ **99**–G
ជាយក្រុង **34**–2
ជាយសំពត់ **73**–1
ជិដូន **24**–2
ជិដូនជីតា **24**–1
ជិដូនទម្មួយ **24**–12
ជិតា **24**–3
ជីវសាស្ត្រ **119**–1
ជីវឡ្ហាវ **119**–12
ជុតកម្រាល **46**–E
ជុតខាងក្តុង **46**–K
ជុតកុជាបំផ្ញ៉ាង **46**–O
ជុតផ្ទះ **27**–N
ជុតលាងកម្រាល **46**–J
ជុបប្រទះការរលាក់ខ្ញាំង **111**–N
ជុង **163**–26
ជុយដៃគូរបស់អ្នក **6**–J
ជុយមេីលអ្នកជំងឺ **140**–B
ជុរ **55**–20
ជុរជេីរ **54**–5
ជុរភ្ញិ **117**–15
ជុលចន្លុបវ្លែង **28**–I
ជុលផ្ញះវ្លែង **35**–1
ជុលមេធាវី **99**–B
ជុសជុលគ្រឿងប្រេីប្រាស់ក្នុងផ្ញះ **140**–G
ជេីង **74**–6
ជេីងច្យេម **52**–14
ជេីងទ្នាក់ប៉ែលមទីក **155**–2
ជេីងទ្រ **163**–21
ជេីងទ្រទេ្យ **41**–8
ជេីងម៉ាស៊ីនថត **165**–20
ជេីងសក់ **23**–7
ជុំវិញកាប់ផ្ញះ **105**–10
ជិធិ **85**
ជិនាញការរផ្ញតការងារ **140**

ជំនិះ **152**–17
ជំរាបស្ងរនេរណាម�្លាុក់ **8**–A
ជំាស្ស្បរក **78**–12
ជិះ **157**–W
ជិះកង់ **91**–E, **159**–4
ជិះកង់នេាភ្ញិ **154**–8
ជិះកាណ្ដោ **154**–2
ជិះក្ដារទីកកក **160**–2
ជិះក្ដាររលេីរលេក **160**–9
ជិះក្ដារស្គេត **159**–12
ជិះទុកក្ដ្រងស៊ីរបែតភូតចា **160**–10
ជិះទុកកោស៊ី **154**–4
ជិះទុកវ៉ៃរ **154**–3
ជិះសេះ **154**–9
ជិះស្គេត **157**–V
ជិះស្ក៉ី **157**–U
ជិះឡ្ហានបិសទេាសាលា **26**–H
ស្រលងជ្រោះ **117**–17
ស្រលងភ្ញិ **117**–18
ជ្រែង **118**–22
ជ្រញ **40**–27
ជ្រក **133**–8
ជ្រែសខេាអារទុកដោយឮកា **72**–A
ជ្រោយ យុកាតាន់ **123**–19
ឈប់ **107**–3
ឈប់ និងផ្ដ្លាក់ចេញ **165**–F
ឈរណេ្លាះជាម្ដាស់ **35**–J
ឈាមច្រមុះ **78**–17
ឈិស្បរ **54**–38
ឈិស្បរ ថែក **53**–12
ឈិស្បរ ឈិជា **53**–10
ឈិស្បរប៉ីហ្ត្លិ **60**–3
ឈិស្បរម្មួយអោស្ត **57**–11
ឈិស្បរ ស្ងាស **53**–11
ឈិស្បរ អាមេរិកាំង **53**–9
ឈិ **30**–14, **82**–A
ឈិរក្បាល **78**–1
ឈិរក្រោ **78**–4
ឈិខ្នង **78**–5
ឈិចាប់ **30**–17
ឈិត្រច្យេរ **78**–3
ឈិផ្ទេញ **78**–2
ឈិប៉ំពង់ក **78**–6
ឈិរោះ **78**–4
ឈ្មូងសមុទ្រ **117**–9
ឈេី **151**–18
ឈេីភ្លុស **154**–21
ឈេីត្រក់ **80**–7
ឈេីចប់ **80**–1
ឈេីចប់ជេីរ **80**–5
ឈេីម៉ាអ្រូច **149**–17
ឈ្លាន់ល្យេ៉ន **109**–47
ឈ្លាន់ប្រ្យ៉ាង **109**–46
ឈេ្លាះ **4**–1
ឈ្ញក់ **82**–L

ញញួរ **150**–1
ញញួរធំ **149**–22
ញាំ **60**–A
ញ៉ាំជាតិទឹក **80**–B
ញ៉ាំកិចចិច **153**–D
ដកកាគចាក់លុយអ្នកចេញពីម៉ាស៊ីន **97**–F
ដកជម្រើសមិនរួច **82**–N
ដកធ្មេញ **85**–M
ដកប្រាក់ **97**–D
ដកស្បោរចេញពីគម្រមផ្លា **39**–A
ដងតម៉ាស៊ីនបូមសំរាម **47**–14
ដងទូរស័ព្ទ **9**–2
ដងរាយហូលហ្វ៉ី **161**–1
ដងសន្ទច **154**–18
ដណ្តាប់ **150**–7
ដណ្តាប់កាត់ខ្សែភ្លើង **151**–37
ដណ្តាប់មួលបិតង់ទឹក **151**–42
ដគ្ររមអំពៅ **132**–21
ដផ្ដៀប **59**–23, **119**–8
ដផ្ដៀបក្រចាប់ **150**–6
ដផ្ដៀបចាប់ **83**–2
ដផ្ដៀបវែង **119**–15
ដផ្ដៀបសក់ **76**–18
ដផ្ដៀបសក់ភ្លូចា **76**–19
ដផ្ដៀបហាលខោអាវ **72**–10
ដប **56**–1, **95**–26
ដបយកត្រឡប់មកវិញ **54**–1
ដប់ **14**
ដប់ដុល្លារ **20**–9
ដប់បី **14**
ដប់ប្អូន **14**
ដប់ប្រាំ **14**
ដប់ប្រាំបី **14**
ដប់ប្រាំប្អូន **14**
ដប់ប្រាំពីរ **14**
ដប់ប្រាំមួយ **14**
ដប់ជាន់ **14**
ដប់ពីរ **14**
ដប់ភាគរយ **15**–7
ដប់មួយ **14**
ដប់សែន **20**–3
ដាក់កាក់ **9**–C
ដាក់ចុះ **94**–A
ដាក់ដងទូរស័ព្ទចុះ **9**–F
ដាក់/បញ្ចូលខោអាវក្នុងម៉ាស៊ីនបោក **72**–C
ដាក់បន្ថែមចូល **58**–Q
ដាក់ប្រាក់កក់ **97**–C
ដាក់ប្រាក់ទឹកតែ **62**–J
ដាក់ពាក្យអោយត្រូវគ្នា **7**–W
ដាក់របស់អោយត្រូវគ្នា **7**–X
ដាច **70**–23
ដិខ្យាច **155**–23
ដិចូល **117**–16
ដិផ្លា **39**
ដិបាក់ផ្ទាំងៗ **102**–6

ដិស **3**–16
ដិស្រេចំការ **34**–13
ដិអិដ្ឋករណី **162**–14
ដឹកជញ្ជូន **146**–C
ដុក **58**–U
ដុកដៅ ៣៥០ អង្សារ ចំនួន ៤៩ នាទី **58**–L
ដុកឡេន **169**–H
ដុសផ្គកក្រមាល **46**–L
ដុស...ធ្មេញ **77**–J
ដុង **50**–22
ដូរកនួប **94**–E
ដូរក្រមាល **46**–P
ដូល **82**–O
ដើម **128**–4
ដើមខ្ចិម **51**–17
ដើមលេបិ **42**–18
ដើមលេបិក្រហម **128**–7
ដើមលេបិ និង រុក្ខជាតិ **128**
ដើមដកវុត **128**–16
ដើមដំងយក្ស **128**–21
ដើមគ្នោតបារាំង **128**–15
ដើមបិច **128**–8
ដើមប្បេរិ **128**–20
ដើមតគយសិនស៊ីម៉ាក់ **128**–24
ដើមតគយសិន អាយវិ **128**–25
ដើមតគយសិនអ្នក **128**–23
ដើមមាក់ណុលា **128**–9
ដើមមេប៉ុល **128**–13
ដើមមិលទ្បូវ **128**–14
ដើមសេន **128**–18
ដើមស្រល់ **128**–10
ដើមស្រល់ណេលដែល **168**–20
ដើមហ្ហល្លិ **128**–19
ដើមដែលម៌ **128**–17
ដើរ **156**–A
ដើរភិសាន្ត **154**–6
ដែកថ្ម[**94**–L
ដែររខោអាវ **140**–I
ដែរដោយដៃ **73**–A
ដែរដោយម៉ាស៊ីន **73**–B
ដែរបញ្ចូល **73**–E
ដែរបញ្ចេញ **73**–F
ដែកក្មែបក្រដាស **143**–44
ដែកគោល **150**–29
ដែកគោលវេញនិងមេដែ **143**–43
ដែកត្រិច **109**–51
ដែកឈ្មស **151**–52
ដែកពន្លាក **151**–51
ដែលទាក់ចិត្ត **22**–23
ដៃ **74**–9
ដៃភូច **11**–1
ដៃដ់ **11**–2
ដៃអាវ **73**–6
ដុ **56**–10, **118**
ដុក្ប្ពួទរំ **144**

ដុ (ចាសហ្គេម) **162**–2
ដុ្ថ្ចពិល **165**–22
ដុ្ប្អូនផ្គង **45**–15
ដុ្ហ្ពិលអគ្លុលលេខ **143**–31
ដ់ **149**–D
ដំណាប់មួលកែវ **56**–14
ដំណេរិដេរិក **28**–29
ដំងវាយក្លុតគោល **161**–11
ដំបវាយបេសុរុបល់ **161**–14
ដំចូល **38**–20
ដំចូលលិច **48**–3
ដំចៅត្រច្បេក **79**–3
ដ់រិ **135**–42
ដ់រិទឹក **135**–43
ដ់ទ្បូងកិច **61**–11
ដ់ទ្បូងច្បេច **60**–2
ដ់ទ្បូងតិប **55**–40
ដ់ទ្បូងផ្លា **51**–22
ដ់ទ្បូងផុត **61**–14
ដ់ទ្បូងបារាំង **51**–21
ដ៉ា **148**–A
ដ៉ាដើមលេបិ **39**–D
ដៅះ **74**–14
ឆិស **144**–5
ឆិស ផ្ដាយ **144**–3
ឆិ ចិ **33**–17
ណាត្ **60**–10
ណែនទាំមិត្តអ្នកអាយគេស្គាល់ **8**–F
តង់ **154**–10
តង់ថ្ម ទិញ **35**–H
តគ្ត្ត **120**
តគ្ត្ទិក្ *138**–41
តម្រង **59**–22
តម្រិមស្តិកលេបិ **39**–E
តម្រក **99**–1
តាក់ស៊ុ **104**–18
តាមផ្លូវក្រោមដិ **105**–11
តាវា **127**–23
តាវាងពេទ្យ **87**–20
តាវាងស្ដង់ក្ភក្ **84**–11
តាវាវិធិ **127**–11
តាវាវិទ្ **127**–20
តិន្ត្និស **159**–14
តឹងច្រមុ **78**–7
តុ **142**–1
តុគ្តាគ្រដាស **163**–30
តុការហ្គេ **42**–23
តុគោអ៊ិនេវារាងហាល **39**–5
តុគុព្ព្ទំរ **143**–21
តុគ្ប្វធច្បោប់យោង **98**–2
តុ្ខាងមុខ **60**–13
តុជាប់និងជញ្ជាំង **40**–22
តុ្ដូរកន្ថច **45**–12
តុ្ទ្លល **60**–13
តុ្ទ្លខាងមុខ **145**–8

គុបតែងផ្ទះ **169**–C
គុបរិភោគអាហារ **153**–8
គុបាយ **41**–17
គុប្ផកន្ទុបក្ដេង **95**–9
គុតិងប៉ុង **159**–13
គុលា **19**–34
គុលាការកំពូល **116**–8
គុល្យការ **97**–11
គុរៈកាត់ **87**–34
គុសរសេរ **2**–6
គុសរាប់ពិនិត្យ **84**–13
គូច **70**–2
គូចបំផុត **70**–1
គូចពោត **70**–20
គូបលក់កាណែម **93**–20
គូបលក់កាសែត **90**–11
គូបលក់អីវ៉ាន់ **152**–23
គ្រៀមការហ្ឡ **88**–2
តែ **61**–24
តែងសេចក្ដី **113**–2
តែតិកកក **60**–5
តែម **96**–10
តោ **135**–36
តោភ្ញី **134**–2
តោសមុទ្រ **131**–34
តំបន់ខ្លស់ ជីជាតិ **123**–18
តំបន់ខ្លស់ផ្នែកខាងគប្ដេង **123**–17
តំបន់ទីក្រុង **34**–1
តំបន់វាលស្មៅ **123**–3
តំបន់អាគ្នេយ៍ទិច **123**–6
តំប្ញើន **120**–19
តំលែធម្មតា **21**–2
តំលៃលក់ចុះចោក **21**–3
តំលៃលក់ធម្មតា **21**–6
តាំងពិតណ៍ **152**–21
ត្ញោក **12**–11
ត្រតាក **74**–5
ត្រង់ **118**–18
ត្រឡ្យក **74**–28
ត្រជាក់ **10**–4, **30**–4
ត្រជាក់ខ្យាង **10**–5
ត្រជាក់ជាប់សែ្អក **82**–G
ត្រជាក់ល្មម **10**–3
ត្របកផ្ដា **129**–8
ត្របកភ្នែក **74**–33
ត្រឡ្យេតសក់ **76**–17
ត្រប់សណ្ដាយ **51**–18
ត្រពាំង **117**–21
ត្រសក់ **51**–12
ត្រសក់ស្រូវ កង់តិមួរូប **50**–15
ត្រសាល់អំពោះ **73**–17
ត្រសេះ **132**–9
ត្រាកបល **144**–15
ត្រាកោស្ដិ៍ **143**–40
ត្រាក់ទ័រ **148**–9

ត្រាក់ទ័រកាយដី **149**–8
ត្រាក់ទ័រល្មេសដី **149**–6
ត្រាប៉ុស្ដ៍ **96**–9
ត្រី **53**
ត្រីកក **53**–30
ត្រីកោណ **118**–7
ត្រីកោណមាត្រសាស្ត្រ **118**–27
ត្រីក្រិមាស **133**–16
ត្រីចក្រយាន **153**–9
ត្រីឆ្យេរ **61**–17
ត្រីចំពុះស្រួច **130**–12
ត្រីឆ្នាម **130**–7
ត្រីដុលហ្វ៊ន **131**–30
ត្រីគុណា **130**–9
ត្រីបាស់ **130**–11
ត្រីបាថ្ញេន **131**–29
ត្រីប្រចែល **130**–6
ត្រីតកតយ **131**–31
ត្រីម៉រុយ **130**–8
ត្រីមានបន្ទាជុវិញ **130**–20
ត្រីមីក **130**–10
ត្រីម៉្យាងស្រដៀងនឹងត្រីព្រាល **53**–16
ត្រីសម្មូទ្រដៃ8 **130**–4
ត្រីស្មុំងទាំងមូល **53**–18
ត្រីស្រស់ **53**–29
ត្រី ហាលិថាត់ **53**–20
ត្រីអណ្ដាតឆ្កែ **130**–13
ត្រីអណ្ដេង **53**–17
ត្រីអានិមោន **130**–21
ត្រូវការកាប្បរជាប់នឹងខ្លួន **101**–C
ត្រូវការពារកាប្បបណ្ដក **101**–D
ត្រូវចាក់សោទ្វារ **101**–E
ត្រូវដេរជាមួយមិត្តភក្ដិ **101**–A
ត្រូវដេរតាមផ្លូវដែលមានភ្លើងភ្លឺច្បាស់ **101**–B
ត្រូវដោះរែលង **99**–H
ត្រូវតិបតស្ត្ញា **107**–9
ត្រូវមានអាយុ ១៨ ឆ្នាំ **116**–A
ត្រូវឡ្បស់ **82**–A
ត្រូវរាយការណ៍ប្រាប់អំពើឧក្រិដ្ឋទៅប៉ូលិស **101**–H
ត្រូវសន្ទប់មិនដឹងខ្លួន **82**–B
ត្រូវសុគស្មារតិ **82**–C
 វៃត្រគ្រមបើក **120**–13
វៃត្របាវាំង **120**–15
វៃត្រសាក់សូហ្ឡុន **120**–7
វៃត្រសំលេងធំ **120**–14
ត្រីស្មន **120**–12
ថង់ **56**–7, **135**–50
ថង់ក្រដាស **55**–22
ថង់ខ្យល់ **108**–16
ថង់គេង **154**–12
ថង់ថ្នាំសំរក់/IV **87**–27
ថង់ប្លាស្ទិក **55**–23
ថង់ប្លាស្ទិកសំរាប់ខ្ចប់ **55**–54
ថង់ម៉ាស្ទិចប្មសំរាម **47**–15
ថង់សម្រាប់អ្នកគុលយន្តហោះ **110**–15

ថង់សំរាម **47**–12
ថជលិក **130**
ថក **40**–23, **44**–3, **165**–A
ថកដោយប្រើភ្លើងស្រួល **165**–34
ថកដោយប្រើភ្លើងតិច **165**–35
ថករូប **32**–D
ថទិកសត្ត **134**–135
ថទិកសត្តសម្ម្ទ្រ **131**
ថាក្ត **60**–9
ថាពាក្យ **6**–C
ថាពាក្យម្ដងឡ្យេត **6**–D
ថាមពល **126**
ថាមពលចំហាយកំដៅផែនដី **126**–7
ថាមពលបរមាណូ **126**–8
ថាមពលព្រះអាទិត្យ **126**–1
ថាមពលវារីអគ្គិសនី **126**–5
ថាស **41**–10
ថាស CD **98**–14
ថាសចោល **161**–27
ថាសចំអ្ឆេង **98**–15
ថាសដាក់បាយលីវៃត្រ **86**–9
ថាសដុតធំ **59**–26
ថាសដុតធំផាយ **59**–28
ថាសឆ្នា **87**–23, **151**–45
ថាសបង្ឈម **63**–7
ថាសម្មម **110**–16
ថាសុបបញ្ច្ចាំង **165**–30
ថាសសាថ **59**–13
ថាស ស៊ីឌី រ៉ម **144**–2
ថ្ម **41**–9
ថ្មដាក់ក្រែម **41**–13
ថើច **33**–F
វៃថទាំក្មេង **140**–L
វៃថមសាថ្ម **72**–B
ថាំង **155**–22
ថ្ញាម **74**–23
ថ្ញាស **74**–20
ថ្ម **4**, **18**–10
ថ្ងៃកំណើត **19**–41
ថ្ងៃក្ដុងសប្ដាហ៍ **18**–12
ថ្ងៃខ្ចុច **19**–42
ថ្ងៃខែឆ្នាំ **18**–14
ថ្ងៃលប់សម្រាកតាមច្បាប់ **19**–43
ថ្ងៃត្រង់ **17**–17
ថ្ងៃនេះ **18**–15
ថ្ងៃបុណ្យ **168**
ថ្ងៃបុណ្យចូលឆ្នាំ **168**–1
ថ្ងៃបុណ្យសាសនា **19**–44
ថ្ងៃប្រចាំសប្ដាហ៍ **18**
ថ្ងៃរ៉ាឆ្ញិនថែទ **168**–4
ថ្ងៃឈ្បក **18**–16
ថ្ងៃឯងករាជ្យ **168**–7
ថ្នាក់ត្រូវបញ្ចប់ការសិក្សា **32**–1
ថ្នាក់រៀនចេរិកម **121**–5
ថ្នាក់សេដ្ឋកិច្ច **121**–6

ផ្ទេរ **73**–11
ផ្ទាលស្ព័ **161**–25
ថ្នាំក្រមួន **81**–24
ថ្នាំភ្នែក **81**–20
ថ្នាំឧសច្បាប់ **100**–4
ថ្នាំគ្រាប់ទ្រវែង **81**–26
ថ្នាំគ្រាប់មូល **81**–25
ថ្នាំផ្តតុទ្ធអោយរលោង **47**–18
ថ្នាំដុសធ្មេញ **77**–21
ថ្ញាំដុសធ្មេញមួយដប **56**–24
ថ្នាំទឹក **163**–25
ថ្នាំចន្ទក់ភ្នែក **81**–22
ថ្នាំបាញ់ច្រមុះ **81**–23
ថ្នាំបាញ់សក់ **76**–12
ថ្នាំបាញ់សគ្គល្អិត **154**–23
ថ្នាំបំពុលសគ្គល្អិត **126**–14
ថ្នាំប្រឆាំងជាតិអាស៊ីដ (អាន់ជាស៊ីដ) **81**–18
ថ្នាំប្រេង **163**–24
ថ្នាំផ្សាសាយ **81**–17
ថ្នាំផ្សើមស្បែក **76**–8
ថ្នាំមានសំបុត្រពេទ្យ **80**–11
ថ្នាំម្សៅប់ការណើចាប់ **81**–16
ថ្នាំលាងកញ្ចាក់ **47**–8
ថ្នាំលាងក្រចក **77**–32
ថ្នាំលាងចង្ក្រានអាំង **47**–3
ថ្នាំលាប **81**–24, **149**–A, **151**–20
ថ្នាំលាបការពារកំដៅ **155**–13
ថ្នាំលាបការពារមេរោគចាប់គើរ **83**–9
ថ្នាំលាបក្រចក **77**–31
ថ្នាំលាបភ្នែក **76**–4
ថ្នាំលាបរោមភ្នែក **77**–38
ថ្នាំលាបសក់អោយរឹង **76**–11
ថ្នាំលាបសំរាប់ការពារស្បែក **76**–6
ថ្នាំលាបសំរាប់ប្រតិកម្មលើស្បែក **83**–10
ថ្នាំលាបស្បែក **155**–13
ថ្នាំលាប អាត្រិលិក **162**–9
ថ្នាំហាម្រៃហ្បេនៈដៃកសាយ **83**–8
ថ្នាំឥតមានសំបុត្រពេទ្យ **80**–12
ថ្នាល់ **74**–29
ថ្ម **155**–24
ថ្មកបាល **151**–40
ថ្ចង់ **22**–27
ថ្មីងម្មប **57**–B
ថ្មើម **52**–7, **75**–39
ថែងសុន្ទរកថា **32**–E
ថែទ **131**–41
ថែយានជំនិៈ **104**–5
ទ **38**–19
ទង **129**–4
ទង់ជ័យ **168**–9
ទផ្ចិតវៃក្តា **33**–I
ទទឹង **15**–17
ទទូលការបញ្ចាយកម៉ុខម្មប **62**–E
ទទូលការអោយយោបល់ **113**–C
ទទូលសំបុត្រ **96**–D

ទទ្យាយគល់ **133**–13
ទម្មន់ **57, 161**–19
ទម្មាក់ទុក **94**–A
ស្យនាវផ្គ **98**–7
ទស្យតិកជន **32**–10
ទា **52**–18, **132**–13
ទាញរទេៈ **153**–A
ទាត់ **156**–L
ទាប **22**–18
ទារក **22**–2
ទាស់ **79**–8
ទាសករ **114, 115**
ទាសករជាតិអាប្រ្ចិក លើកទី១ ត្រូវគេលក់ផ្ទេរ ទៅ វិជិនញ៉ា **114**
ទិញ ដៃទៅល្ចិស្សាណា **114**
ទិញផ្ទៈ **29**–O, **35**
ទិញម្មូបតាមបង្ខងបើកឡ្បាន **90**–13
ទិញ្ចាល់បុត្រ **111**–A
ទិស **107**
ទឹកទៃងកំណើត **4**–17
ទឹកក្រេង **4**–7, **34**–1
ទិសដប **14**
ទិសបថិ **14**
ទិសប់បួន **14**
ទិសប់ប្រាំ **14**
ទិសប់ប្រាំបី **14**
ទិសប់ប្រាំបួន **14**
ទិសប់ប្រាំពីរ **14**
ទិសប់ប្រាំមួយ **14**
ទិសបពីរ **14**
ទិសប់ម្មួយ **14**
ទិទុយ **132**–6
ទិផ្ថា **37**–18
ទិផ្ថាខាងក្រោយ **38**–2
ទិផ្ថាខាងមុខ **38**–15
ទិផ្ថាលេខ **36**–6
ទិប **14**
ទិបួន **14**
ទិប្រាំ **14**
ទិប្រាំបី **14**
ទិប្រាំបួន **14**
ទិប្រាំពីរ **14**
ទិប្រាំម្មួយ **14**
ទិពីរ **14**
ទិម្មួយ **14**
ទិម្ម **14**
ទិលក់ម្មុប **93**–14
ទិរាល **117**–19
ទឹក **155**–1
ទឹកភ្លា **43**–5
ទឹកក្រខុត់ **126**–12
ទឹកក្រអូបធ្មើអោយខោអាវទេៈ **72**–6
ទឹកធំនន់ **103**–16
ទឹកដប **55**–53
ទឹកដោៈគោ **54**–35, **95**–25
ទឹកដោៈគោក្រឡ្អក **60**–12

ទឹកដោៈគោម្មយក្រុត **57**–4
ទឹកត្រជាក់ **43**–7
ទឹកផ្ទាំងខូរមាត់ **77**–23
ទឹកផ្អាក់ **117**–2
ទឹកបៃងចោៈ **60**–23
ទឹកផ្ទៃច្ចោម **55**–50
ទឹកផ្ទៃច្ចោមម្មួយហ្នាឡ្អង **57**–5
ទឹកម្ភិតាក **60**–24
ទឹកម្មយអោាប្ន **57**–1
ទឹកលប់ **143**–33
ទឹកសាប្ម៉ាស្ចិលលាងចាន **47**–21
ទឹកសាឡ្នាត់ **60**–18
ទឹកអប់ **76**–5
ទឹកអប់ក្ខួញ **76**–5
ទឹកអប់ម្រើក្រោយពេលកោរ **77**–28
ទុកខ្មៅដៃញ **2**–L
ទុកចងខ្យួរវស់អ្នក **111**–H
ទុករបស់ក្មេងលេង **46**–H
ទុកសារផ្ទាំផ្ថិក្ខុម៉ាស៊ិន **9**–E
ទុកក្ក្លាង **155**–4
ទូខោអារមានគ្រឿងសំភិតសំអាង **44**–2
ទូចារមកពិតិច **41**–1
ទូដាក់តាំងក្ខុងបុន្ខប់ទូលភ្ថើរ **42**–13
ទូដាក់ផ្ទ័ **43**–19
ទូដាក់របស់តាំងលក់ **69**–7
ទូដាក់របស់របរនេ, ទាចផ្គាៗបាយ **40**–1
ទូដាក់សំណុំរៀង/ឯកសារ **142**–10
ទូដែកដាក់ផ្ទ័ក **97**–2
ម្មូដែកសម្រាប់ដាក់ផ្ទ័ក **97**–13
ទូទឹកកក **40**–9
ទូមានថតច្ចើន **45**–8
ទូរស្ច្ចូរ **42**–26, **164**–6
ទូរស្ច្ចូរ៌ប្រជាប្រិយ **115**
ទូរស្ច្ចូរ៌យូរបាន **164**–7
ទូរស្ច្ចូ **9, 9**–1, **115**
ទូរស្ច្ចូរ៉ាវ **9**–7
ទូរស្ច្ចូបង់ថៃ្ម **9**–11
ទូរស្ច្ចូរ៌ច្ចិច **9**–13
ទូរស្ច្ចូសាធារណៈ **91**–21
ទូរស្ច្ចូស្មរកតិមាន **141**–E
ទូរស្ច្ចូតផ្គនៃខ្យ **9**–12
ទូរាយបាំយ **11**–16
ទូស្មូរគោ **3**–8, **42**–1
ទូស្មួរៈ **142**–13
ទូស្កាត **11**–15
ទូរណិរស **150**–25
ទូរណិរសក្សាលផ្ទ័ង **150**–26
ទេ្យន **41**–7
ទេសភាពល្អ **11**–21
ទេសភាពអាក្រក់ **11**–22
ទោៈ **153**–12
ទៅផ្គ្ខ **27**–X
ទៅផ្គ្ខបុពេទ្យចាប់សរវៃស **81**–H
ទៅរដេក បុទៅគេង **27**–Y
ទៅត្រង់ **107**–A

ទៅផ្ទៃការ **26**–I
ទៅល្បោរ **26**–L
ទៅយក **94**–G
ទៅយកកូន **27**–O
ទៅរៀននៅមហាវិទ្យាល័យ **28**–J
ទៅសម្ភាសន៍ **141**–H
ទៅសំរាន្ត **27**–X
ទុំ **50**–29
ទំនិញ **152**–24
ទំពក់ថ្នក់ **73**–23
ទំពក់មូល **150**–34
ទំពក់មូលក្បាលជិត **150**–35
ទំពែក **23**–12
ទំពាំងបាយជូរ **50**–1
ទំពាំងបាយជូរក្រៀម **50**–27
ទំពាំងបាយជូរក្រៀម កន្ទុះ រ៉ែច **57**–9
ទំពាំងបាវាំង **51**–24
ទំហំ **70**
ទះដៃ **32**–B
ទ្រនាប់កោស្ស៊ីសំឡី **154**–13
ទ្រនាប់កំដៅ **80**–3, **149**–13
ទ្រនាប់ចាន **41**–20
ទ្រនាប់ឆ្នាំង **59**–29
ទ្រនាប់មេដិត **67**–6, **68**–69
ទ្រនាប់តុ **142**–7
ទ្រនាក់រែច **63**–22
ទ្រនាប់ស្ទូងជើង **161**–13
ទ្រនាប់ស្មា **161**–21
ទ្រង់ក្នុងលេខ **95**–11
ទ្រង **74**–13
ឡារក្រៅ **38**–12
ឡាមុខ **38**–11
ឡារោងឡាន **38**–7
ឡារសំណាញ់ **38**–8
ទិច **124**
ធនាគរវិនថាមពល **126**
ធនាគរ **88**–3, **97**–1
ធម្មញ្ញាសហរដ្ឋ **115**
ធរណីមាត្រសាស្ត្រ **118**–26
ផាក់កំប៉ោង **22**–20
ផាត់មធ្យម **22**–21
ផាតុអាកាស **10**
ផុង **47**–20, **56**–5, **155**–22
ផុងកន្ធប **45**–13, **95**–23
ផុងកាកសំណល់ពេទ្យ **86**–14
ផុងចោលសំរាម **43**–25
ផុងដាក់ខ្យល់សម្រាប់មុជទឹក **155**–8
ផុងដាក់របស់ក្នុងលេខ **45**–24
ផុងដាក់របស់សម្រាប់ផ្ទុះឡើងក្មួងឡ្បែត **47**–2
ផុងមីកកក **155**–11
ផុងទឹកភ្លោខ្ពច **48**–1
ផុងសំរាម **37**–20, **39**–3
ផុងសាំង **108**–12
ផុងស្រោចផ្កា **39**–17
ផុញទ្រាប់ **31**–26
ផុលណា **54**–25

ធូរស្បើយ **30**–16
ធំ **70**–4
ធំបំផុត **70**–5
ធិពោក **70**–21
ធ្មើម **149**–3
ធ្ម **19**–36, **161**–6
ផ្ទឹ **40**–8
ផ្ទះខាងលើ **110**–10
ផ្ទេញ **74**–25
ផ្ទេញដង្ហូស្ប៊ី **84**–20
ផ្ទុង **126**–4
ផ្ទាក់វិទ្យា **5**–12
ផ្ទាខ្យាច់សម្រាប់ក្នុងលេង **153**–15
ផ្ទាក់ **82**–O
ផ្ទាក់ក្នុងភ្ដិស្សេហា **28**–K
ផ្ទាក់ទឹកកក **10**–9
ផ្ទៃការ **26**–K
ផ្ទៃការដោយដៃ **140**–D
ផ្ទៃការណោក់ផ្ដុប **85**–A
ផ្ទៃការពិសោធន៍ **119**–A
ផ្ទៃឆ្ដុការសាលា **27**–T
ផ្ទៃគ្រៀងសិប្បកម្ម **162**–D
ផ្ទៃជាក្រម **6**
ផ្ទៃជាម្ងងដៃគ្ **6**
ផ្ទៃឪណេវិ **29**–N
ផ្ទៃតាមសេចក្ដីណែនាំ **7**
ផ្ទៃប្រដុង **163**–G
ផ្ទៃមួ **140**–C
ផ្ទៃមួបពេលល្ងាច **27**–P
ផ្ទៃឆ្វិយទ្រ **73**–D
ផ្ទៃឆ្វិយវេង **73**–C
នាទិ **16**–2
នាមកណ្ដាល **4**–3
នាមខ្លួន **4**–2
នាមត្រកួល **4**–4
នាយការិយាល័យ **143**–25
នាយតម្រួត **138**–44
នារាចំទ្យេង **104**–23
នាទ្យីកា **3**–10
នាទ្យីកាកត់ម៉ោង **146**–4
នាទ្យីកាតិតថ្ងៃឈ្មួល **104**–21
នាទ្យីកា(ដៃ) **69**–34
នាទ្យីកាដាំស់ **59**–18
នាទ្យីការណ្ដៀន **108**–20
នាទ្យីការាស់កំដៅ **108**–23
នាទ្យីការាស់ចម្ងាយ **108**–21
នាទ្យីការាស់ខេ្ស្ឌិន **48**–14
នាទ្យីកាវិទ្យុ **164**–1
ចិម្មាបចិត **136**–4
និយមប្រើ Internet **115**
និយាយជាមួយគ្នា **7**–P
និយាយជាមួយអ្នកមើលការខុសត្រូវផ្ដះផ្ដួល **35**–B
និយាយជាមួយអ្នកសណ-ទិញផ្ដះបុដិ **35**–G
និយាយទូរស័ព្ទក្នុងតំបន់ **9**–4
និយាយទូរស័ព្ទក្រៅតំបន់ **9**–5
និយាយទូរស័ព្ទឆ្ងាយប្រទេស **9**–6

និយាយទៅត្រ **2**–B
និយាយទៅរកមិត្តក្ម៉ែ្រ **141**–A
និយាយតិបចិបសោធនីរបស់អ្នក **141**–I
និយាយភាសាសាមួយឡ្បែត **140**–J
ទឹកផ្ដះ **31**–21
ទឹកផ្ឈ្មម **169**–J
ន្ធុ អ៊ុងតូ្រ **123**–11
នេសាទពាណិវ្ឋកម្ម **136**–15
នៅក្នុង **13**–5
នៅវិញ្ញ្រ **13**–1, **13**–2
នៅក្រោម **13**–9
នៅខាងក្ដេង **13**–1
នៅខាងមុខ **13**–4
នៅខាងស្ដា **13**–2
នៅចន្លោះ **13**–10
នៅពិក្រោម **13**–7
នៅពិក្រោយ **13**–3
នៅពិលើ **13**–6
នៅលើ **13**–8
នៅសាលា **26**–J
និ **54**–32, **61**–19
និស្សុតឃី **54**–31
និស្សុតឃីមមុខកញ្ចប់ **56**–20
និចាក់ចុល **61**–6
និដុលភាគ **60**–15
និប៉ុង **54**–29
និប៉ុងគ្រាប់ធញ្ញជាតិ **53**–3
និប៉ុងភ្ជើរ/ឆុត **61**–3
និប៉ុងមួលភតុច **54**–30
និប៉ុងមួបចង់ **56**–22
និប៉ុងលាយខ្ទិម **61**–16
និប៉ុងស **53**–1
និប៉ុងស្រុសសាម្ប៊ី **53**–2
និផ្ដាយ **61**–21
និផ្ដម **61**–4
បតិសំខ្យា **14**
បងប្រុស (ប្ដូនប្រុស) **24**–9
បង/ប្ដូនថ្ងៃប្រុស **24**–16
បង/ប្ដូនថ្ងៃស្រី **24**–15
បង/ប្ដូនប្រុស ដែលជាកូន ឪពុក បុម្ឋាយចុង **25**–33
បង/ប្ដូនប្រុស ឪពុក បុម្ឋាយគែមុម **25**–29
បង/ប្ដូនស្រី ដែលជាកូនឪពុក បុម្ឋាយចុង **25**–32
បង/ប្ដូនស្រី ឪពុកបុម្ឋាយគែមុយ **25**–30
បងស្រី (ប្ដូនស្រី) **24**–8
បង់ថ្ងៃផ្សលផ្ដះ **35**–F
បង់ថ្ងៃទិក្ដេច **35**–L
បង់ថ្ងៃមួ **62**–I
បង់កន្ធជារ **116**–E
បង់រ្ៀបអប់ផាំ **143**–42
បង់ស្ដើតខ្យាភ្គិន **151**–38
បង់ស្ដើថ្ងា **143**–39
បង់ស្ដើបិត **83**–5
បង់ស្ដើតុំរួបស **83**–3
បង់ស្ដើតសម្រាប់បិទការពារ **151**–49
បងងសម្មត្រ **53**–23
បធ្ដិតក្ស៊ូ **162**–C

បង្គន់ **5–8, 43–17**
បង្គន់ស្ងួចចាល់ **49–18**
បង្គួយ **131–41**
បង្ការបញ្ហា **144–9**
បង្ក្រ (បង្គុច) **38–18**
បង្ការការសន្ធនា និងវែកញែក **167–20**
បង្ការមុខចំពោះគុលាការ **99–C**
បង្ការសំបុត្រនៅច្រកចូល **111–D**
បង្កុច **38–17, 42–17**
បង្កុចបាត់ **48–5**
បង្កែមម្សៅាង **61–20**
បញ្ចុប **157–Z**
បញ្ចុប់ការសន្ធនា **8–C**
បញ្ចុកចំណី **148–D**
បញ្ចូលភាគតាក់លុយអ្នកក្នុងម៉ាស៊ីន **97–A**
បញ្ចេញគំនិតគ្រួសា កិបញ្ចី **6–K**
បញ្ច្រមុម **62–3**
បញ្ជីវាយឈ្មោះរបស់តាមកុំព្យួទ័រ **98–9**
បញ្ចា **70**
បញ្ញាក្នុងផ្ទះ **48–49**
បញ្ញាពិបាក **11–1**
បញ្ញាស្រួល **11–23**
បជា **33–15**
បណ្ឌាញតុំក្រៀង **146–8**
បណ្ណរិបាល **156–K**
បណ្ណោយ **15–16**
ប័ណ្ណផ្ទះឡាន **104–12**
ប័ណ្ណផ្ទល់ទោស **96–4**
ប័ណ្ណដាក់ប្រាក់កក់ **97–12**
ប័ណ្ណធានារ៉ាប់រង **84–4**
ប័ណ្ណបណ្ណាល័យ **98–19**
ប័ណ្ណបេីកតាក់សុី **104–22**
ប័ណ្ណបេីកបរ **29–4**
បណ្ណាគារ **92–4**
បណ្ណារក្សុតច្បោប់ **98–1**
បណ្ណាល័យ **5–6, 89–28, 98**
បត់ខោអាវ **72–F**
បត់ខ្លន **157–R**
បត់ផ្សេង **107–C**
បត់ទៅក្រោយបាន **107–7**
បត់ស្ដាំ **107–B**
បទឧក្រិដ្ឋ **100**
បន្ធោងខ្សែក **69–33**
បថ្នមម៉ាង **17–33**
បន្ទប់ក្នុងក្មេង **94–4**
បន្ទប់គេង **44**
បន្ទប់គេងរបស់ក្មេង **45**
បន្ទប់ដាក់ចាន **63–12**
បន្ទប់ដាំកូនឈេី/រុក្ខជាតិ **152–5**
បន្ទប់គុលាការ **99–7**
បន្ទប់ទទួលទានអាហារ **62–2**
បន្ទប់ទទួលភ្ញៀវ **42**
បន្ទប់ទឹក **43**
បន្ទប់ទុមានសោ **5–7**
បន្ទប់បាយ **41**
បន្ទប់ប្រជុំ **145–19**

បន្ទប់ពិនិត្យ **84–9**
បន្ទប់ភាពអាសន្ន **87**
បន្ទប់ភ្ញៀវ **145–10**
បន្ទប់ដង់ចៅ **84–1**
បន្ទប់រេៀន **2–3, 5–1**
បន្ទប់រ៉ា **145–20**
បន្ទប់លេខ **4–6**
បន្ទប់ៈកោត់ **87**
បន្ទប់អ្នកជម្ងឺ **86**
បន្ទាត់ **3–27, 118**
បន្ទរកេរ **119–5**
បន្ទៈសាច់គោអាំង **61–13**
បន្ទៈសាច់ផ្ដេកបិដាន់ **61–7**
បន្ទា **129–28**
បន្ធៃ **51**
បន្ធៃកក **55–43**
បបួរម៉ាត់ **74–30**
បិមបញ្ញាយនូហោស **110–7**
បិមអ្នកចាំសង្ឃោៈ **155–20**
បរាសិកក្នុងពោៈរេៀន **79–16**
បិរយោការ **126**
បសុសត្ត **133, 148–21**
បាត់ខ្សែរត **70–24**
បាត់ភ្ល័ត **82–P**
បាំក់ **163–F**
បាកុ **21–4**
បាចផ្ចា **129–27**
ប៉ាំណូបរិធានស្ងំ **108–17**
បាតដៃ **75–59**
បាត់ស្បែកជេីង **68–12**
បាត់ក្មេង **102–1**
បាត់ទ្បេរ **70–25**
បានការធ្លេ **28–G**
បានធ្វើការ **141–L**
ប៉ាំន់វៃ **41–11**
បាយ ភិទ្យាហ្គ **61–18**
បាល់ **45–16**
បាល់ទាត់ **158–12, 161–12**
បាល់ៈ **158–14, 161–3**
បាល់ៈក្នុងទឹក **158–15**
បាល់ម្ម្លលិង **161–5**
បាល់ពោៈ **158–8, 161–4**
បាល់រ៉ាយដំបង **158–9, 161–18**
បាល់អោរ **158–11, 161–22**
បាស់ **120–10**
បាស់ស៊ីន **120–6**
ប៉ាំស្ដោ **61–15**
ប៉ាំស្រ្តាមី **53–6**
បិត **3–18**
បិទសេរូវតៅ **2–J**
បិ **14**
បិដងម្មយសច្ចហ៍ **18–24**
បិដងម្មយអាទិត្យ **18–24**
បិត **51–6**
បិភាគបួន **15–5**
បិយ៉ា **159–2**

បិង **117–13**
បិរ **54–36**
បគ្ឆលីកពោទ្យ **86**
បគ្ឆនសញ្ញា **113–7**
បុណ្យកំណេីតគ្រោះយេស៊ូ **168–18**
បុណ្យថ្ងៃងឥណួរគុណព្រៈ **168–15**
បុណ្យពិណាណិតាមនោរាជធិ **152–19**
បុណ្យលេងល្បែងកំសាន្ត **152–16**
បុណ្យហាល់ទ្បវ៉ីន **168–10**
ប៊ុស្ស្រផ្តេកក្ដាប់របស់ **96–14**
ប៊ុស្ស្រ្ទប្រសណិយ័ **89–29**
ប្ក **69–40**
បុក **135–51**
ប្រ៊ម្រិ **46–I**
ប្រ៊មយក...ឈ្មាម **85–G**
ប្ូលិស **99–1**
ប្ូរណសំខ្សា **14**
ប្លុងស្ងួង **169–J**
ប្ូន **14**
ប្ូផ្ត្រងទ្រវៃង **118–8**
ប្ូផ្ត្រងស្មៃ **118–6**
បេីក់ថ្ម **10–6**
បេីកបរទាំងស្រវឹង **100–3**
បេីកមេីលពាក្យ **6–A**
បេីកទ្យាន **90–C**
បេីកទ្យាន ក្រៀងម៉ាស៊ីនដំ/ទ្យានស្ទួច **140–F**
បេីកទ្យានទៅធ្វេីការ **26–I**
បេីកទ្យានធំ **140–E**
បេីកសេរូវគៅ **2–I**
បេីកអំណោយ **169–L**
ប៉េងប៉ោៈ **51–23**
ប៉ៃតសំប **14**
ប៉ៃតសំបភាគរេយ័ **15–10**
បៃបផៃន **70**
បិំល **39–13, 149–21**
បៃគង **12–8**
បៃគងសួន **70–6**
បោកខោអាវ **72**
បោកចំបាល់ **159–16**
បោសសំអាតគម្ម **46–A**
បំបាត់ទាសករ **115**
បំបែកពងទាបិ **58–A**
បំពៅ **94–D**
បំបង់ **56–12**
បំបង់ក **75–36**
បំបង់គិលាណ **151–17**
បំបង់ទឹក **39–9, 151–16**
បំបង់ទឹកកក្ស្ងៈ **49–19**
បំបង់ទឹកស្ខាយ **154–24**
បំបង់បិក **60–20**
បំបង់ផ្ស្ងែង **38–21, 108–11**
បំពេញក្នុងចន្លោៈ **7–R**
បំពេញក្រដាស **4–B**
បំពេញក្រដាសសុំធ្វេីការងារ **141–G**
បំពេញប្រហោង (ធ្មេញ) **84–22**
បំជិ នៅក្នុងគណៈៈវិទិផ្ទីយ **116–G**

ច្រើម៉ាស៊ូតកលុយ **140**–N
ច្រើឡើងវិញ **126**–A
ច្រេង **55**–49, **126**–6
ច្រេងកាគ **126**–6
ច្រេងមួយពែង **57**–2
ច្រាំ **14**
ច្រាំដុល្លារ **20**–8
ច្រាំបិ **14**
ច្រាំបួន **14**
ច្រាំបីរ **14**
ច្រាំមួយ **14**
ច្រាំមួយដប/កំប៉ុង **56**–9
ច្រាំសែន **20**–2
ច្បង់ចន្ទុប ច្បង់ផ្ទះ **38**–1
ច្បុក **107**–2
ច្បើបើរ **50**–19
ច្បេច **132**–7
ច្បេកនោម **75**–47
ផលដំណាំ **148**
ផលិត **146**–B
ផាត់គិន្ទរ **163**–E
នីក **60**–B
នេីងផ្ងា **39**–18
ផៃ **155**–16
ផៃនដី **127**–7
ផៃនទិ **3**–12
ផៃនទិមួល **3**–9
ផ្ងា **39**–19, **129**, **129**–7
ផ្ងាកូឡាប **129**–15
ផ្ងាក្រដាស **168**–3
ផ្ងាក្រកុស **129**–25
ផ្ងាខានេសៀន **129**–18
ផ្ងាក្រិស្សុងតៃម **129**–19
ផ្ងាឈូក **12**–10
ផ្ងាឈូករតន៍ **129**–10
ផ្ងាជាហ្ខិល **129**–26
ផ្ងាដេហ្ប៉ី **129**–14
ផ្ងាទូលិប **129**–11
ផ្ងាឧនស្រី **129**–16
ផ្ងាផ័យសេតគ្លា **129**–23
ផ្ងាម៉ិះ **129**–21
ផ្ងាយដុះកន្ទុយ **127**–25
ផ្ងាយណិចទូន **127**–2
ផ្ងាយព្រះពុត **127**–9
ផ្ងាយព្រះសុក្រ **127**–8
ផ្ងាយព្រះសៅរ៍ **127**–4
ផ្ងាយព្រះហស្ប្តី **127**–5
ផ្ងាយព្រះអង្គារ **127**–6
ផ្ងាយភូត **127**–1
ផ្ងាយយូអេនិស **127**–3
ផ្ងាវាំយោល **129**–12
ផ្ងាលិលី **129**–24
ផ្ងាឡ្យិច្ឆេ **129**–22
ផ្ងាស្បៀង **129**–13
ផ្ងាស្តស **51**–16

ផ្ងាអគីដេ **129**–17
ផ្ងាអិះ **129**–20
ផ្កុំគ្រៀង **140**–A
ផ្ធើក្រដាសតាមម៉ាស៊ូ ទូរុក្ម **142**–B
ផ្ធើស៍ប្ត្រ **96**–B
ផ្ធាសាយធំ **79**–2
ផ្ធៃមការសន្ទនា **8**–B
ផ្ធៃមរាយបាល **157**–N
ផ្ធៃវព្រាក់ **97**–E
ផ្ងាងសំរក្ស **165**–28
ផ្ងាងសំរក់សំរាប់តូ **163**–22
ផ្ងះ **34**–6, 38
ផ្ងះក្រេង **34**–7
ផ្ងះចលៃត **34**–8
ផ្ងះគុក្កុតា **45**–14
ផ្ងះបាយ **40**
ផ្ងះឈ្លៃងផ្សល **34**–5, **36**–37
ផ្ងះ **102**–4
ផ្ងកខ្ញ្រាច់ **117**–5
ផ្ងៃក **140**–A, **146**–7
ផ្ងៃកគ្រៀងឧប្ធាន **108**–109
ផ្ងៃកនៃដេមលេី **128**
ផ្ងៃកនៃរធ្មង់ **118**
ផ្ងៃកនៃរាងបួនផ្ដ្រងស្ម៉ី **118**
ផ្ងៃកបព្ញាន (ស៊ី.ភី.យ) **144**–1
ផ្ងៃកបស្ម៉ីមកណ្ញាល **123**–9
ផ្ងៃកម្រាមជេីង **68**–15
ផ្ងៃករបស់ត្រី **130**
ផ្ងៃកសផ្សស្វាប **132**
ផ្ងបត **144**–5
ផ្ងាកគិលៃ **21**–1
ផ្ងាកចិត **143**–35
ផ្ងាកបំរាម **80**–15
ផ្ងាកពាក់សំគាល់ពេលអាសន្ន **83**–14
ផ្ងាកលេខឧប្ធាន **108**–15
ផ្ងាកសំប៉ុត្រឆ្ងាំ **80**–14
ផ្ងាស់ប៉ូវម្ភេបចំណិ **80**–C
ផ្ងាស់លៃនៅ **29**–P
ផ្ងូ **104**–2
ផ្ងូគេតពេលភ្លៃងភេះ **36**–7
ផ្ងូចាល់ **107**–8
ផ្ងូចេញពេលភ្លៃងភេះ **37**–23
ផ្ងូច្រកគុត **37**–21
ផ្ងូឆ្មងកាត់ **90**–8
ផ្ងូជៃះគង់ **153**–2
ផ្ងូជៃរ **91**–26
ផ្ងូជៃរខាងមុង **38**–14
ផ្ងូដៃក **104**–10
ផ្ងូផ្ងល **90**–9
ផ្ងូផ្ងល់ទិក្រុង **88**–89
ផ្ងូប្រជព្ធុក្ម **90**–91
ផ្ងូវក់ **5**–11
ផ្ងូវចធ្លគ្លិងក្នុងស្រុក **115**
ផ្ងូវចធ្លគ្លិងធ្លុងកាត់ **107**–11
ផ្ងូវលិទិក្រិភេក្រជាតិយ៉ាវ៉ីត **114**

ផ្ងូវឡ្ញានចូល **38**–5
ផ្ងូវជៃងកទិស **107**–6
ផ្ងៃកបឡ្ញារ **10**–17
ផ្ងៃកគាំបិតគោរ **77**–26
ផ្ងៃខៃ **150**–23
ផ្ងៃលេី **50**
ផ្ងៃលេ្យរិ **50**–16
ផ្ងៃដៃកខ្ងង **150**–23
ផ្ងៃលុភ **50**–23
ផ្ងៃប៉ោម **50**–4
ផ្ងៃផ្ធុ **50**–8
ផ្ងៃព្រាន **50**–26
ផ្ងៃភា **50**–6
ផ្ងៃណោរ **150**–11
ផ្ងៃវាស់បើរ **50**–18
ផ្ងៃស្រល **128**–11
ផ្ងុំខ្ញ្បល់សរផ្ងៃះ **83**–16
ផ្ងៃកនុត់ឡ្ញេន **169**–K
ផ្ងុំ...សក់ **76**–H
ផ្ងៃរ **54**–55, **89**–20
ផ្ងៃរធំ **92**–93
ផ្ងៃរមេម **152**–22
ផ្ងៃរលក់របស់ចាស់នៅខាងក្រៅ **152**–22
ផ្ងៃរហ៉ិនរល់ដុល **114**
ផ្ងៃរិត **51**–26
ផ្ងៃង **10**–14
ផ្ងៃងសាយអ៉ុ **126**–10
ផ្ងៃរាត **131**–30
ពង **54**–34
ពងទារាយបព្ញាលគ្ម **58**
ពងទារាយបព្ញាលគ្ម **61**–1
ពងបៃក **78**–15
ពងមួយកាតុង **56**–16
ពញ្ស្រល **134**–8
ពណិ **12**
ពត់ខ្ញុនព្រាណ **157**–Q
ពតិមាន **167**–17
ពតិមានផ្ងាល់ខ្ញន **4**
ពន្ធៃថ្ងល់ក់ **21**–7
ពន្ធ្យៀនទៅមុង **165**–C
ពតៃ **133**–1
ពស់កគ្ងិត **131**–39
ពស់ផៃក **131**–40
ពស់ផសតិស **131**–38
ពាក់កណ្ញាលយប់ **17**–21
ពាក់កណ្ញាលអាយុ **22**–14
ពាក្យទាក់ទងនឹងចលនា **105**–1
ពាល់ **75**–E
ពិការ **22**–25
ពិការវ័ត **22**–26
ពិជសណ្ញិត **118**–25
ពិតាន **42**–5
ពិនិត្យ...គម្រៃគលាម **85**–B
ពិនិត្យមេីលកិច្ចការរបស់អ្នក **7**–Y
ពិនិត្យមេីល...វ័ត **85**–F

តិចិត្យមេីលគរ៉ាធ់ **111**–B
តិន្ទ **158**–1
តិភពផ្ទាយ **127**
តិគតលោក **124–125**
តិភាក្បាពិបព្ធ **6**–L
តិល **151**–39
តិសារបាយពេលល្ងាច **27**–R
តិងពាង **132**–30
តិរ **14**
តិរដងធ្មេយសញ្ចារ៉ិ **18**–23
តិរដងធ្មេយអាទិត្យ **18**–23
ពុកចង្កា **23**–6
ពុកមាត់ **23**–5
ពុត **18**–4
ពុល **147**–3
ពុក **44**–25
ពុកយា៉ងកុំអោយទឡ្ឍចនឹងក្រែ **45**–7
ពូថៅ **150**–3
ពួកអេស្បាញ នៅ សាគតា ហ្គេ **114**
ពូន **169**–E
ពេឡ្យផ្ចេញ **84**–18, **137**–20
ពេឡ្យផ្ទែកចំណិអាហារ **87**–25
ពេឡ្យសគ្ន **139**–62
ពេលណវាត់ដួច **19**–45
ពេលបង្ខយ **17**–33
ពេលវេលា **16–17**
ពេលសេដ្ឋកិច្ចធ្លាក់ឱិនភាព **114**
ពែង **63**–21
ពែងការហ្គេ **41**–27
ពោត **51**–27, **148**–4
ពោះ **74**–3
ពោះគោ **52**–8
ពោះវៀន **75**–42
ព្យុរខោអាវ **72**–H
ព្យុះទឹកកក **10**–20, **103**–11
ព្យុះធូលី **10**–21
ព្យុះត្រិល **10**–18
ព្យុះសង្ឃរា **103**–13
ព្រហស្បត្ត **18**–5
ព្រាប **132**–16
ព្រិល **10**–19, **165**–33
ព្រិស្ត៍ **119**–20
ព្រិក **17**–16
ព្រឹត្តិការណ៍ប្រវត្តិសាស្ត្រ និងនយោបាយ **114**
ព្រឹទ្ធសភា **116**–3
ព្រយ **130**–1
ព្រយមាត់ **134**–18
ព្រញ **161**–7
ព្រយ **30**–13
ព្រយចិត្ត **31**–20
ព្រៃ **117**–1
ព្រៃឈេី **117**–11
ព្រោន **130**–19
ព្រ៉ **44**–23
ព្រះចន្ទឌិតសូន្យ **127**–13

ព្រះចន្ទពេញវង់ **127**–16
ព្រះវិហារត្រីស្ត **88**–6
ព្រះវិហារសស្លាម **89**–23
ព្រះអាទិត្យ **127**–10
ភស្តុតាង **99**–9
ភាគនិគតិ **123**–12
ភាគបាយព្យព៍សុីហ្ហ្រិត **123**–14
ភាគរយ **15**
ភាគអគ្គេយ៍ **123**–13
ភាគ **144**–17
ភាន់ច្រឡ្យ **31**–27
ភាពយន្ត **152**–10, **166**–1
ភាពយន្តខោច្ម៉យ **166**–9
ភាពវាំងសួគ **103**–10
ភាពអាស្ថ **102–103**
ភាពអាស្ថផ្ទែកពេឡ្យ **82**
ភាសាបរទេស **121**–8
ភាសាអង់គ្លេសជាភាសាទីពីរ **121**–7
ភិគ **163**–28
ភិចនិទ **153**–D
ភិនភ្គិត **132**–12
ភិច **50**–5
ភិគសា **60**–7
ភិសាម៉ា **67**–4
ភូគោល **3**–9
ភូមិសាស្ត្រ **117**
ភូយ **44**–12
ភូយញាក់សំម៉ឬ **45**–2
ភេ **131**–35
ភេគ្ត **9**–16
ភេគ **4**–12
ភោជនីយដ្ឋាន **62–63**
ភ្ញាក់ដឹងខ្លួ **26**–A
ភ្ញាក់ផ្ផែល **31**–31
ភ្នំភ្ថា **70**–13
ភ្ស្រ៉ **33**–14
ភ្ស្រ៉ **145**–11
ភ្ស្រ៉វាគ្ប្ន **32**–9
ភ្ភក់ភ្ថិង **154**–11
ភ្ភាក់ងារ **99**–1
ភ្ភាក់ងារគេយ **110**–21
ភ្ភាក់ងារប៉ូលិស **138**–44
វ៉ែក្ត **74**–27
ភ្ភំភិគផ្គ៍ **103**–14
ភ្ភក់ **75**–D
ភ្ភក **135**–48
ភ្ភិត **42**–10
ភ្ភ៉ិងចនាគ **90**–6
ភ្ភ៉ិងគេះ **102**–7
ភ្ភ៉ិងឆាថ់ (រលត់) **48**–2
ភ្ភ៉ិងថ្គួល **91**–23
ភ្ភ៉ិងបថ់ **108**–4, **108**–18
ភ្ភ៉ិងមានអំពូលត្រេថ **42**–3
ភ្ភ៉ិងវាគហាល **38**–9
ភ្ភ៉ិងព្រា្ងថ **108**–13

ភ្ភ៉ិង **10**–8
ភ្ភ៉ិងព្ស្រៈ **10**–16
ភ្ភ៉ិងមានជាតិអាស៉ិដ **126**–11
ភ្ភ៉ា **52**–21, **74**–16
មកផល **111**–O
មកផ្ទៈ **27**–Q
មកា **19**–25
ម្ឆ្លួមឆ្លណលកុមារ **94–95**
មគ្គេយ្យសាលា **112**–4
មគ្ផ្លាបាយឆង់ព្រាត់ **20**
មនុស្បចាស់ជរា **22**–12
មនុស្បចាស់ទំ **22**–15
មនុស្បគំ **22**–9
ម៉ិនិផ័រ **144**–6
មន្ឌិរពេទ្យ **86–87**, **88**–7
មន្ឌិរក្ស្បាជនជរា-ពិការ **34**–11
មន្ឌិរសេដ្ឋកិគភពផ្ទាយ **127**–19
មហាវាយរ៉យធម្មជាតិ **102–103**
មហារ៉ិគខ្មរក្បាស **79**–12
មហាវិទ្យាល័យ **112**–10
មហាសមុទ្រ **117**–6
មហោស្រព **166**–6
មា (ក្ងូ) **24**–11
មាត់ **74**–22
មាត់ទន្ថេ **117**–10
ចាត់សប្ផ្រ **155**
មានឆន **29**–M
មានចៅ **29**–Q
មានប្រតិកម្មនឹងការមិនត្រូវធាតុ **82**–E
មាន់ផ្ផ្រោះ **22**–19
មាន់គគ **133**–6
មាន់ឡេបាល **133**–6
មាន់ញ **133**–5
មាន់បាវាគ **52**–17
មាន់បាវាគ **168**–17
មាន់បាវាគ្ភ្ភិរ **53**–4
មាន់ស្ម៉ារ **58**
មាន់អ៉ាង **61**–12
ម៉ិញ **164**–2
ម៉ាញ្ញឡ្ប្ហាន **108**–30
ម៉ានជឹបេគ **144**–18
ម៉ាញ្ប៉ុវេនេស **60**–25
ម៉ានគ៍ **3**–19
មាស ដែលគេរកឃេីញនៅ កាលិហ្ប៉ វៃ **115**
ម៉ាស់ពាក់ការបារមុខជៈ ស្ថ **66**–14
ម៉ាស់សម្រាប់អ្នកឆាប់បាល់ពាក់ការពារ **161**–15
ម៉ាស់អ្នកស៉ិសែន **110**–14
ម៉ាស៉ុន **109**–41
ម៉ាស៉ុនគាត់ស្ម៉៊ **39**–22
ម៉ាស៉ុនគិត **40**–12
ម៉ាស៉ុនគិតភាគសំណល់ **40**–5
ម៉ាស៉ុនគិតសាថ/បថ្ន **40**–26
ម៉ាស៉ុនគំដេរ **108**–29
ម៉ាស៉ុនគំដេរខ្ចុគ **49**–15
ម៉ាស៉ុនខាត់ **150**–9

ម៉ាស៊ីនខៃវ័ខ្យរភ្លើង **150**–8
ម៉ាស៊ីនខៃដី **149**–9
ម៉ាស៊ីនគាស់ថ្ម **149**–9
ម៉ាស៊ីនកិតលុយ **55**–18
ម៉ាស៊ីនចាក់កាសែត **3**–11, **164**–15
ម៉ាស៊ីនចាក់ចាស **164**–12
ម៉ាស៊ីនចាក់ស៊ីឌី **164**–14
ម៉ាស៊ីនចិតខ្ចៅដៃ **142**–9
ម៉ាស៊ីនច្រៀក **150**–12
ម៉ាស៊ីនភ្ញៀយទូរស័ព្ទ **9**–14
ម៉ាស៊ីនដាក់កាតឯកសារលុយ **97**–3
ម៉ាស៊ីនដេរ **73**–10
ម៉ាស៊ីនត្រជាក់ **37**–19, **108**–28
ម៉ាស៊ីនថតកុន **165**–19
ម៉ាស៊ីនថត រេមួតគន្លង **165**–21
ម៉ាស៊ីនថត ទំហំ 35 មម **165**–24
ម៉ាស៊ីនថតវីដ្យួ **164**–8
ម៉ាស៊ីនទាញ **146**–10
ម៉ាស៊ីនទឹកកក **145**–18
ម៉ាស៊ីនទូរ្ស័ម្ម **143**–23
ម៉ាស៊ីនភ្ញើអោយកក **40**–10
ម៉ាស៊ីនបន្លួតខ្យល់ **80**–4
ម៉ាស៊ីនបូមសំរាម **47**–13
ម៉ាស៊ីនបោក **72**–3
ម៉ាស៊ីនផ្គុំកូនបថត **142**–14
ម៉ាស៊ីនផ្គុំស្ព័កលេ **39**–4
ម៉ាស៊ីនផ្សើម **80**–2
ម៉ាស៊ីនព្ពម្ម **144**–12
ម៉ាស៊ីនមើលម៉ៃក្រូហ្វីល **98**–4
ម៉ាស៊ីនលាងចាន **40**–4
ម៉ាស៊ីនលាយគ្រឿង **40**–25
ម៉ាស៊ីនលើក **146**–14
ម៉ាស៊ីនរាយអក្តលើលេខ **142**–2
ម៉ាស៊ីនលួតនាំរ័វ៉ាន់ **110**–18
ម៉ាស៊ីនស្កេន **144**–13
ម៉ាស៊ីនហាលខោអាវ **72**–4
ម៉ាស៊ីនអាត់កាសែត **164**–3
ម៉ាហ្ស៊ីន **54**–39
ម៉ាហ្ស៊ីន **60**–14
ម៉ាទ្បូតទុល្យោ **151**–42
ម៉ាទ្បូតមួល **151**–43
មុកសិត្ត **123**
មិនទាន់ទុំ **50**–28
មិនប្រយ័ត្ន **147**–23
មិនស្រួល **30**–8
មិនា **19**–27
មិថុនា **19**–30
មិត្រ **164**–4
មិង **24**–10
មុខ **74**
មុខរបរ **136**–139
មុខវិជ្ជាសិក្សាផ្សេងៗទៀត **121**
មុខទឹក ពាក់ត្រៀងផកផដឡើម **160**–12
មុខទឹកពាក់មុខ **160**–11

មុត **78**–13
មុម **118**–24
ម៉ូដិម **144**–11
ម្ងត្ **91**–19
ម៉្លួតិអដ៏រ **20**–16
មូលទ្រវែង **118**–9
ម៉្លិតុល **119**–18
មូស **132**–23
មួហ្ប **134**–1
មួក **32**–3, **66**–1, **68**–5
មួកក្តិប **66**–6
មួកក្តុបកិឡា **66**–27
មួកជះស្ពី **66**–10
មួកបាល់អោម **161**–20
មួកិង **147**–19
មួករៈកាត់ **87**–31
មួកស្ព័រ **66**–23
មួកស្រោបក្បាល (ងុតទឹក) **76**–1
មួម៉ា **31**–28
មួយ **14**
មួយដុល្លារ **20**–7
មួយពាន់ **14**
មួយពាន់មួយ **14**
មួយភាគបី **15**–3
មួយភាគបួន **15**–2
មួយភាគប្រាំបី **15**–1
មួយភាគពីរ **15**–4
មួយមុិន **14**
មួយរយ **14**
មួយរយកោដិ **14**
មួយរយដុល្លារ **20**–12
មួយរយភាគរយ **15**–11
មួយរយមួយ **14**
មួយលាន **14**
មួយសប្បាហ៍មុង **18**–22
មួយសែន **14**, **20**–1
មួយអាទិត្យមួង **18**–22
មេម **129**–9
មេល **75**–A
មេមិលការខុសត្រ **140**–K
មេលិក្នុងទព័រផ្សាយដណ្ណិង **141**–D
មេលិក្នុង...បំបង់ត **85**–E
មេលិទូរទស្សន៏ **27**–S
មេលិប្រកាសចិទ្ធផ្សាយការងារ **141**–B
មេលិមិនឃើញ **22**–26
មេលិស្បៀវភៅរាំសំរាប់ភាពអាសន្ត **111**–K
មេយពកកប្រេិទ **10**–7
មេយស្រឡះ **10**–6
មេដែក **119**–21
មេដៃ **75**–56
មេធាវី **138**–36
មេធាវីផ្ត **99**–10
មេធាវីរបស់ចុងចោទ **99**–4
មេធ្ផ **137**–32

មេសា **19**–28
មេអំបៅ **132**–20
មេអំបៅយប់ **132**–22
មែក **128**–2
មែកគុចចា **128**–1
ម៉ែត្រលេិ **151**–15
ម៉ែត្រវាស់ **150**–22
ម៉ៃក្រូដើរ **40**–13
ម៉ៃក្រូហ្វិល **98**–5
ម៉ោង **16**–3
ម៉ោងតំបន់កណ្ណាល **17**–28
ម៉ោង តំបន់ផាស៊ីហ្វិក **17**–26
ម៉ោងតំបន់ភាពខាងកេិត **17**–29
ម៉ោងតំបន់ភ្ពុ **17**–27
ម៉ោងតំបន់អាទ្សុំទិក **17**–30
ម៉ោងទូទោ **17**–32
ម៉ោងនោរតំបន់ ដ៏រកឃើញថ្ម **17**–31
ម៉ោងពីរខ្វះដប់នាទិ **16**–14
ម៉ោងពីរខ្វះ ដប់ប្រាំនាទិ **16**–13
ម៉ោងពីរ ខ្វះប្រាំនាទិ **16**–15
ម៉ោងពីរខ្វះៃម្ភនាទិ **16**–12
ម៉ោងពីរខ្វះៃម្ភប្រាំនាទិ **16**–11
ម៉ោងមួយ **16**–4
ម៉ោងមួយកន្លះ **16**–10
ម៉ោងមួយ ដប់នាទិ **16**–6
ម៉ោងមួយ ដប់ប្រាំនាទិ **16**–7
ម៉ោងមួយ ប្រាំនាទិ **16**–5
ម៉ោងមួយ ៃម្ភនាទិ **16**–8
ម៉ោងមួយ ៃម្ភប្រាំនាទិ **16**–9
ម៉ោងមួយ សាមសិបប្រាំនាទិ **16**–11
ម៉ោងមួយ សែសិបនាទិ **16**–12
ម៉ោងមួយសែសិបប្រាំនាទិ **16**–13
ម៉ោងមួយហាសិបនាទិ **16**–14
ម៉ោងមួយ ហាសិបប្រាំនាទិ **16**–15
ម៉ោង ហាវ៉ៃ-អេឡ្យូៃស្យេន **17**–24
ម៉ោង អាឡ្យាស្កា **17**–25
ម្ងាស់ផ្ទះ **37**–32
ម្ងាស់អោងចក្រ **146**–2
ម្ងាស់វាលចិ៍ផ្តើមសត្ត **148**–22
ម្ងាស់ហាង **139**–56
ម្ងុលខ្លាស់ **69**–36, **73**–24
ម្ងុលចាក់ **163**–18
ម្ងុលចាក់ថ្ម **84**–14
ម្ងុលដេរ **73**–22
ម្ងុលសំរាប់ខ្ញាស់ **73**–14
ម្ងាយ **24**–5
ម្ងាយក្មេក **24**–13
ម្ងាយចុង **25**–31
ម្ងាយថ្មីលែង **25**–25
ម្ងុសផ្ទាក **51**–7
ម្ងុសហិរ **51**–8
ម្ងាក់ឯង **30**–18
ម្ងាល **50**–2
ម្ងែ **14**

រៀងផ្សងក្រោង **166**–13
រៀងវិទ្យាសាស្ត្រប្រឌិត **166**–12
រៀងស្នេហា **166**–16
រៀងអាថិ៍កំបាំង **166**–15
អៀន **6–7, 26**–J
អៀនបើកបរ **28**–E
អៀនផ្នែកពាណិជ្ជកម្ម **121**–2
អៀបការ **28**–L
អៀបការគ្នា **25**–23
អៀបការឡើងវិញ **25**–27
អៀបក្រដាសតាមលំដាប់ **142**–H
អៀបប្រែ **46**–G
អៀបចានស្មាបប្រា **63**–14
អៀបចំ ក្រៀងឥតូ **35**–K
អៀបតាមមំព័រ **142**–F
អៀបតុ **62**–A
អៀបបាយ **26**–F
អៀបរាប់ពិវត្ត **11**
អៀបរាប់អំពិសក់ **23**
អៀបរាប់អំពិសំឡេកបំពាក់ **70–71**
អៀប ឋម្ព **149**–B
អាគ្រុទ្បរៃទេ **79**–7
អាគ HIV **79**–10
អាគលើសលោម **79**–15
អាងចក្រ **146**
អាងជាង **121**–10
អាងភាពយន្ត **88**–11
អាងឡោន **88**–10
អាងឡ្ហាន **38**–6
អាម **132–5, 134–19**
អាមភ្នែក **74**–34
អាល័រ ខ្ទស្ទិ **152**–15
អិតិប **31**–23
វាំ **33**–J
លក់ **21**–B
លក់ឡ្ហាន **140**–H
លក្ខណៈជម្មិ **79**
លក្ខណៈជម្មិ និង ជម្មិផ្ទន់ធូរ **79**
លក្ខណៈរាងកាយ **22**
លង់ទិក **82**–I
លប់ភ្នារខ្វេន **2**–H
លា **133**–2
លាក់ **169**–E
លាងចាន **46**–M
លាងបង្គន់ **46**–D
លាង...សក់ **76**–F
លាម...ក្រចក **77**–O
លាបខ្វាញ់ខ្ញុះ **58**–C
លាបថ្នាំសំរាប់ការពារវែក្ស **76**–D
លាបពណ៌ **163**–E
លាបពណ៌ិសក់ **23**–D
លាប...ម្សៅរែតខ្លួន **77**–P
លាយក្រៀងស្យិ **58**–K
លាសសមុទ្រ **53**–28
លាសសមុទ្រម្យ៉ាង **130**–18

លិខិតឥតងដែន **29**–9
លុយសុទ្ធ **20**–13
លើស្ពាន **105**–2
លើកដងទូរស័ព្ទ **9**–A
លើកដៃ **2**–A
លើកទម្ងន់ **159**–15
លើកសរសើរមិត្តអ្នក **8**–G
ល្បៀង **12**–12
លេខ **3–31, 14–15**
លេខក្បាលទូរសព្ទ **4**–10
លេខគណនីសន្សំ **97**–6
លេខគណនីសែក **97**–8
លេខកតិ **15**–6
លេខគុណ **118**–3
លេខចែក **118**–4
លេខតំបន់ **4**–9
លេខទូរសព្ទ **4**–11
លេខបូក **118**–1
លេខរ៉ូម៉ាំង **14**
លេខសង **118**–2
លេខាធិការ **139**–52
លេខាធិការ **142**–3
លេង **94–K, 165–B**
លេងប្ប **163**–H
លេងភ្នេក **120**–A
លេងល្បែង **162**–B
លេងស្កេតលើទឹកកក **160**–4
លេងស្កេតលើទឹកកកផ្តើកាយវិការ **160**–5
លេងស្ពិចុះផិអេល **160**–1
លេងស្ពីលើទឹក **160**–7
លេចបថ្នាំ **80**–F
លេចបថ្នាំពូល **82**–J
លេចបថ្នាំហ្គសកម្រិត **82**–K
លែងលះគ្នា **25**–24
ឡោកខ៉ងខាងខ្ទិត **127**–14
ឡោកខៃមួយភាគបួន **127**–15
ឡោកយឺញ្ញត្រកេសម្ងាប់ **115**
ឡោក វ៉ាស៊ិងតុន ប្រធានាធិបតិទ៉ **115**
ឡោក អាមស្ទ្រងទៅដល់ចានព្រះចន្ទ **115**
ឡោក **156**–J
ឡោកបោះឆ្នោត **157**–S
ឡោមមត្តា **131**–32
លំពែង **75**–46
លំហាតអាកាស **127**–22
លំហាត់សរសេរ **113**–1
ឡ្ហាន **166**–8
ឡ្ហាន / កុនឥត្ភូតា **152**–14
ឡ្ហានសម៉ើយ **167**–21
ឡ្ហាច **17**–19
ឡ្ហាក់ទិក **117**–2
ល្ហែង **152–18, 162–163**
ល្ហែង / ចំណោមស្ខរភ្នេងវៃទ្យុបួនរស្សវិ **167**–23
ល្ហែងបេសស្បាល **152**–25
ល្ហែងឥត្ក្បា **45**–22
ឡ្ហា **51**–13

ស្លិ **50**–25
ស្លេងច្រេក **145**–13
ស្លង **50**–20
ស្លិ **42**–2
ផ្កែ **113**–5
រស់ភ្លេង **120**–1
រស់ភ្លេងប៉ិក **120**–2
រថនាឡ្ហក្រម **3**–28
រថនាឡ្ហក្រមរូបភាព **3**–29
រ័ណ្ឌមណ្ឌល **118**–15
រល្បិ **128**–22
វ៉ាន់ស៊ុយជារាំង **51**–10
រាលឡ្ហាច **117**–4
រាលភ្លេងមួងសម្ងុត្រ **123**–16
រាលលេខបាល់ **153**–1
រាលស្មៅ **117**–20
រាម **156**–G
រាមបាល់ **157**–O
រាយស័ប្ត្រ **142**–D
រាយអក្សរ **140**–M
រាយអាយសព្ទ **58**–B
រាស់ **149**–C
រាស់គ្រៀងស្លិម្ងប **57**–A
វិការដ្ឋាន **32**–4
វិចិត្រករ **136**–5
វិត្តិកា **19**–35
វិជ្ជមេផ្ទៈ **121**–9
វិជ្ជហាត់ព្រាលា **121**–11
វ៉ិជ្ញុកោណ **118**–23
វ៉ិជ្ញុមាត្រ **118**–17
វិទ្យាល័យ **112**–7
វិទ្យាសាស្ត្រ **119**
វិទ្យាសាស្ត្រកុំព្យូទ័រ **121**–4
វិទ្ប **108**–31
វិទ្ប្ហាប់រលេកឋាអាតុអាកាសចាយ **164**–5
វិទ្ប្ហត្ត **164**–15
វិទ្ប្ហមានទ្យៀផ្ទិក **44**–16
វិទ្ប្ហុរុចាន **164**–2
វិធិផ្ទេលេខ **118**
វិតិផ្ទើនិយមបេះដូងដើរអ្ឡើងវិញ **83**–17
វិតិ្ប្រិវណ្ណយុត្តិ **113**
វ៉ីតិសង្គ្រោះ Heimlich **83**–18
វិនាទិ **16**–1
វិលមុខ **78**–C
វិស្វករ **137**–23
វិស្សមកាល **19**–46
វិតាមិន **81**–19
វិល្ល៉ប្ហុង **120**–8
វិសសលេបិ បូខ្វៅមួលឡេបិ **150**–28
វិស៊ូអា **164**–8
វេទិកា **32**–5
វេក **59**–7
វេកករ **59**–19
វេកចំហៀង **23**–4
វេកឡេបិ **59**–9

អ៊ីនតាការពារ **147**–10
អ៊ីនតាជំនួយភ្ញៀវ **81**–35
អ៊ីនតាផំការពារ **147**–9
អ៊ីនតាពាក់ការពារវ៉ៃថ្ម **66**–21
រាំងនន **44**–5
រាំងននបង្អួច **42**–16
ស **12**–14
សក់ **74**–19
សក់ក្រញាញ់ **23**–11
សក់ក្រហម **23**–14
សក់ខ្ចៅ **23**–15
សក់ខ្លី **23**–1
សក់ជង់ដែង **23**–16
សក់តណ្ហិត្ឆោត **23**–17
សក់ប្រិញ **23**–11
សក់វែង **23**–3
សក់វែងប្រស្មា **23**–2
សក់សិង្ហ **135**–49
សក់ស្អួរ **23**–13
សក់ស្តួត **23**–9
សក់អង្កាញ់ **23**–10
សង្កតមើល **119**–B
សង្គ្រាមភូមិ **115**
សង្គ្រាមឆ្នាំ ១៩១២ **114**
សង្គ្រាមត្រជាក់ **114**
សង្គ្រាមបដិវត្តន៍ **115**
សង្គ្រាមបារាំង ពលរ៉ាន **115**
សង្គ្រាមមជ្ឈិមបុរាណ **115**
សង្គ្រាមរវាងអេស្ប៉ាញ៉ូល និងអាមេរិកាំង **115**
សង្គ្រាមលោកលើកទី១ **114**
សង្គ្រាមលោកលើកទី២ **114**
សង្គ្រាមវៀតណាម **115**
សង្គ្រាមស៊ីវិល **115**
សង្គ្រាមអាមេរិក និងម៉ិកស៊ិក **114**
សង្ស័រម៉ែត្រ (សម) **15**–12
សញ្ញា **91**–29, **107**
សញ្ញាចរាចរ **107**
សញ្ញាប័ត្រមធ្យមសិក្សា **29**–2
សញ្ញាប័ត្រមធ្យមសិក្សា **32**–7
សញ្ញាប័ត្រមហាវិទ្យាល័យ **29**–7
សញ្ញាបន្ទុក **113**–11
សញ្ញាប្រាប់ថាមានកន្ថែងទំនេរ **36**–11
សព័ណ្ណកក់ប៉ុង **54**–26
សព័ណ្ណកត្ត **51**–25
សព័ណ្ណកបារាំង **51**–19
សព័ណ្ណកសេវ្រា **148**–3
សណ្ហោតារ **88**–5, **145**
សណ្ហោតារត្ថច **89**–22
សត្ត **152**–2
សត្តកករ **133**
សត្តកករម្យ៉ាងសណ្ហោនដូចកំប្រុក ជាដើម **133**–22
សត្តកព្ញ **132**–19
សត្តកវែង **135**–33
សត្តកែងការ **135**–44
សត្តកៅឡ្លា **135**–45

សត្តចង្រៃក្នុងផ្ទះ **49**
សត្តចិញ្ចឹមក្នុងផ្ទះ **133**
សត្តចិញ្ចឹមយកសាច់ **148**–13
សត្តណិបម៉ុង **133**–20
សត្តញ៉ាត់សំឡ្បី **45**–23
សត្តត្រកួត **130**–26
សត្តបិរិវ័ **134**–9
សត្តផាន់ផា **135**–41
សត្តផ្តេកផិតិកិស **135**–46
សត្តពង្រុល **135**–24
សត្តរស់ក្នុងទឹកនិងលើគោក **130–131**
សត្តល្អិត **132**
សត្តល្អិតទេច / វ៉ា **78**–11
សត្តវិស **131**–32
សត្តសន្ធានខ្យងខ្ទា **53**
សត្តសម្ទ្រ **130, 130–131**
សត្តស៊ីស្រេមាច **135**–24
សត្តស្រេល **131**–33
សត្តស្រាម្យៀងឈ្មួស **135**–35
សត្តស្រុក **133**
សត្តស្វាប **132**
សត្តស្វាន **135**–31
សត្តហ្គោហ្ស៊ី **133**–19
សត្តហ្ស៊ីរ៉ាហ្ស **135**–33
សត្តអន្ទង **130**–27
សត្តអាទិទ្យូប **135**–35
សត្តឆ្លិ **132**–10
សង្ឆិសុខសាធារណៈ: **101**–1
សន្ធឹកស្សេវរកៅ **3**–25
សឡ្ស **126**–B, **126**–C
សឡ្ស៍វត្ត **162**–A
សឆ្យោហ៍ **18**–11
សឆ្យោហ៍ក្រោយ **18**–20
សឆ្យោហ៍នេះ **18**–19
សឆ្យោហ៍មុន **18**–18
សឆ្យោយ **31**–32
សឆ្ញចនាធិប្បាយ **98**–18
សភាតំណាងរាស្ត្រ **116**–1
សម **41**–21, **63**–25
សមមូរ **15**
សមរភូមិ នៅពំបនផ្គងំរួស **115**
សមសាឡ្តាត **63**–24
សមាជិកព្រឹទ្ធសភា **116**–4
សមាជិកសភាស្រី / សមាជិកសភាប្រុស **116**–2
សម្បូរ **155**–1
សម្តចាន **46**–N
សម្ព៉ាះកិឡ្បា **161**
សម្ព៉ាះជំនួយជាបន្ធាន់ **83**–1
សម្ព៉ាះធ្វើចំការ **148**–10
សម្ព៉ាះបង្ខែម **68–69**
សម្ព៉ាះផ្ទះបាយ **59**
សម្ព៉ាះសំណាំ **150–151**
សម្ព៉ាះសំរាប់សំអាត **47**
សម្រាក **165**–E
សម **54**–24

សមយដ្ឋាននិស្សិតមហាវិទ្យាល័យ **34**–9
សរសេរក្រដាសព្រាងទិម្ម័យ **113**–A
សរសេរណស្មៅះអ្នកជានអក្សរពុម្ព **4**–C
សរសេរលើក្តារូច្រួន **2**–G
សរសេរអត្ថបទអ្នកឆ្ល្បើងវិញ **113**–D
សរ័សលោនាម្រកហាម **75**–43
សរ័សលោនាមខ្ចៅ **75**–44
សរ័សប្រសាទ **75**–50
សរុប **21**–8
សរនដ្ឋាន **5**–3
សហរដ្ឋអាមេរិក **123**
សហរដ្ឋអាមេរិកបិទព្រុំដែន **114**
សហុបាល **158**–10
សាកលលោក **127**
សាកលវិទ្យាល័យ **112**–10
សាក្សី **99**–11
សាច់ក្រក **52**–12, **61**–2
សាច់ក្តូនគោកាត់បន្ធ:ស្ត្រីង៉ា **52**–6
សាច់កំតួនឈវជិឆ្យេម **52**–13
សាច់គោ **52**
សាច់គោកាត់ជាជុំត្ថចៗ **52**–3
សាច់គោកិន **52**–4
សាច់គោសំរាប់អាំង **52**–1
សាច់គោស្សោរ **53**–8
សាច់គោអាំង **53**–7
សាច់គោអាំងមួយនោរន្ត **57**–12
សាច់ឆ្យេម **52**
សាច់ឆ្ញិនផ្តិនឆ្យេមកាត់ជុំៗ **52**–15
សាច់ជាប់ផ្តិនធិផ្ញែកកាត់ជុំៗ **52**–10
សាច់ជ្រុក **52**
សាច់ជ្រុកបិជាន **52**–11
សាច់ផ្ញ៉ **75**–48
សាច់ត្រីស្ម៉ុងមួយន្ង:ៗ **53**–19
សាច់ត្រីអ័ណ្ហាត់ផ្តកន្ង: **53**–21
សាច់�្ធេន **52**–19
សាច់ធម្មតា **52**
សាច់ឆន្ន: **52**–2
សាច **បសុបក្តិ **52**
សាច់ភ្ញៅ **52**–9
សាច់មាន **52**–16
សាច់មាន់នៅ **52**–24
សាច់មាន់ត្តិន **52**–25
សាជិ **118**–11
សាជិផ្លុង **118**–13
សាប្ច្ **43**–23, **76**–2
សាប្ច្កក់សត់ **76**–9
សាប្ច្កាត់ **72**–8
សាប្ច្ធ្វើឆ្ងិយសក់ទន់ **76**–10
សាប្ច្បោកខោអាវ **72**–7
សាមសិប **14**
សារពតិមាន **98**–8
សារាឝុក្រម **98**–18
សាឝ័នខោអាវ **73**
សាឝ:មធ្ជ្ឃសិល្ប: **152**–7
សាឝាឝ្ណ្ណ **89**–18

សាលាក្រុង **89**–17
សាលាប្រជុំរបស់ធិហ្ម **88**–9
សាលារៀន **5, 89**–27
សាលាបបមសិក្សា **112**–5
សាលាមនុស្សចាស់ **112**–8
សាលាសាធារណៈ **112**–1
សាលាសាសនា **112**–3
សាលាហ្វឹកហ្វឹនការងារ/ពាណិជ្ជកម្ម **112**–9
សាលាឯកជន **112**–2
សាឡាង **104**–23
សាឡាត់ **51**–1, **60**–8
សាឡាត់ដំឡូងបារាំង **53**–13
សាឡាត់ ប៉ាស្ថា **53**–15
សាឡាត់ពិសេស **61**–9
សាឡាម **53**–5
សិង្ហ **135**–36
សិត...សក់ **76**–G, **76**–I
សិទ្ធិ និងការទទួលខុសត្រូវ **116**
សិទ្ធិស្ត្រីបោះឆ្នោត **114**
សិល្បៈ **121**–1
សិល្បៈឈ្លោន **121**–12
សិល្បៈ, ឧស្សាហកម្ម **121**–10
សិស្ស **2**–3, **139**–57
សិស្សឆ្នូងកាព **107**–13
សិស្សដែលថ្មឹងសុន្ទរកថា ពេលបញ្ចប់ការសិក្សា **32**–8
សិដ៏ទម **167**–18
សិតុណ្ណភាព **10**
សិុផ្ទ **108**–24
សិុមិងង **149**–10
សិុមិងង្ក្រឹមៗ **149**–14
សិុអ៊ីប **61**–5
សិហា **19**–32
សិុទ្ធហ្ហន **120**–17
សិុតិទ្ធអ៊ីន **131**–34
សិុឡៃវង **118**–12
សុក្រ **18**–6
សុិត **54**–34
សុិបកំប៉ុង **54**–24
សុិប (ប្រចាំថ្ងៃ) **61**–10
សុិបមួយកំប៉ុង **56**–15
សុដា **55**–52, **60**–4
សុដាច្រាំមួយកំប៉ុង **56**–21
សុដាមួយដប **56**–13
សុប្ស **14**
សុ្បហ្សា **42**–19
សួត **75**–37
សូនកំសាន្ត **88**–8
សូនកំសាន្ត **152**–13
សូនច្បារជំរែសរុក្ខជាតិ **152**–4
សូនច្បារនៅរលើដំបូល **36**–5
សូនសត្វ **152**–1
សូនៃអំពីកឹរ **141**–J
សូ្ពិម៉ាឯងធ្វើការ **141**–F
សូរសំណូរ **6**–G

សេិច **33**–H
សេ្ិបស្សពិប្រាក់ប្យេវត្ស **141**–K
ស្យេរភាពកំណត់ជួប **143**–27
ស្យេរភាពក្រាស់ **11**–7
ស្យេរភាពគួ្រចាប់អារម្មណ៍ **167**–30
ស្យេរភាពទ្វេសុខ្វ **9**–15
ស្យេរភាពធនាគារ **97**–5
ស្យេរភាពបណ្ណាល័យ **98**–20
ស្យេរភាពប្រក្រិតិចិត្ត **142**–6
ស្យេរភាពផតទី **98**–3
ស្យេរភាពមេរ្យេន **3**–23
ស្យេរភាពរាយឈ្មោះហាង **93**–19
ស្យេរភាពរូបថត **165**–32
ស្យេរភាពរូបភាព **45**–17
ស្យេរភាពរៀងកំប្លង **167**–27
ស្យេរភាពរៀងកម្មុត **167**–28
ស្យេរភាពរៀងគួ្រឆ្លេញទ្រាន់ **167**–29
ស្យេរភាពរៀងិត **167**–26
ស្យេរភាពរូបសំរុល **143**–30
ស្យេរភាពសរសេរ **3**–24
ស្យេរភាពសរសេរស្ដាំមុ៉ល **3**–26
ស្យេរភាពសៃក **97**–7
ស្យេរភាពសំរាប់ផាត់ពណ៌ **45**–20
ស្យេរភាពស្តីពីខ្លុះ្នូគ្រជាររគ្នាន់ **83**–7
ស្យេរភាពស្តឹង **11**–8
ស្យេរភាពអាន **3**–22
សេកត្ត **133**–15
សេកវិមាន **116**–5
សេរីរ៉ាលមួយប្រអប់ **56**–18
សេរ៉ឹម **87**–27
សៃកផ្ដាល់ខ្លន **20**–14
សៃកអ្នកដំណឹរ **20**–17
សៃនិចដាក់លិស្សប **61**–8
សៃលឡ្ពីរ **51**–9
សៃសិប **14**
សៃា **37**–31
សៃាកនាដកម្ម **166**–11
សៃាខ្ចិ **48**–6
សៃាទ្វា **109**–34
សៃាបញ្ជោះម៉ាស្ុន **108**–25
សៃាមានគន្លឹះ្ខ្វស់ដោយដៃ **37**–29
សៃរ៍ **18**–7
សុំទៅាស **8**–I
សុំភូយ **111**–M
សំណង់ **149**
សំណាញ់ជាងភ្គិ **42**–11
សំណាញ់សក់ **147**–18
សំបកលាស បុខ្លាច **155**–21
សំបុក **132**–3
សំបុត្រ **96**–2, **104**–14
សំបុត្រកំណើត **29**–1
សំបុត្រគុណប្បញ្ញប្រចាំខែ **97**–10
សំបុត្រទិញធ្មើ **80**–13
សំបុត្របញ្ចាក់ចូលសញ្ញាតិ **29**–6

សំបុត្របន្ឋ **104**–6
សំបុត្រឆ្នើតាមផ្ លអាកាស **96**–13
សំបុត្រឆ្ើតានលើរៀន **96**–12
សំបុត្រឆ្ើមួយយប់ដល់ **96**–15
សំបុត្ររហ័ស **96**–15
សំបុត្រអនុស្ឋ **96**–11
សំបុត្រអាពាហ៍ពិពាហ៍ **29**–8
សិកព់ឝ្ម **71**–35
សិកពត់្រួនាប់ **67**–23
សិកពត់បញ្ាំងរូប **152**–12
សិកពត់រូប **64**–3
សិកពត់វៃង **71**–34
សិកពត់សសរាប់បញ្ាំង **2**–2
សិកពត់បុ្រឹប **64**–10
សំពោច **134**–13
សិរាក **27**–U
សិរាកលើ្រៃ **80**–A
សំល្ពេកចំពាក់គេងស្ត្រី **67**–5
សំល្ពេកចំពាក់ឌុគទឹក **66**–26
សំល្ពេកចំពាក់ផ្ុរការ **71**–36
សំល្ពេកចំពាក់ ភាគ **64**–67
សំល្ពេកចំពាក់សាម៉ិញ្ **71**–37
សំល្ពេកចំពាក់ស្ត្រីមានផ្ទៃពោះ **65**–19
សំល្ពេកចំពាក់ហាត់ប្រាណ **67**–1
សំល្ពេកចំពាក់ហាល់ទ្បរិន **168**–13
សំឡ្បិជុំគសម្ាប់មេរោក **83**–4
សំអាចចង្ក្រានអ៉ាង **46**–C
សំអាតក្រមង្ម៉ាស្ុនហបាល **72**–D
សំអាតកុ **62**–G
សំអាត...ធ្មេញ **85**–I
សំអាតផ្ះ **27**–N
សៃ៖ **133**–4
សៃ៖បង្គង **135**–34
សៃ៖សម្ម្ទ **130**–23
សុរ **55**–48, **60**–21
សុរគោស្ត្ី **55**–42
សុ្រក្រាប់ **168**–14
សុ្រជិន្ុស **60**–22
សុ្រផ្ុ **55**–41
សុ្ររត្នាត ៩/៩ វាង **57**–8
សុ្រមួយស្ថាបប្រាបាយ **57**–7
ស្ថាក់, អាយរៈ, ងាល្មិងង **115**
ស្ុង **134**–12
ស្ុរកតាមខ្ា **159**–9
ស្ុរកស្រេចំការ **34**–4
ស្រ្ **148**–1
ស្រ្សាឡ្ី **148**–2
ស្រ្ុល **30**–7
ស្ រក **30**–2
វំសៃក "ពញ្ាក់!" **169**–G
ស្រ្ាចដើមលើ **39**–B
ស្រ្ាមខ្ៃម **44**–10
ស្រ្ាមដើក **67**–15
ស្រ្ាមដើក្រឹមធង្ក់ **67**–25

អាងលាងដៃ **43**–22
អាងលាងដៃ មានទឹកហូរហូរ **49**–17
អាងហែលទឹក **37**–16
អាចធាបនេះ **147**–2
អាចម៍ដែកសម្រាប់ដុសឆ្នាំង **47**–5
អាផ្ទាកណ្តាល **158**–6
អាផ្ទាសាលា **99**–13
អាណាទិតមគមតាមបណ្តោយផ្គូរសម្បុត្រ អាគ្នុទិក បង្កើតឡើងដោយ ពួកអឺរ៉ុបខាងជើង **114**
អាណាទិតមទិយម **114**
អាណាទិតមទិយម និងការដោះលែងជាតិស្បែកខ្មៅ **115**
អាគត់ចំទ្បូង **165**–A
អាត្ថម **119**–17
អាទិត្បុក **51**–20
អាទិត្បួ **18**–1
អាទិត្បុក្រោយ **18**–20
អាទិត្បួនេះ **18**–19
អាទិត្បុមុន **18**–18
អាតកាវែសត **27**–V
អានតាក្ប **6**–B
អានវៀង **94**–F
អាប់លុយ **21**–9
អាប៊ីសុ **134**–4
អាត្រិកុត **50**–7
អាគ្រិខេត្បិន **144**–21
អាមេរិកកណ្តាល **122**–123
អាមេរិកខាងជើង **122**–123, **124**–1
អាមេរិកខាងត្បួង **124**–2
អាមេរិកទិញ្ញដីអាឡាស្ក្លា **115**
អាយគតិបាត **13**
អាយុ **22**
អាម្ពូណ៌ **30**–31
អាល់ហ្ក្លាល់ហ្ក្លា **148**–5
អាវកាក់ **65**–24
អាវកាក់ជោមឥត់ដៃ **66**–13
អាវកិឡ្បាដៃវែង **64**–14
អាវកិឡ្បាធិ **64**–6
អាវចាក់ **65**–20
អាវត្រកសំរាប់ក្មេងក្មេង **67**–7
អាវជាប់ខោ **71**–30
អាវដៃខ្លី **71**–30
អាវដៃវែង **71**–31
អាវតុកស្បិម **65**–28
អាវទប់ខ្បួល **66**–24
អាវទ្រនាប់ដៃង **67**–21
អាវទ្រនាប់ស្រី **67**–20
អាវធិមានទ្បាំងអាវកាក់ **64**–1
អាវនិងសំពត់ទ្រនាប់ជាប់គ្នា **67**–22
អាវផ្លាយ **65**–22
អាវពាក់ការពារ **147**–15
អាវពាក់ទៅបន្ទប់ទឹក **67**–8
អាវពាក់ពេលយប់ **67**–9
អាវភ្បៀង **66**–17
អាវភ្បៀងដៃវែង **66**–20

អាយ៊ិតកខ្ទិ **71**–26
អាយ៊ិតកស្រួច **71**–27
អាយ៊ិតកិឡ្បា **65**–26
អាយ៊ិតកិឡ្បារ្ប្វលគ្បើក **67**–2
អាយ៊ិតក្រាស់ **64**–11
អាយ៊ិតខាធិការ **65**–27
អាយ៊ិតជ្រះស្ថាប **72**–16
អាវយ៊ិតទ្រនាប់រួលគ្បើក **67**–10
អាវយ៊ិតប្រទាក់ **72**–15
អាយ៊ិតមួរក **64**–7, **71**–28
អាយ៊ិតដោមឃ្យម **70**–14
អាយ៊ិតសើម **72**–17
អាយ៊ិតស្បូត **72**–18
អាយ៊ិតស្ពីង៉ា **64**–12
អាយ៊ិតអំបោះ **70**–16
អារងា **66**–7
អារងាក្រាស់ **71**–41
អារងាជាតិកោវស្ប **70**–17
អារងាផ្តក្រាស់ **66**–15
អារងាមានមួក **66**–8
អារងាវែង **66**–2
អារងាស្បិង **71**–40
អារងាវស្បួក **66**–3
អារញ្ញ **72**–19
អារវ្បលគ្បើក **71**–29
អារ្បួលគ្បើកស្រី **67**–21
អារវែង **32**–2
អារវែងទាក់ខាងក្រោរ **66**–25
អារវែងសម្រាប់រាត្រីសមោសរ **65**–29
អារសង្គ្រោះជីវិត **154**–14
អារសីមិស **64**–4
អារស្រី **64**–9
អារស្រីធើរធាយ **71**–39
អារស្រីលាត **71**–38
អារហែលទឹក **154**–14
អារអ៊ុតហើយ **72**–20
អារ្បើមក្មេង **65**–18
អារអ្នកជម្ងឺគេងពេទ្ប **86**–15
អារ៉ូកាផ្ម **50**–14
អាសយដ្ឋាន **4**–5
អាសយដ្ឋានអ្នកទទួល **96**–8
អាសយដ្ឋានអ្នកផ្ញើ **96**–7
អាស្ច **125**–4
អាគ្រ្ខិត **125**–5
អិង (អិង្គ) **15**–13
អីរ៉ុម **125**–3
អុក **162**–6
អុដធាប៊ូ **123**–4
អុកស្ថាយ **79**–6
អិតខោអាវ **72**–G
អិតសក់ **23**–B
អុដ្ម **135**–38
អុប្ប **120**–5
អុស្ក្លាល់ **125**–6

អ្បល **82**–L
អេប៊ុំ **47**–24
អោម **33**–G
អោយ **21**–D
អោយចំណិ **148**–D
អោយជាក់ផ្លាស់ថាមអ្នកយល់ **8**–E
អោយថ្មសម្រាប់/ទិញ **21**–C
អុំ **24**–10, **24**–11
អំណោម **33**–18
អំចិលសយស្ថាបាត្រាការហ្ម **57**–6
អំបោល **47**–10
អំបោលសជុតទឹកសើម **47**–16
អំបោលសបោសធ្មាន **47**–17
អំបោលសស្បាបសុក្ត **47**–1
អំបោះចាក់ **163**–17
អំបោះដេរពេលរៈកាត់ **83**–15
អិត្រាយ៉ាហ្ប **109**–45
អំពូលភ្លើង **42**–4, **115**
អំពើយោរាយោរំវែនជនពាល **100**–2
អាំង **58**–V
អាំងឆ្គួង/ឧស្បុំង **58**–T
អ្នកភ្លិសេចក្ត្បិនគុណាការ **99**–12
អ្នកកាត់ខោអារស្បិ **73**–2
អ្នកកាត់ដេរស្រួល **73**–9
អ្នកកាត់សាថ់ **136**–11
អ្នកកាន់បញ្ជីដីកជ្ញ្ម **146**–15
អ្នកកាន់ម៉ាស៊ិន **138**–37
អ្នកកំប្បែងម្ពាំងង **166**–5
អ្នកខ្បប់ **146**–13
អ្នកគិតលុយ **55**–19, **136**–14
អ្នកគូរ **137**–29
អ្នកគូរប្បង់ **146**–3
អ្នកចប់ការសិក្ស្បា **32**–6
អ្នកចាត់ការជំនួយ **136**–3
អ្នកចិទ្បងកាវ្ពតិកាវ៉សៃតអាត់តុចៗ **142**–4
អ្នកចាំកន្ឆ្ងៃ្មង្គល **145**–9
អ្នកចាំសង្ផ្ដោះ **155**–18
អ្នកច្រកលវ៉ាន **55**–21
អ្នកផែកសំបុត្រ **104**–16
អ្នកជិតខាង **37**–22
អ្នកជិះកង់ **153**–3
អ្នកជួលផ្ទះ **37**–33
អ្នកជួយយកវ៉ឿន **138**–40
អ្នកជួយធើរការពេទ្ប **87**–18
អ្នកជួយពិ **138**–40
អ្នកជួលជុល **48**–10, **138**–48
អ្នកជិគី **84**–3
អ្នកជញ្ជ្ទ្បួយ្ប្រស/ស្រី **136**–10
អ្នកជំនួយខាងបេះទូរសព្ត **9**–8
អ្នកជំនួយពេទ្ប្យ្រញ្ញ **84**–19, **137**–19
អ្នកជាក់សំបុត្រ **96**–6
អ្នកជើរ **90**–7
អ្នកជើរភ្ត **136**–2
អ្នកដេកហាលៃថ្ងៃ **155**–17

Index លិបិក្រម

អ្នកដំណើរ **104**–7, **110**–23
អ្នកដាំដំណាំ **148**–15
អ្នកតំណាងអាកាសយាន **110**–2
អ្នកត្រួតពិនិត្យ **54**–8
អ្នកថតរូប **32**–11
អ្នកថែក្មេង **94**–3
អ្នកថែទាំ **138**–35
អ្នកថែទាំផ្ទះ **138**–33
អ្នកថែទាំសួនច្បារ **137**–26
អ្នកថែសួនច្បារ **152**–6
អ្នកថ្មើរជើងឆ្លងកាត់ **107**–10
អ្នកទទួលសុគ្រូវផ្នែកបណ្ណាញ **146**–5
អ្នកទទួលភ្ញៀវ **62**–1, **84**–2, **138**–47, **145**–4
អ្នកធ្វើការក្នុងចំការ **148**–8
អ្នកធ្វើការខាងសំលៀកបំពាក់ **137**–27
អ្នកធ្វើការនៅកំពង់ផែ **137**–21
អ្នកធ្វើការប្រិសណិយ **138**–45
អ្នកធ្វើការផ្នែកអនាម័យ **139**–51
អ្នកធ្វើដំបូលផ្ទះ **48**–8
អ្នកធ្វើនំ **136**–8
អ្នកធ្វើសក់ **137**–30
អ្នកចិត្ត **98**–22, **139**–64
អ្នកទាំសារ **138**–38
អ្នកទាំសំបុត្រ **138**–38
អ្នកបកប្រែភាសា **138**–34
អ្នកបង្ហាញម៉ូដដែលសំលៀកបំពាក់ **138**–39
អ្នកបើកតាក់ស៊ី **104**–20
អ្នកបើកយន្តហោះ **110**–12
អ្នកបើកឡានឈ្នួល **104**–8
អ្នកបើកឡានផ្ទាំ **139**–61
អ្នកបើកឡានលៀន **11**–3
អ្នកបើកឡានយឺត **11**–4
អ្នកបើកបូមទូលប្រាក់ **97**–1
អ្នកបោសសំអាត **138**–35
អ្នកបំរើ **62**–4, **63**–6, **139**–53
អ្នកបំអិកក្នុងយន្តហោះ **110**–13
អ្នកកំរៃកករកៅស៊ូ **145**–1
អ្នកបំអិតាមបន្ទប់ **145**–12

អ្នកបំរើប្រុស **62**–4
អ្នកបំរើស្រី **63**–6
អ្នកចោះពុក្ខ **138**–46
អ្នកប្រកាស **152**–27
អ្នកផ្តល់ម្ហូបអាហារ **33**–12
អ្នកផ្តុំគ្រឿង **136**–6
អ្នកផ្គត់ផ្គង់របស់របរ **139**–55
អ្នកពន្លត់ភ្លើង **102**–8, **137**–24
អ្នកព្យាបាលអោកប្រើកាយឬហាត់ **81**–30
អ្នកមេញា **62**–5
អ្នកមើលការខុសត្រូវផ្ទះជួល **36**–12
អ្នកមើលវិទ្យា **158**–4
អ្នកមើលក្មេង **136**–12
អ្នកមើលថែទាំតាមផ្ទះ **137**–31
អ្នកយក/ដឹកទាំរបស់អោយភ្ញៀវ **137**–18
អ្នកយាម **99**–3, **97**–4
អ្នកយាមទ្វារ **36**–10, **145**–2
អ្នករក្សាបញ្ជី **142**–12
អ្នករក្សាសុវត្ថិភាព **152**–3
អ្នករថនា **146**–3
អ្នករាយការណ៍ **139**–49
អ្នករុករកជាតិបារាំង, អេស្ប៉ាញ, អង់គ្លេស **114**
អ្នករញាត់វ៉ាន់ **145**–5
អ្នកលក់ **68**–1, **139**–50
អ្នកលក់តាមទូរស័ព្ទ **139**–59
អ្នកលក់តាមផ្លូវ **91**–30
អ្នកលក់ផ្កា **137**–25
អ្នកលក់សំបុត្រធ្វើដំណើរ **139**–60
អ្នកលក់សាំង **137**–28
អ្នកលាងចាន **63**–13
អ្នកលាបថ្នាំ **138**–43
អ្នកលើកចានពិតុ **63**–9
អ្នកលើករបស់ **139**–55
អ្នកលេខវិទ្យា **158**–5
អ្នកលេងភ្លេង **138**–41
អ្នកសរសេរ **139**–64
អ្នកសមេសរប្រមូលវុំស្មន **136**–16
អ្នកសិល្បួលផ្ធីស្រេចចំការ **148**–20

អ្នកសំដែង **136**–2
អ្នកសម្ពាប់សត្វល្អិត **49**–21
អ្នកសំអាតឆ្អេញ **84**–16
អ្នកសំអាតបន្ទប់ **145**–15
អ្នកស្ម៉ៃគ្រចិត្ត **87**–19
អ្នកហ្វឹកហ្វឺន **139**–58
អ្នកអវកាស **127**–17
អ្នកអោយឱវាទ **5**–16
អ្នកឯកទេសខាងពិសោធន៍ **86**–16
អ្នកឯកទេសផ្នែកភ្នែ **86**–8
អ្នកឯកទេសពេទ្យសង្គ្រោះក្នុងពេលអាសន្ន (EMT) **87**–26
ឥដ្ឋ **149**–11
ឧទានសព្ទា **113**–8
ខណ្ឌមាតចក្រ **110**–8
ឧទ្យាន និង កន្លែងក្មេងលេង **153**
ឧបករណ៍ **150–151**
ឧបករណ៍សម្រាប់តោងឡើង **153**–14
ឧបទ្ទិប **117**–7
ឧង្គសត្វ **130–131, 131**
ឧស **42**–12
ឧសថការី **80**–10
ឧសភា **19**–29
ឧស្សិនធម្មជាតិ **126**–3
ឦពុក **24**–6
ឦពុកក្មេក **24**–14
ឦពុកចុង **25**–28
ឦពុកប្រពន្ធលែង **25**–26
ឦពុកម្តាយ **24**–4
ឦពុក/ម្តាយ **94**–1
ឦឡ្ហីក **50**–24
ឧស **128**–5, **129**–3
ឫ **75**–B
ឍកសណ្ឋាន **65**–17, **161**–16
ឍគោ **30**–18
ឦម៉ាល់ **132**–18
ឧសថស្ថាន **80**–9, **90**–2